Las Vegas

Scott Doggett

LONELY PLANET PUBLICATIONS
Melbourne · Oakland · London · Paris

Las Vegas
1st edition – January 2000

Published by
Lonely Planet Publications Pty Ltd A.C.N. 005 607 983
192 Burwood Rd, Hawthorn, Victoria 3122, Australia

Lonely Planet Offices
Australia PO Box 617, Hawthorn, Victoria 3122
USA 150 Linden St, Oakland, CA 94607
UK 10a Spring Place, London NW5 3BH
France 1 rue du Dahomey, 75011 Paris

Photographs
Boyd Gaming, Scott Doggett, John Elk III, Lee Foster, Rick Gerharter,
Norman Godwin, Imperial Palace, *Jubilee!*, Bonnie Kamin, Las Vegas
News Bureau, Henia Miedzinski, David Peevers, Al Seib, Johnny
Stockshooter/International Stock
Some of the images in this guide are available for licensing from
Lonely Planet Images.
email: lpi@lonelyplanet.com.au

Front cover photograph
Lightbulbs in Las Vegas (Rick Gerharter/Lonely Planet Images)

ISBN 1 86450 086 7

text & maps © Lonely Planet 2000
photos © photographers as indicated 2000

Printed by The Bookmaker Pty Ltd
Printed in China

Contents

The Author

Scott Doggett

Scott's interest in exotic cultures (Las Vegas included) dates from 1979, when the travel bug bit him good during a high school graduation trip to Europe. The itch to travel remained strong in Scott when he graduated from UC Berkeley four years later; within weeks he'd ridden buses all the way to San Salvador, where he shot film as a freelance photographer for the next six months. His initial career was followed by postgraduate work at Stanford University; reporting assignments for United Press International in Los Angeles, Pakistan and Afghanistan; and, from 1989 through 1996, seven years as a staff editor for the *Los Angeles Times*. During his free time, Scott toured more than 60 countries, often writing stories about his travels for the *Times*, the *Washington Post*, the *Miami Herald* and *Escape* magazine. In 1996, he coauthored and coedited (with his future wife, Annette Haddad) the anthology *Travelers' Tales: Brazil*. Scott began writing for Lonely Planet the next year. Today, he is the author of Lonely Planet's *Panama* guide and coauthor of Lonely Planet's *Mexico* and *Dominican Republic & Haiti* guides. Scott has also written guidebooks to Amsterdam and Los Angeles. At the time this book went to press, Scott was finishing work on Lonely Planet's first guide to Yucatán and preparing to start researching Lonely Planet's first Nicaragua guide.

Dedication

Most American teenagers have no idea what they want to be when they grow up, and I was that way until the Rev Thomas G Piquado, SJ, entered my life. Father Piquado was my English teacher during my senior year at Jesuit High in Sacramento, CA, and during that year (1979) he convinced me that I had a gift for writing. Because of him, my future suddenly had direction: I'd major in English in college and pursue a career that involved lots of writing. Perhaps I'd become a journalist.

That summer, Father Piquado led a group of students, including me, on a trip to Europe. Many of the values I hold dear today I formed during those four weeks in Europe. I remember, for example, wondering why anyone would buy a fancy car when they could travel for years on that kind of money. That trip affected me in many ways, mostly because of the enthusiasm Father Piquado instilled in me as we toured Western Europe.

Father Piquado was no less compelling in the classroom. If an essay impressed him, he let you know by telling the entire class – and he always did it with flare, often clenching the student's paper in his left hand and raising his right hand for emphasis as he spoke in a voice that was pure authority. His style had an impact on us at an age when most kids are only concerned about the impressions they are making on other kids. You did your best work for Father

Piquado because you wanted his respect and because you wanted him to recognize you in front of your peers.

It's been 20 years since I've spoken with Father Piquado, and he long ago left Jesuit High. Today, he is the associate pastor at St. Ignatius Church in San Francisco. I think about Father Piquado often for the confidence and guidance he gave me at a critical time in my life and for introducing me to the joys of travel. With profound respect and appreciation, this book is dedicated to him.

FROM THE AUTHOR

Jeff Campbell edited this book, and for that I am very grateful. Jeff demonstrated a sharp eye for exposing inconsistencies when he edited portions of *Dominican Republic & Haiti*, but I didn't know how thorough he was until he picked this sucker apart. Not only did he find discrepancies and suggest many ways the book might be improved, but he also wrote some of the text that appears here (the excellent sidebar 'Nuclear Waste in the Nevada Desert' leaps to mind, and the Things to See & Do and Entertainment chapters are much stronger because of him). Jeff deserves much of the credit for this book.

A sincere thank you also to Tom Downs, the senior editor of this book, who supervised Jeff's work and offered valuable guidance. A sincere thank you also to senior editor Carolyn Hubbard, who helped with the book's planning, and to Charlotte Hindle, the general manager of Lonely Planet's UK office, who provides a very personal perspective on Sin City with her sidebar 'Getting Hitched in Vegas: A True Story.'

In Las Vegas, many people aided me. Chief among them was Karen Silveroli, News Bureau Coordinator of the Las Vegas Convention & Visitors Authority, who supplied me with scores of slides. Many other people also provided me with slides or otherwise helped me, and I'd be remiss if I didn't mention the following publicists: Dan Bradley (New York-New York); Dave Brendmoen (Boyd Gaming); Maria Gladowski (Monte Carlo); Alan Hopper (Circus Circus); Larry Houck (Imperial Palace); Pien Koopman (*Mystère*); Jennifer Michaels (The Mirage, Treasure Island); Cheryl Miles (Barbary Coast, Gold Coast, The Orleans); John Neeland (Riviera); Candie Priest (Bally's); Michelle Rosen (Stardust); Yale Rowe (Sahara); Patricia Schneck (Las Vegas Hilton); Paul Speirs (Luxor, Excalibur); Laura Sugden (Rio); and Lance Taylor (O). A heartfelt thank you to all of you.

This Book

FROM THE PUBLISHER

Many people contributed their time, energy and patience to this book. It was edited by Jeff Campbell, proofed by Kevin Anglin, mapped by Monica Lepe, and designed by Henia Miedzinski. Senior editor Tom Downs, senior cartographer Amy Dennis and senior designer Margaret Livingston offered guidance and assistance. Hayden Foell wrangled a small army of illustrators – including Wendy Yanagihara, Hugh D'Andrade, Jim Swanson and John Fadeff – and he created several illustrations himself. Joshua Schefers did photo research, and Rini Keagy created the cover.

Foreword

ABOUT LONELY PLANET GUIDEBOOKS

The story begins with a classic travel adventure: Tony and Maureen Wheeler's 1972 journey across Europe and Asia to Australia. Useful information about the overland trail did not exist at that time, so Tony and Maureen published the first Lonely Planet guidebook to meet a growing need.

From a kitchen table, then from a tiny office in Melbourne (Australia), Lonely Planet has become the largest independent travel publisher in the world, an international company with offices in Melbourne, Oakland (USA), London (UK) and Paris (France).

Today Lonely Planet guidebooks cover the globe. There is an ever-growing list of books, and there's information in a variety of forms and media. Some things haven't changed. The main aim is still to help make it possible for adventurous travelers to get out there – to explore and better understand the world.

At Lonely Planet we believe travelers can make a positive contribution to the countries they visit – if they respect their host communities and spend their money wisely. Since 1986 a percentage of the income from each book has been donated to aid projects and human-rights campaigns.

Updates Lonely Planet thoroughly updates each guidebook as often as possible. This usually means there are around two years between editions, although for more unusual or more stable destinations the gap can be longer. Check the imprint page (following the color map at the beginning of the book) for publication dates.

Between editions, up-to-date information is available in two free newsletters – the paper *Planet Talk* and email *Comet* (to subscribe, contact any Lonely Planet office) – and on our website at www.lonelyplanet.com. The *Upgrades* section of the website covers a number of important and volatile destinations and is regularly updated by Lonely Planet authors. *Scoop* covers news and current affairs relevant to travelers. And, lastly, the *Thorn Tree* bulletin board and *Postcards* section of the site carry unverified, but fascinating, reports from travelers.

Correspondence The process of creating new editions begins with the letters, postcards and emails received from travelers. This correspondence often includes suggestions, criticisms and comments about the current editions. Interesting excerpts are immediately passed on via newsletters and the website, and everything goes to our authors to be verified when they're researching on the road. We're keen to get more feedback from organizations or individuals who represent communities visited by travelers.

Lonely Planet gathers information for everyone who's curious about the planet – and especially for those who explore it firsthand. Through guidebooks, phrasebooks, activity guides, maps, literature, newsletters, image library, TV series and website, we act as an information exchange for a worldwide community of travelers.

Research Authors aim to gather sufficient practical information to enable travelers to make informed choices and to make the mechanics of a journey run smoothly. They also research historical and cultural background to help enrich the travel experience and allow travelers to understand and respond appropriately to cultural and environmental issues.

Authors don't stay in every hotel because that would mean spending a couple of months in each medium-size city and, no, they don't eat at every restaurant because that would mean stretching belts beyond capacity. They do visit hotels and restaurants to check standards and prices, but feedback based on readers' direct experiences can be very helpful.

Many of our authors work undercover; others aren't so secretive. None of them accept freebies in exchange for positive write-ups. And none of our guidebooks contain any advertising.

Production Authors submit their raw manuscripts and maps to offices in Australia, the USA, the UK or France. Editors and cartographers – all experienced travelers themselves – then begin the process of assembling the pieces. When the book finally hits the shops, some things are already out of date, we start getting feedback from readers and the process begins again....

WARNING & REQUEST

Things change – prices go up, schedules change, good places go bad and bad places go bankrupt – nothing stays the same. So, if you find things better or worse, recently opened or long since closed, please tell us and help make the next edition even more accurate and useful. We genuinely value all the feedback we receive. Julie Young coordinates a well-traveled team that reads and acknowledges every letter, postcard and email and ensures that every morsel of information finds its way to the appropriate authors, editors and cartographers for verification.

Everyone who writes to us will find their name in the next edition of the appropriate guidebook. They will also receive the latest issue of *Planet Talk*, our quarterly printed newsletter, or *Comet*, our monthly email newsletter. Subscriptions to both newsletters are free. The very best contributions will be rewarded with a free guidebook.

Excerpts from your correspondence may appear in new editions of Lonely Planet guidebooks, the Lonely Planet website, *Planet Talk* or *Comet*, so please let us know if you *don't* want your letter published or your name acknowledged.

Send all correspondence to the Lonely Planet office closest to you:

Australia: PO Box 617, Hawthorn, Victoria 3122
USA: 150 Linden St, Oakland, CA 94607
UK: 10A Spring Place, London NW5 3BH
France: 1 rue du Dahomey, 75011 Paris

Or email us at: talk2us@lonelyplanet.com.au

For news, views and updates, see our website: www.lonelyplanet.com

HOW TO USE A LONELY PLANET GUIDEBOOK

The best way to use a Lonely Planet guidebook is any way you choose. At Lonely Planet, we believe the most memorable travel experiences are often those that are unexpected, and the finest discoveries are those you make yourself. Guidebooks are not intended to be used as if they provided a detailed set of infallible instructions!

Contents All Lonely Planet guidebooks follow the same format. The Facts about the Country chapters or sections give background information ranging from history to weather. Facts for the Visitor gives practical information on issues like visas and health. Getting There & Away gives a brief starting point for researching travel to and from the destination. Getting Around gives an overview of the transport options available when you arrive.

The peculiar demands of each destination determine how subsequent chapters are broken up, but some things remain constant. We always start with background, then proceed to sights, places to stay, places to eat, entertainment, getting there and away, and getting around information – in that order.

Heading Hierarchy Lonely Planet headings are used in a strict hierarchical structure that can be visualized as a set of Russian dolls. Each heading (and its following text) is encompassed by any preceding heading that is higher on the hierarchical ladder.

Entry Points We do not assume guidebooks will be read from beginning to end, but that people will dip into them. The traditional entry points are the list of contents and the index. In addition, however, some books have a complete list of maps and an index map illustrating map coverage.

There may also be a color map that shows highlights. These highlights are dealt with in greater detail later in the book, along with planning questions and suggested itineraries. Each chapter covering a geographical region usually begins with a locator map and another list of highlights. Once you find something of interest in a list of highlights, turn to the index.

Maps Maps play a crucial role in Lonely Planet guidebooks and include a huge amount of information. A legend is printed on the back page. We seek to have complete consistency between maps and text, and to have every important place in the text captured on a map. Map key numbers usually start in the top left corner.

> Although inclusion in a guidebook usually implies a recommendation, we cannot list every good place. Exclusion does not necessarily imply criticism. In fact, there are a number of reasons why we might exclude a place – sometimes it is simply inappropriate to encourage an influx of travelers.

Introduction

Go ahead. Get it out of your system. Say it, even if you don't mean it. It's what everybody expects: 'Las Vegas. It's tasteless, cheap, sleazy and cheesy.'

Ah, feel better? But to be honest, Las Vegas no longer lives up to its long-held reputation. It's become a remarkable and unique city that – like every other big city on our glorious planet – has its tasteless, cheap, sleazy and cheesy elements. Consider Paris, San Francisco, Tokyo, Rome. Every great city mixes the tacky with the sublime.

However, only Las Vegas exists chiefly to satisfy the needs and desires of its visitors, and this it does in spectacular fashion. Sin City has taken or re-created the best that other great cities have to offer and then upped the ante – making it bigger, grander, flashier.

What other city has so many superb restaurants? What other city has so much world-class entertainment? What other city has a Manhattan skyline *and* a Parisian skyline *and* a Venetian skyline? What other city has produced more instant millionaires?

The truth is, no other city has. And while many cities call themselves the 'Entertainment Capital of the World,' Las Vegas is now the reigning heavyweight champion of that title. Las Vegas is in a league of its own.

Given what we've always been told about Las Vegas, it's almost shocking and disturbing to realize this is true. Then again, with Las Vegas' hotel-casinos making so much money, resort owners have the freedom to scour the globe and say, 'I want one of *those*.' No, not a Ferrari. Not an estate house on a hill. Not the stuff regular Joes and Janes like us dream about.

Listen. When Steve Wynn, the $6-zillion man behind The Mirage, decided to create Bellagio, he set out to awe the most discerning individuals. 'The challenge,' he said, 'became building a place so preemptive, so overwhelmingly attractive and delicious, that it would attract people who do not

Now entering Sin City

come to Las Vegas now – people who are not that impressed with gaming.'

Wynn built a resort that's an aesthetic knockout and that contains an art collection even Las Vegas' staunchest detractors reluctantly admit is first-rate. For entertainment, Wynn turned to Montreal's Cirque du Soleil to create a show 'that people would talk about in Singapore, Rome, Hong Kong, London, New York and Buenos Aires.' Out of Cirque sprang the critically acclaimed *O*.

For food, Wynn's dream was to hire the best chefs on Earth and put them to work for him. Today, there are seven James Beard award-winning chefs at Bellagio, each with his own restaurant. Perhaps never before has such an exceptional group of chefs and restaurants been assembled under one roof.

Wynn is an exceptional man, but his approach to Bellagio, which opened in late 1998, is not exceptional. To compete with Wynn: David Cacci opened New York-New York, which captures the excitement and beauty of Manhattan without, ironically, any of its sleaze. Glenn Schaeffer opened Mandalay Bay, home to the Broadway musical smash *Chicago*, several superb restaurants and one of the nation's premiere blues clubs. Arthur Goldberg opened Paris-Las Vegas, which reproduces in exquisite detail the City of Lights' most famous landmarks and contains not less than eight outstanding *restaurants français* with a French-trained culinary staff of 500.

Wynn, Cacci, Schaeffer, Goldberg and others you've probably never heard of (there's no reason why you should have) have created a Las Vegas that, at the dawn of the 21st century, can no longer be easily dismissed by its derogators. Not only does the gallery at Bellagio contain fine art, but its Picasso restaurant is filled with original Picassos and the decor was selected by the artist's son. (Bellagio contains many such surprises.)

Likewise, in re-creating some of the magic found in the thrill rides at New York's (now-defunct) Coney Island amusement park, New York-New York not only built a roller coaster, but it built one with a blazing top speed of 67mph and a twist-and-dive maneuver that produces the weightless sensation a pilot feels during a barrel roll. Nearby, Stratosphere has a roller coaster too – one that's more than a hundred floors above The Strip and is the highest thrill ride in the world.

And so it goes with dozens of Las Vegas attractions. It's impossible to talk about Las Vegas without using the word 'world' because so many of the city's hotels, restaurants and entertainment options are truly world-class.

Even the natural and human-created splendors around Las Vegas are world-class. There's only one Grand Canyon and only one Hoover Dam, which was built more than 60 years ago and is still one of the world's tallest. The 1450-mile-long Colorado River, which carved the Grand Canyon, attracts white-water rafters from across the globe, and not a road leaves Las Vegas that doesn't stumble through the sparse, wind- and water-carved landscapes of the Southwest's famous red rock desert. All these sites are easy excursions from Sin City and shouldn't be missed.

True, Las Vegas hasn't changed completely. It still has its topless revues, but with increasing frequency they're being replaced by shows featuring the greatest stage performers of our time. Yes, Las Vegas still has its notoriously huge buffets, but these days the mounds of spaghetti and the piles of cheap cuts of meat have been replaced with grilled salmon, NY steaks, king crab and sushi.

Nor will Las Vegas let you down if you're searching for all things tasteless, cheap, sleazy and cheesy. But if you arrive with an open mind, you'll find it has a sizzling nightlife, extraordinary restaurants, outstanding production shows and incomparable hotel-casinos – and you'll likely leave town feeling like you've just had the best amusement ride of your life.

Facts about Las Vegas

HISTORY

Contrary to legend and Hollywood movies, there was a lot more to Las Vegas than a dumpy gambling house, some tumbleweeds and cacti the day mobster Benjamin Siegel drove into the Mojave Desert and decided to build a glamorous, tropical-themed casino under the searing sun. Humans had been living in Las Vegas Valley an entire millennium before the celebrated gangster opened the Flamingo in 1946.

The Paiutes Tough It Out

It was a full thousand years ago – or at about the time Byzantine monarch Basil II ordered the blinding of thousands of Bulgarian prisoners and Asian king Machmud of Ghazni retained 400 poets to entertain him – that a small band of weary Indians followed a bend in the Colorado River to Nevada's Black Mountains, where they crossed the jutting beige peaks and settled in the valley below. These hard-bitten Indians were Southern Paiutes, members of the Uto-Aztecan language family that also contains the better-known Shoshones and Utes of Wyoming and Utah, respectively.

The Paiutes pitched tents near an oasis where the city of Las Vegas now stands. The desert Indians spent their days roaming about the Mojave in small groups, harvesting everything they could eat. Nearly 40 varieties of seeds were gathered and stored in tightly woven baskets. Wild celery, sweet sage and the blazing star were eaten, as were the roots and bulbs of the sego lily, camas and wild caraway. Insects such as crickets and locusts, and their larvae, were relished. The rattlesnake was a special treat.

As time passed the Paiutes came to occupy the mountains and valleys spreading in all directions from Las Vegas for 50 miles, and they became expert hunters. The Sheep Range, the Spring Mountains, the El Dorado Mountains and the Black Mountains ringing Las Vegas Valley contained elk, bear, deer and antelope, which the Indians felled with arrows and clubs. To protect their skin against the blistering desert sun, the Paiutes smeared red paint on their faces and bodies.

The Rat Pack – icons of Sin City's swingin' past

To protect their soles from the broiling earth, they wore moccasins made of yucca leaves.

Despite the rigors of their surroundings, the Paiutes were a disciplined people who adhered to certain practices without waver. Birth took place in circular brush enclosures. Boys were required to surrender first kills to parents. Though marriage was unimportant, funerals were four-day affairs involving cremation or cave burials, the killing of eagles and abandonment of homes. Elected headmen discoursed on morality and had advisory, not authoritative, functions. In the unforgiving desert, the Paiutes not only endured, but they advanced as a culture.

Just how forbidding was their territory? The Spanish, who were the first Caucasians to claim jurisdiction over southern Nevada, skirted this region during their extensive exploration of North America during the 16th and 17th centuries. They were content to leave this section of their 'domain' uncharted, calling the blank space left on their maps the 'Northern Mystery.' Despite its proximity to well-trodden Mexico and California, Las Vegas Valley and the land around it in all directions for at least two weeks' hike was the last part of the US to be penetrated and explored by white settlers.

Trappers & Traders

Except for infrequent raids by Navajo and Ute slave traders during the 18th century, the Southern Paiutes lived a peaceful, if arduous, existence in and around Las Vegas Valley for more than 800 years. Their undoing as the dominant people of the region began with the arrival of white men seeking buck-toothed rodents with flat tails, beady eyes and a penchant for turning rivers into ponds. Beavers were abundant in the Southwest, and beaver fur was prized for its warmth and beauty. During the 1820s anybody who was anybody in Europe wore a beaver-pelt hat. Making matters worse for the busy herbivores, a secretion from their musk glands was thought to be a cure-all and was as sought after as the fur. Europe couldn't get enough of the fur and musk of the little dam-makers, and some American

fur traders went to extreme lengths to meet the demand.

One of those traders was Jedediah Smith, who left his trapping areas along the Utah-Idaho border in mid-1826 in search of untouched beaver country. Heading toward the Pacific, Smith blazed a trail southwest along the Virgin River. While following the river out of Utah, Smith intersected the Nevada border in November 1826 at a point near the modern city of Mesquite, NV, 80 miles east of Las Vegas. Smith thus became the first Caucasian American to enter present-day Nevada.

Incidentally, the moniker 'first white person to enter Nevada' belongs to British explorer Peter Skene Ogden, who made a brief foray into northern Nevada earlier in 1826. Smith is also credited with having opened up a major segment of the Spanish Trail – a trading route between Santa Fe, NM, and Los Angeles, CA. The Spanish Trail existed from 1830 until the middle of the 20th century, when large segments of it were paved and became sections of Interstate 15.

Jedediah Smith continued on to California (he was anxious to sell his furs in Los Angeles), and it wasn't long before other adventurers traced his steps into the Northern Mystery. Most were traders, some were settlers anxious to get to California, and all were looking for greener pastures of one kind or another.

At least a few green pastures were found: In the diaries of many Spanish Trail travelers arises an image of Las Vegas in the 1830s and 1840s as a string of lush meadows linked by a picturesque year-round creek that emerged from a series of springs. (This explains the city's name; Las Vegas is Spanish for 'The Meadows.') Shade created by cottonwoods and willows near the creek allowed grass to grow, and the grass fed the mules, horses and oxen of Spanish Trail caravans.

Among the Trail's most famous travelers was John C Fremont (after whom the main street of downtown Las Vegas is named), an army officer who spent several years exploring and mapping the area around Las Vegas. The beauty of the region awed Fremont, and his favorable reports, which appeared in part in many US newspapers, encouraged scores of people on the East Coast of the US to seek opportunity in the West. The encouragement took on a sense of urgency in 1849, when gold was discovered in California. By year's end the Spanish Trail no longer served mostly fur traders; it had been overtaken by men hungry for gold.

Mormons on the Move

Amid the legions of hard-drinking Rockefeller wanna-bes responding to the gold strike was a group of men hell-bent on doing God's work in Indian country. These Mormons were sent from Salt Lake City, UT, by leader Brigham Young to colonize the expanding state of Deseret, as they called their homeland. The faithful were dispatched to Las Vegas to help secure a string of Mormon settlements that would stretch from church headquarters in Utah all the way to the Pacific Ocean. In the process, the Mormons began occupying land that had belonged to the Southern Paiutes for 850 years.

To keep the Indians in check, Young instructed the missionaries to convert them to Mormonism. The Mormon gospel has two underlying principles: church officers believe that they are divinely called to be leaders and, second, that there must be unquestioned obedience to their orders. Devotion to that system was so strong that only two of the 30 men ordered to go to Las Vegas to build a fort and convert Indians refused to make the trip. On May 10, 1855, a party of Las Vegas-bound missionary-colonists left Salt Lake City after each man had sold sufficient possessions to buy a wagon load of provisions and had said good-bye to his family.

During their first months in Las Vegas the missionary-colonists built a fort made of adobe, and they planted corn, squash and other crops. Although the Paiutes tolerated the white men because the missionaries gave them grain and squash, they failed to become evangelized. For instance, when the Paiutes showed the Mormons a cliff near the summit of Potosi Mountain, 27 miles southwest of Las Vegas, that contained large quantities of silver ore, the Mormons tried

William Bringhurst

to enlist the Indians into mining the ore. The Mormons offered a thousand Indians a total of 10 shirts and a small amount of food to remove the ore from the mountain. The natives hauled only one load of rock on their backs before they quit. Overlooking the facts that the work was demanding and the pay absurdly low, one missionary involved with the silver venture had only this to say about the Indians: 'There seems to be but little Mormon in them, and they showed me on their finger nails how much.'

The missionary's high opinion of Mormons may have slipped a little over the next few months. During that time, intense conflicts arose among the Las Vegas Mormons, who were anxious to get their hands on the wealth that seemed so near but were unable to get the Indians to agree to be beasts of burden. Fueling passions further was a power struggle that developed between two church officers. One of them, William Bringhurst, was among the original missionary-colonists. The other, Nathaniel Jones, was dispatched from Salt Lake City after Young had been informed about the silver ore.

Bringhurst was in charge of the mission; there was no denying that. But Jones had a letter from Young saying he could borrow men from the mission to help him extract silver from the Potosi mine, and Young had instructed Jones to bring the silver to Salt Lake City. Bringhurst didn't want to relinquish control of the mine and the riches within it, so he initially denied Jones the men he needed. Because Salt Lake City was a 45-day hike away, whoever controlled the men temporarily controlled the mine.

Dissension arose within the ranks of the missionaries when some announced they wanted to help Jones at the mine and perhaps become rich in the process. Others sided with Bringhurst, who dispatched a messenger to Salt Lake City with a letter asking Young to name a director of the silver mine. But before a reply arrived, frustration got the better of Bringhurst: Although he had advised gentle treatment of the Indians, Bringhurst kicked a Paiute from his house and from the mission when he caught the famished man stealing bread. Word of the incident spread like fire through the Paiute community, and the Mormons lost all credibility with the people they were hoping to evangelize.

At about the same time, some of the missionaries announced a desire to build a church. Others thought a fence around the mission was more important and should be erected first. After much bickering the men agreed to build a church and then build a fence, but the team spirit that had existed at the mission was lost. Then came news that Young had decided to excommunicate Bringhurst, which in turn resulted in some ill will toward the church leader.

In the meantime, Jones and a handful of missionaries had begun mining the silver, but finding the work extremely painstaking and the heat unbearable, Jones abandoned the mine after only five weeks and returned to Salt Lake City with unfavorable reports concerning the mine and the mission.

Citing the inability of the Las Vegas missionaries to solve social problems, their unsuccessful efforts to convert the Indians and the dissension that arose over the mine, Young ordered the mission closed in February 1857, less than two years after it had first

been established. Although the mission failed in all of its objectives, it paved the way for settlement of southern Nevada the following decade. And for what it's worth, the mission represented the first concerted effort by white men to occupy Las Vegas.

A Silver Mine & a Golden Spike

Many gold miners en route to California via the Spanish Trail learned of the silver in Potosi Mountain as they passed through Las Vegas. When word reached them that the Mormons had abandoned the lode, some of the miners returned to Nevada to try their hand at Potosi. In 1860, these miners, unlike Jones and his men, worked Potosi expertly and extracted lots of silver. Some of the Potosi miners, when returning to Los Angeles for provisions, showed off impressive chunks of silver ore, which fueled excitement about the mine. Soon up to 35 miners a day were arriving at Potosi. Some men got rich. Most did poorly. A few took to farming in Las Vegas Valley.

After the Potosi silver boom subsided in late 1861, those who had tried to farm Las Vegas left their generally uncooperative fields for more fertile ground elsewhere. For four years the valley again belonged solely to the Paiutes. Then, in 1865, an on-again, off-again miner from Ohio named Octavius Decatur Gass and two associates reconstructed the buildings that had been the Mormon mission and revived the fields once used by the missionaries. The resulting 2000-acre Las Vegas Ranch flourished for the rest of the century and its success encouraged other settlers to stake claims in the valley.

No railroads crossed southern Nevada in 1900, but plans had by then been worked up to link Los Angeles and Salt Lake City by rail, with a stop in Las Vegas. In January 1905, the final spike, a golden one, was driven in just south of Las Vegas, and train service commenced. By this time Las Vegas was more than just a ranch ringed by cacti and barren foothills. A post office had opened, as had a meat market, a general store and a hotel. But with the new railroad, the town was destined for much more, and the railroad company cleared off a patch of desert and staked out 40-blocks' worth of lots in the dirt. Then they held an auction. Over two frenzied days local settlers as well as speculators and real estate investors from Los Angeles and the East Coast bid and out-bid each other for the land, and the barren lots sold for twice to ten times their original price. The railroad company made a killing. As the dust settled, on May 15, 1905, the City of Las Vegas was officially founded – as was the town's personality.

The young city was quickly transformed as new buildings and businesses sprung up almost overnight. Railroad freight cars pro-vided easy access to provisions that had pre-viously taken weeks to bring in. After a few months, the initial excitement dimmed somewhat as people coped with the difficul-ties of desert life, but by January 1906, Las Vegas was home to dozens of businesses, including two banks, a drug store, a school and a jail. Tent homes made of canvas and lumber spread everywhere. The *Los Angeles Times* put the city's population at more than 1500. Electricity arrived by year's end.

By the start of WWI, which had little effect on the Las Vegas economy, ranches and small farms flourished throughout the valley, and the downtown area was develop-ing rapidly. A well had to be sunk at each farm to provide for irrigation, as rainfall was insufficient, but beneath the surface of the desert there proved to be no shortage of water. Except for citrus, many types of fruit, as well as grains and vegetables, were grown. Construction financed mostly by outsiders kept employment high. Anderson Field, Las Vegas' first airport, opened in 1920; sched-uled passenger service to Salt Lake City and Los Angeles commenced soon after.

Sin also flourished in Las Vegas during this period, in the infamous red-light district known as Block 16 (between 1st and 2nd Sts and Ogden and Stewart Sts downtown). Home to gambling, booze and prostitution, this row of saloons, with their makeshift 'cribs' out back, survived Nevada's 1911 ban on gambling and the 'dry years' of Prohibi-tion, as it did the occasional civic effort to stamp it out.

Prosperity, or at least opportunity, had embraced everyone – everyone except the Paiutes. Unable to speak English and pres-sured into giving up their land by numerous business interests, including the railroad, the Indians withdrew from the valley they had occupied since 1000 AD. Their withdrawal

Desert Survival Tips

Octavius Decatur Gass, who founded Las Vegas Ranch in 1865 and at one point in the mid-1870s owned almost all the water rights in Las Vegas Valley, offered the following desert-travel advice to late-19th-century readers of the *San Bernardino Guardian*:

Never travel alone; have a large canteen; rest before crossing the desert; feed your animal on all occasions where you can get supplies. If you have no means to do this, don't start until you have, as your life is at stake; drink, gorge yourself with water before starting to cross a desert, like an Indian; then keep cool; don't get scared and imagine yourself thirsty the first five miles and commence to gorge your water before you really need any. Ever remember that your life is in your canteen; draw it out with a zealous eye . . . .

Never play with the Indians, like some rattle-brained boy and show them your guns, etc, as many have forfeited their lives for this imprudence . . . . Invariably [before beginning your travels] get full directions about location of water, which side of the road, etc, etc. Never leave a plain wagon road in search of water (as some have done), thinking vainly that they knew more about water than a road. All wagon roads lead to springs and creeks. If you can-not follow these directions, stay at home with the gal you love so much and drink lager beer.

from desirable land occurred throughout Nevada as years passed. Today, most of the Paiutes live in reservations scattered across the state. All of the reservations would easily fit within the Nevada Test Site – an area in southern Nevada presently used by the US Air Force for weapons testing.

Dam Offsets Depression

Many small American cities managed to duck the socioeconomic bullets that struck the United States during WWI, but few escaped the country's Great Depression, which began with an unprecedented stock market crash in 1929 and lasted until the advent of US involvement in WWII. One of the few lucky cities was Las Vegas. The reason: Hoover Dam. Finished at a total cost of $165 million, the world's largest dam was built on the 1450-mile-long Colorado River a mere 25 miles east of Las Vegas. The dam not only provided, as it still does, a reliable source of water to the seven states through which the river runs, but it also put an end to widespread annual flooding caused by melting snow in the Rocky Mountains.

The dam benefited Las Vegas in many ways. For one thing, a virtual army of well-paid construction workers lived in the area for five years until the dam's completion in 1936, two years ahead of schedule. To aid construction, a good supply road was built from Las Vegas to the project site in the Black Mountains. Once the road was completed, the city's saw mills and cement factories could barely keep pace with demand. The railroad increased the number of rail lines in the region to facilitate the work, and installation of those lines meant more jobs for Las Vegas residents and more money going into the city's economy.

In 1931, that economy once again included gambling. That year, Nevada relegalized casino gambling and dropped the state's divorce residency requirement to six weeks; both decisions ran counter to the country's prevailing moralistic fervor and set the course of the state's, and especially Las Vegas', sin-filled future. Dam workers flocked to Las Vegas at night to partake in the flowing illegal booze, the rampant pros-

titution and the numerous, newly legal gambling halls that quickly sprouted downtown.

After 1936, as construction forces left, some businessmen viewed the 726-foot-high dam and newly created Lake Mead as potential big-time tourist attractions; thanks to the federally funded supply road, Las Vegas had easy access to them. Los Angeles hotelman Thomas Hull, more than anyone else, deserves credit for the Las Vegas we see today. In 1941, Hull opened the city's first plush casino-hotel, El Rancho Vegas, south of town along the two-lane highway that eventually became Las Vegas Boulevard, otherwise known as The Strip. Hull promoted the dam and Lake Mead like no one else. As a result, people came in droves to see the colossal dam, to relax by the lake and to gamble at his establishment.

In addition, El Rancho Vegas attracted a new element to the desert – Hollywood movie stars, who enjoyed gambling and rubbing elbows with the 'characters' it attracted. One of these characters was mobster Benjamin 'Bugsy' Siegel, who, along with partner Meyer Lansky, had a dream of building an even more luxurious resort in the desert that would draw 'high-rollers from all over the world,' Lansky said. Backed by Lansky's East Coast mob money, Siegel built the $6-million Flamingo hotel in 1946, and with its incandescent pastel paint job, tuxedoed janitors, Hollywood entertainers, and eight-story flashing neon-covered towers out front, it became the model for the new Las Vegas casino-hotel that was soon to come.

Unfortunately for Siegel, the Flamingo didn't make a profit, at least not immediately, and that was too long to wait as far as Siegel's backers were concerned. On June 23, 1947, he was gunned down by his associates, and the Flamingo had an instant 'change in ownership.' But the resultant national scandal had a curious effect: more people than ever came to Las Vegas to see its stunning gaming palaces and to consort with their notorious patrons and owners. An explosion of new casino-hotels erupted along The Strip, beginning with the Thunderbird in 1948, and it has continued with only a few short pauses to this day.

At the same time that the first hotel-casinos were going up, the Las Vegas economy got a boost from the army. In 1941, the year the United States entered WWII, the US military opened the Las Vegas Aerial Gunnery School, which was expanded the next year into Nellis Air Force Base, 10 miles northeast of downtown Las Vegas. Initially the site contained only a few shacks, but soon a large complex was constructed to train aerial gunners for combat duty in Europe and the Pacific. The airfield's mission quickly grew to include training copilots for B-17 and B-29 bombers. At the height of the war the base housed several thousand troops. The arrival of the troops also meant, interestingly enough, the end of prostitution on Block 16. The commander of the gunnery school threatened to make the city off-limits to soldiers if the city didn't clean up its act, and so the city did, effectively putting the illicit 'cribs' out of business for good.

That same year, 1941, Las Vegas also benefited greatly from the building of a $150-million magnesium plant in Henderson, NV, 15 miles southeast of Las Vegas. Metallic magnesium is the key component of incendiary bombs, which were widely used by the Allies. The quick, intense heat resulting from such bombs made fire control almost impossible and destroyed scores of munitions plants and other strategic targets in Germany and Japan.

Spectacular Las Vegas

By the 1950s, Las Vegas felt like a boomtown again, with casino-hotels popping up at an ever more rapid pace, and everyone – gamblers and hotel owners alike – trying to strike it rich before the good times ended. The lavish $4.5-million Desert Inn set the tone in 1950 by throwing Las Vegas' biggest party yet for its grand opening. The hotel was run by Wilbur Clark, a small-time gambler who enjoyed the media limelight, and it was funded and primarily owned by Moe Dalitz, head of a Cleveland-based organized crime syndicate. In fact, a federal investigation at the beginning of the decade made this emerging trend crystal clear: the Las Vegas casino industry enjoyed ties to

Fremont Street in the 1950s

LAS VEGAS NEWS BUREAU

Bugsy's Baby, the Flamingo hotel

and the hidden backing of organized crime from across the nation. And why not? The mob loved Las Vegas. It gave them a legitimacy and a glamorous cachet they'd never experienced before, and by fixing the games, fixing the local politicians and skimming profits both under and over the table, they were getting rich in a hurry. For their part, Las Vegans loved them back: everyone, from low-rolling 'grinds' to Tinseltown starlets, flocked to the desert town to soak up the glittering, extravagant spectacle – a gangster's vision of paradise – and the promise of instant wealth.

After the Flamingo and the Desert Inn, practically every new hotel-casino in Las Vegas tried to best the rest in terms of size and/or services, flash or taste, entertainment extravaganza or the quality and/or number of shops and restaurants. There was the Horseshoe (1951), the Sahara (1952), the Sands (1952), the Showboat (1954) and the Riviera, Dunes and New Frontier, all in 1955. Revenue from the gaming tables permitted the casinos to feature the biggest names in show business, which in turn allowed the hotel-casinos to appeal to gamblers and nongamblers alike. The Sands

attracted Frank Sinatra and Dean Martin, and later the entire Rat Pack; the Riveria nabbed Liberace; other headliners included Jimmy Durante and Sammy Davis Jr.

By the mid-1950s, Vegas had overbuilt, and a number of casinos had already gone under or changed hands, but that didn't stop new, ever-larger casino-hotels from opening, each one topping the last. The Fremont and the Hacienda opened in 1956, the Tropicana in 1957 and the Stardust in 1958 – at the time the biggest hotel in the world (1056 rooms) with the biggest electric sign. In 1957, the Dunes grabbed the spotlight when it introduced bare-breasted showgirls in its revue, *Minsky Goes to Paris*, then the next year the Stardust grabbed it back when it boasted that it had *real* French showgirls in its bare-breasted revue, *Lido de Paris*.

The 1950s also heralded the testing of nuclear weapons just 65 miles northwest of Las Vegas. Beginning in January 1951 and over the next 41 years, approximately a thousand nuclear explosions were initiated at the Nevada Test Site for national defense and peacetime purposes. For the first 12 years these tests were mostly above ground, at a rate of about one a month, until the 1963

Nuclear Test Ban Treaty forced them below ground, where they continued until 1992. Initially unconcerned about radiation fallout, Las Vegans took the atomic bomb blasts in stride – and even celebrated the publicity and notoriety they brought by selling atomburgers and crowning a Miss Atomic Bomb. One photo taken from Fremont Street at the heart of downtown shows people casually going about their business while a mushroom cloud rises ominously in the distance. The decade ended with the opening of the Las Vegas Convention Center, which presaged the city's future as a major convention city.

By 1960 the population of Las Vegas had risen to 64,406 residents (up from about 17,000 in 1945), which constituted more than half of the population of Nevada. That same year the Convention Center hosted a championship boxing match (the first of many to be held in Las Vegas), and El Rancho Vegas – the grand dame of Sin City – caught fire and burned to the ground. Hotel construction slowed considerably through the first half of the turbulent '60s, with no new grand hotels until the Aladdin opened in 1966; a year later Elvis Presley married Priscilla Beaulieu in the hotel. The Aladdin was followed in short order by Caesars Palace (1966), Circus Circus (1968), the Landmark (1969) and the $60-million International (1969; today the Las Vegas Hilton), which featured Barbra Streisand on opening night.

The slowdown in construction during the first part of the '60s allowed federal and state regulators a chance to redouble their efforts to 'clean up' the gambling industry. Scandal after scandal had plagued the casinos, as charges of mob corruption, racketeering, influence peddling and tax evasion were continually raised and investigated by federal agencies, and Nevada's elected officials were finding it increasingly difficult to maintain the fiction that their stringent casino licensing standards and vigilant enforcement were keeping the criminal element at bay. There wasn't a handful of casinos without some proven or alleged link to organized crime, and all the bad publicity was beginning to hurt tourism. Then, in 1966, into the picture stepped eccentric billionaire Howard Hughes.

Hughes arrived at the Desert Inn on Thanksgiving night in the back of an ambulance (for security reasons), and he didn't set foot outside the hotel again for the next four years. He took over the high-roller suites of the ninth floor, and when he'd worn out his welcome, rather than move, he simply bought the Desert Inn from Moe Dalitz for $13.2 million. He eventually dropped $300 million in a Las Vegas buying spree: he also purchased the Sands, the Castaways, the New Frontier, the Silver Slipper and the Landmark, as well as a TV station, the North Las Vegas Airport and other land along The

Miss Atomic Bomb made nukes sexy.

LAS VEGAS NEWS BUREAU

Eccentric billionaire Howard Hughes

Strip and around the state. It was a public relations boon for Nevada officials, as Hughes immediately lent the casino business a much-needed patina of legitimacy. If gambling was a dirty business, local papers declared, then an industrialist like Hughes wouldn't be getting into it.

Hughes received special dispensations to do business in the city, and these led to 1967 and 1969 Nevada legislation that allowed for corporate ownership of casinos. This encouraged publicly traded corporations, such as Hilton, Holiday Inn and MGM, to get involved in the gambling industry, which spurred a new round of construction in the late '60s and '70s. Most important, Las Vegas could finally begin to distance itself, in the public's mind anyway, from its notorious link to organized crime. In the end the only loser was Hughes, who in one short span of time became Las Vegas' largest operator of hotel-casinos but who ultimately got the short end of his many deals and left town several million dollars poorer.

The Age of the Megaresort

With the arrival in 1973 of the magnificent $120-million MGM Grand, Las Vegas experienced the dawn of the megaresort. At 2100 rooms, or roughly double the number at the Stardust, the MGM Grand captured the mantle 'world's largest resort.' A slew of smaller hotels also popped up along The Strip during the decade, including the Holiday Hotel, the Continental, the California, the Barbary Coast, the Imperial Palace and Bob Stupak's Vegas World (which became the Stratosphere in 1996). Master illusionists Siegfried and Roy began turning women into tigers at the Tropicana (a practice they continue today at the Mirage); Dean Martin made a surprise appearance on Jerry Lewis' *National Muscular Dystrophy Telethon* at the Sahara, thus ending a 20-year falling-out between the two comedians; and Tina Turner, Bill Cosby, Steve Martin, Johnny Cash and Sonny and Cher entertained crowds in Las Vegas' many showrooms.

However, the '70s were also a difficult decade for the city. A flash flood swept down a section of The Strip, damaging or destroying hundreds of cars; Atlantic City legalized gambling, causing Vegas tourism to dip; and state and federal investigations into illegalities in the gaming industry continued to unwind before the public. This remaining taint of corruption kept many traditional banking institutions from freely financing corporate gaming – making it sometimes difficult to raise the enormous funds necessary to build the huge resorts.

The 1980s began tragically for Las Vegas – when fire swept through the MGM Grand, killing 84 guests and injuring 700 (Bally's took over the property and quickly reopened it) – but the decade ended with a celebration, also of fire – in the form of a 50-foot volcano that erupts every 15 minutes from sunset till midnight in front of the gleaming Mirage hotel-casino. As the US economy recovered, and Vegas overcame the competition from Atlantic City, the town experienced a new boom. All the *known* mobsters were finally run out of town, and Las Vegas was declared sufficiently 'sanitized.' Nothing signaled the rearrival of good times like Steve Wynn's 3000-room Mirage, which was also home to a white-tiger garden, a dolphin habitat, a 20,000-gallon aquarium and a rainforest. Frequent Las Vegas headliners during the '80s included singers Dolly

When the Lights Went Out

In the history of Las Vegas the city's casino chieftains have turned off their marquee lights on only five occasions. The first time was in 1963, when the casinos closed for three hours following the assassination of President John F Kennedy. The casinos closed their doors again in 1968, after an assassin's bullet claimed the life of the Rev Martin Luther King Jr. The casinos remained open for business the day Sammy Davis Jr died of throat cancer on May 16, 1990, but their marquee lights were shut off in unison for 10 minutes. Their lights were dimmed again for two more Rat Pack brothers – when Dean Martin succumbed to acute respiratory failure on December 25, 1995, and when Frank Sinatra was silenced by a heart attack on May 14, 1998.

Parton and Willie Nelson and funnymen Rodney Dangerfield, Eddie Murphy and Don Rickles.

The 1990s saw the boom get bigger. The Excalibur, a giant medieval-castle-themed hotel complete with moat and staffed with valiant knights and fair damsels, ushered in the decade with trumpets blaring. And blare they should have, because the city's most spectacular megaresort casinos were just around the bend. The new MGM Grand re-appeared from a massive renovation with 5000 rooms in 1993, reclaiming its status as the largest hotel in the world. The same year, the Luxor's black pyramid rose from the desert, Treasure Island launched its pirate battle on The Strip, and the Dunes was intentionally blown to bits. Then came the Hard Rock Café & Hotel (the self-proclaimed world's first rock 'n' roll hotel), the French Riviera-themed Monte Carlo resort and New York-New York, replete with Manhattan skyline. Even more impressive were late arrivals Bellagio, one of the most opulent hotels in the world and home to $300 million in fine art; Stratosphere, which is a hotel, a casino and an elegant, white viewing tower that is the tallest building in the western United States; Mandalay Bay, which takes 'bundling' into uncharted territory with gourmet restaurants, a world-class spa, a terrific blues club and six-time Tony Award-winning musical *Chicago*; and two more awesome, city-themed megaresorts, the Venetian and Paris-Las Vegas.

As the Second Millennium AD neared its conclusion, Las Vegas boasted 19 of the world's 20 largest hotels, it attracted 32 million visitors a year (more than any other US city), and annual reported gaming revenue from Sin City's gambling establishments topped $5 billion (or more than $10,000 every 60 seconds!). Over 100,000 marriage licenses were issued in Las Vegas yearly, which is an average of one 'I do'

Liberace's smile defined Las Vegas style.

LAS VEGAS NEWS BUREAU

Nuclear Waste in the Nevada Desert

The US government stopped exploding nuclear bombs underground at the Nevada Test Site in 1992, but that hasn't meant the end of a possible nuclear future for state residents. In 1998, a US Department of Energy report – which took 15 years and $6 billion to research – recommended Yucca Mountain, near the test site and about 90 miles northeast of Las Vegas, as the best possible location for the nation's only long-term high-level nuclear waste repository.

Did we say long-term? The proposed site – which would eventually hold 80,000 tons of used reactor fuel from nuclear power plants across the country – would remain deadly for 300,000 years. In that time, Earth itself may experience the next ice age, and Yucca Mountain, currently one of the driest and most remote places in the United States, may no longer be a desert.

And that's a problem. Scientists agree that water poses the greatest risk to radiation leakage at the site – a far more serious risk than earthquakes (mild ones are common) or volcanic eruptions (which haven't occurred here in 7.5 million years). If ground water seeps down and contacts the waste a thousand feet below the surface, it can carry radiation relatively quickly (in less than 50 years, a recent study found) into a water basin below the underground site and into the surrounding countryside.

The Department of Energy acknowledges this risk, but maintains that the corrosion-resistance metal casks will last for at least 10,000 to 100,000 years, even if they get wet, and after that escaped radiation won't rise above background amounts.

However, no one is arguing that the containers won't deteriorate. And once they do, the only thing keeping the radiation from spreading in substantial amounts is the bone-dry mountain rock – so long as it stays dry.

Anyone care to predict the weather 200,000 years from now?

Not surprisingly, Nevada officials are fighting the proposed waste site tooth and nail. The problem is that nuclear power plants already have enormous piles of spent fuel rods and radioactive waste they have to put somewhere – a total of about 40,000 tons of high-level waste in 34 states. Unless another solution is found, the Energy Department is on schedule to make a formal recommendation on the suitability of Yucca Mountain to the president in 2001.

If approved, the Yucca Mountain repository would begin taking nuclear waste in 2010; it would continue to receive atomic waste for around a hundred years, and then its 100 miles of tunnels would be capped. The proposed project carries an estimated price tag of $43 billion (in 1998 dollars).

every five minutes. There were more than 16 miles of lighted neon tubing in the city. In 1997, Suzanne Henley won $12,510,559 at a Vegas slot machine with a $3 bet. At any time of day or night in Las Vegas you could buy a refrigerator, get divorced, rent a date, sell your car, pick up your cleaning or arrange for a caterer. It took two people 75 hours a week just to maintain the 325 human-hair wigs used in Bally's *Jubilee!* revue. As the Third Millennium AD gets underway, there is no city in the world like

Las Vegas, and no city even attempting to catch it.

GEOGRAPHY

Las Vegas is in the Great Basin, a vast region that includes most of Nevada and parts of California, Idaho, Utah, Wyoming and Oregon. It's called a 'basin' because its rivers drain into inland lakes and sinks, not to a sea. Within the Nevada portion of the basin are dozens of north-south mountain ranges, such as those that surround Las Vegas on all sides for more than 200 miles.

The principal life zone of the Great Basin is high desert, with most of the basins at over 4000 feet and most of the ranges topping 10,000 feet. The geographic area of the Great Basin that contains Las Vegas is the 15,000-sq-mile Mojave Desert, which covers parts of southern Nevada, southeastern California, northwestern Arizona and southeastern Utah. The city sits in the middle of a valley that's 2174 feet above sea level and ringed by barren foothills. There are no year-round rivers in the valley.

CLIMATE

Las Vegas receives a mere 4.13 inches of rainfall and enjoys 310 sunny days during a typical year. The dry weather acts as a magnet for sun-starved retirees and others seeking refuge from blizzards at home, but the heat can be oppressive, particularly from May through September. Tourism officials are quick to note it's 'a dry heat,' which is true; relative humidity rarely tops 20%. But be forewarned: daily temperatures approach 100°F half of the year, and highs during July and August routinely hover around 105°F. August is Las Vegas' 'wettest' month, receiving an average of .49 inches of rain. June is the driest month, receiving an average of .12 inches of rain.

Las Vegas doesn't cool off much after sunset. Concrete and asphalt retain and radiate heat. Due to the billions of tons of concrete and asphalt in Las Vegas, temperatures within the city often exceed 75°F well after nightfall. That said, chilly days and cold nights occasionally visit Las Vegas during winter. To everyone's surprise, Las Vegas

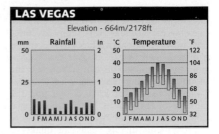

even experienced a white Christmas in 1998. If you'll be in Las Vegas during November, December or January, you'd be wise to bring a jacket.

ECOLOGY & ENVIRONMENT

Las Vegas is an environmentalist's nightmare. Water usage is the chief concern. The city receives 85% of its water from the Colorado River, which supplies Lake Mead, and 15% from the ground. Las Vegas residents use, on average, 178 gallons of water per day per person; this figure includes the tremendous amounts of water used by hotel-casinos.

The Las Vegas Valley is expected to use its entire water supply by the year 2010. It presently shares Colorado River water with California and Arizona, and none of the communities that currently receive water from the Colorado River want to give up any of it. What's going to happen in the years to come when there's not enough water to go around is anyone's guess.

Water pollution is another big problem. Lake Mead, despite being the largest human-made lake in the Western Hemisphere, is experiencing rising levels of pollution. The lake receives partially treated effluent pumped back by Las Vegas' sewage plants. More partially treated effluent is going into the lake than ever before, and the amount of water leaving the lake exceeds the amount entering it. This situation is particularly alarming when you consider that Las Vegas is one of the fastest-growing cities in the US.

Air pollution is another unpopular subject in Las Vegas. The city is surrounded by mountains that trap hazardous particulates. Prior to 1980, the view of those mountains was crystal clear every sunny day; most days now the sky above Las Vegas contains a dirty brown inversion layer that's occasionally so thick you can't even see the mountains. With average daily traffic in Las Vegas increasing at 5.8% a year and the number of takeoffs at McCarran International Airport on the rise, the probability of improvements in Las Vegas' air quality is poor.

FLORA & FAUNA

There are 370 recorded species of birds, 129 species of mammals and 64 species of reptiles in Nevada, and the state boasts an equally impressive variety of plantlife. But no one's got a clue how many species of birds, mammals, reptiles or plants can be found *in the wild* in Las Vegas Valley.

In Las Vegas, domesticated critters include white tigers, black jaguars, bottle-

Brittlebrush

nosed dolphins, Asian elephants – and those represent only the exotic animals found at The Mirage. The Flamingo Hilton is home to African penguins, Chilean flamingos, sacred ibises and wood ducks. And there's also a zoo in town – lions and tigers and bears, oh my!

GOVERNMENT & POLITICS

Las Vegas has operated under a council-manager form of government since January 1, 1944. Under this form of government the citizens elect four council members and a mayor who make up the City Council. The mayor is elected at large by all the voters of the city. Each council member is elected from one of four wards in the city. The mayor and the council members serve four-year terms.

A city manager, hired by the City Council, is responsible for the day-to-day operation of the city government. Below the city manager is the city attorney's office and two deputy city managers, responsible for the 14 major departments within the government. Departments are further divided into logistical divisions to perform their respective functions.

On June 8, 1999, in a major blow to official efforts to clean up Sin City's image, Las Vegas voters picked longtime mob lawyer Oscar Goodman to be their mayor. Goodman, who gained fame defending mafia figures such as Meyer Lansky and Tony 'The Ant' Spilotro, caught the voters' fancy with a populist platform that called for developers to pay fees to help solve city traffic and air pollution woes.

The alleged 'barrister-to-butchers,' as an editorial in the *Las Vegas Review-Journal* described him, makes no effort to hide his past. Indeed, the purported 'mouthpiece of the mafia' loves to talk about the old days, when he busted up dozens of government attacks on reputed mobsters and kept Spilotro out of jail despite suspicions that the feared mafia enforcer had committed nearly two dozen murders.

As Lansky's attorney, Goodman got the mafia's financial genius dropped from a casino cash-skimming trial because of

Lansky's failing health. Goodman similarly evoked the disgust of law enforcement officers nationwide when, in 1970, he persuaded a judge to throw out wiretap evidence obtained in 19 cities around the country, crippling a federal campaign against bookmaking.

In his defense, Goodman, whose office is chock-full of photos of reputed mobsters and toy rats in traps, has devoted much of his practice to the poor and the dispossessed, often pro bono. In 1998, he won the release from prison of a cancer-ridden woman who had murdered her abusive husband – a noble thing in the minds of many. And the National Association of Criminal Defense Lawyers once hailed Goodman as 'Liberty's last champion.'

What kind of mayor Goodman will make has yet to be seen (this was written as he was being elected). Goodman was fond of saying in the weeks leading to his victory, 'They can call me the mob lawyer, but there are so many other things about me. When I am through they are going to say, "He is a hell of a mayor."'

ECONOMY

Tourism drives the Las Vegas economy. That's no surprise, given that 32 million-plus tourists a year spend an average of four days in town, and most of those people come with money to gamble; the average Vegas visitor in 1997 had a per-trip gambling budget of $515. During the same year more than 50% of the city's workforce was employed in the service industry.

The stability of Las Vegas' economy is open to debate. The US economy during the late 1990s was record setting: the stock market reached new highs, unemployment was at a 40-year low, and interest rates and inflation were very favorable. Eighty percent of Las Vegas' visitors are American, and with Americans doing so well it wasn't surprising that Las Vegas did well, too.

It remains to be seen what will happen to Las Vegas when the US slips into a recession and Americans aren't so anxious to gamble. Las Vegas' casinos were taking in $5 billion in gaming revenues annually by 1999. How Las Vegas and its ultra-expensive megaresorts will fair if that figure is halved is anybody's guess, but it likely won't be pretty.

POPULATION & PEOPLE

Las Vegas had a population of 401,702 in 1998, the most recent year a population figure was available for the city. However, the number of people living in Las Vegas Valley (which would include the residents of North Las Vegas, Henderson and several other unincorporated communities) exceeded 1 million.

Of Las Vegas' 401,702 residents, 24.5% were under the age of 18, 10.5% were 65 or older, the median age was 33.1 years and the median household income was $30,986. The ethnic origin of Las Vegans broke down as follows: 73.5% European, 11.7% Hispanic, 9.3% African, 4% Asian, 1% Indian and 0.5% other.

EDUCATION

State law requires all children ages 7 to 17 to attend school. Students attend 180 days of school for the year. In 1999 there were 142 elementary schools, 31 middle schools and 28 high schools in the Clark County School District, which includes Las Vegas. In that year the district predicted 110 new schools would be needed over the next 10 years.

Las Vegas has two institutions of higher learning: the University of Nevada at Las Vegas (UNLV) and the Community College of Southern Nevada (CCSN). The 335-acre UNLV campus has a student body of 20,000.

Not So Learned

Nevada ranks last among US states in sending its high school graduates to college. Nationwide, 53.5% of high school graduates go on to college. In Nevada, the rate is only 32.8%. Nevada also has the highest percentage of high school dropouts in the country. Figures for Las Vegas are unavailable.

Its admission requirements are low, and none of its 148 undergraduate, master's and doctoral programs is held in high regard nationally.

Enrollment at CCSN's three campuses hovers around 26,000 students. Sounding somewhat defensive in its literature, the college maintains that its 'students are serious about education and demonstrate a strong work ethic.' In fact, 90% of CCSN's students are employed. As the college says, 'They are dedicated part-time scholars with full-time jobs.'

ARTS
Like clean government in Chicago or sizzling nightlife in Salt Lake City, until recently cultural arts in Las Vegas would have been just another urban oxymoron. But that's not the case anymore. A glimpse of Vegas' art scenes is provided here; see the Things to See & Do chapter for details.

Dance
It might surprise you to know that Nevada has a professional ballet company, and it presents both classical and contemporary ballet performances. The Nevada Ballet Theatre (☎ 702-898-6306, 1651 Inner Circle Drive) offers performances year-round.

Music
Las Vegas is home to the Nevada Symphony Orchestra, the Nevada Opera Theatre, the Las Vegas Civic Symphony and the Nevada Chamber Symphony. Like jazz? You can hear it live every day of the week in Las Vegas. Rhythm and blues? Same deal.

The greatest names in rock 'n' roll appear at The Joint, the 1400-seat state-of-the-art concert venue at the Hard Rock Hotel. Lounge acts playing old favorites? Las Vegas has a million of them. Live country music? Live hip-hop? Big band sound? Karaoke? Las Vegas has got it all.

Sculpture
Many of the nonprofit and for-profit galleries have ceramic and wooden sculptures on display. Most of the megaresorts contain statues in their casinos or adjacent shopping

JOHN ELK III

Flashlight by Claus Olderberg
on the UNLV campus

wing. The campus of the University of Nevada at Las Vegas has a rather illuminating piece called *The Flashlight* by Claes Oldenberg; yes, it's a flashlight – a jet-black three-story-tall flashlight located beside the university's Performing Arts Center.

Painting
Caesars Palace still has its kitschy exterior copies of the *Venus de Milo* and other sculptural icons, but Las Vegas now has the Bellagio Gallery of Fine Art – with $300 million in *great* art. And seeing a Monet water lily, Cézanne's *Portrait of a Woman* and Renoir's *La Loge* in a setting renown for glitz actually gives the paintings more power, not less.

The masterpieces at the Bellagio are the pride of Vegas' artistic community these days, but they certainly aren't the only artworks in town. There are no fewer than 22 other private art galleries and 29 nonprofit art galleries in Las Vegas. Among them are the Gallerie Michelangelo, where original works by contemporary artists such as LeRoy Neiman and Erté can be found.

Architecture

In Las Vegas, structures that predate 1950 cling to life like a trailer park in a tornado. Until recently, buildings with historic value were being blown to pieces or slammed apart by wrecking balls as often as Don Rickles comes to town.

Okay, so Las Vegas doesn't have any masterpieces of architecture, but the Huntridge Theater does have a splendid example of Streamline Moderne architecture, a style of clean, austere lines born in the 1930s. The building now housing the Las Vegas Academy of International Studies and Performing Arts is the only full-scale art deco structure in the city.

New monoliths along The Strip celebrate just about every metropolis and epoch except modern-day Nevada. There is a pyramid of ancient Egypt at the Luxor, the famous high-rises at New York-New York, an ersatz Eiffel Tower at Paris-Las Vegas and a *palazzo* at The Venetian. Buildings come in all sizes, shapes and designs in the city of cash and flash.

Literature

One thing Las Vegas isn't known for is literature. Books by Las Vegas writers or about Las Vegas tend to focus on two topics: beating the casinos at their game *(Henry Tamburin on Casino Gambling* et al) and doing Las Vegas on a dime *(The Cheapskate's Guide to Las Vegas* et al). For these kinds of titles, see Books in the Facts for the Visitor chapter.

In 1971 Hunter S Thompson wrote *Fear and Loathing in Las Vegas*. In many minds, it is the only major literary work linked to Las Vegas. In *Fear and Loathing*, Thompson recounts the humorous story of his trip to Las Vegas to cover the Mint 400 Off-Road Race. The book defined the counterculture of its day.

Literary Las Vegas is an anthology edited by Mike Tronnos and published in 1995 that contains 24 pieces about Las Vegas penned by Thompson, Tom Wolfe and Noel Coward, to name a few.

Film

Hollywood *loves* Las Vegas. Between 1980 and 1998, no fewer than 86 major motion pictures were shot in Las Vegas or in the desert on the edge of town, and dozens of other movies were made in the area prior to then (see Hollywood Comes to Vegas). In addition to the films mentioned in the boxed text, the following movies were also shot in or near Sin City, some of which now function as time capsules of previous incarnations of this ever-changing place: *Wild Is the Wind* (1957), *The Professionals* (1966), *The Gauntlet* (1977), *Electric Horseman* (1979), *Romancing the Stone* (1984) and *Vegas Vacation* (1997).

Movie Theaters

There are many movie theaters of the typical variety (flat screen, nothing special) in Las Vegas. At the Omnimax Theater at Caesars Palace specially made films create

Hunter S Thompson

Hollywood Comes to Vegas

More than 130 motion pictures have been filmed in the Las Vegas area since 1932, when John Ford et al visited and made *Airmail*, a routine story of pioneer airmail pilots starring Pat O'Brien and Ralph Bellamy. Here's a look at some of the famous and infamous movies featuring Sin City.

Love Las Vegas Style
Viva Las Vegas (1964) – Elvis Presley's a race car driver and Ann-Margret is the sexy Rusty Martin. Can Elvis win the race and the girl? Of course! But only after a few musical numbers.

Kiss Me, Stupid (1964) – Dean Martin stars as a crooner making the moves on a songwriter's wife in the Nevada desert town of Climax in this lewd farce by Billy Wilder.

Indecent Proposal (1993) – High roller Robert Redford offers $1 million to a needy couple (Demi Moore and Woody Harrelson) if the wife will have sex with him. It proves to be a poor bargain. Filmed partly in the Las Vegas Hilton.

Betting the Farm
Lost in America (1985) – This hilarious film starring Albert Brooks finds a middle-class couple looking to escape their yuppie lifestyle only to lose their 'nest egg' at the Desert Inn.

Rain Man (1988) – Tom Cruise takes his autistic brother (Dustin Hoffman) on a cross-country roadtrip that ends with a triumphant round of cards at Caesars Palace. Many scenes in this Oscar-winning movie were shot in nearby rural Nevada.

Mobsters & Crooks
711 Ocean Drive (1950) – Joseph Newman directs and Edmond O'Brien, Joanne Dru and Otto Kruger star in this racketeer tale with a nail-biting climax at Hoover Dam.

Ocean's Eleven (1960) – This is the movie that gave birth to the Rat Pack: Frank Sinatra, Sammy Davis Jr, Dean Martin, and Peter Lawford attempt to rob five casinos at once. Overlong and sometimes dull, it's still a quintessential Vegas film.

The Godfather (1972) – There's a brief Vegas interlude in this Oscar-winning tale of an East Coast mafia family.

Bugsy (1991) – Hollywood's take on the Benjamin 'Bugsy' Siegel story. A compelling film starring Warren Beatty that takes great pains to recreate the original Flamingo.

Casino (1995) – This Scorsese film follows casino chief Robert De Niro as Las Vegas changes from a mob-run heaven to a family-fun theme park. Sharon Stone shines amid a heavyweight cast.

an awesome visual display projected via 70 mm film, which is 10 times the frame size of regular projection film. The screen isn't your standard wall-mounted white rectangle either, but instead the theater has a dome ceiling and films are projected against it; the seats are designed to allow you to lie back and stare up at the movies. Complementing the visual projection is a nine-channel 'sensaround' sound system emanating from a total of 89 speakers.

RELIGION
No one group dominates the Las Vegas religious community. The breakdown: 31.2% Catholic, 24.4% Protestant, 17.8% no affiliation, 16.8% other, 5.4% Latter-Day Saints and 4.4% Jewish.

There are 584 houses of worship in the Las Vegas area. Here are the denominations with churches and the number of churches belonging to each: Apostolic (17), Assembly of God (16), Baptist (83), Catholic (23),

Hollywood Comes to Vegas

Overcoming All Odds

Diamonds Are Forever (1971) – Sean Connery is up to his usual tricks and sexual hijinks as Agent 007 in this James Bond comic-book adventure, which has scenes in Circus Circus and the Las Vegas Hilton.

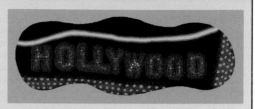

Rocky IV (1985) – Sly Stallone fights for the USA and Dolph Lundgren the USSR – and James Brown borrows *Jubilee!* props for his musical number – in the third unnecessary sequel to an American classic.

Destroying Vegas

The Amazing Colossal Man (1957) – In this camp thriller, a man turned into a giant by a nuclear explosion terrorizes Vegas. Extremely silly, but there's vintage footage of The Strip.

Honey, I Blew Up the Kid (1992) – See this Disney flick only for its homage to *The Amazing Colossal Man*, in which a giant baby toddles down Fremont St.

Showgirls (1995) – The makers of this film didn't set out to destroy Vegas, but that's what happened. Voted worst movie about Vegas in the *Las Vegas Review-Journal*'s 1999 readers' poll.

Mars Attacks! (1996) – Martians attack Earth in this cheeky farce, and Sin City is a prime target. Watch Tom Jones and a bevy of Vegas oddballs fend for their lives!

The Nicolas Cage Series

Honeymoon in Vegas (1992) – Nicolas Cage must love this town. Here, he's a detective on the brink of losing his new wife to sleazy Vegas mobster James Caan. The climax of this engaging farce features the Flying Elvii.

Leaving Las Vegas (1995) – Nick plays an alcoholic bent on drinking himself to death in Vegas in this disturbing movie. Cage won a Best Actor Oscar for his role.

Con Air (1997) – In this stupid action flick, Nick plays a good convict who spoils the plans of bad ones. Their plane crashes into the now-demolished Sands hotel-casino, and there's a climactic chase down Fremont St.

Episcopal (10), interdenominational (7), Jewish (13), Lutheran (18), Latter-Day Saints (162), Methodist (15), nondenominational (57), Pentecostal (13) and other (150).

Most tourists seeking religious services while in Las Vegas visit the Guardian Angel Cathedral (☎ 702-735-5241), conveniently located 300 feet from Las Vegas Blvd at 302 Cathedral Way (beside the Desert Inn Hotel). Mass is held at 8 am and 12:10 pm weekdays. Mass is also held at 2:30, 4 and 5:15 pm Saturday, and at 8, 9:30 and 11 am, and 12:30 and 5 pm Sunday. It's quite all right to drop casino chips in the collection plate; a lot of people do.

For the locations and phone numbers of hundreds of churches in the Las Vegas area, see the listings that appear under 'Churches' in the Las Vegas Yellow Pages (a phone directory should be stashed somewhere in your hotel room; if not, ask for one at the reception desk). For the same information for synagogues, look under 'Synagogues' in the Yellow Pages.

LANGUAGE

English is the primary spoken language in Las Vegas. Most of the major casino-hotels have translators on staff to assist guests who are not fluent in English. Also, there are dozens of ethnic/cultural organizations in Las Vegas, including the Cambodian Association, the Deutsche-American Society, the Las Vegas Korean Association and the Polish American Center. Contact Aird & Associates (☎ 702-456-3838) for further information regarding these and many other ethnic/cultural communities and organizations in the Las Vegas area. If you need to communicate with someone who speaks your native language, Aird & Associates can likely assist you.

Gambling in Las Vegas

Gambling can be an exhilarating experience – every lucky roll of the dice providing an electric rush of adrenaline – but when it comes to Vegas casinos, it's important to remember one thing: the house advantage. For every game except poker the house has a statistical winning edge (the 'percentage') over the gambler, and for nearly every payout in nearly every game the house 'holds' a small portion of the winnings. These amounts vary with the game and with individual bets, but they add up to what's referred to as a 'long-term negative expectation' – or the assurance that over the long haul the gambler will lose everything.

As such, you should approach gambling only as entertainment – one for which you pay a fee – and not as a way to fund your children's education. Understand the game you are playing, don't bet more than you are prepared to lose, and learn to leave when you are up. These three 'rules' are the best way to ensure that your time spent gambling will remain enjoyable and fun.

The Casino

The minimum age to enter the gambling pit is 18, but you must be at least 21 years old in order to play. The traditional casino games include baccarat, blackjack, craps, keno, the money wheel, poker, roulette, slot machines, the sports book and video poker. Each game has its own customs, traditions and strategies, and you should read about the games you want to play beforehand (see Books in the Facts for the Visitor chapter for recommendations). Also check out the free gambling lessons at the large casinos.

It's also acceptable to ask your dealer for help and advice. For instance, he or she should gladly tell you the odds on a particular bet at craps or what the strategy is for the blackjack hand you've just been dealt. An entertaining dealer can make your time at the tables an unforgettable experience, and you shouldn't be shy about finding another table if yours is surly or unhelpful. It's also polite to 'toke,' or tip, your dealer if you are winning. Either place a chip on the layout (the area where you place your bet) for the dealer to collect, or place a side bet for the dealer, which he or she collects if it wins. Keno runners and slot attendants also expect a small tip.

Baccarat

Nothing conjures the image of high stakes, black tuxedoes and James Bond like baccarat, and yet, of the card games, it possesses the least strategy – none. The rules are quite fixed, the house edge is low, and there are no decisions for the player except for how to bet. The only thing special about the game, other than its mystique, is that minimum bets are usually

$20 or $25, ensuring that only those with large bankrolls sit down to play. However, you can now often find less-formal minibaccarat tables near the blackjack pit with $2 to $5 minimum bets; these make good places to learn the game.

One player and the banker are each dealt two cards from a 'shoe' that contains eight complete decks of cards. The hand closest to 9 points wins. Aces through 9s count at face value; 10s and face cards are worth zero. If the cards exceed 10 points, only the second digit is counted. For instance, a king plus a 5 card equals 5; a 7 plus a 6 equals 3. A third card must be drawn under specific rules: a player must draw if the score of the two cards is 0, 1, 2, 3, 4 or 5; the player must stand with 6 or 7. Neither the player nor the banker can draw with a score of 8 or 9. If there's a tie, the hands are redealt. There are only three bets: on the bank, the player or a tie.

In baccarat, the 'bank' is passed around among the players; the player holds the shoe and continues as the banker as long as the bank hand wins. When the player's hand wins, the shoe is then passed to the next player, who then becomes the banker. A player can choose to pass the shoe. When you bet on the bank and the bank wins, you are charged a 5% commission that must be paid at the start of a new game or when you leave the table.

Blackjack

Blackjack is the most popular table game in Las Vegas because it is the one game bet against the house where the skill of the player affects the odds, and so it has become the most scrutinized and ana lyzed game of all – by both players and casinos. In fact, it's the only game where memory plays a role – where skilled card counters can track cards played and calculate the probabilities for future cards – and this has created a sometimes antagonistic relationship between players and pit bosses. However, even without card counting, it's possible to follow a basic strategy that can reduce the house advantage to almost nothing in certain situations.

Players bet against the dealer, and the object is to draw cards that total as close to 21 as possible without going over. Jacks, queens and kings count as 10, an ace is worth either 11 or 1 (the choice is yours), and other cards are counted at face value. The player places a bet and is dealt two cards. The dealer then gets two cards, one facing up and the other concealed. The player now has four choices: either to 'stand' (take no more cards), 'hit' (take more cards one at a time), 'double down' (double your bet and take one more card), or 'split' – in which, if you are dealt an original pair (such as two 8s), you create two new separate hands and play them individually.

Players draw cards until they stand on their total or 'bust' (go over 21 and lose immediately). The dealer then reveals the downturned card and must either hit on any total of 16 or less or stand on any total of 17 or more – the house rules here are strict. If the player's hand is higher than the dealer's, he or she wins; if less, the player loses. Ties are called a 'push,' and no money changes hands. All wins are paid at even money, except 'blackjack' (a natural 21, when the first two cards are an ace plus a 10-value card), which pays 3 to 2 – or $3 for every $2 bet.

Many gambling books provide a chart of the 'basic strategy' that outlines the best percentage play for every single card combination, and it's perfectly acceptable to consult a copy of this chart at the gaming table. Basic strategy can be boiled down to a few general rules:

- If you have 12 to 16 and the dealer's up card is 2 to 6, stand.
- If you have 12 to 16 and the dealer's up card is 7, 8, 9, 10 or ace, hit.
- If you have 17 to 21, stand, no matter what the dealer's up card is.
- Double down if you have 10 or 11 and the dealer's up card is 2 to 9.
- Always split a pair of aces or 8s.

Craps

Undoubtedly the most fun and noise in a casino will be generated at a lively, fast-paced craps table – with players shouting, crowds gathering and everyone hoping for that lucky hot streak. Tossing dice is a completely random activity, but that doesn't stop people from betting their 'hunches' and believing that certain numbers are 'due' – even though the odds are exactly the same on every roll. Craps can also be the most intimidating game to step up to for the first time, since the betting possibilities are very complicated and shift as play continues. It's important to spend some time studying a betting guide and begin playing with the simplest wager (on the pass/don't pass line), which also happens to be one of better bets in the casino.

To begin, the 'stickman' hands the dice to a player, who becomes the 'shooter' for that round. A 'pass line' bet is that on the first roll (the 'come-out' roll) the dice will total 7 or 11. If the dice total 2, 3 or 12 (called 'craps'), the player loses. Any other number becomes the 'point,' and the dice are rolled again until either a 7 or the point number comes up – if a 7 comes up first, the player loses; if the point comes up, the player wins.

A 'don't pass' bet is basically the reverse – if the come-out roll totals 7 or 11, the player loses; if it's 2 or 3, the player wins; 12 is a push. If a point is established, the don't-pass bettor wins on a 7 and loses if the point is rolled again. All these bets pay even money.

'Come' bets are placed after a point is established; 7 and 11 win, while 2, 3, 12 lose. If none of these come up, the dice are thrown again until the point is thrown, and the player wins, or a 7 is thrown and the player loses. The don't-come bet is the reverse, except that 12 is a push. Come and don't-come bets also pay even money.

If you've already made a pass or come bet, and a point has been established, you can bet that the point will come up before a 7 is thrown. These bets pay off at a rate that is equal to the statistical chance of a win, so the house has no edge – this is called a 'free-odds' bet (or just an 'odds' bet), and it is the best chance you'll get in a casino. You don't have an advantage against the house, but at least the odds aren't against you.

Then there are even more betting options: 'place,' 'field' and 'buy' bets, and the one-roll 'sucker bets' – the big 6 or big 8, 'hard ways,' any 7 and any craps. Despite big payoffs, these last bets have long odds and a house edge between 9% and 17% – and are avoided by most craps players.

Keno

This slow-paced game with bad odds is a lot like lotto; there are 80 numbered squares on a card, a player picks from 1 to 15 numbers and bets $1 or so per number or number combination. You can bet straight, split, 'way' or combination. At the draw, the casino randomly selects 20 numbers, and winners are paid off according to how many of the winning numbers they chose, as shown on a 'payoff chart.' Payoffs range from $3 to $100,000. The amount paid off is distinctly less than the probability of selecting the numbers by chance, so the odds favor the house by over 20%. Keno runners circulate throughout the casino, and keno lounges serve refreshments while you watch the monitors.

The Money Wheel

Also known as the 'wheel of fortune' or 'big six,' this old carnival midway game is usually near the slot machines. Place your bet on one of 54 positions or slots, spin the wheel and, in most cases, lose your money. The prohibitive house advantage is only slightly less than at keno, making these lonely outposts.

Poker

Poker is unusual for casino games because players bet directly against one another. The house provides the table, the cards and the dealer, who sells the chips, deals the hands and collects a 'rake' from each pot. If you're not already a good poker player, don't even think about getting involved in a Vegas casino game. There are a number of different types of games, including high-low, seven-card stud and straight poker, but one of the most popular is hold 'em, in which five cards are dealt faceup on the table and two cards are dealt to each player. The person with the best five-card hand out of the seven cards wins.

Pai gow poker is a variation on regular poker: a joker is added to a regular 52-card deck, and players play against the bank. The joker is used as an ace or to complete a straight or flush. Players are dealt seven cards each, which are then arranged into two hands. One hand contains five cards and is known as the 'high hand.' The second hand contains two cards and is the 'low hand.' The object of the game is to have both the high and low hands rank higher than the respective hands of the banker.

The ranking is determined by traditional poker rules. If both hands rank lower, the wager is lost to the banker. If either hand wins while the other loses, this is a 'push' and the wager is refunded. If either one of the player's hands ties the banker, then the bank wins. The house handles all bets and charges a 5% commission on all winning wages.

Roulette

This ancient game is easy to under-
stand and often hypnotic to play.
You can use either casino chips or
special 'wheel chips,' which are
dispensed at the roulette table
and are a different color for each
player. Roulette provides the
most clear demonstration of the
house edge. The roulette wheel has
38 numbers – from 1 to 36, plus 0 and
00. Half the numbers are colored red, the other
half are black, while the two zeros are green. The table layout is marked with the numbers and the various combinations that can be bet.

You can bet that a result will be odd or even, red or black, high (19 to 36) or low (1 to 18). All of these bets pay off at even money, but the chances of a win are less than 50% because the 0 and 00 don't count as odd or even, red or black, high or low. Your chances are 18 in 38 (47.37%), not 18 in 36.

Further, a bet on a single number (including the 0 and 00) pays out at 35 to 1, though true odds would be 37 to 1. You can also bet on pairs of numbers, or groups of 4, 5, 6 or 12 numbers, which all have a house advantage of 5.26% (the 5-number bet is actually slightly worse). These aren't the best odds in the casino, but they're far from the worst.

Slot Machines

The 'slots' are mind-numbingly simple – you put in a coin and pull the handle (or push a button) – but they are also wildly popular. Most machines take quarters, some take nickels or pennies and a few take

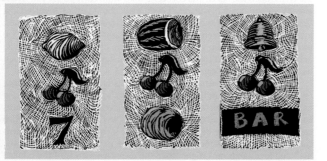

tokens of $1, $5 and even more. Machines have various types of spinning wheels and payouts, but there is no effect a player has on the outcome. The probabilities are programmed into the machine, and the chances of winning are the same on every pull.

The only important decisions are which machine to play and when to stop. Some machines pay back a higher proportion of the money deposited than others (though by law slot machines must return at least 75%). Those that return a lot to the player, as much as 97%, are called 'loose' – hence the signs advertising 'the loosest slots in town.' Loose slots are more likely to be found in the highly visible areas of big casinos. Slots with a lower return, down to 84% or even less, are more common in impulse gambling locations like waiting rooms, bars and bathrooms.

'Progressive slots' offer a jackpot that accumulates, and many slots are now linked in networks to generate bigger jackpots. Often these pay off in the form of a new car, which is prominently displayed in the casino. The jackpots are factored into the payout percentage, so there's no extra statistical advantage to the player, except that a payout of a few thousand dollars may induce someone to quit while he or she is ahead, instead of putting all the winnings back into the slot.

The Sports Book

The bigger casinos usually have a 'sports book' room, where sporting events from around the country are displayed on video screens covering most of a wall. Players can bet on just about any ball game, boxing match, horse race or hockey game in the country, except for events taking place in Nevada. Sports books are best during major sporting events, when everyone is captivated by, betting on and yelling about the same game.

Video Poker

Increasingly popular, video poker games are often built into a bar. Like regular poker, they deal you five electronic cards; you hold the cards you want and then draw again to complete a five-card hand. Quarter machines are common, though they can range from a nickel to $5 per bet. Employing correct strategy and finding machines with the best payout sched-

ules, it's possible to improve your chances of winning and reduce the house advantage to nothing in some situations. Basically, make sure the machine you play pays back your bet for a pair of jacks or better and has a one-coin payout of nine coins for a full house and six coins for a flush (a 9/6 machine). Much has been written recently about video poker strategy (since there is a modicum of player control), and it's worth reading if you enjoy these machines.

Facts for the Visitor

WHEN TO GO

You should factor at least two criteria into your travel plans: the weather and conventions. Unless you're cold-blooded or you just really like to perspire, you might want to avoid Las Vegas from May through September. During this time, afternoon temperatures often hit 100°F, and highs during July and August usually hover around 105°F – in the shade. Sun temperatures can be *much* higher.

You'll also want to avoid Sin City during a big convention (see 'Major Convention Dates') – unless you'll be arriving wearing a conventioneer's hat yourself. Not only are colossal crowds annoying – reaching the shrimp pile at the Big Buffet is never more nerve-racking – but they're costly, too; hotels jack up room rates and buffet prices when the Buggy Whip Manufacturers and other large groups come to town. A room that usually fetches $79 at the Las Vegas Hilton can easily cost $109.

Also be aware of certain holidays when you plan your trip. If you don't like crowds, pass on New Year's Eve in Las Vegas; even the mice are bumping shoulders that night. Also, most of the city's revues are 'dark' (shut down) the week before Christmas. If you'll be in town for only a few days, it might interest you to know that hotel rates are typically 10% to 20% less Sunday through Thursday.

ORIENTATION

Two main highways come into Las Vegas, I-15 and Hwy 95. For downtown, exit Hwy 95 at Las Vegas Blvd (The Strip) or I-15 at Charleston Blvd. I-15 parallels The Strip, so work out which cross street will bring you closest to your destination. If it's your first time in Las Vegas and you're not in a hurry, you might want to exit the I-15 at Blue Diamond Rd and cruise the length of The Strip from south to north, right up to downtown.

Downtown Las Vegas, the original town center, is a compact grid. Its main artery, Fremont St, is for five city blocks a covered pedestrian mall lined with low-brow casinos

BONNIE KAMIN

BONNIE KAMIN

JOHNNY STOCKSHOOTER

and hotels. This portion of the street is called the Fremont St Experience because of the overhead light show that takes place nightly. Public buildings, like the post office and city hall, are a few blocks north. Shopping is mostly limited to cheap souvenirs.

The blocks around the intersection of Main and Fremont Sts are known as Glitter Gulch and feature those long-time grinning neon icons, Vegas Vic and Sassy Sally.

Las Vegas Blvd goes through downtown and continues southward for about 10 miles. The Strip, a 4½-mile stretch of this boulevard, has most of the really big hotel-casinos, which are interspersed with parking lots, garish shopping malls and fast-food outlets. Smaller motels are slotted in between the big places, occupying sites still awaiting a grander fate.

The colossal, three-legged Stratosphere Tower marks the northern terminus of The Strip. From there to downtown, Las Vegas Blvd is mostly lined with tatty-looking buildings – cheap motels, strip clubs, quickie wedding chapels and so on. Locals refer to the 15-block-long neighborhood as 'Naked City' for its proclivity to prostitution. At the south end of The Strip, toward the airport, the bright lights peter out a block past the spectacular Mandalay Bay hotel-casino.

Traffic can be heavy on The Strip at times. This is particularly true on Friday and Saturday nights. Unless you want to be part of the street action, use one of the parallel roads (such as Industrial Rd or Paradise Rd), or take the local buses to travel along here.

Aside from the major casinos near The Strip, most of Las Vegas consists of typical residential neighborhoods. North Las Vegas is a pretty tough area, while the city's western fringe has some of the biggest, fanciest houses. Southeast of Vegas, Henderson is a satellite suburb with some traditional industries, such as chemical manufacturing and metal processing.

MAPS

Maps are widely sold at hotels, gas stations and newsstands. All of the maps described here can be obtained with little difficulty around town.

For ease of use, Rand McNally's 'Las Vegas' is hard to beat. It actually contains several fold-out maps, including Las Vegas Vicinity, Las Vegas Region and Las Vegas Central (which shows the downtown area and The Strip on one long, easy-to-read

NORMAN GODWIN   BONNIE KAMIN   NORMAN GODWIN

Major Convention Dates

Listed below are Las Vegas' major annual conventions, their approximate dates and estimated attendance figures. For exact dates, contact the Las Vegas Convention & Visitors Authority (☎ 702-892-7575, or from anywhere in North America 800-332-5333, www .lasvegas24hours.com) or the Las Vegas Chamber of Commerce (☎ 702-735-1616).

Consumer Electronics Shows
First week of January
100,000 conventioneers

World Floor Covering Association
Last week of January
30,000 conventioneers

Western Shoes Associates
Second week of February
25,000 conventioneers

Associated Surplus Dealers
Third week of February
50,000 conventioneers

Men's Apparel Guild in California
First week of March
70,000 conventioneers

Snowsports Industries of America
Second week of March
30,000 conventioneers

Networld/Interop
Second week of May
60,000 conventioneers

Intl Council of Shopping Centers
Last week of May
35,000 conventioneers

Associated Surplus Dealers
Third week of August
35,000 conventioneers

Softbank Comdex
Third week of November
200,000 conventioneers

map). Among the sites shown are the city's major hotel-casinos, 10 shopping centers, 37 family attractions and 19 golf courses.

For detail, the 'Las Vegas City Map' by Compass Maps is topflight. It shows every single street in the city on one large fold-out map on one side, and has a street and road index on the other. Beside the index is a thorough but not particularly user-friendly Casino Map and a Glitter Gulch/Downtown Map. The large city map is so detailed it nearly requires a magnifying glass to use. If you think you'll be traveling into the suburbs, this is the map for you.

The Las Vegas Convention & Visitors Authority puts out a fold-out 'Las Vegas Maps & Area Information' map that emphasizes The Strip and downtown and contains only the major boulevards in the vicinity of The Strip. This side of the map also has an easy-to-use hotel and motel guide and a small regional map. The reverse side contains the names, addresses and phone numbers of shopping malls, museums, wedding chapels and so on.

The 'Official State Map' produced by the Nevada Commission of Tourism is, like the Visitors Authority map, distributed freely. It folds out and contains on one side a very detailed map of the state, maps of the Lake Tahoe and Las Vegas regions, a map of the Reno-Sparks area, a distance chart and a box showing the location of all of Nevada's campgrounds and recreational areas. The flip side contains lots of good information about the state's history and its attractions.

RESPONSIBLE TOURISM

Las Vegas is the fastest-growing city in the US, with 5000-plus newcomers arriving every month and births outpacing deaths by a margin of 2 to 1. In addition, it seems like every month somebody is opening yet another hotel-casino with several thousand guestrooms. As a result, local officials face enormous challenges with traffic congestion, water conservation and keeping water and air pollution at acceptable levels.

Tap water is a big concern at City Hall. Nevada receives only 10% of the annual allocation of Colorado River water, and that's barely enough to keep up with demand. Increased water usage has led to a rise in the level of pollutants in Lake Mead. Steps are being taken to curb usage. For example, lawn watering is prohibited from May to October between the peak evaporation hours of noon to 7 pm.

You can help Las Vegas maintain its water reservoir by taking short showers and by being miserly with your use of towels; don't use three towels when one will suffice. Unnecessary towel washing not only wastes precious tap water, but it also needlessly adds bleach to the area's water supply. Likewise, before leaving your room, be sure to turn off all the lights and the air-con; inefficient use of electricity results in the needless consumption of unrenewable resources.

TOURIST OFFICES
Local Tourist Offices
There are quite a number of tour operators around town with 'Tourist Information' signs posted out front, but the city's only true tourist office (and a very good one) is just inside the Las Vegas Convention Center, 3150 Paradise Rd (where Paradise meets Convention Center Drive). The tourist office is managed by the Las Vegas Convention & Visitors Authority (☎ 702-892-7575, 800-332-5333, www.lasvegas24 hours.com). Its friendly staff is extremely knowledgeable and the office contains so many free brochures, magazines and maps that one copy of each could easily fill a shopping bag – and the staff will even provide the shopping bag if you ask. The office is open from 8 am to 6 pm weekdays and from 8 am to 5 pm on weekends.

Tourist Offices Abroad
Las Vegas maintains three overseas visitor information centers – in Japan, England and Germany. The Japan office (☎ 3-3358-3265, fax 3-3358-3287) is at Okada Associates, Gyoen Building 8F, 1-5-6 Shinjuku,

Shinjuku-ku, Tokyo 160. The England office (☎ 1-564-79-4999, fax 1-564-79-5333) is at Callet Travel Services, Brook House, 47 High St, Henley in Arden, Warwickshire B95 5AA. The Germany office (☎ 89-260-7895, fax 89-260-4009) is at Mangum Management GmbH, Herzogspitalstr. 5, 80331, Munich.

DOCUMENTS
Passport
With the exception of Canadians, who need only proof of Canadian citizenship with photo ID, all visitors to the US must have a valid passport and may also be required to have a US visa (see Visas below). Check these regulations carefully with the US embassy in your country before you depart. The US government has recently enacted laws that allow Immigration and Naturalization Service (INS) officials at airports to ship you home on the first flight out without a chance for appeal if you are caught without proper entry papers.

Your passport should be valid for at least six months longer than your intended stay in the US, and you'll need to submit a recent photo with your visa application. Documents of financial stability or guarantees from a US resident (in special cases, the INS can demand that someone entering the country be 'sponsored' by a citizen who promises to provide them with financial support) are sometimes required, particularly for people from developing countries.

Although most visitors to the US have no problem entering the country, you should tread carefully from the time you exit your international flight until you have passed through all the formalities and are in the actual arrivals area of the terminal. In addition to the INS people, who will inspect your passport and 'papers,' you will encounter customs officials, who may search your bags, and a Drug Enforcement Agency dog that may sniff your leg and luggage.

The vast majority of these personnel are polite, and in the case of the animals, well behaved. However, if you have problems with any of them, the last thing you should do is argue or otherwise cause them further irritation. The simple truth is that until you have passed through the last formality, you have few if any rights. If various government officers so desire, they can find an excuse to detain you and make your life miserable. It is not uncommon for foreign nationals to be detained for hours over minor procedural questions. If that happens, try to get word to an airline official or even another traveler, who can then notify the people waiting for you outside.

Your passport may also prove useful after arrival, as the drinking age of 21 is universally enforced. If reality or nature allows you to pass for younger than 35, bring some form of age identification with you when you go out (such as your passport) so as to assuage the concerns of any bouncers you might encounter.

Visas

A reciprocal visa-waiver program applies to citizens of certain countries, who may enter the US for stays of 90 days or fewer without having to obtain a visa. Currently these countries are Andorra, Austria, Belgium, Brunei, Denmark, Finland, France, Germany, Iceland, Italy, Japan, Liechtenstein, Luxembourg, Monaco, the Netherlands, New Zealand, Norway, San Marino, Spain, Sweden, Switzerland and the UK. Under the visa-waiver program, you must have a round-trip ticket on an airline that participates in the program; you need proof of financial solvency, such as credit cards, a bank account with evidence of a balance beyond two figures, or employment in your home country; you must sign a form waiving the right to a hearing over deportation; and you will not be allowed to extend your stay beyond 90 days. Consult with your airline or the closest US consulate or embassy for more information.

Other travelers (except those from Canada) will need to obtain a visa from a US consulate or embassy. In most countries the process can be done by mail, but in some countries, notably Turkey, Poland and Russia, you'll need to go to a US consulate or embassy in person. Visa applicants may be required to 'demonstrate binding obligations' that will ensure their return back

HIV & Entering the USA

Anyone entering the US who is not a US citizen is subject to the authority of the Immigration and Naturalization Service (INS), which has the final say about whether you enter or not and has full power to send you back to where you came from. Being HIV-positive is not grounds for deportation, but it is grounds for exclusion. What this means is that once in the US, you cannot be deported for being HIV-positive, but you can be prevented from entering the US.

The INS does not test people for the AIDS virus when they try to enter the US, but the form for nonimmigrant visas asks, 'Have you ever been afflicted with a communicable disease of public health significance?' If you answer yes to this question, the INS may try to exclude you when you reach the US.

If you are HIV-positive but can prove to the consular officials to whom you have applied for a visa that you are the spouse, parent or child of a US citizen or legal resident (green-card holder), you are exempt from the exclusionary rule.

For legal information and referrals to immigrant advocates, potential visitors should contact the National Immigration Project of the National Lawyers Guild (☎ 617-227-9727), 14 Beacon St, Suite 506, Boston, MA 02108, and the Immigrant HIV Assistance Project, Bar Association of San Francisco (☎ 415-267-0795), 685 Market St, Suite 700, San Francisco, CA 94105.

home. Because of this requirement, those planning to travel through other countries before arriving in the US are generally better off applying for their US visa while still in their home country, rather than while on the road.

The validity period for US visitor visas depends on what country you're from. The length of time you'll be allowed to stay in the US is ultimately determined by the INS officers at the port of entry, such as an airport.

Visa Extensions Tourists using visas are usually granted a six-month stay on first arrival. If you try to extend that time, the first assumption will be that you are working illegally, so come prepared with concrete evidence that you've been behaving like a model tourist: receipts to demonstrate you've been spending lots of your money from home in the US, or ticket stubs that show you've been traveling extensively. Visa extensions in Las Vegas are pondered at the INS office (☎ 702-451-3597), 3373 Pepper Lane, at Pecos Rd. If you need to speak with an INS agent and are having trouble getting one on the phone at that location (the line is generally busy), try calling the customs and immigration office at McCarran International Airport (☎ 702-388-6480).

Travel Insurance

No matter how you're traveling, make sure you take out travel insurance. This should cover you not only for medical expenses and luggage theft or loss, but also for cancellations or delays in your travel arrangements, and everyone should be covered for the worst possible case, such as an accident that requires hospital treatment and a flight home. Of course, coverage depends on your insurance and type of ticket, so ask both your insurer and your ticket-issuing agency to explain the finer points. STA Travel and Council Travel offer travel insurance options at reasonable prices. Ticket loss is also covered by travel insurance. Make sure you have a separate record of all your ticket details – or better still, a photocopy of them. Also make a copy of your policy, in case the original is lost.

Buy travel insurance as early as possible. If you buy it the week before you fly, you may find, for instance, that you're not covered for delays to your flight caused by strikes or other industrial action that may have been in force before you took out the insurance.

Driver's License

Planning to drive? Bring your driver's license and check with your country's national auto club to see if they recommend obtaining an International Driver's License. Note that this document alone won't let you drive; you will need a valid license from your home country as well.

Hostel Card

The Las Vegas International Hostel is a member of Hostelling International/American Youth Hostel (HI/AYH), which is affiliated with the International Youth Hostel Federation (IYHF). You do not need to have an HI/AYH card to stay at this hostel, but if you do present the card, you'll save $2 a night for the length of your stay.

The only other hostel in town is the Las Vegas Backpackers Hostel, which is not a member of HI/AYH. Foreigners need only present a valid passport. Americans wishing to stay at the hostel who are not traveling with foreigners are required to present a student ID or a card belonging to one of the various international hostelling groups, such as IYHF.

Student Cards

If you are a student, by all means obtain and carry an International Student Identification Card (ISIC), which can get you substantial discounts at museums, tourist attractions and on some plane fares.

Seniors' Cards

Seniors are Las Vegas' fastest-growing population group. Retirees make up about 20% of Vegas households. About 12% of Vegas' seniors moved here to retire, attracted by the dry climate, mild winters and affordable retirement developments. Many businesses offer senior discounts. Seniors need not have a seniors' card to obtain these discounts. They need only request them. A senior could be asked for proof of age, but ice ages come and go with greater frequency.

Photocopies

Whatever documents you're required to bring, carry photocopies of them separately from the originals. This will speed replacement in case the originals are lost or stolen. It's also a good idea to leave photocopies of each of your travel documents with someone at home.

EMBASSIES & CONSULATES
US Embassies & Consulates

US diplomatic offices abroad include the following:

Australia 21
(☎ 6-270-5900)
Moonah Place Yarralumla, ACT 2600
There are consulates in Melbourne, Perth and Sydney.

Canada
(☎ 613-238-5335)
100 Wellington St, Ottawa, K1P 5T1
There are consulates in Calgary, Halifax, Montreal, Toronto and Vancouver.

France
(☎ 01-42-96-12-02)
2 rue Saint Florentin, 75001 Paris
There is a consulate in Marseilles.

Germany
(☎ 228-3391)
Deichmanns Aue 29, 53179 Bonn
There are consulates in Berlin, Frankfurt, Hamburg and Munich.

Ireland
(☎ 1-687-122)
42 Elgin Rd, Ballsbridge, Dublin

Japan
(☎ 3-3224-5000)
1-10-5 Akasaka chome, Minato-Ku, Tokyo
There are consulates in Fukuoka, Osaka-Kobe and Sapporo.

Mexico
(☎ 5-211-0042)
Paseo de la Reforma 305, 06500 Mexico City
There are consulates in Ciudad Juárez, Guadalajara, Hermosillo, Matamoros, Mérida, Monterrey and Tijuana.

New Zealand
(☎ 4-722-068)
29 Fitzherbert Terrace Thorndon, Wellington
There is a consulate in Auckland.

UK
(☎ 0171-499-9000)
5 Upper Grosvenor St London W1
There are consulates in Belfast, Northern Ireland, and Edinburgh, Scotland.

Embassies & Consulates in Las Vegas

Las Vegas has got a lot of things, but it hasn't got a single embassy or consulate. All embassies are located in the nation's capital, Washington, DC. Quite a number of countries also maintain consulates in New York, Miami, San Francisco, Los Angeles and Chicago.

If you would like to speak with a government representative of a particular foreign country and don't know the location of the country's nearest diplomatic mission, you can call directory assistance for Washington, DC (☎ 202-555-1212), and request a telephone number for that country's embassy. The fee for directory assistance is $1.

CUSTOMS

International travelers who haven't already cleared US customs must clear customs at McCarran International Airport. If you have

The New Money

The US is updating its greenbacks. The longtime $20 bill (top), for example, is being replaced with a new one (bottom). However, there is no difference in the value of the bills. An old $100 bill is just as valuable as a new one, same with the fifties, tens, fives and ones.

nothing to declare, just follow the green line on the floor of the terminal; you may or may not be singled out for a spot inspection as you head toward the exit. If you have something to declare, follow the red line and be sure to declare the article, because if you fail to do so and are caught, you could find yourself in serious trouble. If you have illegal drugs, discard them immediately.

Non-US citizens over the age of 21 are allowed to import one liter of liquor and 200 cigarettes duty free. Gifts may amount to no more than $100 in value. You may bring any amount of money less than $10,000 into or out of the US without declaration. Amounts greater than $10,000 must be declared. There is no legal limit to the amount of US and foreign cash and traveler's checks you can bring in, but undeclared amounts of more than $10,000 can be confiscated.

MONEY

Nothing works like cash, but in Las Vegas you will find that most forms of payment are welcome. How to get cash is another matter. Read below to consider your options.

Currency

US currency is the only one accepted in Las Vegas. The dollar ($) is divided into 100 cents (¢). Coins come in the following denominations, with these names and descriptions:

1¢ – penny, copper colored

5¢ – nickel, fat and silver colored

10¢ – dime, the smallest coin, thin and silver colored

25¢ – quarter, silver colored with rough edges

50¢ – half-dollar, larger than a quarter and silver colored, with a profile of John F Kennedy

$1 – dollar, comes in one of two coins, neither as common as the dollar bill: a large, silver-colored coin with a profile of Dwight D Eisenhower (often called a silver dollar), or almost quarter-size, with a profile of Susan B Anthony (called the Susan B Anthony Dollar)

You are unlikely to see either the half-dollar or dollar coins, unless you go gambling and play the slots.

Bills – paper currency – are confusing to many foreign visitors. They are all the same size and color, regardless of denomination. Be careful to check the denomination in the corners of the bills so you don't pay the wrong amount or receive the wrong amount in change. Bills come in denominations of $1, $2 (rare), $5, $10, $20, $50 and $100. Many places won't accept bills larger than $20, so if you are going out, break large bills at your hotel, at a casino or at a bank.

In 1996, the US Treasury began redesigning the bills to thwart counterfeiters, starting with the $100 bill and proceeding down through the valuations, one bill each year. If you find yourself in possession of both new and old bills, don't worry; the old-design currency will remain valid for at least the next several years.

As for carrying money, you should do with it as you do at home; extreme precautions are not necessary in Las Vegas. If you have more than a few hundred dollars in cash, it would be prudent to place it in a hotel safe. You can avoid the whole problem of carrying large sums of money by using an ATM card to withdraw only a few days' worth of cash at a time (see ATMs).

Exchange Rates

Exchange rates fluctuate daily. At press time, exchange rates for some of the major currencies were as follows:

country	unit		dollars
Australia	A$1	=	$0.64
Canada	C$1	=	$0.66
euro	€1	=	$1.13
France	FF1	=	$0.17
Germany	DM1	=	$0.58
Hong Kong	HK$10	=	$1.29
Japan	¥114	=	$1.00
New Zealand	NZ$1	=	$0.54
United Kingdom	UK£1	=	$1.51

Exchanging Money

Cash Casinos exist to separate you from your money, and they will facilitate that end any way they can. This includes swapping major foreign currencies for US dollars. The casinos will charge a fee to exchange money, but it's usually not very high. Most banks will also change major currencies, and their

Need more money?

exchange rates tend to be more favorable than those offered by the casinos.

There is no shortage of foreign exchange brokers in Las Vegas. The American Express Travel Agency (☎ 702-739-8474) inside the MGM Grand Hotel changes many foreign currencies at competitive rates. The Foreign Money Exchange (☎ 702-791-3301), on The Strip opposite the Stardust Hotel, also changes many foreign currencies at competitive rates.

Traveler's Checks Traveler's checks can be cashed at all hotel-casinos and are accepted by all businesses. If you intend to gamble, you must cash the checks at the casino cashier first, as they are not accepted at the tables. A valid photo identification, such as a current passport or driver's license, is usually required.

American Express cardholders can cash personal checks for traveler's checks at American Express offices. You can cash a check for up to $1000 for any seven-day period with a green American Express card, $5000 with a gold card and $10,000 with a platinum card. If you don't have a check, you can use a counter check; all you need to know is the name of your bank. The funds are charged to your checking account, not your card.

Personal Checks Few businesses accept personal out-of-state checks. However, most hotels will cash a check at the casino cashier if you are a guest of the hotel and have a valid driver's license or passport and major credit card. The hotel-casinos are linked to a central credit system, and $500 is about the most you can cash for any single trip unless you have completed a check-cashing application in advance and they approve the limit you set for your stay in the city.

ATMs Every hotel-casino, every bank branch and most convenience stores in Las Vegas have at least one automated teller machine. You will find ready access to ATMs if you are a member of Plus, Cirrus or Instant-Teller networks (check your card for mention of one of these three). When using ATMs at locations other than your bank, a service charge of $1 or $2 will be charged to your account.

Credit & Debit Cards Major credit cards and most debit cards are widely accepted by car rental firms, hotels, restaurants, gas stations, shops, grocery stores, movie theaters, ticket vendors and so on. Only the least sophisticated businesses in Las Vegas aren't accepting plastic money these days.

Cash advances against your Visa or MasterCard are available at all casinos, but the fee is generally high: about $50 for each $1000. Local banks will give a cash advance on both cards and the fee isn't as high. American Express cardholders should see the Traveler's Checks section, above.

International Transfers Two words: No problem. In keeping with the notion that they don't want to deny you the chance to fritter your money away on their gaming tables and slot machines, most casino cages are equipped to receive wired money (but they won't assist you in sending money from the casino).

Security

Pickpockets *love* Las Vegas. With so many people carrying so much cash on them and drinking like fish as they gamble the day away, what's a pickpocket not to like about Las Vegas? If you intend to carry lots of cash on you, carry it in large-denomination bills to minimize the size of the wad. If you must carry it all in your wallet, be sure to keep your wallet in a front pocket of your trousers or a zippered inside pocket of a jacket. Better yet, keep some money in your wallet and the majority of it in an inside pouch. Never leave money unsecured in a hotel room.

Costs

A trip to Las Vegas can either be fairly inexpensive or outrageously costly. It mostly depends upon you.

If you don't need to be in town during a major convention (when room rates are jacked up), it's possible to find a room on or near The Strip in a major hotel-casino for as little as $29.95, double-occupancy. However, without special deals, basic rooms are usually $69.95 a night or more (see Places to Stay for more advice on finding cheap lodging), and if you want to stay in a premium room, the sky's the limit on price.

Gone are the days when most hotel-casinos offered spectacular meal buffets for slightly more than you'd pay for a beer at a regular bar. However, it's still possible to find cheap eats in Las Vegas, and if quality rather than cost is your primary concern, you'll be pleased to know that there's a plethora of gourmet restaurants in town.

As for prices in general, items targeted for tourists – film, sunglasses, jewelry and so on – will cost more on The Strip than they will in areas of the city less frequented by tourists. If you're looking for snacks or sodas to bring back to your room, expect to pay much more for them at the store inside your hotel-casino than at a neighborhood grocery store.

There's plenty of free entertainment in Las Vegas, and lots of pricey entertainment as well. If you're driving and from outside the US, you'll likely be surprised by the relatively low costs of gasoline in Nevada. Phone calls can cost a lot or a little; see the Telephone section later in this chapter.

In short, unless you come during a convention or during a special event or holiday that's big business for Las Vegas, you can spend as little as $45 a day for room, food and entertainment – or you can spend as much as you've ever had in your checking account at one time.

Tipping

Many people employed in tourist-intensive service industries are poorly paid and rely on tips to bring their incomes up to decent or enviable levels. However, tips should only be given as a reward for good service. If you receive lousy service, leave a poor tip or none at all; to do otherwise defeats the purpose behind tipping, which is to provide a financial incentive for superior service. Here is a guide to customary tipping amounts in Las Vegas.

Bartenders – 15% to 20% of the total check.

Bellhops – From $2 total to $1 a bag, depending on the distance covered.

Change persons – 10% of winnings when a hint on a slot machine pays off for you.

Cocktail servers – 10% to 15%. If drinking for free in a casino, $1 per round.

Concierges – Nothing for information to $20 for securing tickets to a sold-out show.

Doormen – $1 or $2 for summoning you a cab, depending on weather.

Hotel maids – $1 to $2 a day, left on the pillow each day.

Keno runners – 15% if you're winning and a few dollars during play.

Limo drivers – 15% of the total fare.

Skycaps – At least $1 per bag.

Taxi drivers – 10% to 15%.

Valet parking attendants – $2, paid when the keys to the car are handed to you.

Waiters – 15% to 20% of the total check when the service warrants it.

Who not to tip: cashiers, ticket vendors working in booths, hotel front desk employees.

Taxes

Many of the taxes you pay in Las Vegas are included in stated prices and fees. For example, a gallon of gasoline in Las Vegas with a posted price of $1 will cost you exactly $1, but from this amount the gasoline station has to pay the US government 18.4¢, the Nevada government 23¢, and the government of Las Vegas 10¢. More than half of the cost of gasoline in Las Vegas goes to pay taxes, but you won't see any sign or receipt saying so.

Not-so-hidden taxes include a sales tax of 7% that is added to the posted price of most goods and services (gasoline is one of the exceptions) and a 9% tax added to posted hotel rates. The restaurant meal tax is 7%. Car rental agencies add taxes *and* fees: they add a 7% sales tax and a 6% license tag fee to their advertised rental rates, and they often assess a 10% airport surcharge; be sure to ask about additional taxes and costs when reserving a rental car.

There is no value-added tax in the US.

POST & COMMUNICATIONS
Postal Rates
US postal rates are among the lowest in the industrialized world. Beginning in 1999, it cost 33¢ to mail a one-ounce first-class letter – which includes your typical letter or birthday card – within the US. It's another 24¢ for each additional ounce, and postcards cost 21¢.

International rates (except for those to Canada and Mexico, which are slightly cheaper) were 60¢ for a half-ounce letter, $1 for the full ounce and 40¢ for each additional half ounce. Postcards and aerogrammes each cost 50¢.

Several rate options are available for parcels mailed overseas from the US. First class is the most expensive, but delivery anywhere rarely takes more than 10 days. If speedy delivery is not important to you, consider fourth class. Fourth-class rates can be very low, but delivery can take many weeks. If all you are sending is a published work such as a book or magazine, tell the postmaster. Special low rates apply to 'printed matter,' as postal workers call it.

Sending Mail
The US Postal Service handles 41% of the world's mail volume and is very efficient and reliable. It is extremely rare for a piece of mail sent from one part of the US to another to disappear in the process. However, important parcels shipped overseas should be sent via Federal Express (☎ 800-463-3339) or UPS (☎ 800-742-5877) because the US Postal Service does not control mail once it has left America. Call the numbers provided here for the FedEx or UPS office nearest you.

Most of the hotel-casinos sell stamps and will allow you to mail letters and packages from them. Caesars Palace even boasts a full-service US Post Office in its Forum Shops wing; its hours are 10 am to 11 pm Sunday through Thursday, and 10 am to midnight Friday and Saturday. Just west of The Strip is the US Post Office at 3100 S Industrial Rd, near Circus Circus Drive; its hours are 8:30 am to 5 pm weekdays, closed weekends. The downtown post office is at 301 Stewart Ave; its hours are 9 am to 5 pm weekdays, and 9 am to 1 pm Saturday. For Las Vegas postal information, call ☎ 800-275-8777.

Receiving Mail
The best way to receive mail in Las Vegas is to have it sent to your place of residence. If that happens to be a hotel, simply add 'c/o (your name)' beneath the name of the hotel in the address ('c/o' stands for 'care of'). Be sure to include the zip code, as the US Postal Service occasionally returns mail that doesn't have a zip code. Example: Flamingo Hilton, c/o Jack Frost, 3555 S Las Vegas Blvd, Las Vegas, NV 89109. Front-desk staff will alert you when the parcel arrives.

If you won't be in town very long but need to receive a parcel quickly, ask the sender to use one of the major express mail services (or to send the parcel 'priority mail' or 'express mail' from a US post office). Beware that all of the express mail companies require a street address (no post office boxes) and a phone number for the recipient (the hotel's main phone number if you're staying at a hotel).

Telephone
Area Codes There are only two area codes in Nevada: 702, which serves southern

Well Hello There

The first telephone in Nevada was installed in 1907 in a cigar store at the Nevada Hotel in Las Vegas. The telephone number was 1.

Nevada (and, therefore, all of Las Vegas), and 775, which serves the rest of the state.

Dialing All phone numbers within the US and Canada consist of the three-digit area code followed by a seven-digit local number. If you are calling locally, just dial the seven-digit number. If you are calling to another area code, dial 1 + the three-digit area code + the seven-digit local number.

The country code for the US is 1. The international access code is 011 for calls you dial directly, 01 for calls made collect or on a calling card; dial it first, before you dial the country code.

Calls that are free have area codes of 800 or 888; they are generally good throughout the USA and Canada. Numbers that begin with 900 are charged at a premium rate. You most often will see them advertised late at night on TV in ads asking, 'Lonely? Want to have some hot talk?'

Local directory assistance can be reached by calling ☎ 411 or ☎ 555-1212. If you are looking for a number out of your local area code and are sure of the code it's in, dial 1 + the area code + 555-1212. Directory assistance calls cost between 85¢ and $1, depending on the phone company used.

To obtain a toll-free (800 or 888) number, dial ☎ 800-555-1212.

Pay Phones Coin phones have been deregulated and charge what the market will bear. A variety of companies operate them. Those from Ameritech are the most reliable and cost 35¢ for a local call. However, some pay phones are operated by companies run by unethical human beings, and they charge exorbitant rates, especially for long-distance or international calls. Always check the rates

carefully. If you use one of these phones to call long-distance using your credit card or calling card number, you may later be horrified to find that the operator charged you $5 a minute, or some other outrageous rate.

Prepaid Calling Cards A wide range of phonecards is available, but Lonely Planet's eKno Communication Card (see the insert at the back of this book) is aimed specifically at travelers. It provides cheap international calls, a range of message services and free email. For local calls, you're usually better off with a local card. You can join online at www.ekno.lonely planet.com, or by phone from Las Vegas by dialing ☎ 1-800-707-0031. Once you have joined, to use eKno from the USA, dial ☎ 1-800-706-1333.

Hotel Phones The paradox about hotel room phone charges is that the cheaper the hotel, the more likely phone calls from your room will be free. On the dubious theory that if you're paying $100 a night for your room, then you won't mind being gouged for a call, some of the finest hotels nick you for $1 or more for local and toll-free calls. Worse, they often add an exorbitant surcharge to long-distance calls. Always inquire about such charges from the hotel operator or from the front desk before calling Japan or wherever for 30 minutes.

International Calls Americans can contract with long-distance companies for some very cheap international rates. If you are staying with someone local, use his or her phone and reimburse the charges. Every other method will cost much more. To get an international line, dial ☎ 011 + the country code + the city or area code (you don't need to dial 0) + the number. From a pay phone, first dial your number, then wait to hear how much it will be. After depositing your first $1.50 to $3 for the first three minutes, be prepared to keep feeding the slot at a rate of $1 to $2 a minute. If the pay phone has a sign saying it accepts credit cards for long-distance or international calls, check the rates very carefully before you punch your credit card number in.

Collect & Country Direct You can call collect (reverse the charges) from any phone. The main service providers are AT&T (☎ 800-225-5288) and MCI (☎ 800-365-5328). These generally have rates less stressful to the lucky recipient of your call than local phone companies or the dreaded third-party firms.

Fax
Pay fax machines are located at shipping outlets such as Mail Boxes Etc, copy places such as Kinko's and hotel business centers. Prices can be high, as much as $1 an outgoing page to a US number or $4 a page to Europe. Receiving faxes costs about half that.

Email & Internet Access
If you set up an email account through a free service such as hotmail (www.hotmail.com), you can access your email from any computer with a Web connection. Otherwise check with the provider of your account to see how, if possible, you can access it from Las Vegas.

Most of the casino-hotels have business centers that provide Internet access to their guests. The Las Vegas Backpackers Hostel offers Internet access, and the Las Vegas International Hostel told Lonely Planet it intended to install an Internet-accessible computer for its guests in the near future. Unfortunately, at the time of writing there were no dedicated Internet cafés on The Strip or in downtown.

INTERNET RESOURCES
Web resources abound for Las Vegas. The following websites are very informative and could prove useful to you in planning a trip to Las Vegas.

Las Vegas Convention & Visitors Authority This tourist-oriented website (www.lasvegas 24hours.com) contains lots of information on Las Vegas and definitely deserves a look. This is *the* place to find Las Vegas convention, show and event dates. Be forewarned that the hotel reservations service advertised at the website adds a 5%

to 10% surcharge to the rack rates charged by the hotels it represents.

Las Vegas Review-Journal This is the very impressive website (www.lvrj.com/) of Nevada's largest and most respected newspaper. Here, you'll find scores of articles on local news, sports, business, lifestyles, special events, weather and so on. There's even an 'Implosions Index,' where you can download videos showing landmark Vegas hotel-casinos being blown to bits.

Virtual Las Vegas Strip This fun site (www.intermind.net/strip/strip.html) shows a map of The Strip, upon which are photographs of the major tourist attractions that flank Las Vegas Blvd. Click on the photographs and you'll be linked to pertinent information about each one. It's a good website to visit if you're unfamiliar with Las Vegas and want to acquaint yourself with the location of The Strip's chief attractions.

Las Vegas Hack Attack This is the official cab driver's guide to Las Vegas (www.las vegastaxi.com/). It purports to give 'honest Las Vegas cab driver advice on gambling, getting free comps, shows, adult scene, casinos and hotels, brothels, prostitution, nightlife, weddings, entertainment, shows and a whole lot more!' View this information at your own risk.

Gay Vegas This website (www.gayvegas .com/index.html) isn't nearly as thorough as it could be, but it is as it claims the most complete site for gay locals and visitors to Las Vegas. If you look under the heading Frequently Asked Questions, you'll find some good information, such as directions to a nude gay beach at Lake Mead.

Yahoo Las Vegas Yahoo Las Vegas (dir .yahoo.com/Regional/U_S__States/Nevada/ Cities/Las_Vegas/) contains scores of links to sites in more than 20 categories relating to the city, plus its own extensive guides.

BOOKS
For literature, see the section of that name in the Facts about Las Vegas chapter.

Most of the books listed here are available in the US, although some may need to be special ordered. Elsewhere your choices are more limited. Internet surfers often have good luck finding obscure titles on Amazon.com.

Lonely Planet
Lonely Planet's *Travel with Children*, by Maureen Wheeler, will tell you what to do with the little ones while you're on the road.

Guidebooks
Comp City: A Guide to Free Las Vegas Vacations, by Max Rubin, is perfect for anyone interested in garnering casino freebies such as rooms, meals and shows.

Hiking Las Vegas, by Anthony Curtis, contains descriptions of 60 hikes within 60 minutes of The Strip.

Las Vegas Ride Guide, by Lamont J Singley, provides maps and information for more than 30 trails and destinations that you can explore by mountain bike in the Las Vegas area.

Gambling
The Everything Casino Gambling Book, by George Mandos, describes the rules and etiquette for all the casino games played in Las Vegas and offers 'tips and strategies you need to beat the house.'

Casino Gambling the Smart Way: How to Have More Fun and Win More Money, by

Andrew Glazer, provides easy-to-remember tips for recreational gamblers.

Las Vegas: Behind the Tables!, by Barney Vinson, presents a behind-the-scenes look at casino management. Contains lots of stories, as does *Las Vegas: Behind the Tables! Part 2*.

The Las Vegas Advisor Guide to Slot Clubs, by Jeffery Compton, takes readers on an opinionated tour of southern Nevada slot clubs and presents some valuable casino tips.

Welcome to the Pleasuredome, by David Spanmier, profiles some of Las Vegas' high rollers, its movers and shakers and its excesses.

History & Politics
Casino, by Nicholas Pileggi, is an intriguing book that describes the fall of organized crime in Las Vegas' casinos.

Las Vegas: As It Began, As It Grew, by Stanley W Paner, gives the history of Las Vegas from the Spanish Trail days up through the building of the Hoover Dam.

Bombs in the Backyard: Atomic Testing and American Politics, by Costandina Titus, examines the 30-year history of atomic detonations outside Las Vegas.

General
Viva Las Vegas: After-Hours Architecture, by Alan Hess, examines the history and reviews the architecture of Las Vegas from the 1940s to The Mirage.

A Pictorial History of Las Vegas, published by the *Las Vegas Review-Journal*, tells the story of modern Las Vegas through hundreds of captivating photographs.

Starting a Business in Las Vegas, by Wendy Cole, begins with tips on how to select a business for Las Vegas and proceeds with marketing, location and franchising tips.

NEWSPAPERS & MAGAZINES
Nevada's largest and most respected newspaper is the *Las Vegas Review-Journal*, which hits the streets in the morning. The city also has an afternoon paper, the *Las Vegas Sun*. Widely available are the *Los*

Angeles Times, the *New York Times* and the *Wall Street Journal*. Abbreviated national and international news can also be found in *USA Today*.

There are numerous local magazines available in Las Vegas, in addition to the wide variety of US-based magazines available at newsstands throughout America. *Casino Player* is a monthly magazine written for Las Vegas and Atlantic City gamblers. It contains lots of casino and gambling news as well as opinion pieces; a typical opinion piece might address the pros and cons of 'doubling up,' an optional built-in feature on most video poker machines.

Another information-packed magazine that's distributed freely to guestrooms in most Vegas hotel-casinos is *What's On*, which is a weekly guide to current and upcoming shows and events in Las Vegas. Other informative guides available for free at most hotel-casinos and at the Las Vegas Convention & Visitors Authority office at the Convention Center include *Las Vegas: Official Visitors Guide*, *Las Vegas Today* and *Nevada Events & Shows*.

RADIO

Las Vegas' broadcast media are well suited to the interests of the city's listeners. Las Vegas is a sports-betting mecca, and to satisfy the appetites of fans there are no fewer than five sports-talk radio stations: KBAD at 920 AM, which carries UCLA football games; KENO at 1460 AM, which carries NFL and USC football games; KFSN at 1140 AM, which carries Notre Dame football and Phoenix Diamondbacks, Suns and Coyotes games; KLAV at 1230 AM, which carries Nebraska football games; and KRLV at 1340 AM. In addition, news-talk stations KDWN at 720 AM and KXNT at 840 AM carry Los Angeles Dodgers games and NFL games, respectively. Vegas sports junkies program their digital radios to only those stations.

As the cynics will have suspected, there is no 24-hour news station in Las Vegas. There are many other formats, including: adult contemporary (KMXB at 94.1 FM, KMZQ at 100.5 FM, KSNE at 106.5 FM); alternative

rock (KEDG at 103.5 FM, KXTE at 107.5 FM); Christian (KILA at 90.5 FM, KKVV at 1060 AM); country (KFMS at 1410 AM and 102 FM, KWNR at 95.5 FM); jazz (KUNV at 91.5 FM); news talk (KDWN at 720 AM, KXNT at 840 AM, KNUU at 960 AM, KNPR at 89.5 FM, KVBC at 105.1 FM); oldies (KBGO at 93.1 FM, KJUL at 104.3 FM, KQOL at 105.5 FM); rock (KKLZ at 96.3 FM, KOMP at 92.3 FM, KXPT at 97.1 FM); Spanish (KDOL at 1280 AM, KLSQ at 870 AM); and soul and rap (KCEP at 88.1 FM).

TV

All seven major US television networks – ABC, CBS, NBC, PBS, Fox, UPN and WB – and several independents broadcast in the valley. In addition to the over-the-air channels available via your standard 'bunny-ear' antennae, most Vegas hotels are linked to the city's sole cable provider, Prime Cable, and an increasing number subscribe to DirecTV.

Here's an abbreviated channel listing of Sin City's major broadcast network stations and a few of the main cable stations for news:

channel	station	type
2	KUPN	independent station
3	KVBC	NBC affiliate station
4	UNLV	university's station
5	KVVU	local Fox station
6	KFBT	Warner Bros station
7	WTBS	Atlanta station
8	KLAS	CBS affiliate station
9	KBLR	Telemundo (Spanish)
10	KLVX	public station
13	KTNV	ABC affiliate station
14	The Weather Channel	
19	ESPN	sports
20	CNN	Headline News
4	MSNBC	business
49	C-Span	news

For a complete list of local and cable programming, check the back pages of the weekly entertainment guide *What's On*, which is usually placed in hotel guestrooms free of charge (note that not all hotels offer the full range of cable channels). If you don't find a copy in your room when you arrive, ask the front desk for one. For DirecTV programming, search the various DirecTV channels until you find the one that displays scheduled shows and times.

PHOTOGRAPHY & VIDEO
Film & Equipment
Kodak print film is readily available in Las Vegas. You'll find it in every minimarket in town. Professional print and color transparency films, however, are not available on The Strip or in downtown. For them you need to go to Nevada Photo Merchandising (☎ 702 735 2211) at 3217 Industrial Rd, a half block south of Desert Inn Rd, or Sahara Camera Center (☎ 702-457-3333) at 2305 E Sahara Ave at Eastern Ave, in the Albertson's Shopping Center. Both stores also stock a wide selection of cameras and lenses. If you're looking for a particular camera or lens, call first.

For processing or enlargements (and for many professional films, including Fuji Velvia but not Fuji MS 100/1000), the place to go is Photo Finish (☎ 702-732-1878, 800-945-0056, http://photofinish.com), 3121 S Industrial Rd, one block north of Desert Inn Rd. The folks at Photo Finish do top-quality work quickly (usually within 24 hours), and their rates are very competitive. Photo Finish is only 100m from Nevada Photo Merchandising, so if you need film that Photo Finish doesn't stock, you needn't go far to find it. If you're not finicky about your images, use any of the many 'One-Hour Photo' places in town.

Video Systems
If you are from overseas and wish to purchase a video here, remember that the USA uses the NTSC video format, which will look like so much static in the PAL format that's common elsewhere in the world. Make sure to check what will work in your country before you buy. Blank film and videotapes are readily available; see Malls in the Shopping chapter.

Restrictions
Taking pictures inside a casino is a big no-no. The folks manipulating the ceiling-mounted cameras over the card tables and slot machines will immediately suspect that you are plotting a theft against the casino, and this makes them *really* annoyed. If you're caught taking pictures in a gaming area, it's unlikely three huge goons will come out of nowhere to haul you off to a back room for a little 'conversation,' but it is likely you'll get a stern warning and your film may be confiscated.

Photographing People
Tourists should apply the same rules of polite behavior when taking pictures of people in Las Vegas as they would anywhere in the world. Indeed, Americans can sometimes be an overly suspicious people, a fact no doubt linked to the USA's No 1 ranking in many violent-crime categories. When strangers start snapping photographs, some tend to take the attitude, 'Why the hell is that person photographing me?' However, most Americans delight in being photographed if they are asked and told why. Example: 'Can I ask you to stand next to the grizzly bear so my friends can have some idea how big it is?'

Airport Security
Other than casinos, airports are the only public places in the state of Nevada where photography is off-limits. Very few acts of terrorism have been successfully attempted in the US, and police in Las Vegas want to keep it that way. To thwart any attempt to undermine the security measures at McCarran International Airport, the taking of photographs inside the airport is strictly prohibited.

X-Ray Machines
You needn't fear the X-ray machines at the airport damaging your film. The machines, new in 1998, were specifically designed not to harm film. However, if you're still nervous, store your film in a lead pouch (they're available at most camera shops) when traveling or ask the security personnel

monitoring the X-ray machines to hand inspect your film.

TIME

All of Nevada is in the Pacific time zone. Nevada shares this time zone with California, Washington, Oregon and western Montana. The Pacific time zone is one hour behind mountain time, which is respected by Nevada's eastern neighbors Arizona, Utah and Idaho; be sure to change your watch if you're entering Nevada from the east. Nevada is three hours behind the Eastern time zone states (New York and Florida among them).

For half of the year – from the first Sunday in April till the last Sunday in October – Americans set their clocks ahead one hour to give themselves an extra hour of sunlight in the evening so that they can be more productive. Americans call this period 'daylight savings time.' Near the end of October, Americans set their clocks back an hour and call the six months that follow 'standard time'; during this period, Nevada is eight hours behind GMT/UTC. Few countries adjust their clocks like the Americans. Few people are as concerned about time as Americans.

ELECTRICITY

Electric current in the US is 110-120 volts, 60 Hz AC. Outlets accept North American standard plugs, which have two flat prongs and an occasional third round one. If your appliance is made for another system, you will need a converter or adapter. These are best bought in your home country. They can sometimes be found in the giftshops at McCarran International Airport.

WEIGHTS & MEASURES

The US continues to resist the imposition of the metric system. Distances are measured in inches, feet, yards and miles; weights are measured in ounces, pounds and tons.

Here are some common measurements you will encounter: Gasoline is sold in US gallons, which are 20% smaller than the Imperial version and the equivalent of 3.79 liters. Once you have that down, it will become apparent what a bargain gas is in the US. Beer on tap in bars is often sold in US pints, which are three sips short of international ones. Sandwiches often have a quarter-pound of meats or cheese on them. Temperatures are given in degrees Fahrenheit. When it is 65° to 85°F outside, it's nice. Water freezes at 32°F. Your body is normally 98.6°F.

LAUNDRY

Every hostel, motel and hotel mentioned in this book offers laundry service or has a laundry room for guests' use. Additionally, many of Las Vegas' hotel-casinos provide an iron and ironing board in each guestroom.

If you must wash your own clothes and you're staying somewhere that doesn't permit it, either ask the front desk for directions to the nearest Laundromat or look under 'Laundries' in the Las Vegas Yellow Pages (a huge red directory that's provided in most guestrooms; if you don't have one, ask the front desk).

TOILETS

Public restrooms abound in Las Vegas. Every restaurant, casino and bar has them. Some, such as the restrooms in the casino at the Bellagio on The Strip, are elegant. Others are historic; the men's room in the casino at Main Street Station in downtown contains a 15-foot-long, 5-foot-tall slab of graffiti-covered concrete that was formerly part of the Berlin Wall. The restrooms at Pink E's bar contain dozens of neatly framed pin-ups; those in the women's room are from Playgirl, those in the men's room are from Playboy.

LUGGAGE STORAGE

At McCarran International Airport it's possible to place your baggage in temporary storage at the Passenger Service Center, located under the escalators between the ticket counters. Lockers are also available near the A, B, C and D gates – on the 'safe' side of the X-ray machines. Bag storage and lockers are an option at the Greyhound bus station. Likewise, most hotels will allow guests to store luggage, but usually not for more than 24 hours. Luggage storage rarely exceeds $2 per item per day.

HEALTH

Las Vegas is a typical developed-nation destination when it comes to health. The only foreign visitors who may be required to have immunizations are those coming from areas currently experiencing an outbreak of cholera or yellow fever.

Excellent medical care is readily available, but if you are not properly insured, a collision with the US health care system could prove fatal to your budget. The need for travel insurance when traveling abroad cannot be overemphasized.

Precautions

The water is fit to drink, and restaurant sanitation is high. The only health risks you face in Las Vegas are related to accident, violence or the weather. The first is somewhat preventable by paying attention to your surroundings. The second can be minimized; see Dangers & Annoyances later in this chapter. Weather can be almost entirely eliminated as a health risk by behaving intelligently: If it's cold out, bundle up. If it's hot out, don't overexert yourself or get too much sun. If you're going to be in the sun a lot, wear plenty of sunscreen and drink lots of water.

Medical Kit

Most medications are readily available, and there's no reason to pack extras; they just weigh on you. If you take a prescription medicine, bring an adequate supply along with your prescription, in case you lose your supply. Other than that, you might want to pack the following:

Aspirin, acetaminophen or Panadol.

Antihistamine (such as Benadryl), which is useful as a decongestant for colds, to ease the itch from allergies and to help prevent motion sickness.

Bismuth subsalicylate preparation (Pepto-Bismol), Imodium or Lomotil, for stomach upsets.

Rehydration mixture, to treat severe diarrhea, particularly important if you're traveling with children.

Antiseptic, mercurochrome and antibiotic powder or similar 'dry' spray, for cuts and grazes.

Bandages, for minor injuries.

Scissors, tweezers and a thermometer (airlines prohibit mercury thermometers).

Sunscreen and lip balm.

Insurance

Traveling to or within the US without health insurance is foolhardy. One small mishap can drain you of thousands of dollars. Visitors from abroad should carefully check to see what their national or private health insurance will cover. In many cases, you will need to purchase additional travel insurance; read the fine print and make certain that it will cover you for any activity you're likely to engage in.

Americans traveling within the US should check carefully to see what conditions are covered in their policy. This is especially true for HMO members, who may have to call a special number to get approval for health care away from home.

No matter who you are, save all receipts, records and anything else related to your treatment. You'll undoubtedly need them for reimbursement. When in doubt about your insurance, call your carrier no matter where you are and see what they recommend. It could save you thousands of dollars later.

Medical Attention

If you are ill or injured and suspect that the situation is in any way life-threatening, call ☎ 911 immediately. This is a free call from any phone, and you don't have to make a deposit in a pay phone first. It will connect you to an emergency services operator, who will dispatch the appropriate people to assist you.

If you have a less serious malady, such as the flu or a sprained ankle, and just want to see a doctor, ask your hotel for a recommendation. Las Vegas is filled with clinics and doctors who will treat you. However, none of their services come cheap, so carry travel insurance.

The following hospitals offer medical services through their emergency rooms. If

Helpful Hotlines

These crisis hotlines are open 24 hours:

Addiction Treatment Center	702-383-1347
AIDS Hotline	800-342-2437
AIDS Information	702-383-1319
Alcoholics Anonymous	702-598-1888
Domestic Violence Hotline	800-500-1556
Gamblers Anonymous	702-385-7732
Mental Health Crisis	702-486-8020
Narcotics Anonymous	702-369-3362
Pregnancy Hotline	800-322-1020
Poison Center	702-732-4989
Rape Hotline	702-385-2153
Secret Witness	702-385-5555
Suicide Prevention	702-731-2990
Toughlove Hotline	702-386-5632
Youth Crisis Hotline	800-448-4663

your condition is not acute, call first, because many also have clinics that can see you in a more timely and convenient manner.

Desert Springs Hospital – 24-hour emergency services, 225 beds with 16-bed maternity ward. At 2075 E Flamingo Rd (☎ 702-733-6875).

Sunrise Hospital & Medical Center – 24-hour emergency services, 688 beds, poison center, children's hospital. At 3186 S Maryland Parkway (☎ 702-731-8000).

University Medical Center of Southern Nevada – 24-hour emergency services, 545-bed medical-surgical hospital. At 1800 W Charleston Blvd (☎ 702-383-2000).

Valley Hospital Medical Center – 24-hour emergency services, 416-bed medical-surgical hospital. At 620 Shadow Lane (☎ 702-388-4000).

WOMEN TRAVELERS

Women should not be particularly concerned about traveling on their own in Las Vegas, though they should be alert to their surroundings. In bars some men will see a woman alone as a bid for companionship. A polite 'No, thank you' should suffice to send them off. If it doesn't, don't be afraid to protest loudly. It will likely send the offend-

ing party away and bring good Samaritans to your side.

Rape is always a threat to women travelers. The best way to deal with this threat is to avoid the same kinds of risky situations that might leave you open to other violent crimes. Don't walk down poorly lit streets or corridors. Be alert to being followed. Self-defense experts say that if you are attacked in any way, immediately start screaming as loudly as possible.

If you are attacked, call ☎ 911 from any phone. You will be connected with an operator who can dispatch the appropriate assistance to help you.

Organizations

The following organizations may be of particular interest to some women:

American League of Pen Women
    Founded in 1897, this club is composed of artists, writers and musicians. Contact Mary Shaw (☎ 702-363-9920) for information.

Jewish Women's International Club
    This club meets for breakfast the third Wednesday of each month at the Santa Fe Coffee Co., 4949 N Rancho Drive. Contact Lillian Goodman (☎ 702-242-0842).

Southern Nevada NOW
    This is the local branch of the National Organization for Women, a political action group for women's rights. Contact Patricia Ireland (☎ 702-387-7552).

GAY & LESBIAN TRAVELERS

Las Vegas attracts all kinds of people, from the outlandishly liberal to the narrowly conservative, including a large number of Mormons, Midwestern cowboys and others with a skin-deep tolerance for people who aren't one of them. Public displays of affection aren't much appreciated in this generally conservative town, and such displays are *strongly* frowned upon when the people doing the hugging and kissing are of the same sex.

That's not to say that the gay scene in Las Vegas isn't active. It is. There are numerous gay and lesbian dance clubs (see the Entertainment chapter), and the city has a monthly gay newspaper – the *Las Vegas Bugle*

(☎ 702-369-6260, www.lvbugle.com) – which is free and appears in news racks around town.

There's a Las Vegas Gay and Lesbian Chorus, and there's Alternatives, the nation's oldest gay-owned-and-operated alcohol, drug and mental health recovery program. There are several long-running female-impersonator shows in town, and numerous annual events such as the Gay New Year's Eve party and the Fig Leaf Christmas Fashion Show (see the *Bugle* for events information).

Despite all of this, the wisdom of not flaunting your homosexuality in public in Las Vegas cannot be overemphasized. Until the expression 'gay bashing' has slipped into history, a real and present danger exists, particularly for gay men.

Organizations

Unlike some cities, where the gay community feels a need to be secretive, there are several established gay-oriented organizations in Las Vegas.

Gay & Lesbian Community Center
Located at 912 E Sahara Ave, this non-profit group supports the well-being of the gay and lesbian community through projects and programs. Contact Holly Lee (☎ 702-733-9800).

Golden Rainbow
Located at 1130 S Martin Luther King Blvd, the Golden Rainbow provides housing and financial assistance to people with AIDS. Contact Sue Melfi (☎ 702-384-2899).

Lambda Business Association
Located at 1801 E Tropicana Ave, Suite 9, the association consists of gay and gay-friendly business owners. Contact Paul Sanchez (☎ 702-593-2875, www.lambdalv.com).

DISABLED TRAVELERS

Las Vegas is a fairly accommodating place for people with reduced mobility. For one thing, nearly every casino in town is on the ground floor. For another, because so many gamblers are senior citizens, the hotel-casinos and area restaurants have in most instances taken the steps to make their establishments wheelchair accessible. Same goes for public restrooms. Where stairs exist, so does an elevator or a ramp. Automatic doors and shaved curbs are standard.

Organizations

There are a number of organizations and tour providers around the world that specialize in the needs of disabled travelers.

In Australia, try *Independent Travelers* (☎ 08-232-2555), 167 Gilles St, Adelaide, SA 5000.

In the UK, try *RADAR* (☎ 0171-250-3222), 250 City Rd, London, or *Mobility International* (☎ 0171-403-5688).

In the US, try Mobility International USA (☎ 541-343-1284, fax 541-343-6812), an organization that advises disabled travelers on mobility issues and runs an educational exchange program. Write them at PO Box 10767, Eugene, OR 97440.

Also in the US, try the Society for the Advancement of Travel for the Handicapped (or SATH, ☎ 212-447-7284), 347 5th Ave No 610, New York, NY 10016.

Twin Peaks Press (☎ 360-694-2462, 800-637-2256) publishes several useful handbooks for disabled travelers, including

Lied Discovery Children's Museum

Travel for the Disabled and *Directory of Travel Agencies for the Disabled*. Write to them at PO Box 129, Vancouver, WA 98666 USA.

SENIOR TRAVELERS

Though the age at which senior benefits begin varies, travelers 62 and older (though sometimes 50 and older) can expect to receive discounts from hotels, museums, tours, restaurants and other places. Here are some national advocacy groups that help seniors in planning their travels:

American Association of Retired Persons (AARP)
  (☎ 702-386-8661, 800-424-3410)
  601 E St NW, Washington DC 20049
Elderhostel
  (☎ 617-426-8056)
  75 Federal St, Boston, MA 02110
National Council of Senior Citizens
  (☎ 202-347-8800)
  1331 F St, NW, Washington DC 20004

Grand Circle Travel (☎ 800-248-3737) has a brochure called '101 Tips for Mature Travelers.' Call and leave your name and address if you would like to receive it.

LAS VEGAS FOR CHILDREN

The Las Vegas of downtown and The Strip exists for gamblers, and since the gambling age is 21, most casinos would rather you left the little ones at home. State law prohibits people under age 21 from being in gaming areas, and several casinos deny minors entry into any part of their establishments unless they are registered guests. With increasing frequency, hotel-casinos are prohibiting strollers on their grounds. Anyone considering bringing children to Las Vegas should inquire about house rules pertaining to minors before booking a reservation at a particular hotel-casino.

That said, not every hotel-casino looks upon children like so many rats. Circus Circus has gone to great lengths to appeal to kids and to parents with kids, providing free children's entertainment within earshot of the casino. The setup allows one parent to gamble while the other baby-sits Janet and

Joey in a circus environment that's fun for adults, too. Out back is a theme park for kids; the MGM Grand has one as well. There's a waterpark on The Strip that's open half the year, and two museums were designed for kids. There are several spectacular roller coasters in town, and no shortage of arcades, movie theaters and animal attractions. There are even a couple of children-friendly production shows. See the Things to See & Do chapter for details.

Child Care

Only three hotels in town have child-care centers: the Gold Coast (☎ 800-331-5334), the MGM Grand (☎ 800-929-1111) and The Orleans (☎ 702-365-7111). All others encourage parents to contact child-care agencies such as Around the Clock Childcare (☎ 702-365-1040), which has a four-hour minimum of $38 per child and $8 for each additional hour, and Precious Commodities (☎ 702-871-1191), which has a four-hour minimum of $37 per child and $7 for each hour thereafter.

The Gold Coast child-care center is open from 9 am till midnight daily. Kids must be potty trained, healthy and between the ages of 2 and 8. Parents must remain on the premises, and they must leave a photo identification while their kids are being attended to. The service is available only to children of hotel guests. There is no fee. A three-hour daily limit applies. The center features a story-telling center, a movie theater and a toy room.

The MGM Grand accepts only potty-trained kids, ages 3 to 12. Its kids activity center features tumbling mats, a playhouse, puppets and so on for the youngest of the bunch, and small pool tables, Foosball and Ping Pong for the older kids. All kids can play in the arts and crafts room. The child-care center is open from 11 am to 11 pm Sunday through Thursday, and from 11 am till midnight Friday and Saturday. The cost is $7 per hour per child. Maximum stay per day is five hours.

The Orleans' child-care center isn't nearly as impressive as the MGM Grand's, but the attendants are as enthusiastic and the kids seem to really enjoy themselves there. Parents must stay on the premises while the kids are being looked after, and the maximum daily length of each visit is 3½ hours. The center is open from 9 am to 1 am daily. The cost is $5 per hour per child. The center accepts children ages 3 months through 12 years.

LIBRARIES
The Clark County Library (☎ 702-733-7810), 1401 E Flamingo Rd, is the largest library in Las Vegas. Available for check-out are books, videos, CDs and tapes. A library card is issued free of charge to US citizens. Photo identification with current address is requested. Hours are 9 am to 9 pm Monday through Thursday, 9 am to 5 pm Friday and Saturday, and 1 to 5 pm on Sunday.

The James R Dickinson Library (☎ 702-895 3286) on the campus of the University of Nevada at Las Vegas has a collection of nearly 2 million books and photographs. You must live in Clark County to be able to check out materials. Hours vary with the university's schedule.

Military buffs might like to visit the Nellis Air Force Base Library (☎ 702-652-4484), 4311 N Washington Blvd, on the base. The highlight of the library is the collection of photos documenting weapons testing at the

base and at the nearby proving ground. Hours are 10 am to 8 pm Monday through Thursday, and 10 am to 6 pm Friday and Saturday. Note that except for the library, the base is generally off-limits to the public.

CULTURAL CENTERS
The Reed Whipple Cultural Center (☎ 702-229-6211), 821 N Las Vegas Blvd, offers classes for children, teens and adults in dance, theater, music, painting, photography, pottery and weaving. Call for a free brochure detailing all classes. The classes are open to anyone.

The Las Vegas Art Centre (☎ 702-227-0220), 3979 Spring Mountain Rd, conducts classes in drawing, oil painting, calligraphy, watercolor, acrylics and pencil. Call for details. The classes are open to anyone.

DANGERS & ANNOYANCES
Las Vegas survives on tourism. The last thing the city wants is a reputation for crime. To prevent that, more police and private security officers are out and about than you've probably seen anywhere else. They are in cars, on bicycles, on horses and on foot. Surveillance cameras are everywhere.

If you stick to tourist areas, which are well lit and hopping with visitors, you have little to fear in the way of violent crime. Still, pick-

University of Nevada, Dickinson Library

pockets thrive in heavily touristed places, and Las Vegas has its share of them. Keep your money in places that are difficult for pickpockets to access, and never leave money or valuables in your hotel room.

A common complaint registered by tourists is cigarette smoke. 'Smoke-free' and 'Las Vegas' are never in the same sentence: there are ashtrays at every telephone, elevator, pool and shower, in toilets and taxis, and at the movies.

Other complaints include traffic and lines, which often accompany big conventions, and the No 1 annoyance: losing money in casinos. Usually it's an annoyance you can live with, but betting the farm and losing it won't be. Don't bet more than you can afford to lose.

EMERGENCY

For urgent police, fire and ambulance calls, dial ☎ 911; no coins are required if dialing this number at a pay phone. To report a picked pocket or other minor crime for which you don't need immediate police response, dial ☎ 702-795-3111. You will need a police report in most cases to file for an insurance claim.

If your traveler's checks are lost or stolen, call the check issuer:

American Express	☎ 800-221-7282
MasterCard	☎ 800-223-9920
Thomas Cook	☎ 800-223-7373
Visa	☎ 800-227-6811

If your credit card is lost or stolen, call the card issuer:

American Express	☎ 800-992-3404
Diners Club	☎ 800-234-6377
Discover	☎ 800-347-2683
MasterCard Emergency Assistance	☎ 800-307-7309
Visa	☎ 800-336-8472

LEGAL MATTERS

In tourist-dependent Las Vegas, the cops are on their best behavior. However, if at any time a police officer gives you an order of any kind, do not seize upon that moment for a debate. He or she may have mistaken you for someone else. In Las Vegas, police don't act aggressively toward visitors or residents unless they've done something wrong or someone has been mistaken for someone else.

If you are arrested, you have the right to remain silent. There is no legal requirement to speak to a police officer if you don't want to, but never walk away from one until given permission. Anyone who is arrested is legally allowed (and given) the right to make one phone call. If you're from overseas and don't have a lawyer or friend or family member to help you, call your consulate. The police will give you the number upon request.

It's against the law to have an open container of an alcoholic beverage while walking down the street, but in Las Vegas this rule is generally waived in the spirit of good public relations. However, if you're *staggering* down a street with a drink in your hand, you may find yourself being led away to jail to sober up. Be advised: drunk-driving laws are strictly enforced. Even having an open container of an alcoholic beverage in a car is a big no-no, whether or not it's the driver who's drinking.

The drinking age of 21 is pretty strictly enforced. If you're younger than 35 (or just look like it), carry an ID to fend off overzealous barkeeps and the like. In Las Vegas, it is legal to purchase alcohol at any time of day or night.

There is zero tolerance at all times for any kind of illegal drug use. If police find marijuana, cocaine or any other illegal substance on you, you will be led to jail.

BUSINESS HOURS

Office hours in Las Vegas are typically 8 am to 5 pm. Shops are usually open at least until 7 pm, and most keep Sunday hours. You'll find plenty of convenience stores and supermarkets open 24 hours a day. Banks increasingly keep hours like stores. Fortunately, ATMs never sleep.

Movie theaters and many bars and restaurants are open every day of the year. Smaller restaurants are often closed one or two days a week, frequently early in the week. Most production shows are closed one day a week; the 'dark' day, as show business folks call it in Las Vegas, varies from show to show.

PUBLIC HOLIDAYS

Christmas is one of the few holidays left for which most stores close. Those holidays marked with an asterisk (*) are widely observed, with most businesses closed. When some of these holidays fall on the weekend, they are celebrated on the following Monday.

New Year's Day*	January 1
Martin Luther King Jr's Birthday	3rd Monday in January
Presidents' Day	3rd Monday in February
Memorial Day*	last Monday in May
Independence Day*	July 4
Labor Day*	1st Monday in September
Columbus Day	2nd Monday in October
Veterans Day	November 11
Thanksgiving Day*	4th Thursday in November
Christmas Day*	December 25

The festive annual Christmas season traditionally runs from the Friday after Thanksgiving through the big day itself. Purists will be horrified to note that Christmas decorations – and even sales – start in September.

SPECIAL EVENTS

The months in which annual special events are held can shift from year to year, and promoters have been known to move their 'shows' as finances dictate, so if an event is important to you, be sure to contact the Las Vegas Convention & Visitors Authority (☎ 702-892-7575, 800-332-5333, www .lasvegas24hours.com) or the numbers provided to obtain dates and times.

Throughout the year dozens of ethnic festivals are held in Las Vegas. Many are one-time deals. The ones included here are usually held in the months indicated. If ethnic events are your cup of tea, be sure to contact the Ethnic & Cultural Information's 24-hour hotline (☎ 702-225-5555) to get the

Trivial Las Vegas

Persons per household:	2.6
Median home price:	$130,000
Average apartment rent:	$631
Percentage of homeowners:	62
Number of doctors:	1800
Number of dentists:	419
Number of lawyers:	2300
Number of taxis:	1181
Median household income:	$48,329
Sister City:	An San, South Korea

nitty-gritty on all of the multicultural events taking place during your stay.

January

Super Bowl High Rollers – Amateur bowlers compete for $1 million in prize money at this weeklong tournament held at the Showboat Hotel (☎ 702-385-9150 to enter the contest, 800-257-6179 for reservations), 2800 Fremont St. Entry fee is $500 for one person, $750 for two or three people.

OKC Gun Show – One of the largest gun shows in the country (☎ 800-333-4867), held at the Cashman Field Center (702-258-8961), 350 N Las Vegas Blvd. Approximately 1500 sales and display booths attract more than 20,000 attendees each year. Admission is $7.

Chinese New Year – Day-long festivities involving entertainers from throughout Asia and Hawaii mark the beginning of the Chinese New Year. Held at the Asian Pacific Cultural Center (☎ 702-252-0400), 4215 Spring Mountain Rd.

February

Las Vegas International Marathon – This 26.2-mile event begins in Sloan and finishes at the south end of The Strip. A half marathon and relays also are run during the two-day event. Entry fees are $30 for the half marathon and $40 for the big race. Call ☎ 702-876-3870.

Mardi Gras – A big Cajun buffet, ballroom dancing and attendees in costumes make this festival a particularly good one to attend. Held at the Charleston Heights Arts Center (☎ 702-229-6383), 800 S Brush St, on the Saturday evening before Ash Wednesday.

March

Kite Carnival – This popular event is held the first Saturday in March at Freedom Park, at the intersection of E Washington Ave and Mojave Rd. There's no entry fee and everyone's encouraged to help themselves to a free kite and fly it. Call ☎ 702-229-6729 for details.

Busch Grand National – NASCAR's Busch Grand National Series 300 runs at the 1.5-mile oval at Las Vegas Motor Speedway (☎ 702-644-4443, 800-644-4444), 7000 N Las Vegas Blvd. Ticket prices are $15 for children and $45 for adults.

Corporate Challenge – Twenty thousand amateur athletes compete on behalf of their companies in 27 sporting events held throughout town. The competition begins in mid-March and lasts through April. Entry fees are paid by the companies. Call ☎ 702-229-6706 for details.

St Patrick's Day Parade – Downtown is the site of a raucous parade replete with floats every March 17. Notice the color of the beer in most of the casinos along Fremont St on this day: green. Yikes! The six-block procession starts at 8 am and typically ends by 9:30 am.

April

Mardi Gras – The Rio hotel-casino (☎ 702-252-7777), The Orleans hotel-casino (☎ 702-365-7111) and Fremont Street Experience (☎ 702-678-5724) are the site of elaborate New Orleans-style carnivals in early April featuring Cajun food, parades and stage shows.

World Series of Poker – More than 4000 players match wits in 21 tournaments at Binion's Horseshoe hotel-casino (☎ 702-382-1600), 128 E Fremont St, from mid-April to early May to compete for $4 million in cash. Buy-ins cost $1000 for women, $10,000 for men. Public viewing is allowed.

Las Vegas Senior Classic – Some of the top golfers on the seniors tour tee off for $1 million in prize money at the Tournament Players Club at The Canyons (☎ 702-242-3000), 1951 Canyon Run Drive. Tickets for the four-day event begin at $15 a day.

Earth Fair – Held on the Saturday nearest Earth Day (April 22), Earth Fair draws 50,000 people. There are impersonators, a carnival for kids, and free plants and pine seedlings are given away. It's at Sunset Park (☎ 702-455-8206), 2601 E Sunset Rd, southeast of the airport.

May

Cinco de Mayo – On or near May 5, Mexicans celebrate Mexico's victory against French forces in 1862 at Puebla. (French reinforcements later crushed the Mexican army.) Day-long festivities at Freedom Park (☎ 702-649-8553) commemorate the anniversary.

Cinco de Mayo Dos – Fremont Street Experience (☎ 702-678-5724) hosts a three-day celebration of Cinco de Mayo around May 5 with performances by a variety of Hispanic entertainers, including mariachis. Cinco de Mayo is, basically, an excuse for a party.

Craft Fair and Rib Burnoff – This self-explanatory mid-May event at Sunset Park (☎ 702-455-8206), 2601 E Sunset Rd, is a big crowd-pleaser. The featured attractions: handicrafts, country music, people having fun, and food – lots of food. Most meals run about $10.

AMA Supercross – The top dirt bike racers in the US rev it up every May at Sam Boyd Stadium Park (☎ 702-434-0848) at the end of E Russell Rd, past Boulder Hwy. General admission fees start at $10.

June

Helldorado Days – This four-day event at Thomas and Mack Center (☎ 702-870-1221 for Helldorado info, 702-895-3900 for the center), at Tropicana Ave and Swenson St, features nightly rodeos, barbecues and bull riding. Admission is $12 to the bull ride and $11 to the rodeo. Proceeds go to charity.

Winston Cup West – NASCAR racing returns to the Las Vegas Motor Speedway (☎ 800-644-

4444), 7000 N Las Vegas Blvd, with this 150-mile race under the lights. General admission prices range from $15 to $45.

International Food Festival – Culinary offerings from two dozen countries highlight this delicious event held at Cashman Field Center (702-258-8961), 350 N Las Vegas Blvd. Cultural displays and ethnic dances add to the fun. Admission is $2; meals range from $3 to $10.

July

High Rollers – This is the second (and the biggest) of three annual amateur bowling contests held at the Showboat hotel-casino (☎ 702-385-9150, 800-257-6179), 2800 E Fremont St. More than $2.5 million is on the line. Entry fee is $1100. Spectators get in free.

World Figure Skating Champions – Some of the biggest names in ice skating put on a summer show at the Thomas and Mack Center (☎ 702-895-3900), Tropicana Ave at Swenson St. Admission ranges from $20 to $30.

August

Sundown Bluegrass Concerts – Some of the best bluegrass music in the southwestern US fills the air at Jaycee Park (☎ 702-229-6511), 2100 E St Louis St, the first two Sunday evenings in August. Bring a picnic basket and come early. The entertainment is free.

Kidzmania – This two-day, air-conditioned event (☎ 702-233-8388) at Cashman Field Center (702-258-8961), 350 N Las Vegas Blvd, is geared for youngsters. Attractions include a petting zone, game shows and karate demonstrations. Admission is $5 for adults, kids get in free.

Police Olympics – Cops from around the world compete in 22 events held at various Vegas venues during a five-day period (☎ 702-259-6350). PO isn't likely to ever overshadow the real Games (one of the biggest events is a softball tournament), but it's fun and free to watch. Entrants pay $40.

September

Las Vegas Cup Hydroplane Race – Despite its name, this two-day event (☎ 702-892-2874) involving some of the world's fastest boats is held out front of Boulder Beach, Lake Mead. Some of the boats top 200 mph, and then break up! There's no charge to watch.

Greek Food Festival – The name says it all. Held late September or early October at St John's Orthodox Church (☎ 702-221-8245), 5300 El Camino Rd near W Hacienda Ave, this festival also features Greek music and dancing. Admission costs $2; dining is a la carte.

October

Jaycee State Fair – This six-day event (☎ 702-457-3247) held at Cashman Field (702-258-8961), 350 N Las Vegas Blvd, attracts some 65,000 visitors drawn to a slew of exhibits, food booths and big-name bands playing rock, jazz and Latin music. Admission is $6 for adults, $4 for kids.

Las Vegas 500K – Indy cars traveling in circles at high speeds for 500 km are the centerpiece of this event, held at Las Vegas Motor Speedway (☎ 800-644-4444), 7000 N Las Vegas Blvd. Ticket prices range from $15 to $45.

Las Vegas Balloon Classic – This three-day event at Sam Boyd Stadium Park (☎ 702-434-0848), at the end of E Russell Rd, past Boulder Hwy, features more than a hundred hot-air balloons from around the world. Also displayed are vintage cars, handicrafts and antique machinery. Admission is free.

Rio's Italian Festival – The Rio hotel-casino (☎ 702-252-7777), 3700 W Flamingo Rd, maintains a Carnaval theme all year except on the weekend preceding Columbus Day. Then, the Rio hosts a celebration of Italian food and entertainment. Entry is free. Dinner is a la carte.

November

Craftsman Truck Series – These two NASCAR races at the Las Vegas Motor Speedway (☎ 800-644-4444), 7000 N Las Vegas Blvd, involve 70 highly modified pickup trucks racing at speeds exceeding 150 mph. Tickets start at $25.

LPGA Tour Championship – The top 30 money winners on the women's tour compete for $800,000 in prize money at the Desert Inn Country Club (☎ 702-733-4653), 3145 S Las Vegas Blvd. Passes for the four-day event, held the week before Thanksgiving, run $15 daily.

Strut You Mutt Day – This dog show, which features a howling contest and a best-dressed-dog contest among many others, attracts hundreds of doggies and their humorous owners. Held at Dog Fancier's Park (☎ 702-455-8206), 5800 E Flamingo Rd. Entry is $3, spectators pay $1.

Thanksgiving Senior High Roller – This weeklong holiday tournament attracts several hundred amateur bowlers over age 50 who pay a $400 entry fee and compete for $500,000 in prize money. At the Showboat hotel-casino (☎ 800-257-6179), 2800 Fremont St.

December

National Finals Rodeo – This hugely popular 10-day event features the top 15 rodeo performers in seven events, including steer wrestling and bull riding. Tickets to the rodeo, held at Thomas and Mack Center (☎ 702-895-3900), Tropicana Ave at Swenson St, are tough to obtain.

Las Vegas Rugby Challenge – Rugby teams from around the world vie for prize money at Freedom Park (☎ 702-656-7401), Washington Ave at Mojave Rd, during the first weekend of December. There's no charge for watching the two days of fun. Scrum!

New Year's Eve – Fremont Street Experience becomes a huge party scene every December 31 as thousands of celebrants turn out to hear live music, people watch and be dazzled by an overhead light show. Did I mention 'drink like fish'? They do that too. Admission is $10.

Bad Guys Need Not Apply

To work at any hotel-casino in Las Vegas, a prospective employee needs to obtain a 'sheriff's card' from the police department. The process starts with the applicant getting a signed referral from his or her prospective employer and presenting it and two photo IDs at the police department. The police department charges $5 for fingerprinting and running a background check, and $35 more for the card. The card is good for five years. Renewals are $20.

WORK

US law makes it difficult to work in the country without a prearranged permit from an employer. It is possible to overstay a J1 summer work visa, and thousands of students do that every year. But remember, the day the visa expires, you become an illegal alien in the eyes of US authorities.

If you're a visitor from abroad, word of mouth is usually the way to find out about working illegally at restaurants and bars. It helps if you do not have a discernible accent. Illegal white collar work is almost never available, since employers who hire undocumented workers are subject to big fines.

If you are caught working illegally, you will be immediately deported and barred from the US for at least five years. Gone are the days when US immigration agents gave undocumented workers time to gather belongings and notify loved ones. Deportation now occurs the same day an agent finds you working without a green card or proof of citizenship.

If you have a green card or are a US citizen, it may interest you to know that, on average, 110 new jobs become available daily in America's fastest-growing city. To the disappointment of many people, most of those jobs pay only minimum wage. In 1999, that amount was $5.15 an hour for persons age 18 and up, and just $4.38 an hour for persons under 18. State law prohibits an employer from applying tips against the minimum wage.

Getting There & Away

AIR

Las Vegas is served by four airports: McCarran International, Las Vegas Executive, Quail Air Center and Signature Flight Support. The last three are private airports, and unless you'll be arriving in your own plane, they won't concern you.

McCarran International (☎ 702-261-5743, http://McCarran.com), at the southern end of The Strip, is the city's public airport, serving 30 million passengers annually. It is the 15th busiest airport in the world, yet it's centrally located and extremely easy to navigate. Additional information on McCarran appears below.

The Getting Around chapter has full details on the myriad options for getting from McCarran to your hotel.

Departure Tax

You do not have to pay an airport departure tax before leaving. That tax is included in the price of your ticket.

Other Parts of the USA

The following is a list of the nonstop domestic flights to major cities from McCarran, and the airlines providing the service. Call for current prices and departure and arrival times.

Albuquerque – Southwest Airlines.

Atlanta – America West Airlines, Delta Air Lines.

Austin – Southwest Airlines.

Baltimore – Southwest Airlines.

Boston – America West Airlines, Delta Air Lines.

Charlotte – US Airways.

Chicago (Midway) – America West Airlines, American Trans Air.

Chicago (O'Hare) – America West Airlines, American Airlines, United Airlines.

Cincinnati – Delta Air Lines.

Cleveland – Continental Airlines.

Columbus – America West Airlines.

Dallas/Ft Worth – America West Airlines, American Airlines, Delta Air Lines.

Services at McCarran

ATM Between esplanades E and W.
Bag Storage Under escalators between ticketing.
Currency Exchange Under escalators between ticketing.
First Aid South mezzanine above ticketing.
Food 31 food and beverage outlets in airport.
Gambling 571 slot machines inside airport.
Information Gate C, esplanade east, rotunda, baggage claim.
Lockers Near gates A, B, C and D.
Lost & Found South mezzanine above ticketing.
Notary Under escalators between ticketing.
Photocopies Under escalators between ticketing.
Police South mezzanine above ticketing.
Post Office Esplanade east.
Travel Insurance Under escalators between ticketing.
Western Union Under escalators between ticketing.

Denver – America West Airlines, Condor German Airlines, United Airlines.

Detroit – America West Airlines, Northwest Airlines.

Grand Canyon – Eagle Canyon

Houston – Southwest Airlines.

Indianapolis – America West Airlines, American Trans Air.

Kansas City – America West Airlines, Southwest Airlines.

Los Angeles – America West Airlines, American Eagle, Alaska Airlines, Delta Air Lines, Hawaiian Airlines, Northwest Airlines, Reno Air, Southwest Airlines, United Airlines

Memphis – Northwest Airlines.

Miami – America West Airlines.

Milwaukee – America West Airlines, Midwest Express.

Airlines Serving McCarran

Air Canada	☎ 800-776-3000
America West Airlines	☎ 800-235-9292
American Airlines	☎ 800-433-7300
American Eagle	☎ 800-433-7300
American Trans Air	☎ 800-435-9282
Canada 3000	☎ 888-241-1997
Canadian Airlines	☎ 800-426-7000
Condor German Airlines	☎ 800-524-6975
Continental Airlines	☎ 800-523-3273
Delta Air Lines	☎ 800-221-1212
Eagle Canyon Airlines	☎ 800-293-2453
Hawaiian Airlines	☎ 800-367-5320
Japan Airlines	☎ 800-525-3663
Mesa Airlines	☎ 800-637-2247
Mexicana Airlines	☎ 800-531-7921
Midwest Express	☎ 800-452-2022
Northwest Airlines	☎ 800-225-2525
Reno Air	☎ 800-736-6247
Southwest Airlines	☎ 800-435-9792
Trans World Airlines	☎ 800-221-2000
United Airlines	☎ 800-241-6522
United Express	☎ 800-241-6522
US Airways	☎ 800-428-4322

Minneapolis – America West Airlines, Southwest Airlines.

Nashville – Southwest Airlines.

New Orleans – Southwest Airlines, Delta Air Lines.

New York (JFK) – Delta Air Lines, Trans World Airlines.

Newark – America West Airlines, Continental Airlines.

Oakland – America West Airlines, Southwest Airlines.

Oklahoma City – Reno Air.

Orlando – America West Airlines, Delta Air Lines, Southwest Airlines.

Philadelphia – America West Airlines, US Airways.

Phoenix – America West Airlines, Southwest Airlines.

Pittsburgh – US Airways.

Portland – America West Airlines, Alaska Airlines, Delta Air Lines, Southwest Airlines.

Reno – America West Airlines, Reno Air, Southwest Airlines.

Salt Lake City – America West Airlines, Delta Air Lines, Southwest Airlines.

San Diego – America West Airlines, Southwest Airlines.

San Francisco – America West Airlines, United Airlines.

San Jose – Reno Air, Southwest Airlines.

Seattle – America West Airlines, Alaska Airlines, Southwest Airlines.

St Louis – America West Airlines, Southwest Airlines, Trans World Airlines.

Tampa – America West Airlines, Southwest Airlines.

Tucson – America West Airlines, Reno Air, Southwest Airlines.

Washington DC – United Airlines.

Outside the USA

The following is a complete list of the airlines that provide nonstop service between Las Vegas and cities outside the US. If you'll be arriving from a foreign city other than those listed, or on an airline other than those specified, you must first clear customs elsewhere (in Houston, Los Angeles, Miami or New York, for example). After clearing customs, you can then board a domestic airplane bound for McCarran (see Airlines Serving McCarran for a complete list of airlines with flights into and out of Las Vegas).

Calgary – Canada 3000.

Edmonton – Canada 3000.

Mexico City – America West Airlines.

Ontario – America West Airlines, Southwest Airlines.

Tokyo – Japan Airlines, Northwest Airlines.

Toronto – America West Airlines, Canadian Airlines.

Vancouver – Alaska Airlines, Canadian Airlines, Canada 3000.

Winnipeg – Canada 3000.

Flight schedules and ticket prices change all the time. If you're visiting Las Vegas from abroad, call several travel agents or ticket consolidators to obtain current air route information and to get the best price. Check the travel sections of major newspapers for the names and phone numbers of consolidators nearest you.

McCarran International Airport

The soaring popularity of Las Vegas as a vacation and business destination combined with the tremendous growth of the local population have put pressure on McCarran to expand rapidly. To meet the city's air-transportation needs, McCarran has been adding no fewer than five gates a year for the past decade.

McCarran consists of two terminals: Terminal 1 serves domestic passengers, while the much smaller Terminal 2 serves international passengers. Both terminals are reached from Paradise Rd. Terminal 1 is divided into four main wings, or gates, lettered A through D. Gates A and B are reached by walkways; trams link gates C and D to the domestic terminal.

Covered and reasonably priced long- and short-term parking is a brief stroll from both terminals, and the ticketing counters, gates and baggage claim are easy to find. Departing domestic passengers who are already ticketed may check their bags at curbside and go straight to their respective departure gates for boarding passes. Departing international passengers must check their bags at their airlines' ticket counters before proceeding to their gates.

Airline Offices

All of the airlines mentioned in the preceding pages have counters at the airport. If you need to purchase a ticket or make a change to an existing ticket while you're in town, you may want to see a travel agent; there's at least one travel agency in each megaresort. Or, simply take a taxi or the No 108 CAT bus to the airport. A taxi ride from most parts of The Strip to the airport will cost you less than breakfast, and a bus ride's even cheaper.

BUS

The sole national bus company, Greyhound Lines (☎ 800-231-2222), has a station in downtown Las Vegas at 200 S Main St. The seats on most Greyhound buses are narrow but otherwise comfortable, the windows are big, and air-con/heating is switched on as needed. All Greyhound buses are equipped with toilets.

With the exception of Greyhound's express buses, the vehicles can stop fairly frequently to pick up passengers from countless small towns that otherwise have no connection with the outside world except by car. Those stops can slow progress considerably on some routes.

Slot machines welcome travelers at McCarran International Airport.

Air Travel Glossary

Baggage Allowance This will be written on your ticket and usually includes one 44lb (20kg) item to go in the hold, plus one item of hand luggage.

Bucket Shops These are unbonded travel agencies specializing in discounted airline tickets.

Bumped Just because you have a confirmed seat doesn't mean you're going to get on the plane (see Overbooking).

Cancellation Penalties If you have to cancel or change a ticket you purchased at a discounted rate, there are often heavy penalties involved; insurance can sometimes be taken out against these penalties. Some airlines impose penalties on regular full-fare tickets as well, particularly against 'no-show' passengers.

Check-In Airlines ask you to check in a certain time ahead of the flight departure (usually one to two hours on international flights). If you fail to check in on time and the flight is overbooked, the airline can cancel your booking and give your seat to somebody else.

Confirmation Having a ticket written out with the flight and date you want doesn't mean you have a seat until the agent has checked with the airline that your status is 'OK' or confirmed. Meanwhile you could just be 'on request.'

Courier Fares Businesses often need to send urgent documents or freight securely and quickly. Courier companies hire people to accompany the package through customs and, in return, offer a discount ticket that is sometimes a phenomenal bargain. In effect, what the companies do is ship their freight as your luggage on regular commercial flights. This is a legitimate operation, but there are two shortcomings – the short turnaround time of the ticket (usually not longer than a month) and the limitation on your luggage allowance. You may have to surrender all your allowance and take only carry-on luggage.

ITX An ITX, or 'independent inclusive tour excursion,' is often available on tickets to popular holiday destinations. Officially it's a package deal combined with hotel accommodation, but many agents will sell you one of these for the flight only and give you phony hotel vouchers in the unlikely event that you're challenged at the airport.

Lost Tickets If you lose your airline ticket, an airline will usually treat it like a traveler's check and, after inquiries, issue you another one. Legally, however, an airline is entitled to treat it like cash; and if you lose it, then it's gone forever. Take good care of your tickets.

MCO An MCO, or 'miscellaneous charge order,' is a voucher that looks like an airline ticket but carries no destination or date. It can be exchanged through any International Association of Travel Agents (IATA) airline for a ticket on a specific flight. It's a useful alternative to an onward ticket in those countries that demand one, and is more flexible than an ordinary ticket if you're unsure of your route.

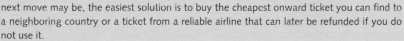

Air Travel Glossary

No-Shows No-shows are passengers who fail to show up for their flight. Full-fare passengers who fail to turn up are sometimes entitled to travel on a later flight. The rest are penalized (see Cancellation Penalties).

On Request This is an unconfirmed booking for a flight.

Onward Tickets An entry requirement for many countries is that you have a ticket out of the country. If you're unsure of what your next move may be, the easiest solution is to buy the cheapest onward ticket you can find to a neighboring country or a ticket from a reliable airline that can later be refunded if you do not use it.

Open Jaw Tickets These are return tickets on which you fly out to one place but return from another. If available, these can save you backtracking to your arrival point.

Overbooking Airlines hate to fly with empty seats and since every flight has some passengers who fail to show up, airlines often book more passengers than they have seats. Usually excess passengers make up for the no-shows, but occasionally somebody gets bumped. Guess who it is most likely to be? The passengers who check in late.

Point-to-Point Tickets These are discount tickets that can be bought on some routes in return for passengers waiving their rights to a stopover.

Reconfirmation At least 72 hours prior to departure time of an onward or return flight, you must contact the airline and 'reconfirm' that you intend to be on the flight. If you don't do this, the airline can delete your name from the passenger list and you could lose your seat.

Restrictions Discounted tickets often have various restrictions on them – such as advance payment, minimum and maximum periods you must be away (eg, a minimum of two weeks or a maximum of one year), and penalties for changing the tickets.

Round-the-World Tickets RTW tickets give you a limited period (usually a year) in which to circumnavigate the globe. You can go anywhere the carrying airlines go, as long as you don't backtrack. The number of stopovers or total number of separate flights is decided before you set off, and they usually cost a bit more than a basic return flight.

Stand-By This is a discounted ticket on which you only fly if there is a seat free at the last moment. Stand-by fares are usually available only on domestic routes.

Travel Periods Ticket prices vary with the time of year. There is a low (off-peak) season and a high (peak) season, and often a low-shoulder season and a high-shoulder season as well. Usually the fare depends on your outward flight – if you depart in the high season and return in the low season, you pay the high-season fare.

Greyhound fares are very low, and reduced seven-day advanced-purchase fares often exist between cities. The 27 weekday (and 29 weekend) buses to Los Angeles, for example, carry a one-way fare of only $31 for the 275-mile trip. A ticket on any of the 10 Phoenix-bound buses is a mere $33 for the 400-mile trip. Las Vegas to Denver, a 1040-mile trip, costs only $84. A one-way ticket to Salt Lake City, 450 miles away, runs $35. San Diego, 425 miles to the southwest, is a $38 option. And if you're in no hurry to reach Chicago, Greyhound will take you those 1935 miles for $120 on a standard bus with many stops or $189 on an express bus.

The fares quoted here are subject to a thicket of bargains and include the option of bringing a companion along for free with three-day advance ticket purchase. If you buy your ticket more than 14 days in advance, no destination in the entire continental US costs more than $59 one way. For budget travelers, Greyhound is a choice.

In addition to the cities mentioned above, Greyhound's Las Vegas station also serves Flagstaff, San Bernardino, Reno, Bakersfield, Fresno, Lake Havasu, Anaheim and Kingman, as well as a host of smaller communities along the way. Call Greyhound for fares, schedules and discount information, or visit the company's impressive website (www.greyhound.com).

TRAIN

Freight trains connect Las Vegas with many other parts of the country, but passenger service was discontinued in 1996. There was talk in mid-1999 of reviving the service, but nothing concrete. If this is disappointing news, call Amtrak (the national rail passenger service, ☎ 800-972-7245) to learn if passenger service to Las Vegas has resumed.

CAR & MOTORCYCLE

Las Vegas makes for a great road trip. It's in the center of a valley that's ringed by picturesque scenery in all directions. Avoid driving at night, when you'd miss out on the scenery, and because you could get very cold very fast if your car or motorcycle broke down on the open highway. Be advised that the mountains that surround Las Vegas Valley cause many vehicles to overheat during days when outside temperatures top 90°F. If you're heading into or out of Las Vegas on a hot day in a car or a truck, consider opening the windows and keeping the air-con off. Air-con taxes the engine and increases the likelihood of overheating.

HITCHHIKING

Hitchhiking in the US is dangerous and is no longer a common practice. It's a sad fact in the US that if you hitchhike, you expose yourself to the risks of robbery, sexual assault and worse. Most decent people are wary of hitchhikers, which makes the credibility of those who would stop extra suspect. As a rule, truckers, once a hitchhiker's best friend, no longer stop for thumb-waggers.

That said, if you still insist on hitchhiking, it helps to follow a few guidelines. If you are a woman, even a group of women, just don't do it (you're right, that's not a guideline, just good advice). Some people in the US assume that a woman hitchhiker is asking for whatever she gets – rape and murder included. If you're a man, your chances of being picked up decrease with each additional person. Carry a neat destination sign and keep baggage to a minimum. Don't look like anyone you yourself wouldn't pick up.

ORGANIZED TOURS

There are many organized tours to Las Vegas. The vast majority appeal to senior citizens who enjoy gambling in Las Vegas for a couple of days at a time and prefer to leave the driving or flying to others. Typically included in the cost are transportation,

The Road Ahead

For highway conditions to/from Las Vegas:

Arizona	☎ 520-573-7623
California	☎ 916-445-1534
Nevada	☎ 702-486-4100
Utah	☎ 801-964-6000

Warning

The information in this chapter is particularly vulnerable to change: Prices for international travel are volatile, new routes are introduced and old ones are canceled, schedules change, special deals come and go, and rules and visa requirements are amended. Airlines seem to take a perverse pleasure in making price structures as complicated as possible. You should check directly with the airline or a travel agent to make sure you understand how a fare (and any ticket you may buy) works. In addition, the travel industry is highly competitive and there are many hidden costs and benefits.

The upshot of this is that you should get opinions, quotes and advice from as many airlines and travel agents as possible before you part with your hard-earned cash. The details given in this chapter should be regarded as pointers and are not a substitute for your own careful, up-to-date research. Shop wisely!

accommodations and airport shuttle; meals are generally excluded.

Some of these tours are led by a director; others are unaccompanied. The accompanied tours mostly consist of chartered bus travel from a retirement community. Round-trip transportation and two nights' stay can cost as little as $99.

Air travel is always a bit more. One unaccompanied tour offered at the time of writing consisted of round-trip travel on Southwest Airlines from Burbank, CA, two nights at the Flamingo Hilton, and airport shuttle. The cost was $177 per person.

The best source of information for organized tours is a local travel agent.

Getting Around

TO/FROM THE AIRPORT

Taxis and walk-up limousine and minibus services are available at McCarran International Airport 24 hours a day. A taxi ride from McCarran to a hotel on The Strip typically costs between $8 and $13 *per party*. A taxi ride to a downtown hotel generally costs $13 to $17. Taxis are metered; in the extremely unlikely event a driver claims his or her meter is broken, take another taxi.

Limousine and minibus service from the airport to a hotel on The Strip usually costs about $4 *per person*. Add another $1 per person to reach a downtown hotel. Bell Trans (☎ 702-739-7990) operates many of the limousines and minibuses at the airport. Call the company to pick you up when you want to return to the airport.

Another option if you're staying at either the Sahara or the Stratosphere at the north end of The Strip or at one of the downtown hotels is to board a No 108 CAT (Citizens Area Transit) bus. From the airport the No 108 proceeds north up Swenson St, then west on Sahara Ave to Las Vegas Blvd, and then north on Main St into downtown.

If your hotel is in downtown, you could also hop aboard a No 109 CAT and ride it north along Maryland Parkway all the way to CAT's downtown station, at the corner of Casino Center Blvd and Stewart Ave. From there it's a short walk to most of the area's hotels. CAT rides cost an even $1 per ride.

If you're staying in downtown or at either the Sahara or the Stratosphere, you could catch a No 108 CAT bus back to the airport. The buses leave at 30-minute intervals from McCarran beginning at 5:09 am daily, with the last one departing the airport at 1:33 am. If you're staying in downtown, you could also take a No 109 bus to the airport. The No 109 buses leave at 15-minute intervals and operate 24 hours a day.

Don't choose the bus option if you're weighed down with a lot of stuff; bus service isn't door-to-door service. If you packed heavy, take a taxi or inquire if your hotel

Up, Up and Away!

If you love to watch jetliners take off and land, McCarran International Airport has got a parking lot for you. Located along Sunset Rd between Paradise Rd and Eastern Ave, the parking lot was created specifically for plane watchers and affords perfect views of McCarran's four parallel runways. Enjoy!

offers airport shuttle service; several of the megaresorts do.

BUS

Citizens Area Transit (CAT) is the local bus company. CAT's general operating hours are from 5:30 am to 1:30 am, although service on some bus routes commences earlier than 5:30 and service on the most popular routes is never ending. CAT provides excellent service along The Strip and in downtown and between the two. At an even $1 per ride, CAT's fares are a bargain.

If you're thinking of getting around town by bus, you'll want to obtain a CAT Guide, which includes all of CAT's time tables and route maps. If you're in the US, you can call CAT (☎ 702-228-7433) and ask for a guide to be mailed free to you. Otherwise, pick up a guide at any convenience store in Las Vegas, at CAT's downtown station or from any CAT driver.

CAT has too many routes to describe here. But the five routes of primary importance to the tourist, by bus number and by name, are: No 108, Paradise Rd/Swenson St; No 109, Maryland Parkway; No 113, N Las Vegas Blvd; No 202, Flamingo Rd; and Nos 301/302, The Strip.

The No 108 bus runs south from CAT's downtown station (at Casino Center Blvd at Stewart Ave) down Main St until it reaches Paradise Rd. From there No 108 runs down

Paradise to McCarran Airport, where it loops through the pick-up area before heading north toward downtown. From the airport No 108 proceeds north on Swenson St and Joe W Brown Drive, then west on Sahara Ave to Main St, and then north on Main St back to the station. The route is in service from 5:09 am to 2:05 am. Frequency: every 30 minutes.

The No 109 bus runs east on Stewart Ave from CAT's downtown station, then south on Maryland Parkway for about 6 miles to Russell Rd, where it heads west into McCarran and loops through the airport's pick-up area. From the airport No 109 doubles back on Russell Rd and Maryland Parkway. At Charleston Blvd the bus travels one block east and then continues north on 13th St to Stewart Ave, turns west and returns to the CAT station 12 blocks away. The route runs 24 hours a day. Frequency: every 15 minutes.

The No 113 is an express bus that goes from the CAT downtown station north on N Las Vegas Blvd to the Las Vegas Speedway, making only one stop and doing that only on event days – at the corner of N Las Vegas and Nellis Blvds. This route runs 24 hours a day. Frequency: every 30 minutes.

The No 202 bus runs along Flamingo Rd from Cimarron Rd to the west to Jimmy Durante Blvd to the east. If you were on The Strip, this is the bus you'd catch to go to the very popular Rio Suites hotel-casino, or to Pink E's bar/pool hall across the street, or to one of a number of good restaurants on or near Flamingo Rd east of The Strip. This route operates 24 hours. Frequency: every 20 minutes.

Buses 301 and 302 follow the same identical route along The Strip, but whereas No 301 makes numerous stops, No 302 is an evening express, stopping only at CAT's downtown station, Fremont St, Stratosphere Tower, Circus Circus, The Mirage, Excalibur and Vacation Village. The northern boundary for these buses is the CAT station on Stewart Ave; the southern boundary is Vacation Village, just south of Sunset Rd.

The No 301 buses operate from 5:30 am to 12:30 am daily, at 10-minute intervals, whereas the No 302 buses operate every 15 minutes from 6 pm to 1 am (southbound) and from 5 pm to midnight (northbound). The fare for the No 301 and 302 buses is $1.50 per ride – 50¢ higher than all of the other CAT routes, but still a good deal.

CAT buses are a good way to tour The Strip.

HENIA MIEDZINSKI

LAS VEGAS STRIP TROLLEY

Competing for a slice of The Strip's transportation action are eight four-wheeled trolleys that strongly resemble the cable cars of San Francisco. These old-fashioned, air-conditioned trolleys with interior oak paneling run the length of The Strip – from the Stratosphere Tower at the northern end to Mandalay Bay hotel-casino on the southern end. They make one digression from The Strip to pick up folks at the Las Vegas Hilton, on Paradise Rd. These trolleys operate every 20 minutes from 9:30 am to 2 am daily. The per-trip fare is $1.30, and exact change is required. The trolleys stop at the front door of each major hotel on The Strip, so the best place to catch one is just outside the main entrance of a big hotel-casino on Las Vegas Blvd. These vehicles are not wheelchair friendly.

Traveling from south to north, the Strip trolley stops at the following places:

Luxor

Excalibur

Tropicana

New York-New York

MGM Grand

Monte Carlo

Jockey Club

Bally's

Flamingo Hilton

Caesars Palace

Imperial Palace

Harrah's

Fashion Show Mall

Desert Inn

Frontier

Stardust

Silver City

Riviera

Slots of Fun

Circus Circus

Las Vegas Hilton

Sahara

Stratosphere Tower

For long-legged VIPs

DOWNTOWN TROLLEY

The several trolleys that operate in the downtown area make an endless loop on Ogden Ave, 4th St, a tiny stretch of Las Vegas Blvd, and Main St. These trolleys make it easy to get from the Fremont Street Experience in the downtown area to the Stratosphere Tower at the northern end of The Strip, and vice versa. The Downtown Trolley operates at 20-minute intervals from 8 am till 9:30 pm daily. The fares: 50¢ for people over the age of 5; 25¢ for seniors and the handicapped.

CAR

Las Vegas is a very easy city in which to drive. The city's streets follow a grid pattern – no simpler street pattern exists – and most motorists drive conservatively due to the presence of many traffic cops and the steep fines they impose on law-breakers. Remember: Pedestrians *always* have the right of way, many people react violently to being honked at, and parking in a blue (handicapped) parking space carries a minimum $271 fine.

Drunk-driving violations are especially frowned upon, and they are punished by mandatory jail time, revocation of driving privileges, court fines, raised insurance premiums and lawyers' fees; a first-time drunk-driving conviction will cost the motorist no less than $5000. Depending on your weight, as few as two beers consumed within an hour could bring your blood-alcohol content to the legally drunk level. If you're planning on going on the drinking binge to end all binges, take taxis.

Las Vegas has an exceptionally large number of jaywalkers. In fact, the number of people in Las Vegas injured by cars as they try to cross a street illegally is much higher than the number of motorists injured in automobile accidents in the entire Las Vegas Valley. If you're driving, overcome the temptation to view the attractions along The Strip; keep your eyes glued to the road ahead of you.

Rental

There are dozens of car-rental companies in Las Vegas. Rates vary but typically start around $25 a day for an economy car. Most companies don't require insurance, but if you want a collision damage waiver, expect to pay an additional $10 a day. Most companies require a major credit card, and some require that the driver be at least 25 years old. The few rental-car agencies that accept cash deposits require customers to provide a round-trip ticket, a cash deposit of at least $250 and proof of employment.

In addition to the rental-car rates, a 7% sales tax (yes, *sales*, even though you're not buying the car) and a 6% license tag fee are added to rental rates. On top of those costs you'll be dinged a 10% airport surcharge if you pick up your car at McCarran. Many agencies maintain rental desks at the airport. Among them: Avis (☎ 702-261-5595, 800-831-2847), Budget (☎ 702-736-1212, 800-527-8006), Thrifty (☎ 702-896-7600, 800-736-8222), Enterprise (☎ 702-795-8842, 800-736-8222), National (☎ 702-261-5391, 800-227-7368) and Dollar (☎ 702-739-8408, 800-4000).

Dollar has counters at Circus Circus (☎ 702-369-9302), Monte Carlo (☎ 702-730-7974), Las Vegas Hilton (☎ 702-733-2171), Flamingo Hilton (☎ 702-732-4180), Excalibur (☎ 702-736-1369), Luxor (☎ 702-730-6988), The Mirage (☎ 702-791-7425), Bellagio (☎ 702-693-8838), Golden Nugget (☎ 702-383-8552), Treasure Island (☎ 702-737-1081) and New York-New York (☎ 702-740-6415). Budget has counters at the Stratosphere and Four Queens (☎ 702-739-

8408 for both). Avis is represented at Sahara (☎ 702-258-3400), Bally's (☎ 702-736-1935) and Caesars Palace (☎ 702-731-7790).

If you'd like to drive something exotic during your stay in Las Vegas, consider renting from Rent-A-Vette (☎ 702-736-2595, 800-372-1981), 5021 Swenson St, near E Tropicana Ave. Among their wide selection (with daily rates): Ferraris ($499 to $699), Dodge Spiders ($299 to $349), Chrysler Prowler ($269), Corvette convertible ($249), Porsche Boxster ($249), Corvette hardtop ($199). BMWs, Jeep Wranglers and other less flashy vehicles are also available. Two major credit cards, in the driver's name, are required. For Vipers and Ferraris, drivers must be at least 30 years old. For weekend use, reserve at least two weeks in advance. Airport pick up and return are provided free of charge.

Don't like the look of those rates? Call Rent-A-Wreck (☎ 702-474-0037), 2310 S Las Vegas Blvd. R-A-W specializes in used cars, but none is older than 1992. Rates are as low as $19.95 a day with no daily mileage charge for the first 100 miles. Weekly rates are available for as little as $119.95.

Buying

Only if you are from another country and planning to spend a long time in the US (six months or more), would it be worth your while to consider buying a car. That's particularly true with regard to used cars. Eventually you'll save money over a rental, but in between you have the hassle of finding a car you can trust and finding a mechanic you can trust to check it out. There are mandatory registration and insurance fees, and then you have to unload the thing when you're done with it. And with the plethora of transit options available in Las Vegas, a car really isn't needed in town and transportation to most other cities is available by bus.

MOTORCYCLE

Motorcycles are great fun to ride in Las Vegas most of the year. The weather's generally fine for it, the streets are in great shape, and most of the drivers respect motorcyclists' right to share the road. Be advised that helmet use is required by law, as is a valid drivers license with motorcycle endorsement.

There are lots of companies in Las Vegas that rent motorcycles. All rent helmets and provide free airport shuttle, and most can rent camping equipment. Company requirements: 25 years of age, a major credit card, proof of current auto insurance (the companies like to see that their customers are insurable) and proof of medical insurance for the rider and passenger.

Iron Eagle Motorcycle Rentals (☎ 702-257-6222, www.iron-eagle.com), 5012 S Arville St near W Tropicana Ave, features a large variety of Harley-Davidson motorcycles. Rates are $150 daily, $950 weekly, and include saddlebags, helmet, basic liability insurance, all necessary locks and 200 free miles a day. A windshield can be provided free of charge.

Rent-A-Vette (☎ 702-736-2595, 800-372-1981), 5021 Swenson St, near E Tropicana Ave, rents Harleys for $100 a day for a 1200cc Sportster and $150 a day for a top-of-the-line hog. For Harleys, Hondas and Buells, contact Cruise America (☎ 702-456-6666, 800-327-7799), 6070 Boulder Hwy.

TAXI

If you don't want to do any more walking than you absolutely have to, you'll find that fairly easy to do. For example, you can catch a cab at the entrance of every hotel-casino; you don't have to go to the roadside and hail one. And taxis, though not inexpensive on a per-mile basis, are quite reasonable on a per-trip basis. The entire length of The Strip, for example, is only 4¹/₂ miles long; a taxi ride from one end to the other runs about $6, more if there's heavy traffic. The distance between downtown and The Strip is only 1 ¹/₂ miles, or $4 by taxi.

It's also possible to call a taxi, or have one called for you. You might want to consider doing this if there's a big convention at the hotel you're staying at and taxis could prove difficult to come by. In this event, your best bet is to ask the concierge (if the hotel has one) or the front desk to call a taxi for

you. If you're somewhere where you'll have to make the call, try any of the following: Deseret Cab (☎ 702-376-2688), Western Cab (☎ 702-736-8000) and Yellow Cab, Checker Cab and Star Cab (all ☎ 702-873-2227).

There are 13 cab companies operating 1181 taxis in the Las Vegas area. Rates are set by the meter and are the same with any area company: minimum fare $2.20, each ¹/₅ mile 30¢ more, waiting time per minute 35¢, trips from McCarran airport add $1.20 to the standard fare. Example of fares: downtown to airport, $13 to $17; airport to mid-Strip, $10 to $11; mid-Strip to downtown, $10 to $12; downtown to Convention Center, $10 to $12.

Yellow, Checker and Star taxis are the only companies that accept credit cards, and they only accept American Express. Companies that have vans with wheelchair lifts are ABC Union (☎ 702-736-8444), Ace Cab (☎ 702-736-8383) and Western Cab (☎ 702-736-8000).

BICYCLE

Las Vegas is very flat, and its streets are wide and in excellent condition. But Las Vegas is not the kind of place you really want to discover on a bicycle. For one thing, the city is hotter than nine kinds of hell half of the year. Unless you're in peak Olympic condition, no matter how far you go in Las Vegas on a bicycle, you'll arrive sweating like some boiler-room grunt aboard a battleship in a WWII movie, your clothes clinging to you like wet gauze.

For another thing, most of the city's attractions are inside its hotel-casinos, and you can't simply park your bike beside the front door and saunter in. Some valet parking attendant with token security-guard duties will figuratively throw a gasket if you try. Bikes, like cars, must be parked in garages, and that often means on the third or fourth floor of a parking structure that's located well behind the hotel-casino. For a little money a taxi will drop you at the front door. For even less money, a bus will drop you at curbside out front.

Of course, riding a bicycle at night in a city where many of the motorists are at least mildly intoxicated and probably distracted by the sights is taking really unnecessary risks. Other factors, such as the chance of rain or theft of the bicycle, should also be taken into account.

But if you're absolutely determined to ride a bike in Las Vegas, you can rent them at several companies in town. Most charge around $30 per day for a mountain, road or BMX bike. Three rental companies worth contacting: Escape the City Streets (☎ 702-596-2953), 8221 W Charleston Blvd; McGhie's, with one store at 4503 W Sahara Ave (☎ 702-252-8077) and another at 3310 E Flamingo Rd (☎ 702-433-1120); and Bikes USA (☎ 702-642-2453), 1539 N Eastern Ave.

WALKING

Often, the best way to get around Las Vegas is by foot. The city is flat and easy to navigate, and most tourists are interested in only two fairly small sectors: downtown and The Strip. Most visitors see little reason to venture to 'the other side of town' – from downtown to The Strip, or vice versa – given all the things to do where they're at. As such, *getting around* Las Vegas often means little more than trekking between three or four casino-hotels in a day.

Topping things off, the megaresorts on The Strip are making it increasingly easy to roam between them without having to work very hard. One way the monoliths have done this is with trams. One tram links Excalibur, Luxor and Mandalay Bay. Another links the MGM Grand with Bally's. A third tram connects Bellagio with Monte Carlo. And still a fourth links Treasure Island with the Mirage.

Movable walkways have also greatly reduced the amount of walking required along The Strip. The Luxor, for example, is further connected to the Excalibur by a movable walkway called the People Mover. Also, it used to be you had a 100-yard walk from roadside to the casino at Bally's; now a series of movable walkways carries you from the sidewalk right into the casino. The same thing at Caesars Palace.

However, if you plan to walk long stretches of The Strip, remember this: Las

On foot? Trams make it easy.

Vegas can get *extremely* hot, especially during the summer, so carry plenty of water and drink often.

ORGANIZED TOURS

Among the myriad companies offering tours of Las Vegas is Gray Line (☎ 702-384-1234, 800-634-6579, fax 702-632-2118, www.pcap.com/grayline.htm), 4020 E Lone Mountain Rd. Gray Line has a 7½-hour tour for $28 per adult, $24 for kids 9 and under, that begins about 9:45 am with hotel pick up. It includes a lecture on the history and growth of the city, a tour of the University of Nevada at Las Vegas campus and Green Valley residential neighborhood, a visit to Ocean Spray Cranberry World, a tour of the Ethel M Chocolate Factory and cactus gardens, a walk through downtown and admission to the top of the Stratosphere Tower for a great city view. Hotel dropoff is about 5:30 pm.

Vegas Tours by Scott (☎ 702-868-4403, 888-268-3427, www.wizard.com/cabbie/) is a mostly one-man operation run by a former Las Vegas taxi driver who specializes in personal tours to a variety of places in and around Las Vegas. Basically, you hop into one of his limousines or Lincoln Town Cars and hit the road. Starting at $35 an hour per group, you and your party can 'see the best roller-coasters, restaurants, hotels, casinos, amusement parks, or nightclubs Las Vegas has to offer.' The company also offers trips to Lake Mead, Hoover Dam, Death Valley, the Valley of Fire, ghost towns, Red Rock Canyon, the Grand Canyon and Bryce Canyon.

The Las Vegas Tour Desk (☎ 702-310-1320, fax 702-312-5543, www.ticketoffice .com/vegas/), 9555 S Las Vegas Blvd, suite 104, offers exhilarating nighttime rides over The Strip and downtown in a glass-bottomed helicopter. The tour begins with hotel pick up and transportation to the Las Vegas Grand Canyon Executive Air Terminal (near the MGM Grand Hotel), followed by a glass of champagne and the narrated flight over Las Vegas. The tour ends back at your hotel, and the whole thing lasts about an hour. The total price is $71 per person.

Things to See & Do

Anyone who hasn't been to Las Vegas in recent years can't claim to know the city. The opening of the Fremont Street Experience in December 1995 converted downtown Las Vegas from an eyesore into a vibrant, open-air pedestrian mall with nightly light shows that stop visitors in their tracks. Also in downtown, three of the four major hotel-casinos along Fremont St recently underwent substantial improvements, and Main Street Station, an elegant Victorian-style resort just two blocks away, was totally renovated. Today, Main Street Station is one of the classiest hotel-casinos in Las Vegas and possibly the best value for the money.

Meanwhile, The Strip has also undergone a transformation. The resorts that opened along S Las Vegas Blvd during the 1990s emphasize themes, size, elegance, fine dining, upscale shopping and, of course, gambling. The trend started in November 1989 with the opening of The Mirage, which continues to wow crowds with its erupting volcano, its glass-enclosed atrium filled with jungle plants, its white tigers and bottle-nosed dolphins, its 20,000-gallon aquarium and its spectacular shows.

Next up was the Excalibur, a gleaming white castle guarded by a moat and a fire-breathing dragon, with a medieval interior to match. Circus Circus, which scored high marks with parents when it brought big-top acts to The Strip in 1968, outdid itself in 1993 when it opened a covered amusement park on five adjacent acres. Also debuting that

Las Vegas at Its Best

Just as beauty is in the eye of the beholder, highlights are a matter of personal taste. Here is my personal list of the highlights of Sin City:

- **Desert Inn Casino** This is where you'd find James Bond if agent 007 was in town.
- **Cirque du Soleil** O at Bellagio or *Mystère* at Treasure Island. Superb entertainment.
- **Luxor** Superb re-creation of the wonders of ancient Egypt without annoying hawkers.
- **Bellagio Gallery of Fine Art** Not just fine art. Truly *great* art.
- **Hard Rock Hotel** Not for everyone, but definitely for every hardcore rock 'n' roller.
- **Stratosphere Tower** For an aerial view of Las Vegas without the costly use of an aircraft.
- **Manhattan Express** The ride of your life at a marvelously impressive mini-Manhattan.
- **Imperial Palace Auto Collection** Not just beautiful old cars, but historic ones as well.
- **The Mirage** A volcano, white tigers, a huge aquarium, an indoor jungle.
- **Star Trek: The Experience** A motion-simulation ride for even the most critical Trekkie.
- **Forum Shops at Caesars Palace** The most elegant shopping mall in the Americas.
- **O'Shea's Magic & Movie Hall of Fame** Possibly the best magic museum in the world.
- **Rio's Masquerade Village** Where Mardi Gras is celebrated all year long.
- **Main Street Station** Lovely Victorian-era antiques abound in this classy hotel.
- **Fremont Street Experience** A light show that always stops pedestrians in their tracks.

Lady Luck Goes Digital

Slot machines, like everything else, have entered the digital age. Computer chips have almost completely replaced spring-driven reels, and the random selection of symbols now takes a split second – though the reels still spin suspensefully, delaying for a few moments the instantaneous result.

HENIA MIEDZINSKI

How else has the microchip changed the billion-dollar slot industry? For one thing, it allows slots to be networked, creating enormous combined jackpots that can reach tens of millions of dollars. It allows for slot club cards that reward regular slot players with prizes depending on how much money they bet. And it allows casinos to track their machines, individually and constantly, and to make them as entertaining as video games.

Indeed, some slot machines have even become 'cable ready,' allowing players to watch their favorite soap operas while they gamble.

year were the architecturally stunning Luxor, the MGM Grand hotel-casino-theme park and Treasure Island with its daily pirate battles.

In the years that followed, the Hard Rock Hotel established Las Vegas as a major player with rock 'n' rollers, the Stratosphere took the city's skyline to new heights, and

New York-New York opened with a fantastic array of attractions, including a world-class high-speed roller coaster. Many other theme-hotels also opened during the late 1990s, including The Venetian, Paris-Las Vegas, Mandalay Bay, Bellagio, Rio and The Orleans. All feature a variety of attractions not usually associated with casinos. Bellagio, for example, boasts a gallery exhibiting $300 million in fine art. Rio hosts Mardi Gras-like parades six days a week. Mandalay Bay is home to a nightclub that features the biggest names in rhythm & blues.

There's no shortage of things to see and do in Las Vegas. Rather, there's often not enough time to see and do everything. That's particularly true of The Strip, where the vast majority of Las Vegas' hotel-casinos can be found, and where the choice of attractions can be overwhelming at times.

In a very real sense, there are two Las Vegases: The older, downtown Las Vegas, which attracts far fewer onlookers than The Strip and is often preferred by gamblers who find white tigers, faux volcanoes and so on a little beneath them (*Real gamblers don't need to be entertained*, they snort). In substance, the downtown casinos have changed very little over the years. Most are still low-ceilinged, with lots of cigarette smoke and little effort at decor. As attractions, they've got little to offer nongamblers.

Then there's the Vegas of South Las Vegas Boulevard, which is constantly reinventing itself, making itself more spectacular (and more of a spectacle) every year. This newer, brighter, shinier Las Vegas is not unlike an adult Disneyland, and it offers plenty of excitement to gamblers and nongamblers alike. Almost every resort on The Strip is an attraction, with splendid decor or thrill rides or other fun things to see or do besides gamble.

Regarding the descriptions below, note that not every hotel-casino in Las Vegas is mentioned, as quite a few are downright unattractive. They are places that should and will eventually be replaced, but so far are hanging on – buoyed by the success of the palaces around them. Also, the descriptions of the hotel-casinos below focus on their attractions, while their recommended restaurants can be found in the Places to Eat chapter, and descriptions of their hotel rooms and other guest-only amenities can be found in the Places to Stay chapter.

THE STRIP
Aladdin
The new Aladdin (☎ 702-736-0111, 800-634-3424, fax 702-734-3583, 3667 S Las Vegas Blvd) is due to open in the spring of 2000 on the site of the original Aladdin hotel-casino – which had been a fixture since the 1950s and was blown up on April 27, 1998, to make way for its new incarnation. This latest megaresort promises to be a major player on The Strip, offering not one but two theme hotels on its 34 acres: a 2600-room Aladdin Hotel & Casino decked out in a desert motif, and a 1000-room Sound Republic Hotel & Casino with 'a multimedia tribute to live music.' The $826-million Aladdin is expected to house a 100,000-sq-foot casino containing 93 gaming tables, 2800 slot machines, a keno lounge and a race and sports book; a 16,000-sq-foot European-style gaming salon operated by London Clubs International and featuring 30 table games, including baccarat, roulette and blackjack; and seven restaurants, a full-service health spa, a sprawling retail complex and a 1500-seat showroom. The $250-million Sound Republic is scheduled to open with a 50,000-sq-foot casino featuring slots, tables games, keno and a race and theater of performing arts to host 'top contemporary and popular artists, major concert tours, award ceremonies and televised music events.' The Aladdin will definitely be worth a look.

Bally's Las Vegas
Bally's hotel-casino (☎ 702-739-4111, 800-634-3434, fax 702-794-2413, www.ballyslv .com, 3645 S Las Vegas Blvd) opened in 1973 as the MGM Grand, which in 1980 was the site of the city's worst disaster – a fire that killed 87 people and injured 700. The resort has since undergone several renovations, and today is one of the most cheerful on The Strip. Set back from Las Vegas Boulevard, Bally's is reached by four 200-foot people movers that transport visitors from The Strip under a neon-lit canopy that's flanked by lush gardens. The moving walkway brings visitors to the entrance of a

People movers lead to the heart of Bally's.

JOHN ELK III

Those Cultured Americans

Attendance at museums in the past few years has exceeded attendance at professional sporting events throughout the US. This little-known fact is one of the reasons cited by Bellagio brainchild Steve Wynn whenever he is asked why he chose to open a spectacular art gallery at his hotel-casino instead of a sports arena.

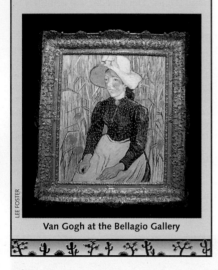

Van Gogh at the Bellagio Gallery

bright and inviting casino that features 100-plus table games, 1500 electronic and video slot machines and a popular sports and race book. The ceiling is high enough and tables and slots are spaced out enough to eliminate the sense of clutter found in many casinos. There's no central theme to Bally's casino, unless that theme is 'big.' Everything in the one-room casino seems oversize – the chandeliers, the velvet chairs, even the casino itself, which is about the size of a football field. *Big* also describes Bally's long-running production show, *Jubilee!*, which is the largest in Las Vegas. Just how large? More than a thousand costumes are worn during the show; no fewer than 70 stagehands are required to operate the stage, sets, lights and sound equipment; and no less than 4200

pounds of dry ice are used each week to create the show's smoke effects. Also of note are Bally's 20 retail shops and the fanciful mural of celebrity faces behind the reception desk.

Barbary Coast

The Barbary Coast hotel-casino (☎ 702-737-7111, 888-227-2279, fax 702-737-6304, www.barbarycoastcasino.com, 3595 S Las Vegas Blvd) opened in March 1979 and has since undergone three major renovations. Today, its relatively intimate 30,000-sq-foot casino with a mere 550 slot machines contains a lavish display of intricately designed stained glass, stately Victorian-era chandeliers and lots of polished dark wood. Except for Main Street Station in downtown, no other gaming establishment in Nevada evokes the image of the West at the turn of the 19th century better than Barbary Coast. The visual highlight of the hotel-casino is its Tiffany-styled stained glass: more than $2 million worth is lavished in the casino, in the hotel's restaurants (particularly in Michael's and Victorian Room) and in every one of its 200 guestrooms. The resort's showpiece is the 'Garden of Earthly Delights,' a 30-by-5-foot stained-glass mural on the casino's west wall, depicting a Victorian-era fantasy. Installed in 1984, the piece required 10 artists working more than 10,000 hours to complete. Barbary Coast contends it's the largest mural of its kind in the world. I wouldn't bet on that, but this hotel-casino is well worth a walk-through.

Bellagio

Built on the site of the legendary Dunes hotel and inspired by the beauty of the lakeside Italian town of the same name, the $1.6-billion Bellagio (☎ 702-693-7111, 888-987-6667, fax 702-693-8546, www.bellagio lasvegas.com, 3600 S Las Vegas Blvd) is the most opulent pleasure palace in Las Vegas. Bellagio, with its Tuscan architecture along an eight-acre artificial lake, is quite different from what most people expect of Las Vegas; it is, in a word, elegant. The view from The Strip is one of a green-blue lake from which spring more than a thousand dancing fountains. At water's edge is a cluster of charming buildings that could have been plucked from Italy's Lake District. Inside them and the butter-yellow, 36-floor hotel-casino behind the lake are 16 upscale restaurants (including the incomparable Le Cirque, imported from New York), an exquisite opera house, a highbrow shopping concourse and a European casino. The lobby is absolutely stunning, highlighted by an 18-foot ceiling adorned with a backlit sculpture composed of giant glass flower petals in every vibrant color. The sculpture was produced by Dale Chihuly, whose work has been exhibited in every major museum in the world. Real flowers, grown in a 90,000-sq-foot greenhouse behind the hotel, fill countless vases throughout Bellagio. Outside, there are six distinctive pool courtyard settings in Mediterranean style. Relaxing pools, soothing spas, garden-vista cafés and private cabañas are accented by artfully formed citrus and parterre gardens. Also at Bellagio is one of the most entertaining, unbelievable shows on The Strip (with prices to match), Cirque du Soleil's *O*. If you can, see it; you'll be glad you did. Be advised that baby strollers are not permitted in Bellagio, and the casino is strictly off limits to persons under 21 years of age.

Bellagio Gallery of Fine Art When the Sahara opened more than 40 years ago, many attendees gasped at its splendor. *Would it ever be topped? Could it?* they asked. Of course, it *was* surpassed in beauty and spectacle many times over in the years that followed. But it's hard to look at Bellagio and not ask the same questions. That's particularly true when you consider its pièce de résistance, the Bellagio Gallery of Fine Art. When Steve Wynn opened Bellagio and the Gallery in late 1998, he brought high culture to an ocean of glitz. And he did it with masterpieces. Among the $300 million in truly great art on display are some amazing paintings: a Monet water lily, Cézanne's *Portrait of a Woman*, Renoir's *La Loge*, Matisse's *Pineapple and Anemones* and Rubens' *The Head of John the Baptist*. Works by Degas, Modigliani, Van Gogh,

Picasso and Pissarro are also on view – and for sale (if you've got the money, you can take home any or all of them!). As befits the quality of the art, the gallery's interior mimics a museum: coffered ceilings, parquet floors, carved frames, discreet lighting and dark walls. Museum-like, too, are the $10 admission and the long lines to get in. It's open from 9 am to 11 pm daily. (Art lovers: Don't overlook, as most people do, the two de Koonings behind the hotel's reception desk.)

Caesars Palace

Caesars Palace (☎ 702-731-7110, 800-634-6661, fax 702-731-6636, www.caesars.com, 3570 S Las Vegas Blvd) set the standard for luxury for Sin City's gaming industry when it opened in 1966. The Greco-Roman fantasyland captured world attention with its full-size marble reproductions of classical statuary, its Strip-side row of towering fountains and its cocktail waitresses costumed as goddesses. Today, bar girls continue to roam the gaming areas in skimpy togas, and

Caesars Centurion

the fountains are still out front – the same ones Evil Knievel made famous when he jumped them on a motorcycle on December 31, 1967. But due to a $600-million renovation completed in 1997, Caesars Palace is more fantastic than ever. Swimming pools inlaid with marble and granite have been added, gardens have been enlarged, façades have been given a cleaner, more modern look. Inside, cheesy mirrors and neon have been replaced with hand-painted murals; dark paint and carpeting have given way to tasteful earth tones. At the center of things are two casinos containing a total of 100 card tables and 1934 slot machines, some of which accept $500 chips. Caesars Palace Race and Sports Book features 90 video screens and state-of-the-art electronic display boards. Other facilities include a movie theater with a dome-shaped screen, three live-entertainment lounges, a 3-D motion-simulated adventure called Race for Atlantis, a multichambered dining and magic experience and a phenomenal shopping concourse (see the Shopping chapter). With all of its attractions, Caesars Palace might be quintessential Las Vegas.

Caesars Magical Empire Caesars Palace opened this impressive facility in 1996, replete with tunnels, grottoes, theaters and dining chambers – and an illusion around every corner. The adventure begins with guests being placed into groups of 24, each of which is then escorted through a maze of misty catacombs by Centurion guards to one of 10 private dining rooms. There, each group is treated to a magic show by its own private magician between servings of a three-course meal. Simple enough. However, most of the entertainment is not so straightforward. Nowhere in this Empire are things as they seem. During dinner and throughout the facility, mysteries abound. You're not even safe in the bathroom; ghosts appear in the mirrors! After dining, visitors are guided through more catacombs to the Sanctum Secorum, a seven-story magical realm with a broken bridge and a bottomless pit. Flanking Sanctum Secorum are two bars, one home to two wisecracking skeletons (Habeus and Corpus), the other to a poltergeist who enjoys spooking guests with interactive magic. Highlighting the experience are two theaters where you can see more magic shows up close and where there's a good chance you'll be asked to be in one. In generally impersonal Las Vegas, the Empire (☎ 702-731-7333, 800-445-4544, fax 702-731-7769 for dinner reservations) emphasizes audience participation in an intimate setting. Free tours are available from 10:45 am to 3:45 pm, Friday through Tuesday. Dinner seating is from 4:30 to 10 pm, Friday through Tuesday. Closed Wednesday and Thursday. Cost: $75 per person.

The Best Tip Ever

Mr C, a very stylish and talented shoeshine at Caesars Palace, has been putting luster on fine footwear for more than 40 years. When asked recently who had given him the best tip since he'd been in business, Mr C didn't need to think hard: 'Sammy Davis Jr. Five hundred dollars – five $100 bills – for a pair of alligator boots. He was on his way to a $5000-a-plate awards dinner, and he wanted to look sharp. Sammy was always doing things like that – giving big tips, making people happy. He was very loved.'

Race for Atlantis IMAX 3-D Ride This virtual-reality ride to the lost city of Atlantis is offered in a domed IMAX theater inside the Forum Shops wing of Caesars Palace. Cutting-edge sound engineering and high-tech motion-simulation equipment combine to immerse riders in a multisensory experience that brings the mythical kingdom of Atlantis to life. The attraction begins with a brief walk through a stone hallway that leads to an underwater palace of sorts. There, you board one of four 27-passenger motion simulators and, after enduring an obnoxious safety warning delivered in rap, your 'chariot' is sent racing toward the lost city in a flight to a finish that will determine the ruler of Atlantis for the next millennium. Each rider is issued a 3-D visor that enables the illusion of debris hurtling past you. Fans and motion (your chariot jolts in all directions in synchronicity with the on-screen images) help create the deception that you're actually going somewhere. Although there is no age restriction, Caesars Palace asks persons with neck, back or heart problems to not race to Atlantis. Furthermore, if you've ever suffered motion sickness, you'd be wise to leave the riding to others. Although the ride lasts only 4½ minutes, that's more than enough time to empty your stomach's contents on 26 total strangers. *Race for Atlantis* welcomes guests continually from 10 am to 11 pm Sunday through Thursday, and from 10 am to midnight Friday and Saturday; $9.50/6.75, adults/kids 12 and under. If you enjoy the ride, you won't want to miss the superior production *Star Trek: The Experience* (see Las Vegas Hilton below).

Caesars Omnimax Theater If you like to go to the movies and have never been to an Omnimax theater, Caesars has got a treat in store for you. The Omnimax theater at Caesars showcases large-format movies on a giant, dome-shaped screen that engulfs the audience. Instead of sitting upright and facing a wall-mounted screen, the seats in this theater are tilted back at a 27-degree angle to allow you to face the domed ceiling in comfort. It is there – and along all of the

A Statue with Punch

Unique among the statues at Caesars Palace is one of former heavyweight boxing champion Joe Louis, the 'Brown Bomber' who did as much for destroying the race barrier in boxing as Jackie Robinson did for baseball. The statue graces the entrance of the sports book. Hewn from Carrara marble by Italian sculptors, it measures 7 feet 6 inches high and weighs 4500 pounds.

After an incomparable professional boxing career that stretched from 1934 to 1951 and included a record 25 title defenses, Louis was for many years employed by Caesars Palace as a casino greeter, holding court with adoring fans at a favorite booth in the Café Roma and sitting ringside with customers during championship fights.

Following his death, at the request of his widow, a memorial service was held at Caesars Palace on April 17, 1981. The service was attended by a host of entertainment and sports celebrities, with eulogies delivered by legendary crooner Frank Sinatra and civil rights activist Jesse Jackson.

walls – that an awesome visual display is projected via 15 perforation/70mm film (the images are *much* more defined than regular theater movies). The panoramic view of *Everest, To Fly, Africa's Elephant Kingdom* and other movies shot with special equipment is at times absolutely breathtaking. Complimenting the visual projection is a sophisticated nine-channel Sensaround sound system that envelops the 368-seat theater with 89 speakers emanating from 10 hidden speaker banks. The only drawback to Omnimax theaters is that there aren't enough of them – once you've experienced one, the old-fashioned wall-mounted screen will never have quite the same appeal. Movie screenings are continuous, from early afternoon until late evening, every day. The theater is in the center of the main casino, up one flight of stairs; ask casino staffers for directions. For show times, call ☎ 702-731-7900. Admission is $7/5, adults/children.

Circus Circus

Few people cruising The Strip overlook Circus Circus hotel-casino (☎ 702-734-0410, 800-444-2472, fax 702-734-2268, www.circuscircus.com, 2880 S Las Vegas Blvd). You can't miss the enormous clown-shaped marquee out front and the tent-shaped casino under a pink-and-white big top. Granted, from outside the sprawling Circus Circus casino, hotel and theme park complex looks pretty cheesy, especially when compared to Bellagio or The Mirage, but under the big top there's plenty of fun to be had for people of all ages. As if you hadn't guessed, a circuslike environment exists inside – as it has since Circus Circus opened in 1968. The ground floor has two casinos containing a total of 2220 slot machines, 72 card tables and a 160-seat lounge. In keeping with its name, the decor is a carnival of colors, mainly pinks and oranges. Directly above the casino and reachable by a circular ramp is Midway, home to an arcade, games and free circus acts. On the center stage, animals, acrobats and magicians perform from 11 am to midnight daily, with usually no more than 30 minutes between performances. Just come on in and take a seat; there's no admission charge or reservations. Nearby are lots of arcades – the video variety *and* old-fashioned carnival games. Among the latter: win a fuzzy space alien by tossing a whiffle ball into a basket, or by hitting a moving target with a cork gun. Another game involves striking a catapult with a wooden mallet, which flings a rubber chicken in the direction of a dozen pots placed on a rotating platform; if the chicken lands in a pot, you win. Circus Circus is a great place for kids and fun-loving adults.

Adventuredome Adventuredome (☎ 702-794-3939, www.circuscircus-lasvegas.com/adventuredome.html, at Circus Circus) is a fully enclosed, five-acre amusement park packed with thrill rides. Amid a desert-canyon setting replete with faux Pueblo cliff dwellings and an archaeological dig are dozens of attractions, including the only indoor, double-loop, double-corkscrew roller coaster in the US; a 20-seat, open-sided toboggan that makes a big splash after rocketing down a four-story slide; and a swinging pirate ship with a heart-pounding swoop. Also popular are a bumper-car arena, a kiddy airplane ride, a Ferris wheel, a laser-tag center and a children's net climb/ball crawl area. In the Extreme Zone are attractions for us older kids, including a four-story rock-climbing wall and a bungee-jumping area. Restaurants, video games and a carousel featuring live animals for your riding pleasure are also on the premises. And what would a Circus Circus amusement park be without clowns? Free clown shows are held throughout the day. While you're in Adventuredome, be sure to admire the 8615 panes of glass that fully enclose the theme park. Each pane weighs more than 300lbs! Adventuredome is open 10 am to 6 pm Sunday through Thursday, and 10 am to midnight Friday and Saturday. Admission to Adventuredome is free. The cost of an all-day ride pass is $16 for persons 48 inches or taller, and $12 for persons shorter than 48 inches (since height restrictions reduce the number of rides a shorter person can go on).

SCOTT DOGGETT

Cat show under the big top at Circus Circus

The Adventuredome at Circus Circus

Tickets for individual rides are available, but for the price of just three individual ride tickets you can purchase an all-day pass.

Desert Inn

The Desert Inn hotel-casino (☎ 702-733-4444, 800-634-6909, fax 702-733-4437, www.thedesertinn.com, 3145 S Las Vegas Blvd) remains one of the classiest resorts in Las Vegas. Construction began in 1946, and it opened to great fanfare in 1950 – and nobody could fault its owners if, over the years, it seemed to decline in the face of wave after wave of stiff new competition. Now, after a $200-million expansion and renovation in December 1997, the Desert Inn looks better than ever. At the heart of the magnificent 715-room resort is a gorgeous casino, which at 32,000 sq feet is rather small by Vegas standards. But its high ceiling and the ample space provided between its 449 state-of-the-art slot machines and 59 gaming tables give the illusion of a much larger casino. Size certainly isn't everything, anyway, and for looks the casino is magazine-cover caliber. The mile-high ceiling, for example, is dome-shaped and hand-painted in royal blue and gold leaf to create a stunning image of stars bursting across a night sky. The architecture is Moorish Mediterranean, illuminated with imported crystal chandeliers and supported by ornate polished marble columns. Don't feel embarrassed if your jaw drops when you enter the casino; it happens to a lot of people. The grand lobby is no less impressive, with its seven-story-high vaulted ceiling, its enormous hand-painted custom-designed murals above a granite reception desk, and its imported-marble floor that's so well polished you can see your reflection in it. The lobby's design reflects the long-lost style of the 1930s Palm Beach era. Don't forget to take a look-see at the 14,500-sq-ft freeform swimming pool, set amid towering palms imported from the Canary Islands and South America. A meandering lagoon with multiple picturesque waterfalls and footbridges adds to the lush and soothing environment. The array of restaurants is top-notch. The Desert Inn also features the only golf course on The Strip. It's on 130 manicured acres directly behind the hotel and casino.

Excalibur

According to legend, Excalibur was a magical sword embedded in stone. During post-Roman Britain, it was proclaimed that whoever could pull the sword from the stone would be crowned King of England. After gallant knights failed in their attempts to free the sword, Arthur, a mere squire, succeeded. The Arthurian legend forms the basis for much of the cheesy decor of the Excalibur hotel-casino (☎ 702-597-7777, 800-937-7777, fax 702-597-7040, www.excalibur-casino.com, 3850 S Las Vegas Blvd). The Excalibur epitomizes low-brow, gaudy Las Vegas. With guestrooms in two nearby towers, the main structure is a caricature of a white castle – it has bright orange- and blue-roofed towers and a faux drawbridge spanning a moat in front of the entrance, where a mechanical fire-breathing dragon does mock battle with Merlin every hour on the hour from dusk till midnight. Inside the castle, which contains a casino, restaurants and shops, the walls are adorned with coats of arms, with cheap stained-glass art of valiant knights and with neon knights

It's cheap, it's kitschy – it's Excalibur.

on neon horses. It's conceivable Excalibur could have been done up in good taste, resembling an elegant English castle, but its owners apparently decided to go the cheap, kitschy route. Even Excalibur's dinner show, *King Arthur's Tournament*, is more like a demolition derby with hooves and armor than a flashy Vegas production. Excalibur is connected to the luxurious Luxor (a classy must-see) by a covered people mover, making it easy to zip over to Excalibur, if only for the snicker factor.

Court Jesters Stage Excalibur is owned by the same folks who own Circus Circus, which has had phenomenal success due in no small part to the free high-quality circus acts that perform there. Following the same winning formula, the management of Excalibur established Court Jesters Stage, where a variety of acts can be seen free of charge every day. On the second floor of the casino a short distance from the people mover to Luxor, the stage boasts a cast of 30 performers dressed in medieval costumes, each

giving contemporary as well as traditional performances. There are musicians, for example, who play period instruments such as mandolin, flute and harp as well as magicians performing feats that medieval alchemists never would have imagined. There are also jugglers and puppeteers. The shows are great fun for everyone, and as with the performances at Circus Circus, you can't beat the price. Daily performances begin at 10 am and continue on the half hour until 10 pm. Acts average 10 minutes.

Flamingo Hilton

When it opened in 1946 with 105 rooms and an elegant casino, the Flamingo (☎ 702-733-3111, 800-732-2111, fax 702-733-3353, www.hilton.com, 3555 S Las Vegas Blvd) was the talk of the town. It was by far the biggest hotel-casino in Las Vegas, and the most expensive; its owners – all members of the New York mafia – shelled out an unprecedented $6 million to build a tropical gaming oasis in the desert. It was prime gangster Americana, initially managed by the infamous mobster Ben 'Bugsy' Siegel. He didn't manage it for long. Siegel died in a hail of bullets at his girlfriend's Beverly Hills home soon after the Flamingo opened, the victim of a contract killing ordered by the casino's investors; the Flamingo had gotten off to a slow start and the investors believed the Flamingo would fail, so they 'took care of business.' With Siegel, the investors made a business mistake: Not only did the Flamingo survive, but it's thrived. In 1970, Hilton purchased the hotel-casino and has expanded it regularly over the years; today it has an incredible 4000 rooms. The casino itself has been remodeled many times since 1946 and it no longer resembles the elegant original, nor does the casino try to invoke images of a tropical paradise or theme – other than a few pink-and-orange neon lights that kind of resemble flamingo feathers. However, just outside the gaming area are the Flamingo's gardens, and they are magnificent: 15 acres of pools, waterfalls and waterways; ponds filled with swans, ducks and koi; islands inhabited by Florida flamingos and African pigeons; and no fewer than 2000 palm trees and jungle plants everywhere you look. The Flamingo isn't what it was in the days when even its janitorial staff wore tuxedos, but its gardens *are* a sight to behold. For entertainment, the Flamingo offers the high-kicking *Great Radio City Music Spectacular*, which is a crowd-pleaser.

GameWorks

GameWorks (☎ 702-597-3122, 3769 S Las Vegas Blvd) is a high-tech entertainment center intended for teens and adults. If you enjoy video games, virtual-reality experiences or just hanging out in places where lots of hip people are having fun, Game-Works is for you. The center has an impressive Hollywood pedigree: GameWorks was conceived by film director Steven Spielberg and created by the entertainment company DreamWorks SKG along with high-end video game maker SEGA Enterprises and Universal Studios. GameWorks consists of one large underground room containing a popular restaurant, a full bar, a 75-foot climbing wall, an intimate pool hall and *lots*

of state-of-the-art video and virtual-reality games. One of the more popular games is *Vertical Reality*, in which eight to 12 players are strapped into seats and divided into groups. The players race the clock to rid a skyscraper of criminals – actually ascending up to 24 feet as they succeed, and descending in a controlled 'free fall' as they get hit. *Vertical Reality* might be the only game of its kind in which players experience physical consequences based on their actions. Also popular is a Jurassic Park attraction that pits groups of four heavily armed players against flesh-eating dinosaurs. Yes, it *is* as fun as it sounds. As GameWorks was designed for social interaction (the best games involve numerous participants), the best time to go is at night, when the facility is most crowded. GameWorks is open daily from 10 am to 4 am; costs vary substantially with games and specials, but expect to pay $25 or more for two hours of play. There's no charge for admission.

Harley-Davidson Café

The Harley-Davidson Café (☎ 702-740-4555, www.harley-davidsoncafe.com, 3725 S Las Vegas Blvd) is mostly a restaurant (and a surprisingly expensive one for a pseudo-biker hangout; see Places to Eat), but it's also a shrine to all things Harley, and that makes it an attraction. Just as the menu

The Harley Davidson Café

jacket states, the café highlights years of Harley-Davidson culture, history and motorcycles – not to mention many of the enthusiasts who have made H-D legendary. A conveyor belt carries a dozen Harley 'hogs' overhead, and the walls are covered with photos of Harley racers and of celebrities beside their Harleys, including *Easy Rider* star Peter Fonda in a black leather jacket and looking oh so cool as he stares way, way off into the distance while seated on his – yes! – Harley. Beside Peter are the words: 'A man went looking for America. And he couldn't find it anywhere . . . ' Somehow the words ring with much greater force when you're reading them in the office-worker-turned-weekend-biker capital of Las Vegas. Or perhaps they just need to be accompanied by the juicy aroma of BBQ ribs, the tinkling of beer glasses and the sounds of people having fun. Found throughout the friendly establishment are dozens of beautifully painted Harley gas tanks, each signed by a celebrity (Goldie Hawn, Sting and Caroll Burnett among them). There's even an adjacent store carrying lots of Harley-Davidson merchandise. Gamblers won't find a single slot machine at this Strip stop, just Harley diehards in Hog Heaven. Open 11:30 am to 11 pm Sunday through Thursday, 11:30 am to midnight Friday and Saturday.

Harrah's

When it opened in 1973, Harrah's (☎ 702-369-5000, 800-634-6765, fax 702-369-5500, www.harrahs.lv.com, 3475 S Las Vegas Blvd) was a Holiday Inn property with a riverboat theme. It wasn't until 1992 that the hotel-casino we know today received its present name and dropped the riverboat look in favor of a whimsical façade and interior reminiscent of Carnival and Mardi Gras. Those changes took place during a $200-million renovation and expansion that turned a mostly forgettable Strip joint into the fun attraction it is today. Unlike some megaresorts that make a half-hearted effort at a theme (Bally's rushes to mind), Harrah's decorators clearly enjoyed their work. Everywhere the visitor looks there's

something playfully suggestive of Carnival in Venice or Mardi Gras in New Orleans. Among the attractions at Harrah's is an enormous backlit mural over the main entrance featuring the greatest Las Vegas entertainers of all time. Photographers will want to see the mural at night, when light passing through the glass mural produces a captivating artwork. Inside, the 103,325-sq-foot casino (one of the city's largest) is nearly always swarming with gamblers who appreciate the bright and uplifting decor, not to mention its great variety of games: 2200 slot and video machines, 51 blackjack tables, eight craps tables, eight roulette wheels, two keno lounges, four minibaccarat, a race and sports book, red dog, eight poker tables, four Pai Gow poker, three Caribbean stud and four Let It Ride games. The facility is also home to a popular lounge, a comedy club, the illusionist show *Spellbound*, six restaurants and 2699 guestrooms.

Holiday Inn Casino Boardwalk

This Holiday Inn hotel-casino (☎ 702-733-2400, 800-635-4581, fax 702-730-3166, www .hiboardwalk.com, 3750 S Las Vegas Blvd) is like any other Holiday Inn except that on The Strip it *had* to have a theme, and so it chose to call itself 'the Coney Island of Las Vegas' and run with that proposition. The façade sports a faux roller coaster, a giant clown's face and the like, while inside a small but bright and pleasant casino goes heavy on clown objets d'art. Unfortunately for the Holiday Inn, the colossal New York-New York opened up a short distance away with Coney Island Emporium, a family entertainment center that's vastly superior to the mild attractions offered by the Holiday Inn (namely, free magic shows in the lounge afternoons and evenings). Still, after spending time in the casinos of the megaresorts, it's refreshing to wander into this bright, airy and cheerfully colored hotel-casino and play a few slots. How long the casino will remain as is is anybody's guess. The Holiday Inn was recently purchased by Steve Wynn, the personality behind The Mirage and Bellagio, and it's unlikely he's going to allow one of his properties to remain low profile.

Imperial Palace

The Imperial Palace hotel-casino (☎ 702-731-3311, 800-634-6441, www.imperial palace.com/vegas/, 3535 S Las Vegas Blvd) has 2700 rooms and turns to the Orient for its inspiration. Though the small, blue-roofed pagoda at the front of the hotel is a bit hokey, the Oriental theme within (lots of wind-chime chandeliers and faux jade, bamboo and curved wood accents) is quite all right. The popular 75,000-sq-foot casino is tastefully done in bamboo and rattan furnishings under a dragon-motif ceiling, and it's packed with 1844 slot and video machines, 26 blackjack tables, four crap tables, three roulette tables, a keno lounge, a big wheel, minibaccarat, a race and sports book, two Pai Gow poker tables, three Let It Ride tables and two Caribbean Stud tables. Special features include an auto collection (see below), men's and women's health clubs, an Olympic-size pool with waterfall and heated spa, and a tour booth. Imperial Palace also has the best celebrity impersonator show on The Strip, *Legends in Concert*. Imperial Palace doesn't have the wow factor of, say, The Venetian or Bellagio, but if you happen to be strolling by and aren't in a hurry, it certainly warrants a look inside.

Imperial Palace Auto Collection At the

back of the hotel-casino, the Imperial Palace Auto Collection is one of the largest privately owned auto collections in the world. A full description of each of the more than 200 cars on display would fill this guide, and serious car buffs could easily spend several hours here. Among the wonderful vehicles on hand: Marilyn Monroe's pink 1955 Lincoln Capri convertible; an armor-plated 1939 Mercedes-Benz 770K convertible used by Adolph Hitler during parades; a 1982 Range Rover 'Popemobile,' custom-built at the factory for the papal visit to the United Kingdom; a 1936 V-16 Cadillac limousine used by Franklin D Roosevelt, US president from 1933-1945 (it is the only unrestored vehicle on display); and a 1981 Zimmer Golden Spirit owned by Liberace, whose 1966 Rolls-Royce Silver Shadow is on display in a plush, gallerylike setting on the

Imperial Palace Auto Collection

fifth floor of the Imperial Palace parking facility. You will also find a gorgeous, guacamole-colored 1929 Duesenberg Murphy convertible coup, a red 1958 Porsche 356A Speedster, a 1925 Studebaker paddy wagon that was used by the Los Angeles Police Department and a 1935 Packard formerly owned by Emperor Hirohito. The gift shop features a wide selection of automobile memorabilia and books. The collection is open from 9:30 am to 11:30 pm daily. Admission is free, and visitors are welcome to take photos of the vehicles.

Luxor

Named after Egypt's splendid city of antiquity, Luxor hotel-casino (☎ 702-262-4000, 800-288-1000, fax 702-262-4452, www.luxor .com, 3900 S Las Vegas Blvd) has the greatest wow factor of Las Vegas' many megaresorts. That's not simply because Luxor houses the world's largest atrium, has 120,000 sq feet of smartly arranged casino space and hosts a stunning array of attractions. Rather, it's that the resort's designers chose a theme that easily could have ended up a pyramid of gaudiness but succeeded in becoming an elegant shrine to Egyptian art, architecture and antiquities. This Luxor evokes the same awe-inspiring sensations as Egypt's Luxor, the site of grand temple monuments on the east bank of the Nile. From an architectural standpoint, Luxor is the most unique resort in town. Built in 1993, the hotel-casino consists of a 30-story

Luxor aims to impress the Pharoahs.

pyramid cloaked in black glass from base to apex; in all, there are 26,783 glass plates totaling 570,000 sq feet. The atrium is so voluminous it could accommodate nine 747 jetliners stacked one atop another and still have room for 50 Cessnas. At its apex a 40-billion-candlepower beacon – the world's most powerful – sends a shaft of blue-white light 10 miles into space. Out front of the pyramid is a 10-story-high crouching sphinx and a sandstone obelisk etched with hieroglyphics. The pyramid's interior is tastefully decorated with enormous Egyptian statues of guards, lions and rams; sandstone walls adorned with hieroglyphic-inscribed tapestries and grand columns; a stunning replica of the great Temple of Ramses II; and a pharaoh's treasure of polished marble. There's a casino, of course, featuring 2530 slot and video machines, 116 gaming tables, poker, keno and a state-of-the-art race and sports book, and for entertainment Luxor offers *Imagine: A Theatrical Odyssey*, a show very similar in style, if not quality, to Cirque du Soleil's *Mystére*.

King Tut's Tomb & Museum When legendary English archaeologist Howard Carter first peered into the tomb of King Tutankhamen in Egypt's Valley of the Kings in 1922, he gazed upon a collection of antiquities representing the finest works of ancient craftsmanship. Today, Luxor's visitors can see exquisite reproductions of the same artifacts Carter discovered on his apocryphal descent into the fabled tomb of an obscure Egyptian dynasty (circa 1350 BC). The museum contains authentic reproductions of more than 500 items discovered in Tutankhamen's tomb, positioned exactly as they were found according to records maintained by the Carter expedition. Dr Omar Mabreuck, a renowned Egyptologist, oversaw the production of the museum pieces, which took more than six months and 50 people to assemble. Among the exhibits: King Tut's innermost gold-leaf coffin, decorated with ornate hieroglyphics and thousands of simulated precious stones; the antechamber, which contains three wooden and gold funerary beds carved in the form of animals; and the treasury, which in addition to golden treasures also contains several miniature wooden boats intended to carry Tutankhamen on his voyage to the afterworld. A 15-minute, self-guided walking tour of the museum allows visitors to view treasures reproduced using the same gold leaf and linens, precious pigments, tools and original 3300-year-old Egyptian methods. If you haven't been to Egypt's famous antiquities museum and don't plan to visit it anytime soon, this attraction provides an excellent reproduction of what you would see there. The museum is open from 9 am to 11 pm Sunday through Thursday, and 9 am to 11:30 pm Friday and Saturday. Admission is $4.

IMAX Theater at Luxor

Unlike the Omnimax Theater at Caesars Palace, which projects movies against a curved overhead screen, the IMAX Theater at Luxor (☎ 702-262-4555 for showtimes) projects its movies the old-fashioned way: on a flat, wall-mounted screen. However, like the films shown at Caesars Palace, the ones shown here employ a technology that permits the projected images to be 10 times more detailed than conventional movies. With such increased detail, a much larger screen can be used without compromising clarity. As a result, the screen at Luxor's theater is nearly seven stories high although the theater contains only 312 seats. The consequence of this is that you feel *very* close to the action. You don't so much watch the movie as experience it. About half of the films shown at Luxor are two dimensional (like regular movies), but the other half are designed to convey three dimensions. Watching a 2-D IMAX film on a huge screen takes film viewing to a new level, but watching a 3-D IMAX film on a huge screen is a galactic leap. The 3-D experience requires that you wear a headset that features 3-D viewing technology (without it, the movie's just a blur). The headset also contains an eight-channel, digital surround-sound system that further immerses you in the film. Ticket prices are $9 for one movie and $14 for a double feature.

M&M's World

M&M's World (☎ 702-597-3122, 3769 S Las Vegas Blvd) is dedicated to the famous candy, and it's primarily intended for kids but is quite entertaining for adults as well. Unlike the neighboring World of Coca-Cola (see below), which is both amusing and edu-

cational, M&M's World isn't meant to be taken seriously. For starters, visitors follow a walkway through a 'candy factory' that's a whole lot more like a fun-house corridor than any real factory. Giant brightly colored gears turn and lights flash and bells go off – and absolutely no candy is manufactured. But kids like it, and that's the intent. After the 'factory' visitors attend a phony class at 'M&M's University,' where a spunky 'professor' lectures about the history and the making of M&M's. It's a whole lot of amusing nonsense. Minutes later visitors are ushered into a theater to watch a short 3-D movie about a candied peanut who lost his 'M' at a craps table and all his travails to get his letter back. If you've never seen a 3-D movie before, you're in for a treat. The 25-minute tour ends at an M&M's gift shop, where lots of M&M's and promotional materials are on sale. M&M's World is probably most appreciated by youngsters ages 5 through 11. Hours are 10 am till midnight Sunday through Thursday, and 10 am to 1 am Friday and Saturday. Admission is $4, free for children 2 and younger.

Mandalay Bay

Las Vegas casinos have long sought to increase their appeal by placing under their roofs popular chain restaurants and restaurants managed by celebrated chefs. The $950-million Mandalay Bay (☎ 702-632-7777, 877-632-7000, fax 702-632-7013, www.mandalaybay.com, 3950 S Las Vegas Blvd) is no exception. Among its 15 restaurants is one managed by chef Wolfgang Puck of Spago fame and another managed by chef Charlie Palmer (Aureole). But when Mandalay Bay made its debut in April 1999 with a special concert performance by legendary tenor Luciano Pavarotti, it carried the bundling strategy two steps further by opening a House of Blues on its premises and by renting its 35th through 39th floors to the Four Seasons Hotel. That's right, an upscale hotel within an upscale hotel – a Las Vegas first. In addition to 424 guestrooms, the Four Seasons features a spa, a convention area and five-star dining. Not content to bring yet another topless revue to Vegas,

Mandalay Bay also presents six-time Tony Award-winning musical *Chicago* in its 1700-seat theater. The quality of entertainment and cuisine Mandalay Bay offers compliments the attention to detail that went into this tropically themed resort. Gamblers will appreciate the vast and classy casino, home to 122 gaming tables, 2400 slot machines and a race and sports book. The Salon Privé caters to high-stakes games. The resort's premiere bar, Rum Jungle, features a wall of fire at its entrance, ceiling-to-floor cascades inside, live Latin jazz most nights of the week, a dance floor for salsa-ing and more than a hundred rums ready to sample. Outside, an 11-acre garden includes a sand-and-surf beach (with actual surfing competitions), a lazy-river ride, a variety of pools and a jogging track. Adding to Mandalay Bay's appeal is its proximity to must-see Luxor.

MGM Grand

With 5005 rooms, the $1-billion MGM Grand (☎ 702-895-1111, 800-929-1111, fax 702-891-1112, www.mgmgrand.com, 3799 S Las Vegas Blvd) is currently the largest hotel in the world. Despite its size, the shimmering emerald-green City of Entertainment – as the MGM Grand bills itself – has done a superb job of making its attractions seem intimate. The megaresort has accomplished this feat by embracing not one but many themes taken from Hollywood movies. The most obvious example of that is the resort's dance club, Studio 54 (of New York nightclub and motion-picture fame). The adjacent casino consists of one gigantic, circular room

with an ornate domed ceiling and replicated 1930s glamour replete with bandstand (live swing and jazz every night, free of charge). At 171,500 sq feet, MGM Grand's casino floor is equal in size to four football fields and offers the full spectrum of table games (around 165) and slots (a whopping 3724) as well as a race and sports book, a poker room and a keno lounge. Other attractions include two shopping concourses, a seasonal amusement park (see MGM Grand Adventures below) and an array of culinary choices with an impressive celebrity chef lineup. For theatrical amusement, MGM Grand offers *EFX*, which is one of the top production shows in Las Vegas (see the Entertainment chapter). The list of headliners who have appeared at the MGM Grand is a virtual who's who of world-class performers. With so much to do in the MGM Grand, many guests choose not to spend their time in Las Vegas anywhere else.

MGM Grand Lion Habitat On July 1, 1999, the MGM Grand opened the company's $9-million, 5345-sq-ft Lion Habitat (☎ 702-891-7777), a swank enclosure with four separate waterfalls, beautifully landscaped overhangs, a pond, Acacia trees, skylights – it's easy to see where the $9 mil went. The featured attractions, of course, are the lions, some of whom are descendants of MGM Studio's famous signature marquee lion, Metro. The MGM owns 18 of the magnificent big cats, but for the comfort of the animals no more than five will be in the enclosure simultaneously. One of the treats of the Lion Habitat is its see-through walkway tunnel, which allows the lions to roam above, below and around their visitors. At times, the lions sleep atop the tunnel, separated from onlookers only by a sheet of Plexiglas and couple of feet of air. No doubt aware that their cat house would be compared to the tiger exhibit at The Mirage, the executives at the MGM Grand really went to town with their multilevel lion home; it definitely warrants a stop. While they're not cared for by a pair of illusionists known 'round the world, the cats' caretaker, Keith Evans, is a 30-year animal trainer with a

Spare Change

When the MGM Grand opened on December 18, 1993, $3.5 million in quarters were needed for its slot machines and to provide change. Thirty-nine armored cars were used to transport the 14 million coins, which were delivered in 3600 sacks. Each sack weighed 60 pounds.

tremendous reputation who lives on 8½ acres just outside of town with 22 big cats. The Lion Habitat is open daily from 11 am till 11 pm. Admission is free. There's a Lion Habitat retail shop next door.

MGM Grand Adventures The seasonal outdoor theme park MGM Grand Adventures (☎ 702-891-7979) features amusement

For outdoorsy-types, MGM offers a fake river.

rides, theatrical performances, themed streets, restaurants and retail shops. But unlike Adventuredome at Circus Circus – a fully enclosed, fully air-conditioned theme park – MGM Grand Adventures looks like it was hastily erected on a parking lot. However, it does offer the inveterate theme-park visitor something to write home about: SkyScreamer. SkyScreamer lifts one to three flyers at a time to a height of 220 feet off the ground. Flyers pull their own ripcords to set into motion a free fall that approaches 70 mph, and a bungee cord keeps each flyer from turning to mush on the ground. Also

popular are Lightning Bolt, a roller coaster featuring exciting twists and turns; Over the Edge, a log-flume ride that coasts on water through a nostalgic old saw mill and leaves most riders soaking wet; and Grand Canyon Rapids, a free-floating raft ride that whirls through gushing white water, a Wild West gun fight and a tunnel explosion. Live entertainment by actors, singers, gymnasts and comedians is also available at outdoor as well as indoor, climate-controlled theaters. MGM Grand Adventures is open during spring and summer only. Hours and rates vary from year to year, so call for exact dates, times and prices. Expect to pay around $2 to enter the park with no rides, $12 to enter the park and take advantage of all rides except SkyScreamer, and up to $23 for all the rides plus one drop on the Sky-Screamer.

The Mirage

When the Mirage opened in 1989, owner Steve Wynn told reporters his goal was to build a hotel-casino 'so overriding in its nature that it would be a reason in and of itself for visitors to come to Las Vegas.' The Mirage (☎ 702-791-7111, 800-627-6667, fax 702-791-7446, www.themirage.com, 3400 S Las Vegas Blvd) is such a place. The $730-million megaresort captures the imaginations of its guests with a tropical setting replete with a huge atrium filled with jungle foliage, picturesque cascades and meandering creeks. Woven into this waterscape are scores of bromeliads enveloped in sunlight and moistened by a computerized misting system. Circling most of the atrium is a Polynesian-themed casino that incorporates the unique design concept of placing gaming areas under separate roofs to invoke a feeling of intimacy. Real and faux tropical plants add to the splendor of the elegant casino. The registration area features an awesome 20,000-gallon aquarium filled with sharks, pufferfish, angelfish and other tropical fish. World-famous illusionists Siegfried & Roy perform in a theater designed just for them. A short distance away is a spacious open-air enclosure where white tigers play. Special slanted glass permits gamblers a

JOHN ELK III

Mirage erupted on The Strip in 1989, and Vegas hasn't been the same since.

glare-free view of the big cats, which are rotated among several lovely habitats throughout the day. The Mirage features an elite collection of fine boutiques presenting men's and women's sports, casual and formal wear. Fine dining is available in five international restaurants. Family dining is featured in four additional restaurants, including a 24-hour coffee shop. Out front of the hotel-casino is a lagoon containing a faux volcano that erupts with a roar, steam and fireballs every 15 minutes from 6 pm till midnight. Few people leave The Mirage unimpressed.

Secret Garden of Siegfried & Roy Illusionists Siegfried & Roy and their white tigers perform to sell-out crowds in a theater adjacent to the Mirage casino twice nightly except Wednesday and Thursday. How the men spend their days is anyone's guess, but the big cats can almost always be found at one of four locations, including the Secret Garden behind the casino. There, visitors can expect to see a black jaguar, a snow leopard, white lions, white tigers, orange tigers and an Asian elephant named Gildah.

The cats are among the 50-plus felines owned by Siegfried & Roy, some of which are used in the duo's extraordinarily popular show. Cats are nocturnal animals, which means they don't move about much during the day. Since the Secret Garden is closed at night, the best time to visit is late afternoon. It's then that the cats start thinking about dinner and are most alert, often chasing one another and otherwise being frisky. Audio guides are available free of charge, and there's a gift shop selling lots of Siegfried & Roy souvenirs. The price of admission allows visitors access to the adjacent Dolphin Habitat, which consists of two huge pools in which eight bottle-nosed dolphins spend their days swimming, leaping and interacting with their keepers. Be sure to visit the underwater viewing rooms; it's in them that you can get the best look at the playful small-toothed whales (yes, dolphins are whales). The Secret Garden and Dolphin Habitat are open from 11 am to 4:30 pm Monday, Tuesday, Thursday and Friday, and 10 am to 4:30 pm weekends (open later during summer). Admission is $10; children under 10 get in free.

Monte Carlo

The Monte Carlo hotel-casino (☎ 702-730-7000, 800-311-8999, www.monte-carlo.com, 3770 S Las Vegas Blvd) is a joint venture between the owners of Bellagio and Circus Circus, and the product reflects the European elegance of the former and the entertainment orientation of the latter. The resort, which debuted in June 1996 at a cost of $344 million, is fronted by Corinthian colonnades, triumphal arches, dancing fountains and allegorical statuary. A gorgeous entryway opens onto a bustling and tastefully appointed casino, just as you'd expect from an establishment trying to reproduce the grandeur of its namesake in Monaco. Behind the casino, where stands a stately tower containing 3000 guestrooms, is a magnificent marble-floored, crystal-chandeliered lobby evocative of a European grand hotel. Palladian windows behind the registration desk overlook the hotel's 2½-acre pool area, replete with 5000-sq-foot wave pool for body surfing, an artificial river for tubing, waterfalls and swimming pools. Other amenities include a unisex styling salon, a full-service spa, a fully equipped exercise room and lighted tennis courts; ah, but these things are only for guests. Open to everyone is a shopping concourse (see the Shopping chapter) and a spacious casino with 97 table games, 2092 slot machines, a high-limit gaming area and a race and sports book. For entertainment, Monte Carlo presents the excellent *Lance Burton: Master Magician*; many people feel Burton is the best illusionist in Vegas. Monte Carlo is definitely worth a look, and if time permits, consider having a beer at casino-level Houdini's Lounge, an intimate bar and gathering place featuring a variety of brews made on the premises.

New York-New York

New in 1997, New York-New York hotel-casino (☎ 702-740-6969, 800-693-6763, www.nynyhotelcasino.com, 3790 S Las Vegas Blvd) is a $460-million must-see. Its façade re-creates the Manhattan skyline, complete with 12 New York-style skyscrapers containing more than 2000 guestrooms and suites. These interconnected structures are approximately one-third the actual size of New York City architecture. The tallest tower replicates the Empire State Building at 529 feet (47 stories). Other icons include a 150-foot replica of the Statue of Liberty; a Coney Island-style roller coaster called Manhattan Express; a 300-foot-long (or one-fifth size) replica of the Brooklyn Bridge; and replicas of the Chrysler, AT&T and CBS buildings. Design elements throughout the property also reflect the history, color and diversity of Manhattan. The 84,000-sq-foot casino is a true marvel of design. Its 71 gaming tables and 2400 slots are set against a rich backdrop of famous New York landmarks, and its race and sports book offers electronic satellite wagering. Ringing most of the impressive casino is a wide array of restaurants and retail shops behind colorful

Lady Liberty, Vegas-style

NORMAN GODWIN

façades that resemble businesses found along Park Avenue, in Greenwich Village and at Times Square. The Bar at Times Square, which features live 'dueling pianos' each evening, is particularly popular with the thirtysomething crowd (see the Entertainment chapter). The attention to detail at New York-New York is remarkable, down to the whiffs of steam that rise from the faux sewer covers along the path to the Chrysler elevator. Not only that, this version of New York can be just as or even more crowded with tourists: for instance, whereas a mere 178,000 pedestrians stride Manhattan's Brooklyn Bridge annually, more than 5 million people each year cross Las Vegas' Brooklyn Bridge. New York-New York claims to be the 'greatest city in Las Vegas.' The folks at The Venetian, The Orleans and Paris-Las Vegas beg to differ. Decide for yourself. You'll have fun in the process.

Manhattan Express Within New York-New York is the Coney Island Emporium, a family entertainment center that re-creates the aura of the Coney Island amusement park in the early 1900s. The 28,000-sq-foot facility features the latest arcade attractions, but the pièce de résistance is Manhattan Express. ME is the world's first roller coaster to feature a heartline twist-and-dive maneuver, and only the second heartline coaster to operate in the world. For the uninitiated, a 'heartline roll' is similar to the sensation felt by a pilot during a barrel roll in a fighter plane, when the center of rotation actually becomes the same as the passenger's center of gravity. In the twist and dive portion of the 230-second ride, the train rolls 180 degrees, suspending its riders 86 feet above the casino roof, before diving directly under itself. To embark on the hair-raising ride, board one of the five four-car, 16-passenger trains from inside the casino. The train's first move will be to ascend 203 feet. Height and speed characterize the first half of the ride. The initial drop of 75 feet is just a warm-up for the 55-degree, 144-foot, 67mph second drop that passes within a few feet of the hotel's valet entrance. Continuing beside Tropicana Boulevard, the train ascends to

152 feet above street level, banks left, and then climbs onto the casino roof. Here, riders encounter a dizzying succession of high-banked turns, camel-back hills, a vertical loop, a 540-degree spiral, and finally, the sensational heartline twist and dive. As the train nears the end of its 4777 feet of track, the coaster disappears through the casino roof and returns to the station. The ride is open from 10 am to 10 pm Sunday through Thursday, and from 10 am to 11 pm Friday and Saturday. Riders must be at least 54 inches tall. The cost is $7.

O'Shea's Magic & Movie Hall of Fame

One glance at sleazy-looking O'Shea's Casino (☎ 702-737-1343, 800-732-2111, 3555 S Las Vegas Blvd) and one might choose to ignore the come-ons to visit the unusual hall of fame inside. That would be a shame because O'Shea's Magic & Movie Hall of Fame provides one of the best dollar-for-dollar entertainment values in town. The well-planned museum, which covers 20,000 sq feet on the second floor of O'Shea's Casino and houses $4 million in exhibits,

HENIA MIEDZINSKI

It may look cheesy, but O'Shea's museum is worthwhile.

contains a large collection of stage props that have been used by the most famous magicians of the 19th and 20th centuries. Throughout the museum are video monitors showing illusions being performed by the legends of magic, including Howard Thurston, Sevais le Roy and Harry Houdini. Also smartly displayed is an impressive collection of dummies used by ventriloquists, as well as videos showing some of the best in action. The Movie Magic section is devoted to historic Hollywood memorabilia; exhibits include a jacket worn by Gene Kelly in *Singing in the Rain* and a dress worn by Elizabeth Taylor in *Cleopatra*. Museum visitors have the option of attending a 30-minute live comedy act and a performance by world-class ventriloquist Valentine Vox at no extra cost. Topping things off, visitors are given a coupon entitling them to a drink in the casino downstairs. All this for less than the cost of a movie ticket ($5). And that's no illusion. Open 1 to 10 pm Tuesday through Sunday. Shows are 4:30 to 8:30 pm.

Paris-Las Vegas

Like so many Las Vegas hotel-casinos, the $760 million, 34-story Paris-Las Vegas (☎ 702-739-4111, 888-266-5687, fax 702 967 3836, www.paris-lv.com, 3645 S Las Vegas Blvd) strives to capture the essence of an international, exotic locale by re-creating its landmarks – in this case, one-third-scale likenesses of the Arc de Triomphe, Champs-Élysées, the Paris Opera House, Parc Monceau and even the Seine River. The signature attraction of the resort, like the signature attraction of the French capital, is a 50-story (half-scale) Eiffel Tower, where visitors can dine in a gourmet restaurant overlooking The Strip or travel on a glass elevator to an observation deck for a panoramic view of Las Vegas Valley. Just how authentic is the tower? Gustave Eiffel's original drawings were used to re-create this Eiffel Tower. The Vegas version is welded together rather than riveted like the original, but designers added cosmetic rivets to the tower for authenticity. And unlike the original, the Paris-Las Vegas landmark is fireproof and able to withstand a major

Paris, just part of the Vegas skyline

earthquake. Paris-Las Vegas is adjacent to Bally's and the two are connected by an extension of the Rue de la Paix, a Parisian street known among jet-setters for its chi-chi French boutiques and restaurants. Paris-Las Vegas features no fewer than eight French restaurants and 31,500 sq feet of upscale French retail shopping set along quaint cobblestone streets and winding alleyways. Surrounded by street scenes of Paris, the 85,000-sq-foot casino contains 100 table games, 2200 slots and a race and sports book. Napoleon Bonaparte once said, 'Secrets travel fast in Paris.' The same can be said for Las Vegas, and Paris-Las Vegas, which opened in 1999, is one secret that made the rounds here in record time.

Riviera

The Riviera (☎ 702-734-5110, 800-634-6753, fax 702-794-9451, 2901 S Las Vegas Blvd) was the first high-rise on The Strip, soaring to a then-impressive nine floors when it opened on April 30, 1955, with Liberace doing the ribbon-cutting honors and Joan Crawford delivering opening remarks. The hotel-casino has been renovated numerous times over the years and today boasts, at an even 100,000 sq feet, one of the largest casinos in the world (albeit a dimly lit and confusing one). When the Riviera opened, it contained a mere 18 gaming tables and 116 slot machines. Today, it has 1576 slots and video machines, 21 blackjack tables, four craps tables, two roulette wheels, a keno lounge, one wheel of fortune and a race and sports book; there's also one baccarat, two Pai Gow poker, Sic-Bo, two Caribbean stud and five poker tables. There are several dozen retail shops on the premises, a handful of restaurants (excluding a fast-food center called Mardi Gras Food Court) and a lounge with nightly entertainment. One thing to keep in mind about this very popular hotel-casino is that it's got spicy ads all over the place for its three adult-theme shows, *Crazy Girls, Splash,* and *An Evening at La Cage*. If you don't want Johnny or Suzy seeing some butt-glorified *Crazy Girls* ads, don't bring them into the hotel-casino. The ads are pretty hard to miss.

Sahara

Together with the Stardust and the Desert Inn, the Sahara (☎ 702-737-2111, 888-696-2121, fax 702-737-2027, 2535 S Las Vegas Blvd) is one of the few old-Vegas hotel-casinos that's survived its own numerous ownership changes and the onslaught of keen competition from newer gaming houses. Over the years the Sahara has undergone many changes, some better than others. The $100 million in modernization steps undertaken in 1997 and '98 gave the Sahara the facelift it needed to be a contender on The Strip at the start of the Third Millennium AD – although, for no intelligent reason, its present owners also replaced the Sahara's landmark marquee with a gaudy one featuring a cheesy caricature of a camel's face. Except for that, the Sahara strengthened its Moroccan theme with a vastly improved Strip-side entrance that features several dozen royal palms, an arched dome with lots of marble, golden chandeliers, tiny dark-blue tiles and other Arabian Nights details. The Moroccan-desert theme continues inside, where the completely revamped casino is guarded by a row of sultan statues. Replacement of tack with elegance is very apparent to any longtime visitor. Improvements include gold-painted ceilings, molded columns laced with colorful vines and jeweled lattice-work soffits. Outside, toward the towers that contain more than 2000 guestrooms (which have been renovated as well), is a new 5000-sq-ft heated swimming pool adorned with Moroccan mosaic tiles and ringed by lots of tanning decks. If you make it to the Sahara, be sure to pass by the resort's Congo Room to see who's performing; the Congo has showcased entertainers from Mae West to The Beatles since the Sahara first opened its doors in 1952, and it's continuing to draw big names. Question: What does the very African Congo have to do with the very Arabian Morocco? Very little, except that they share the same continent. But hey, it's Vegas. Anything goes.

Sahara Speedworld The vastly improved Sahara is the brainchild of developer Bill Bennett. Soon after buying Sahara in 1995, Bennett decided Sahara could benefit from a state-of-the-art motion-based simulator attraction, and he called upon the wizards at Illusion Inc to create a field of Indy car simulators so real they'd excite actual Formula 1 drivers. Illusion Inc, which developed the simulators that trained US tank troops for Desert Storm, was up to the task. Two years and $15 million later they presented Speedworld. Speedworld consists of 24 simulators that are three-quarters the size of actual Indy cars and closely resemble them. Each of these faux racers is bolted to a computer-controlled hydraulic platform, and each is fronted by a 20-foot, wrap-around screen that projects a virtual replica of the Las

Vegas Motor Speedway. When the virtual-reality experience begins, drivers compete in a computer-synchronized race that's simply scary in its realism. When, for example, you turn your steering wheel too abruptly and begin sliding, unless you're able to regain control of your race car the image in front of you will quickly be one of a fast-approaching wall. If you brake hard to avoid it, your car will dip suddenly and speakers all around you will squeal with tires skidding. Most drivers exit their cars sweating and breathing heavily. They are then given a detailed printout showing individual lap record speeds, braking performances and assorted other factors. For drivers who don't meet the 42-inch height requirement, there are two 24-seat 3-D theaters, each with four six-seat motion pods. Like the individual cars, these pods feature a 16-channel sound system and variable wind on board. Sahara Speedworld is open from 10 am to 8 pm Monday through Thursday, and 10 am to 10 pm Friday and Saturday. Cost is $8 per race. Ignore Speedworld if you have a heart condition or suffer from motion sickness. Seriously.

Stardust
When it was completed in 1958 at a cost of $10 million, the Stardust (☎ 702-732-6111, 800-634-6757, fax 702-732-6257, www.star dustlv.com, 3000 S Las Vegas Blvd) was the most spectacular hotel-casino in town. With its 1065 guestrooms, it was also the world's largest resort complex (at least by room count). While the Dunes hotel-casino had brought bare-breasted showgirls to The Strip with its *Minsky Goes to Paris* revue the previous year, the day the Stardust opened it one-upped the Dunes by bringing in actual French showgirls with its *Lido de Paris* revue. No question about it, the Stardust was a 'real class joint' back then, as the mobsters used to say. Today, however, *Lido de Paris* has been replaced by the equally topless but postmodernly bizarre show *Enter the Night*, and the difference between them says just about everything that needs to be about the Stardust of the here and now – which is to say, interesting, but no longer anything

special. It's wisely kept its landmark 188-foot starry sign, recently added a 1500-room tower and expanded its casino to 100,000 sq feet, but there's absolutely nothing spectacular about the place, except maybe for the high level of second-hand cigarette smoke that abounds in the casino (the low ceiling doesn't help matters). In terms of a theme, the casino has a very exciting pseudo-tropical thing going on that's not much of a draw. Nevertheless, the Stardust continues to see as much action as ever, thanks to its legendary status and the fact that its sign appears in every Vegas establishing shot called for by movie directors. For what it's worth, The Strip won't be the same when the Stardust inevitably falls. Maybe that's reason enough to see it while you can.

Don't look down from the High Roller.

Stratosphere
Las Vegas has many buildings exceeding 20 stories, but only one tops 100 stories. Standing 1149 feet, the white, three-legged Stratosphere Tower (☎ 702-380-7777, 800-998-6937, fax 702-383-5334, www.grand casinos.com, 2000 S Las Vegas Blvd) is the tallest building in the western US. At its base is a casino that's got all the usual trappings

of a sprawling Vegas gaming room but little in the way of a theme, and the several dozen retail shops one floor up leave a lot to be desired. However, it's what's atop the elegantly tapered $550-million tower that people have been coming to see since it opened in 1996, and here you'll find a revolving restaurant, a circular bar, an indoor viewing deck and above it an outdoor viewing deck affording spectacular views in all directions. To get you there, the Stratosphere has the fastest elevators in the US: they ascend and descend at 20.5mph, or about three times the speed of regular elevators, taking you 108 floors in a mere 37 ear-popping seconds. Once you've recovered from that ride, head for the world's highest roller coaster, just above the outdoor observation area. Just how high is the High Roller? A whopping 110 stories! And rising above that thrill ride is a second, the Big Shot, consisting of 16 completely exposed and outward-facing seats that zip up and down a steel spire that forms the pinnacle of the tower. Think of the Big Shot as a glass elevator, only there's no glass, and instead of standing, riders are strapped into plastic seats. And, instead of ascending and descending at a barely discernible speed, the Big Shot rockets riders 160 feet in 2.5 seconds, producing a blood-rushing, fighter-aircraft-mimicking four Gs of force. Leave it to Las Vegas to reduce Disneyland to kid's stuff. The rides are in operation – except when there's strong wind or rain – from 10 am to 1 am Sunday through Thursday, and 10 am to 2 am Friday and Saturday. The various costs: the elevator ride to the top of the tower and back down is $6; tower and High Roller, $9; tower and Big Shot, $10; tower, High Roller and Big Shot, $16. Children 3 and younger can ride to the top of the tower for free. Last but not least, the Stratosphere has two good production shows: *American Superstars* and *Viva Las Vegas* (see the Entertainment chapter).

Treasure Island

Although officials at Treasure Island (☎ 702-894-7111, 800-944-7444, fax 702-894-7446, www.treasureislandlasvegas.com, 3300 S Las Vegas Blvd) insist the theme of their hotel-casino is strictly 'elegant Caribbean hideaway,' the similarities between it and Disneyland's famous Pirates of the Caribbean ride are too great to be coincidental. The mock sea battle that takes place at Treasure Island's entryway is ripped straight from Disneyland's how-to book of popular attractions – and that's not necessarily a bad thing, if you're young at heart. From The Strip, the pirate-themed resort announces its presence with a 60-foot-high skull-and-crossbones sign. Coming from Las Vegas Blvd, visitors enter Treasure Island via a drawbridge-style approach that spans artificial Buccaneer Bay, beside which is a replica of an 18th-century sea village. In the bay, two ships – a pirate vessel and a British frigate – set the stage for scheduled mock sea battles. The pirate theme continues inside the resort, with black carpeting emblazoned with colorful images of gold coins, enormous jewels and the like. The walls and ceilings of the casino are covered with paintings of piracy. The casino's one-armed bandits (slot machines) are tightly grouped but no one seems to mind – the sprawling, 75,000-sq-foot casino with 2002 slots and 82 gaming tables is usually packed. Equally popular is Treasure Island's awesome production show, *Mystère*, which is performed by the French-Canadian performing troupe Cirque du Soleil (see the Entertainment chapter). Numerous restaurants such as Lookout Café and a shopping promenade with stores such as Damsels in Dis'Dress are very popular. It's hard not to be swept away by Treasure Island. Easing the journey there or away is a monorail ride to The Mirage, which shares a 100-acre site with Treasure Island.

Battle for Buccaneer Bay A full-scale battle between Treasure Island's pirates and British naval officers takes place no fewer than five times a day at Buccaneer Bay, located between The Strip and the resort's can't-miss casino. From the road you'll spy the two wooden ships and the nearby viewing platforms for bystanders, and like the volcanic eruptions at The Mirage, no tickets are needed for the show, which involves 30 stunt performers and actors and

Las Vegas Free & Fun

Some of the best things in Vegas don't cost nothin'. If you're counting your copper coinage for the penny slots, it may interest you to know that many of Sin City's best attractions are also free.

- **Spectacular Floral Arrangements** Flower lovers will appreciate Bellagio's lobby and casino.

- **Window Shopping** Million-dollar necklaces in Bellagio's shops, high fashion at Caesars.

- **Stage Performances** Acrobats, animals and clowns at Circus Circus, court jesters at Excalibur.

- **For the Birds** The Flamingo Hilton's 15 acres of gardens, Tropicana's Wildlife Walk.

- **Lofty Lounge Acts** Every major hotel-casino has got them, and most are excellent entertainers.

- **Loads of Fun** Just watching the players at GameWorks is enjoyment enough for many people.

- **Manhattan Without the Mugging** New York-New York is perfect for strolling.

- **Tigers and a Volcano** The Mirage is a feast for the eyes – and ears. That's the volcano rumbling.

- **Battle for Buccaneer Bay** High-seas hijinks have never been so much fun to watch.

- **Shrine to Rock Stars** Hard Rock's casino is a temple to the gods and goddesses of rock 'n' roll.

- **Lions, Lions and Lions, Oh My** Roar with MGM Grand's signature animal at its Lion Habitat.

High seas hijinks at Treasure Island

- **Mardi Gras Celebrations** In Rio's Masquerade Village several times a day, six days a week.

- **Brilliant Light Show** When the Fremont Street Experience is on, all eyes look toward heaven.

- **Gold & $1 Million** Golden Nugget has a mega-nugget, Binion's Horseshoe flashes big cash.

a hefty amount of gunpowder. Just saunter up to the viewing area and watch the drama unfold. It all begins when the British frigate, the HMS *Brittania*, rounds Skull Point and spies the pirate ship *Hispaniola* unloading its booty. The British challenge the pirates to surrender; a pompous British captain can be heard shouting, 'I order you brigands to lay down your arms and receive a Marine boarding party.' Pirates don't take kindly to orders, and the pirate leader replies, 'The only thing we'll receive from you is your stores, valuables and whatever rum ye might have on board, you son of a footman's goat.' In the minutes that follow a spectacular pyrotechnic war ensues, including cannon shots that snap a mast, set buildings aflame and force combatants on both sides to hurl themselves into the sea. Just as the pirates' fate appears doomed, the pirate captain swings across his ship from bow to stern, grabs a smoldering ember and lights the fuse on the final cannon. The last-chance shot hits the *Brittania* dead center. The ship tilts to one side and slowly sinks as the British captain stands defiantly on deck and goes down with his ship. Moments later, before everyone's eyes, the ships are returned to their original conditions and positioned for the next big battle. Showtimes are 4, 5:30, 7, 8:30 and 10 pm, Sunday through Thursday, with an additional performance at 11:30 pm Friday and Saturday.

Tropicana

Built in 1957, the Tropicana hotel-casino (☎ 702-739-2222, 800-634-4000, fax 702-739-2469, www.tropicana.lv.com, 3801 S Las Vegas Blvd) has had lots of time to lose its luster, lose its crowds and go the way of the Dunes and the Sands – ashes to ashes, dust to dust. Instead, after more than 40 years, the Tropicana has never looked better. Thanks to a major renovation in 1995, the Trop's entryway resembles a festive Caribbean village, sporting two three-story likenesses of Maori gods, a waterfall, a lagoon, outrigger canoes and a Polynesian longhouse that often hosts Hawaiian musicians. The tropical-paradise theme virtually disappears in the casino, except for a few flower prints and a few exotic plants here and there. Still, the casino is roomy, bright and otherwise appealing. The resort's 1900 rooms reside in two towers, between which are five acres of

Size Matters

In Vegas, size matters. Here are the current records Vegas holds:

- World's biggest hotel, today: the MGM Grand, with 5005 rooms

- World's biggest hotel, tomorrow: the Venetian, with over 6000 rooms by 2001

- World's largest atrium: Luxor

- World's biggest gold nugget: Hand of Faith at the Golden Nugget

- World's highest roller coaster: High Roller at the Stratosphere

- World's first heartline roller coaster: Manhattan Express at New York-New York

- World's largest public wine collection: The Wine Cellar at Rio

- World's most powerful beacon: Luxor

- World's largest race and sports book: Las Vegas Hilton

- World's largest carved emerald: the 430-carat Carved Moghul Indian Emerald at the Fred Leighton store inside Bellagio

- North America's largest bowling alley: Showboat

- Fastest elevator in the United States: Stratosphere

- Tallest building in the Western United States: Stratosphere

LEE FOSTER

swimming pools, five spas, a 110-foot water-slide, thousands of tropical plants, a lovely waterfall and two lagoons that are home to flamingos, swans and ducks. A very popular section of the Tropicana is Wildlife Walk, which is a wide, elevated hallway with views of the pools and gardens below. At one end of the walk, resting in a little inside garden of their own, is a clutch of exotic birds, including a blue-and-gold macaw, an umbrella cockatoo, a green macaw and a greater sulfur-crested cockatoo, among others. Other entertainment offered at the Trop includes the long-running production show *Folies Bergère* and the Comedy Shop comedy club. Pedestrian skywalks link the Tropicana with the MGM Grand, Excalibur and Luxor.

The Venetian

Sheldon Adelson broke ground on The Venetian (☎ 702-733-5539, 888-283-6423, fax 702-733-5190, www.venetian.com, 3355 S Las Vegas Blvd) shortly after closing the 44-year-old Sands Hotel Casino in 1996. This $2-billion, 35-story megaresort inspired by the splendor of Italy's most romantic city is being developed in two phases on the old Sands site. Phase 1 opened in 1999 with 3036 roomy suites, an elegant 116,000-sq-foot casino and a 500,000-sq-foot shopping area known as the Grand Canal Shoppes. A gondola-filled lagoon and full-scale repro-ductions of Venetian landmarks abound. Graceful arched bridges, actual flowing canals, vibrant piazzas and welcoming stone walkways really do capture the spirit of Venice in faithful detail. The casino is linked to the 1.15-million-sq-foot Sands Expo and Convention Center, which features state-of-the-art facilities located at the heart of the ever-popular Strip. This fantastic hotel-casino also has a large health spa and fitness club. Phase 2 of The Venetian's construction, which was scheduled for completion in late 2000, will add 3000 more suites to the site. With more than 6000 suites in all, The Venet-ian will be the world's largest hotel. Even if you've had the good fortune of strolling the cobblestone pathways and plying the romantic canals of the one-and-only Venice,

Gondolas: the only way to travel

you won't want to miss the Las Vegas version. In a city filled with spectacles, this is surely one of the most spectacular.

Wet 'n' Wild

The 26-acre Wet 'n' Wild water park (☎ 702-737-3819, www.wetnwild.com, 2601 S Las Vegas Blvd) is the coolest place on The Strip from early May through September – its months of operation. During this usually hot period, Wet 'n' Wild offers kids and adults alike more than a dozen slides, chutes and floats refreshed by 1.5 million gallons of constantly filtered water. You may have made a splash at a water park before, but it's unlikely you've ever been to one like this. Among the many attractions are Raging Rapids, a simulated white-water rafting adventure on a 500-foot-long river; Blue Niagara, a dizzying six-story descent inside intertwined looping tubes; Willy Willy, a monstrous whirlpool that propels riders around and around on inner tubes in a circular pool; Surf Lagoon, a 500,000-gallon wave pool that's popular with body surfers; Bomb Bay, a bomblike enclosure 76 feet in the air that sends its occupants on a vertical flight into a sparkling pool target; and Banzai Banzai, a roller-coaster-like ride in which riders atop plastic sleds swoosh down a chute at a 45-degree angle into a pool, where they skip like stones for more than 100 feet. There is a leisurely float trip as well, but most of what Wet 'n' Wild has to offer was designed for the wild, not the mild. The park has plenty of food concessions and even a swimwear store. Hours are 10 am to 6 pm daily (later during heat waves). Admission: $24 for persons 10 years or older, $18 for kids ages 3 to 10, and free to children under 3.

World of Coca-Cola

World of Coca-Cola (☎ 702-597-3122, 800-720-2653, 3769 S Las Vegas Blvd), the official museum of the world's leading soft drink maker, is an excellent attraction that takes the visitor well beyond who invented Coke and why (which in itself is pretty interesting stuff). Did you know, for example, that the exact ingredients and process used in making Coca-Cola is a closely guarded secret? Only five people are in the know, and the only written record of how to make the sweet dark syrup that's at the heart of the beverage is kept in a vault in Atlanta. Among the many displays at the World of Coca-Cola are a counter where a soda jerk stirs up a glass of Coca-Cola the old-fashioned way; person-size (and bigger) samples of Coca-Cola bottle art from international competitions; a theater where guests can watch Coca-Cola commercials from the 1950s, '60s and '70s; Coca-Cola advertisements from the 1930s; beautiful Coca-Cola refrigerators and early bottle-dispensing machines; and a sampling station where visitors can try 30 beverages produced by the Coca-Cola Company worldwide, including Krest Ginger Ale from Mozambique, Guaraná Tai from Brazil and Lychee Mello from Thailand. The requisite gift shop contains *lots* of high-quality Coca-Cola promotional products, such as black

leather jackets with an eye-catching Coca-Cola Las Vegas patch on the back. The museum is a very pleasant surprise. Open from 10 am to midnight Sunday through Thursday, and from 10 am to 1 am Friday and Saturday. Admission is $6; children under 6 get in free.

EAST OF THE STRIP
Hard Rock Café & Hotel

The Hard Rock Café & Hotel (☎ 702-693-5000, 800-693-7625, fax 702-693-5010, 800-473-7625, www.hardrockhotel.com, 4455 Paradise Rd) is the world's first rock 'n' roll casino, and it includes the most impressive collection of rock memorabilia ever assembled under one roof. The facility consists of a restaurant and a hotel-casino, with several acres of free parking in between. The restaurant varies little from Hard Rocks scattered across the planet, but the hotel-casino is really something special. The entryway opens up to a roomy circular casino around which are bars, a concert hall, a bank, a sports book and a retail store. Throughout the hotel-casino are the clothes, tools and toys of rock stars. Among the priceless memorabilia: concert attire worn by Elvis, Madonna and Prince; a drum kit used by Alex Van Halen; a custom motorcycle originally owned by Hell's Angels and donated by Nikki Sixx of Mötley Crüe; a 5m-by-3m display case filled with Beatles memorabilia; dozens of jackets and guitars formerly owned by the biggest names in rock 'n' roll; and Jim Morrison's handwritten lyrics to one of The Doors' greatest hits, 'The Changeling.' The list could fill 10 pages, and each item is smartly displayed. The reception desk can give you a hotel-casino guide and foldout map that contains detailed information about every piece of memorabilia on the premises. This place is a must-see for rock 'n' rollers.

Las Vegas Hilton

Not to be mistaken with the Flamingo Hilton, the Las Vegas Hilton (☎ 702-732-5111, 800-732-7117, fax 702-732-5790, www .lvhilton.com, 3000 Paradise Rd) is enormously popular with business travelers, in

Marriages Made in Heaven

Heaven might not be your word choice, but 'Marriages Made in Las Vegas' definitely doesn't have the same magical ring to it. Then again, there must be something magical about it, since more than 300 couples a day tie the knot in Sin City.

The reasons people cite for getting hitched here are countless, but the low licensing fee ($35) and the absence of waiting-period and blood-test requirements are often mentioned. The services themselves can range in quality from a 10-minute drive-thru to a big to-do at a hotel-casino (12 resorts contain wedding chapels).

If you're thinking of 'making it official' in Las Vegas and want to know what's required, call the County Clerk's Office (☎ 702-455-4416, 200 S 3rd St). Be advised that New Year's Eve and Valentine's Day are crush times for Vegas wedding chapels; plan ahead if you want to have your big day on either of these days.

Among the scores of celebrity couples who have exchanged vows in Las Vegas: Whoopi Goldberg and David Claessen, Jon Bon Jovi and Dorothea Hurley, Melanie Griffith and Don Johnson, Richard Gere and Cindy Crawford, Bruce Willis and Demi Moore, and Clint Eastwood and Dina Ruiz.

Another happy wedding...Next!

---

no small part due to its proximity to the Convention Center. Being off The Strip, it also doesn't attract nearly as many glassy-eyed slot jockeys and slobby low-rollers as the casinos on Las Vegas Blvd. The casino, which has been used in many films including *Diamonds Are Forever* and *Indecent Proposal*, is roomy and tastefully appointed; there's nothing phony about the Austrian crystal chandeliers or the Italian marble columns. Off to one side is the $17-million SuperBook, the largest race and sports book in the world. The NightClub at the Las Vegas Hilton is the only dance club in town that offers live music four nights a week (swing on Tuesday and Wednesday, pop dance music Friday and Saturday). Out-of-this-world entertainment is on the ground

floor of the Hilton's North Tower; that's where you'll find the $70-million interactive attraction *Star Trek: The Experience* (see below). The Hilton's excellent production show, however, goes back in time: *Forever Plaid* is an appealing throwback that makes up in musical nostalgia what it lacks in showgirls. The Hilton has a number of fine restaurants, including one that specializes in seafood, another in French cuisine and a third in gourmet Chinese. There's an eight-acre rooftop recreation deck that features a heated pool and a spacious whirlpool spa. A health club on the third floor offers steam rooms, saunas, treadmills and tanning booths, along with weight training equipment and cardiovascular facilities. A massage, manicure, facial and/or body wrap is a phone call away. No wonder so many guests view the Hilton as mixing business with pleasure.

Star Trek: The Experience The highlight of *Star Trek: The Experience* (☎ 702-732-5111, www.startrekexp.com) is a 22-minute motion-simulator Voyage Through Space at – what else? – warp speed aboard – what else? – the starship *Enterprise*. The attraction also includes a complete re-creation of the promenade from *Star Trek: Deep Space Nine*, where guests can dine in Quark's Bar & Restaurant, choose from the largest selection of *Star Trek* merchandise in the known universe, and even converse with a variety of interplanetary visitors. State-of-the-art video games are also on the premises. Did I mention gambling? The gateway to *Star Trek: The Experience* is the 20,000-sq-foot, very futuristic SpaceQuest Casino, where guests step aboard a simulated space ship that is constantly circling the Earth from an orbit of 1500 miles. The focal points of this casino in space are three 10-by-24-foot 'space windows' above the gaming area, which create the illusion of a genteel passage around our happy planet. There's no cost to enter the casino, to investigate the *Star Trek* merchandise or to saunter up to Quark's Bar and be treated just like any other Earthling, but the motion-simulation ride – which begins with a really cool museumlike exhibit featuring authentic *Star Trek* costumes, weaponry, make-up, special effects and props used in the four *Star Trek* television series and eight motion pictures – will set you back $15. Be advised that if you suffer from motion sickness, the motion-simulation ride is instead your ticket to Puke City. The bar and casino are open 24 hours; voyages occur from 11 am to 11 pm daily.

Liberace Museum

Known and loved throughout the world as 'Mr Showmanship,' Liberace was honored during his lifetime with two Emmy Awards, six gold records (each signifying 1 million in record sales) and two stars on the Hollywood Walk of Fame. Following his death in 1987, the late great entertainer was posthu-

LEE FOSTER

The legendary sequins still sparkle.

mously honored with the creation of this off-Strip museum (☎ 702-798-5595, www.liberace.org, 1774 E Tropicana Ave), which houses the most outrageous rhinestone-studded costumes and some of the most ornate cars you'll ever see. While audiences enjoyed listening to Liberace's exuberant keyboard artistry, they were also amazed and amused by his outlandish style. Liberace's favorite stage pianos are not to be missed – a rhinestone-encrusted Baldwin and a concert grand covered in mirror squares are a visual feast. Many rare pianos are on display as well; among them are a hand-painted Pleyel on which Chopin played and a Chickering grand once owned by George Gershwin. Liberace's car gallery includes a hand-painted red, white and blue Rolls-Royce convertible, a Rolls-Royce clad entirely in mirror tiles and a 1934 Mercedes Excalibur covered in Austrian rhinestones. Among the many pieces of outlandish jewelry on display is Liberace's trademark candelabra ring, complete with platinum 'candlesticks' and diamond 'flames.' Many visitors favor the Liberace wardrobe exhibit, where rhinestone-studded costumes, feathered capes and million-dollar furs make for fun viewing. The Liberace Museum is a Las Vegas must-do. Open from 10 am to 5 pm Monday through Saturday, and from 1 to 5 pm Sunday. Admission is $7/5, adults/children.

San Remo

The often-overlooked San Remo hotel-casino (☎ 702-739-9000, 800-522-7366, fax 702-736-1120, www.sanremolasvegas.com, 115 E Tropicana Ave) is a great find for party-hearty budget-conscious gamblers. While the San Remo isn't quite on The Strip, it's only a short walk from it, and that convenient location – behind the Tropicana, across the street from the MGM Grand and a hop, skip and a jump from the Bellagio and Caesars Palace – is one of its attractions. Many Vegas regulars like to stay at the San Remo because it's in the thick of things, yet the room rates are generally much less than those on The Strip. And the lovely swimming pool out back is heated all year. The San Remo's medium-size casino isn't much to look at – it's got low ceilings, a bad floral theme, gaudy chandeliers and lots of second-hand smoke – but (and this is a big *but*) the San Remo pours free champagne in the slot areas round the clock, it has a 2-for-1 drink deal from 4 to 6 pm daily and its slot club is one of the most generous in the city. Given these alcoholic and budgetary attractions, it's easy to see why so many people overlook the cheap flower murals and claustrophobic ceiling. Of course, if you feel the need to breath, a few minutes out by the pool will usually set you right. Not only is the pool ringed by mature palm trees and a flowering desert landscape, but when it's hot out, frozen drinks are brought to you poolside.

WEST OF THE STRIP
Gold Coast

The chief selling points of the Gold Coast hotel-casino (☎ 702-367-7111, 800-331-5334, 888-402-6278 for room reservations, fax 702-365-7505, www.goldcoastcasino.com, 4000 W Flamingo Rd) are its relatively inexpensive rooms, its 72-lane bowling center, its 750-board bingo parlor and its plain-but-high-ceilinged and easily navigated casino (which makes up in size what it lacks in decor). And while it might not be much, there are two features at the Spanish-façade Gold Coast casino you'll find at no other large casino in town: it has windows and it has more video poker machines than it has slot machines. Hey! – you read it here first. A hit with visitors and locals alike are the Gold Coast's two no-cost lounges, which offer a variety of sounds from Dixieland jazz to rock 'n' roll, and its colossal Country & Western dance hall, the largest in Nevada. Bowlers will appreciate the Brunswick 2000 equipment and automatic scoring system at the bowling center, which is open 24 hours and a favorite of families. Amenities include a pro shop with instructor, 1400 equipment lockers, bumper bowling for kiddies and a pizza parlor. Also popular with families are the Gold Coast's Twin Theaters, which show first-run movies (the popcorn is drenched with real butter!). The Gold Coast combats its distance from the ever-popular Strip by offering free shuttle service to and from its sister hotel, the Barbary Coast on Las Vegas Blvd; the service operates every 15 minutes from 9:30 am to 12:30 am daily.

The Orleans

One mile west of The Strip, The Orleans (☎ 702-365-7111, 800-675-3267, fax 702-365-7535, www.orleanscasino.com, 4500 W Tropicana Ave) is a New Orleans-themed hotel-casino that has done only a so-so job of re-creating the Big Easy. Regardless, The Orleans has been a crowd-pleaser since it opened on 88 acres in 1997. Its popularity is due mostly to the fact that its room rates tend to be significantly lower than rates at Strip-side hotels, but The Orleans isn't devoid of attractions either. Among its most popular are a 70-lane bowling alley, a 12-plex movie theater, a selection of seven restaurants, a video arcade, a swimming pool complex with a bubbling spa and numerous specialty bars. The 112,000-sq-foot, first-floor casino consists of one bright and airy rectangular room with a high ceiling. On balconies along the edge of the room are costumed mannequins resembling Mardi Gras celebrants. On the casino floor are more than 2100 slot machines, 60 card tables, a 20-screen race and sports book, a 20-table poker room and a 60-seat keno lounge. Beside the gaming area is the Bourbon Street Cabaret, which features free live entertainment nightly. The Orleans also has an 827-seat showroom that has spotlighted such big-name performers as Willie Nelson and Ray Charles. The decor at The Orleans isn't as magical as it could be, but in many minds its attractions more than make up for its visual shortcomings. Be advised that The Orleans provides free shuttle service to and from The Strip and the airport.

Everyday is Mardi Gras at the Rio.

Rio Suite Hotel & Casino

The name of this wildly popular hotel-casino says a lot about it. Rio (☎ 702-252-7777, 800-752-9746, www.playrio.com, 3700 W Flamingo Rd) offers only suites and its theme is Mardi Gras. The Rio is a strenuous walk from The Strip, and when it opened in January 1990, a lot of people thought it wouldn't survive. They said it was simply too far from Las Vegas Boulevard, and tourists wouldn't make the effort. Well, they were wrong. By 1997 the Rio was running so strong that its owners added a 41-story tower and the enormously festive Masquerade Village, which is now the center of the action and a big hit with tourists and locals. The 'village' occupies the first two floors of Rio's twin towers and offers a hearty mix of food, shopping and gaming choices, as well as loads of free entertainment, that all adds up to an ongoing party atmosphere. Occupying most of the village is a huge casino decked out in a color-filled Rio-esque motif and featuring 2500 slot machines, 100 table games, a poker room and a full-service race and sports book. Ringing the ground-floor casino are two dozen upscale retail shops and the two best buffets in town – one offering international cuisine, the other seafood. Every even hour from 2 pm till midnight

(except Wednesdays), sets modeled after Mardi Gras floats and suspended from tracks in the ceiling parade above the gaming tables; costumed performers dance on the floats and lip-synch to Motown songs. (Yes, Motown, and it *is* a bizarre choice.) Other performers simultaneously appear on a stage that rises from the casino's basement. There's no Ipanema at Rio, but guests will find a beach beside one of the resort's three pools. Fifty floors above the village atop one of Rio's towers (and reached by an exhilarating glass elevator ride) is the VooDoo Lounge, which is a great place to enjoy a drink (see the Entertainment chapter for details). Also, one floor below the village, in an easy-to-overlook cellar, is the world's largest collection of fine wines (see the Shopping chapter). Not only that, but Rio offers excellent evening entertainment with its incomparable celebrity impressionist, *Danny Gans: The Man of Many Voices*. In other words, Rio: Not on The Strip but well worth the trip. And Rio makes it an easy trip by providing free shuttle service to and from The Strip from a pick-up area at the northeast corner of S Las Vegas Blvd at Harmon Ave. A shuttle departs every 20 minutes, from 9 am till midnight daily.

Scandia Family Fun Center

This family amusement center (☎ 702-364-0070, 2900 Sirius Ave), a few blocks west of The Strip, features three 18-hole miniature golf courses, bumper boats, batting cages, midget Indy cars and more than 200 video arcade games. Admission to the park is free, but there's a fee for each game or activity. There is a variety of pricing plans from which to choose. The Unlimited Wristband costs $16 and entitles its wearer to unlimited miniature golf, unlimited rides at the Lil' Indy Raceway, unlimited bumper boat rides and 10 arcade tokens or 10 batting-cage tokens. The Super Saver option costs $11 and allows the wearer 18 holes of miniature golf, a Lil' Indy Raceway Ride, a bumper boat ride and five arcade tokens or five batting-cage tokens. Eighteen holes of miniature golf for the little one will set you back $6 (children 5 years of age and younger play for free with a paying adult). Turns at the Lil' Indy Raceway and the bumper-boat attraction cost $4 each (raceway drivers must be 54 inches tall; bumper boat drivers must be 46 inches tall). The batting cage has 18 automated pitching machines in all, tossing hardballs or softballs depending on the hitter's preference. The cost to use a machine is $1.25 for 25 pitches; discounts are available for 15, 30 and 60 minutes of use. The fun center is open from 10 am to 10 pm daily.

DOWNTOWN
Arts Factory Complex

Las Vegas' art scene received an enormous lift in June 1997 when commercial photographer Wes Isbutt, somewhat by accident, created the Arts Factory Complex (☎ 702-382-3886, 103 E Charleston Blvd). Isbutt was looking for space for his photographic business, Studio West (☎ 702-383-3133), when he came across a block-long 1940s structure that he liked. Although he hadn't set out to establish an art colony in Las Vegas, that's exactly what he did. Isbutt bought the entire building and made most of its space available to local artists as well as galleries exhibiting works mostly by local artists. In a short time a burgeoning arts community developed. Today the building's two floors house several art galleries, an architecture firm, several individual artists' studios, two graphic design firms and other businesses, even a tattoo parlor. While the quality of some of the art is debatable, talent is clearly evident in many of the pieces on display. Anyone interested in art by Las Vegas residents or art of Las Vegas should definitely pay a visit to the Arts Factory Complex. The various businesses do not keep the same hours. To play it safe, arrive between 10 am and noon Monday through Friday, when all of the businesses are definitely open.

California

At many Vegas hotel-casinos, the right spin of the slot will earn you a new BMW Z3, a convertible Jaguar or a red-hot Dodge Viper. At the 'just-call-me Cal' California (☎ 702-385-1222, 800-634-6255, fax 702-388-2610, www.thecal.com, 12 E Ogden Ave), one very lucky nickel player will someday ride home in a – drumroll please – VW Beetle! That simple fact tells you a lot about the 781-room Cal, built in 1975 and lightly attired in tropical apparel – even the casino dealers wear Hawaiian shirts (this last mainly because 85% of the Cal's guests hail from Hawaii). In 1998, just about time the Bellagio opened its $300 million gallery of fine art and Paris-Las Vegas broke ground on the world's second Eiffel Tower, the Cal issued a press release: 'Coin-free Penny Slots come to the Cal!' Beneath that banner headline appeared this riveting subhead: 'New multi-denominational machines bring lots of options.' Sure enough, on the mezzanine level of the Cal is a bank of penny slot machines that accept $1, $5, $10 and $20 bills. But wait, there's more! Instead of paying out a hopper full of coins, the Cal's newest slots pay in vouchers, which can be redeemed for cash at the change cage. Yippee! Okay, enough poking fun. Fact is, penny slots offer superior time-on value (the amount of time a player is able to stay on a machine with a small amount of money), and the Cal's casino, though small by Vegas standards, offers all the usual table games and has more than a thousand slots, video poker and video Keno machines. Few hotel-casinos can boast two $1-million-plus slot wins only a week apart; the Cal can. The Cal can also boast seven jackpots in only four days. Not very many casinos can claim that. There's nothing spectacular about the Cal, but it does make cents. Lots of cents.

Fremont

The legendary Fremont hotel-casino (☎ 702-385-3232, 800-634-6182, fax 702-385-6229, www.boydgaming.com, 200 E Fremont St) has been packin' 'em in since 1956, when it opened as downtown's first high-rise. Also separating it from the pack in 1956 was its wall-to-wall carpeting; at the time, every other downtown casino had sawdust-covered floors in its gaming area. It was here, too, that famous lounge singer Wayne Newton began his career. Despite these firsts, the Fremont has since slipped into mediocrity in most regards – its very good restaurants being the major exception. Like its sister hotel-casino, the California – both are owned by Boyd Gaming, which also owns Main Street Station and the Stardust – it serves a large contingent of travelers from Hawaii and has a weak tropical-island motif. The casino is nothing special, but its location at the heart of the Fremont Street Experience and its wide variety of gaming options has made it a favorite with many gamblers.

The Fremont's casino covers 32,000 sq feet, which means that it's identical in size to the Desert Inn's elegant casino. There are more than a thousand machines to choose from at the Fremont, which features Keno and video-poker machines. Most of the table games permit bets ranging from $20 to $1000. The slot lineup includes denominations ranging from 5¢ to $5. Although the casino is smoky, nonsmoking tables are available.

Fremont Street Experience

Only a few years ago, downtown Las Vegas had lost nearly all of its tourists to the rapidly developing Strip. With the opening of each new megaresort on Las Vegas Boulevard, older downtown hotel-casinos such as Fitzgerald's, Golden Nugget and Binion's Horseshoe lost their luster. With no end to the development of The Strip in sight, something had to be done or downtown would become a ghost town (wandering homeless people not withstanding). The city and the area's businesses came up with a plan, which was realized in December 1995: a $70-million, five-block-long pedestrian mall called Fremont Street Experience that is topped by an arched steel canopy filled with computer-controlled lights. The canopy is 1386 feet long and 90 feet high, and it runs the length of Fremont St from Main St to

Huge Golden Nugget Found in Backyard

The 61lb Hand of Faith nugget on display at the Golden Nugget hotel-casino was found in October 1980 near Wedderburn, Australia, by a man using a metal detector. The man, who has chosen to remain anonymous, was prospecting behind the modest trailer home he shared with his wife and four children when he made the spectacular discovery. The meteor-resembling nugget was in a vertical position a mere six inches below the surface when it was found.

Las Vegas Blvd; its belly is covered from edge to edge with no fewer than 2.1 million multicolored lights, which are controlled by 31 computers. Suspended from the giant light board are 208 concert-quality speakers. Five times nightly (on the hour, every hour, from 8 pm till midnight), the canopy becomes a six-minute light show enhanced by 540,000 watts of wrap-around sound and music. When the lights come on, they usually stop people in their tracks. The shows are quite remarkable, as their 73 programmers have no fewer than 65,536 color combinations of light with which to be creative. Has it helped pick up business downtown? Absolutely. Although the casinos along Fremont St generally aren't as nice as the newer ones on The Strip, their proximity to one another is a real plus and a misting system built into the canopy provides welcome relief on hot days.

Hand of Faith

No, Hand of Faith is not the title of a life-affirming religious tract, nor is it a new brand of dishwashing detergent. Rather, it's the name of the largest single gold nugget in the world, weighing a massive 61lb and 11oz. Along with another nugget weighing 13lbs and a treasury of 26 smaller chunks of the most valuable, ductile, yellow metallic element known to humankind, the Australia-found Hand of Faith is on display under glass at, appropriately enough, the Golden Nugget hotel-casino (☎ 702-385-7111, 129 E Fremont at 1st Sts). Although picture taking is generally not permitted in Las Vegas casinos for security reasons, the management of the Golden Nugget smiles upon visitors who snap away at the mighty rocks. And why not? It's not like any of the other casinos in town can claim to possess the heftiest hunk of gold ever found. Viewing is available 24 hours a day.

$1 Million in Cash

In the grand Las Vegas tradition of one-upmanship, Binion's Horseshoe hotel-casino (☎ 702-382-1600, 128 E Fremont St) responded to the Golden Nugget's display of precious yellow rocks by offering visitors a chance to drool over $1 million in rare $10,000 bills. There are 100 of them in all, kept under glass in a display case shaped, appropriately enough, like a horseshoe. And guess what? You can take as many photographs of the money as you'd like; you just can't leave with any of it. However, you *could* leave the casino with your own million dollars, at least in theory: a no-limit gambling policy has been a fixture at Binion's for years. That's one of the reasons the blackjack tables there are usually filled day and night. The horseshoe of cash is at the back of the ground-floor casino, to the right of the long bar. The casino is directly across Fremont St from the Golden Nugget, so you could see the gold and see the cash in just a matter of minutes.

Jackie Gaughan's Plaza

Built on the site of the old Union Pacific Railroad Depot, the Plaza (☎ 702-386-2110, 800-634-6575, fax 702-382-8281, www.plaza hotelcasino.com, 1 Main St) doesn't look like it's changed much since it opened in 1971. Like most hotel-casinos were back then, its casino is jammed with slot and video machines – nearly 1600 in a 57,120-sq-ft area – and its decor is limited mostly to thousands of tiny recessed lights and mirrors designed to give the illusion of space. Also in the room are 19 blackjack tables, 12 poker tables, five craps tables, three roulette wheels, two keno lounges, minibaccarat, one Pai Gow poker table and a race and sports book. The decor doesn't seem to correspond to a theme, unless the theme is *cheap*. Even the chandeliers – and there are chandeliers – look cheap. And that's just fine with the Plaza's gamblers, many of whom are attracted to the casino because of its penny slots and $1 blackjack tables. The Plaza's room rates are lower than most, and its location – at the western end of Fremont Street Experience – is ideal for an old-Vegas (pre-megaresort) casino like this one. The Greyhound bus depot is next door, and the public train station is actually inside the Plaza, though it's been dormant since Amtrak stopped serving Las Vegas a few years back. Like most of downtown's hotel-casinos, the

Getting Hitched in Vegas: A True Story by Charlotte Hindle

We knew we wanted to get married in Vegas, nowhere else, but apart from booking the flights and our first night's accommodations, we decided to put no planning into the actual day. We just wanted to turn up (from Britain) and do it.

We made a point of flying United – when you get married, little things like the name of an airline seem important. The next morning, we had breakfast in our wedding outfits (cream dress for me, old shorts for Simon) and walked the length of The Strip, checking out the Little Chapel of the West, the Hitching Post, the Little Chapel of Love and many others. To be truthful, the more we saw, the less we were inclined to entrust them with the happiest day of our lives. Many were pretty tacky, full of plastic flowers, fake stained-glass windows and doll's house pews.

We went to get our State of Nevada marriage license at the County Court. As the clerk was typing it up, she recommended we try the registry office across the road. Las Vegas seems

Plaza is intended for hardcore gamblers; it leaves the Parisian, Venetian and New York themes to others, though it does offer an entertaining drag-queen show, *Boy-lesque*. Here, you'll find dealers and cocktail waitresses who treat people well. What the Plaza lacks in elegance, it makes up for in warmth and value. Which goes a long way in explaining why it's seemingly always filled with people.

Las Vegas Motor Speedway

The Las Vegas Motor Speedway (☎ 702-644-4443, 800-644-4444, www.lvms.com, 7000 N Las Vegas Blvd) opened in late 1996 and hosts a variety of motor races on a 1.5-mile super speedway, a 2.5-mile road course, a 4000-foot dragstrip, and paved and dirt short-track ovals; there are also facilities for motorcross and even go-cart competitions. Annual events at the $100-million, state-of-the-art racing complex include Indy car,

NASCAR, dwarf car, classic car, truck, sprint car, dragster and sand-pull competitions. There's something going on every week of the year. Facilities include a restaurant and gift shop. Call for a schedule of upcoming events, or visit the speedway's website, which includes an events schedule, ticket prices and lots of other useful information. Tickets generally cost between $10 and $15, but can go much higher for certain competitions.

Las Vegas Natural History Museum

If you've ever been to a really good natural history museum, you won't be wowed by this one – but your kids might. That's because the Las Vegas Natural History Museum (☎ 702-384-3466, 900 N Las Vegas Blvd) has lots of things youngsters love, but the exhibits aren't well done enough to impress most parents. The museum is

Getting Hitched in Vegas: A True Story by Charlotte Hindle

a long way to come to be married in a registry office, but local advice is usually worth heeding, so we had a look. Though the building itself was positively ugly, we were won over by Flora, a friendly, heavily made-up grandmotherly type who, for US$35, would perform the ceremony – no appointment necessary. A lady was summoned from the typing pool to perform as both witness and official photographer.

Twenty minutes later we emerged newly wed and headed straight for Binion's Horseshoe Casino – not for a gamble but for a tipple. The place was dimly lit, packed with punters and buzzing with atmosphere. We got our picture taken next to its claim to fame – an illuminated horseshoe stacked with a million dollars' worth of real paper bills.

Outside, we were surprised to find the Moscow State Circus performing a free show. As we ooed and aahed with the crowd, I fingered my new Russian wedding ring, trying not to attach too much significance to this post-Soviet coincidence.

Finally, as the sun set, we strolled back down The Strip. Outside Treasure Island, we jostled with parents and children to witness its life-size sea battle. Among the fireworks, the screams, the cannon-fire and the thickening smoke, we slurped champagne straight from the bottle. We walked next door, where the fake volcano at the Mirage Hotel was rumbling and simmering, readying itself for another volcanic eruption. The lava ran, the sky lit up, and we looked at each other. In a Las Vegas sort of way, the earth was moving for both of us.

Charlotte Hindle and Simon Calder were married on September 5, 1997. Charlotte is the general manager of Lonely Planet's UK office.

divided into five main rooms, each about the size of a standard living room and each with a different theme: the international wildlife room contains two dozen or so stuffed exotic animals rather weakly displayed; the marine-life room contains several aquariums and about a dozen stuffed sharks suspended from the ceiling; the Nevada *au natural* room features stuffed state residents of the nonhuman variety; the dinosaur den is quite okay with its animated dinosaurs and fossils; and the young scientist center is a popular interactive area for children of all ages. The young scientist center allows kids to touch lots of cool stuff such as fossils, the leg bone of a dinosaur and a stuffed bobcat (its fur is wearing thin, but kids still pet it with glee). A particularly good exhibit is a sandbox containing a mastodon's tooth, a tooth from a T-rex and so on. Kids are encouraged to play archaeologist and uncover the items, and when they do there

are brushes available for sweeping the objects clean for further investigating. This last exhibit must appeal to some basic human urge, for parents can often be seen 'helping' their children play one Leaky or another. The museum is open from 9 am to 4 pm daily, except Thanksgiving Day and Christmas Day. Admission is $5/2.50, adults/children 4 to 12.

Lied Discovery Children's Museum

Directly across the street from the Natural History Museum is the Lied Discovery Children's Museum (☎ 702-382-5437, 833 N Las Vegas Blvd), which houses exhibits designed for kids ages 3 to 12. Unfortunately, most of the dozen or so exhibits are either too complex for children to understand or work successfully or they are too simple and therefore boring. Example: The Pathway to Music exhibit consists of 13 squares placed on the ground, each representing a musical note that will chime when stepped on. Four kids following precise instructions and acting in unison can play 'Twinkle, Twinkle Little Star' by stepping on specific squares in a specific order. It's a smart exhibit, but that level of coordination is beyond many youngsters. It's never used, except by the hyperactive visitors who like to stomp and make noise. In contrast, the Bubble Art exhibit allows participants to pull a rope that raises a bar from a trough of bubble solution and – *voila!* – create a large bubble. There's no real scientific lesson here, just an activity most kids find amusing for a few minutes. It's a shame, but the Lied's interactive exhibits leave many kids either confused or bored. The Lied is open from 10 am to 5 pm Tuesday through Saturday, and from noon to 5 pm Sunday. Admission is $5/2.50, adults/children.

Main Street Station

This 'old fashioned' hotel-casino recreates Victorian opulence with unique design, detailed craftsmanship and an extensive collection of antiques, architectural artifacts and collectibles. Main Street Station (☎ 702-387-1896, 800-713-8933, fax 702-386-4466, www.mainstreetcasino.com, 200 N Main St) is not only the most beautiful of the downtown establishments, but it is also the most historically interesting. Throughout the lovely 780-room hotel and casino are notable *objets d'histoire*, most keeping to the turn-of-the-19th-century theme; then there are the other pieces of history, such as a large graffiti-covered chunk of the Berlin Wall that now serves one of the walls supporting the urinals in the gentleman's restroom. Other artifacts on display at Main Street are the private rail car Buffalo Bill Cody used to travel the US with his Wild West Show from 1906 until his death in 1917; three exquisite bronze chandeliers above the casino's central pit, which were originally installed in the 1890s in the Coca-Cola Building in Austin, Texas; and the ornate mahogany woodwork that now graces the casino entry, hotel registration desk and the Company Store, which was removed from a 19th-century drugstore in Covington, KY. Additionally, the gorgeous Pullman Grille dining room was built around an ornate carved oak fireplace and wine storage cabinets taken from the Preswick Castle in Scotland (the unique sideboard niche includes panels that depict characters and morals of Aesop's Fables). Main Street Station has old-fashioned elegance and historic treasures most everywhere you look. The registration desk dispenses free copies of *Guide to Artifacts, Antiques & Artworks*, which identifies and describes the historic attractions in the hotel-casino. Also worth checking out is its adjacent Triple 7 BrewPub, which makes its own beer and features excellent music several nights of the week (see Dance Clubs under Downtown in the Entertainment chapter).

Old Las Vegas Mormon Fort State Historic Park

The remains of the Las Vegas Mormon fort (☎ 702-486-3511, 908 N Las Vegas Blvd) are pretty unspectacular compared with the modern metropolis, but this is where it all started in the 1850s. Here, an adobe quadrangle provided a refuge for travelers along the Mormon Trail, between Salt Lake City and San Bernadino. Some of the original walls still stand and a three-room display shows artifacts and photos from the early days. Outside are sample fields of the first crops grown here and an archaeological dig. Volunteer groups worked hard to preserve this site, and there are plans for more research, restoration and reconstruction. The fort is next to the Las Vegas Natural History Museum and the Cashman Field sports center, and is surrounded by a wire fence. It is open most days, and you may have to ring the bell for the attendant.

Showboat

Nearer to downtown than The Strip but really off on its own is the Showboat hotel-casino (☎ 702-385-9123, 800-826-2800, fax 702-383-9238, www.showboat-lv.com, 2800 E Fremont St), which is easy to overlook due to its remoteness. But to overlook the Showboat, which underwent substantial cosmetic surgery a few years ago, would be a pity. The Showboat, with its Mardi Gras and old-time Louisiana decor, is a part of early Vegas casino history and a pleasure to look at. Built in 1954, the Showboat was the first establishment in Las Vegas to offer the three B's: Bowling, Bingo and Buffets. All three B's still exist at the Showboat. In fact, the Showboat has the largest bowling center in North America (see Activities, below), and it's possible to play bingo from 9 am to 1 am everyday. The hotel-casino frequently holds special bingo events (some of their Super Star Bingo games have guaranteed prizes exceeding $100,000). And the establishment that initiated Las Vegas hotel buffets is still offering them – at competitive prices in a cheerful room. The Showboat maintained the look of a showboat for more than four decades until recently, when it decided to smarten up with Victorian moldings, stained-glass windows and distressed paint, magnificent Venetian-glass chandeliers in the lobby and hand-painted murals of Mississippi riverboats and plantations. The result is a bright, pretty and popular Showboat that's well worth a visit if time permits. The 80,300-sq-ft

casino is home to 1548 slot machines, all of the common games, a race and sports book and even computerized bingo.

ACTIVITIES
Gambling

The chief tourist activity in Las Vegas is gambling. There isn't a city in the world that compares to Las Vegas in terms of variety and quantity of games. At the time of writing there were 145 casinos in the city containing a combined total of 197,144 slot machines, 3536 blackjack tables, 463 craps tables, 408 roulette wheels, 174 keno games, 138 Caribbean stud tables, 131 sports pools, 104 race books, 92 minibaccarat tables and 86 baccarat tables. Many more games are available, and most casinos in town never close. See the special Gambling in Las Vegas section (page 35) for descriptions of the games themselves. Anyone intending to do a significant amount of gambling in Las Vegas should consider doing three things:

Join a Slot Club You receive a card, similar to an ATM card, that is inserted into a machine before you begin play. You are

Enjoy swim-up blackjack at the Hard Rock Hotel.

NORMAN GODWIN

awarded points by how much money you put into the machine, and those points are redeemable at the hotel-casino for cash, merchandise or 'comps' (complimentary meals, rooms, limousines and other amenities), or a combination of the three. Membership is free. Requirements: You must be 21 and have a photo identification. All of the megaresorts and some of the smaller casinos have slot clubs. Just go to the main change cage inside the casino where you'll be doing your gambling and ask to join their slot club. You'll have your slot-club card within minutes.

Ask to Be Rated If you play the tables, ask the pit boss to rate your play. Why? Because each year the city's casinos give out more than $500 million in comps to rated players (unrated players get nothing). Generally, if you are playing between $5 and $10 per hand, you can expect to be comped breakfast and/or lunch at the casino's coffee shop. Between $10 and $25 per hand, expect a free meal and a heavily discounted room rate. Between $25 and $100, expect free show tickets, free gourmet meals and a free room. Between $100 and $250, you needn't concern yourself with your room, food or drink bills – the casino will gladly pay them and give you any show tickets you might want. If you're gambling $250 per hand or more, the casino will typically pay for your suite, food, drinks, limousine service, greens fees and even airfare.

Take Some Gaming Lessons Unless you already know how to gamble intelligently, and most people don't, consider getting some free instruction from professionals. Most dealers will be happy to explain the ins and outs of a game or give you a guide that shows how to play the game, but many casinos go a significant step further: they offer free lessons from professional gambling instructors. Among the hotel-casinos that offer free instruction at scheduled times are Bally's, Caesars Palace, Circus Circus, Excalibur, Flamingo Hilton, Harrah's, Imperial Palace, Lady Luck, MGM Grand, Riviera, Sahara, San Remo, Stardust and Tropicana. This list is by no means conclusive. Call the hotel-casino that most interests you for class times and other details.

Golf

There are no fewer than 33 golf courses in Las Vegas Valley, and most are within 10

HENIA MIEDZINSKI

Your typical desert landscape

miles of The Strip. In general, reservations for tee times should be made at least seven days in advance. The following is a partial list of golf courses in the Las Vegas area. Among the courses that do not appear here are those belonging to private country clubs, where membership fees of $30,000 up front plus $350 a month are not uncommon; privately owned courses where play is limited to residents of a particular gated community; and one golf course where play is limited to the 51 members of the Las Vegas Paiute tribe. Call for greens fees, tee times and directions.

Angel Park Golf Course
A 36-hole Arnold Palmer-designed municipal golf course, 100 S Rampart Blvd (☎ 702-254-4653)

Badlands Golf Club
Designed by US Open Champion Johnny Miller amid spectacular terrain, 9119 Alta Drive (☎ 702-242-4653)

Calloway Golf Center
A 42-acre golf training facilty offering instruction and practice, 6730 S Las Vegas Blvd (☎ 702-894-4100)

Desert Inn Golf Club
Resort course for 18 holes, hosting all three major pro golf tours, 3145 S Las Vegas Blvd (☎ 702-733-4290)

Desert Rose Golf Course
Municipal course with moderate length, wide fairways and fast greens, 5483 Clubhouse Drive (☎ 702-431-4653)

Desert Pines Golf Club
Play on water, undulated greens and pot bunkers, 3401 E Bonanza Rd (☎ 702-366-1616)

Highland Falls Golf Club
Designed by course architect Greg Nash and golfer Billy Casper, 10201 Sun City Blvd (☎ 702-254-7010)

Las Vegas Golf Club
Inexpensive municipal golf course with lots of trees and little water, 4300 W Washington Drive (☎ 702-646-3003)

Las Vegas National Club
A public course (reserve weeks in advance) with lots of trees, 1911 E Desert Inn Rd (☎ 702-734-1796)

Legacy Golf Club
One of the top 100 golf courses in the US, located in nearby Henderson, 130 Par Excellence Drive (☎ 702-897-2200)

North Las Vegas Golf Course
A night-lighted municipal course for nine holes on 18 acres, 324 E Brooks Ave (☎ 702-633-1833)

Painted Desert Golf Course
An 18-hole course with lush fairway landing pads amid a desert landscape, 5555 Painted Mirage Rd (☎ 702-645-2568)

Rio Secco Golf Club
An 18-hole, 72-par course set in the foothills of the Black Mountains, 2851 Grand Hills Drive (☎ 702-361-7044)

Wildhorse Golf Club
An 18-hole semi-private course in nearby Henderson, 2100 W Warm Springs Rd (☎ 702-434-9009)

Bowling

Bowling is very big in Las Vegas, and most bowling centers are in hotel-casinos where you can work on your glide and release at any time. All of the bowling centers mentioned here are in hotel-casinos and all rent top-of-the-line equipment. Fees vary but are typically $2 per game and $1.50 for shoe rental. Occasionally a facility will be closed for league bowling. If bowling while in Las Vegas is a priority to you, call ahead to avoid any unpleasant surprises.

Gold Coast
Features: 72 lanes, a pro shop, a resident professional and especially low fees on weekends and holidays. 4000 W Flamingo Rd (☎ 702-367-4700)

The Orleans
Features: 70 lanes and a pro shop. Beware: There's league play nightly at 5:30 and 9:30 pm; lanes can be unavailable then. 4500 W Tropicana Ave (☎ 702-365-7111)

Santa Fe
Features: 60 lanes, a pro shop and Bowlervision (which tracks the speed and path of the ball from the time it leaves your hand). 4949 N Rancho Drive (Business Hwy 95) (☎ 702-658-4995)

Showboat
Features: North America's largest bowling center, with 106 championship lanes, pro shop and a resident professional. 2800 E Fremont St (☎ 702-385-9153)

Places to Stay

There's no shortage of places to stay in Las Vegas, and room options range from filthy wham-bam-thank-you-ma'ams east of downtown to exquisite 9000-sq-foot suites at the Desert Inn Resort & Casino. Rates range from as little as $12 a night at one of the youth hostels to $10,000 or more a night for a penthouse suite at one of the glamorous megaresorts on The Strip.

Las Vegas room rates vary with demand, and they vary wildly. A standard room at the Bellagio, for example, usually goes for $159 a night, Sunday through Thursday. However, the same room will cost $499 when there's a big convention in town. That very same room carried a $2000-a-night price tag on New Year's Eve 1999, and a minimum stay of three nights at a cost of $6000 (plus $540 hotel tax) was required to reserve the room.

In addition, many of the hotel-casinos try to lure customers during slow periods with discounted room rates. These rates are often advertised in the travel or events sections of major US newspapers. Often the low rates involve two companies working together. In early 1999, for example, the Las Vegas Hilton was offering its standard rooms for $29.95 to people possessing Bank of America Visa cards. The standard rate for the same room was $69.95.

What all this means is that the rates shown here should only be viewed as approximates. The amounts you are quoted by the hotels could be substantially higher; it's unlikely they will be substantially lower, unless the US economy suddenly nose-dives. As with so many things in life, timing is everything, particularly when it comes to Las Vegas room rates.

Another thing to remember is that hotel-casinos such as the Flamingo and Excalibur can offer rooms on The Strip for the same price as a dumpy joint on Fremont St east of downtown. That's because the Flamingo and

NORMAN GODWIN

Las Vegas sports more than 100,000 hotel rooms – but reservations are still essential.

Excalibur make their big bucks in their casinos, whereas the dumpy joint hasn't got a casino to recoup room losses. With Las Vegas, it's wrong to assume that a nice, centrally located place must be much pricier than a poorly situated, unappealing little place.

If you'll be visiting Las Vegas on a tight budget, or if you're simply determined to get the best value you can find, be sure to contact at least a handful of places, as you never know who will be running a special when. It takes less time than you might think, and if you're calling from the US or Canada, you can usually use a toll-free number. Most of the hotels also have websites where you can check room rates and availability.

Whatever you do, don't arrive in Las Vegas without a reservation. There are more than 100,000 hotel rooms in Sin City, but you'd be shocked and amazed how often every standard room in town is occupied. If you simply show up at a hotel-casino and ask for a room, you may find the only one available is a two-bedroom suite with a mortgage-payment equivalent for a nightly rate.

THE STRIP

As mentioned above, room rates fluctuate with demand, and nowhere is this more true than with the hotels along The Strip. The room prices shown here are standard midweek rates, and they do not include the 9% hotel tax. Expect to pay a little more on weekends, a lot more during popular events such as National Finals Rodeo, and even more during hotel-filling conventions such as the COMDEX consumer electronics trade show, which attracts 2200 exhibitors and 210,000 delegates each November.

Note that you can find further descriptions of all of the hotel-casinos on The Strip in the Things to See & Do chapter.

Places to Stay – Budget

The **Barbary Coast** (☎ 702-737-7111, 888-227-2279, fax 702-737-6304, www.barbary coastcasino.com, 3595 S Las Vegas Blvd) is an excellent find. This mid-Strip hotel-casino, which shares an intersection with

Room Rate Categories

Budget	$40 and under
Mid-range	$41 to $70
Top End	$71 and above

Caesars Palace, Bally's Las Vegas and Bellagio, not only has a lovely casino but great care has been taken to ensure that the charming Victorian-era decor found elsewhere in the establishment carries into its 400 rooms as well. Guestrooms have half-canopied brass beds, lace-curtained windows, attractive floral carpets, quaint sitting areas and gaslight-style lamps. Rates range from $39 to $140, with many $39 days, especially during the summer.

The ever-popular **Circus Circus** (☎ 702-734-0410, 800-444-2472, fax 702-734-2268, www.circuscircus.com, 2880 S Las Vegas Blvd) has 3744 rooms, 3612 of which are standard and 132 of which are suites. The suites, like clowns, come in all shapes and sizes: there are two-story suites, minisuites, parlor suites, Jacuzzi suites and so on. The standard rooms are all 460 sq feet in size and come with sofas, balconies or patios, and desks. The color scheme varies but is generally a tasteful gray-blue or mauve, and the rooms are very well maintained. Most are designated nonsmoking, 45 were designed for the hearing impaired and 122 are wheelchair accessible. These appealing rooms have an attractive price: they start at $39 much of the time. Don't let the name fool you, either: Circus Circus, like the vast majority of Las Vegas' hotel-casinos, has spent millions of dollars in recent years to replace the kitsch with class.

Looking only slightly like a Japanese temple, the **Imperial Palace** hotel-casino (☎ 702-731-3311, 800-634-6441, www.imperial palace.com/vegas/, 3535 S Las Vegas Blvd) offers 2700 rooms, including 225 suites, in a 19-story tower. The standard rooms are nothing special, and at 280 sq feet are smaller than most. But they all have air-con, satellite TV and even balconies. Given the

A Casino with a Heart

The Imperial Palace has always made a point of hiring people with disabilities, who make up 13 percent of its staff, but this fact was little known until 1991, when the hotel-casino was named Employer of the Year by US President George Bush's Committee on Employment of People with Disabilities.

The Imperial Palace was widely recognized two years later when it opened the Resort Medical Center, a 24-hour medical facility serving hotel employees, their families, and guests of the Imperial Palace and other area hotel-casinos.

The Imperial Palace also hosts a special Christmas party, at which low-income seniors and nonambulatory convalescent center residents are treated to a complimentary dinner and show. The party, the hospital and the drive to hire people with disabilities were all initiated by Ralph Engelstad, the sole owner of this major Las Vegas hotel-casino.

hotel's mid-Strip location and rates often starting at $39, these rooms are an awfully good value. An even better value are the much-larger Luv Tub suites for $30 more. Each features a spacious bedroom with an ego-stroking mirror over a king- or queen-size bed and a 300-gallon sunken 'luv tub' in an oversize, heavily mirrored bathroom.

The recently renovated *Sahara* (☎ 702-737-2111, 888-696-2121, fax 702-737-2027, 2535 S Las Vegas Blvd) contains 2035 guestrooms, which have a relentless Moroccan theme that is either cheerful or gaudy or both, depending on one's taste. The carpeting and drapes are tan, the upholstery appears in earth tones, and each room comes with a wooden desk topped with a brass lamp. Tame enough, classy even. But the rest of each guestroom is done up in a mix of stars and stripes and vivid colors that are a bit too much for some people. On the one hand, the Moroccan overkill adds to the

festive ambiance that pervades the *new* Sahara, which has gone to great lengths to provide a substantial wow factor, but as an authentic reproduction of another place the Sahara scores a big fat 'F.' Rates start at $39 a night.

Places to Stay – Mid-Range

The Arthurian motif that appears in all of the public areas of *Excalibur* (☎ 702-597-7777, 800-937-7777, fax 702-597-7040, www.excalibur-casino.com, 3850 S Las Vegas Blvd) doesn't end at your guestroom door. The Excalibur has a total of 4032 rooms within its two 28-story towers, and all contain walls papered to resemble the interior of a castle. Hung on the walls are prints of knights jousting. The bedspreads have a fleur-de-lis theme, the mirrors are flanked by sconces and the oak furnishings are heraldically embellished. Nonsmoking rooms, rooms with extra-wide doors for wheelchair accessibility and Jacuzzi suites are available. While some hotel-casinos don't welcome kids, the Excalibur is clearly child friendly. And that sentiment is reflected in its room rates: they range from $49 to $119 *for up to four people*. Children under 17 can stay for free in their parents' room.

The centrally located *Flamingo Hilton* (☎ 702-733-3111, 800-732-2111, fax 702-733-3353, www.hilton.com, 3555 S Las Vegas Blvd) underwent a $130-million renovation and expansion in 1996 that included the addition of a 612-room sixth tower, raising the total number of guestrooms at the legendary hotel-casino to 3642, including 36 parlor suites and 150 minisuites. Although each standard guestroom is a mere 333 sq feet in size, because the closet and bathroom are undersize and one wall of the bedroom is a floor-to-ceiling window, the rooms seem much more spacious than they actually are. They are certainly pleasant to return to at the end of the day, in no small way because of the attractive color scheme: soft blues and peach, watercolors of tropical scenes and light-colored wood furnishings. Room rates range from $39 for one or two weeks in December to a more typical $69, but they can reach as high as $299 during a

Today's highrise Flamingo bears little resemblance to Bugsy Siegel's streamlined original.

convention. The Flamingo has lots of faithful customers, and for two good reasons: location and price.

The ***Holiday Inn Casino Boardwalk*** (☎ *702-733-2400, 800-635-4581, fax 702-730-3166, www.hiboardwalk.com, 3750 S Las Vegas Blvd*) has the distinction of being the world's largest Holiday Inn, as well as the world's most bizarre (how else can you describe the enormous fake roller coaster and the enormous fake Ferris wheel out front?). For better or worse, there's nothing unusual about this Holiday Inn's 655 guestrooms, the majority of which are in a new 16-story tower. Except for the vibrant colors and prints of Coney Island, the tower's guestrooms are typical Holiday Inn fare – quite all right but nothing to get excited about. A minority of the hotel's rooms are pleasantly presented in pastels. Rates tend to range from $39 to $109 (with $69 being the norm), though they can go much higher during special events.

The 4467 rooms at ***Luxor*** (☎ *702-262-4000, 800-288-1000, fax 702-262-4452, www.luxor.com, 3900 S Las Vegas Blvd*) are possibly the most distinctive of all of the rooms in Las Vegas. They range in size from 465 sq feet for a standard to 4800 sq feet for the penthouse. All rooms feature art deco and Egyptian furnishings, and the marble bathrooms contain phones, vanity mirrors and hair dryers (but usually only a shower – no tub). Rates range from $49 to $249 for a standard room, and Jacuzzi suites start at $99. Other suites start at $500. Facilities available to guests include the 12,000 sq foot Oasis Pool and Spa with hot whirlpool, steam bath, dry sauna, facials, massages, four body wraps (herbal, aroma, steam and aloe), aromatic sea salt scrubs and soaks, hair and nail appointments and a complete fitness center. By the way, the Luxor's unusual high-speed elevators are calling 'inclinators,' since they must travel at a 39-degree angle due to the Luxor's pyramid shape. Oh, and you must be a guest to ride in one.

Like the rooms at Luxor, those at the ***MGM Grand*** (☎ *702-895-1111, 800-929-1111, fax 702-891-1112, www.mgmgrand .com, 3799 S Las Vegas Blvd*) aren't punched from a cookie cutter despite the fact that there are so many of them (exactly 5005, including 751 suites, housed in four 30-story emerald-green towers). Each of the 446-sq-foot standard guestrooms is done up in what the hotel-casino seriously refers to as a *classic motif* – 'Wizard of Oz,' 'Hollywood,' 'Southern' or 'Casablanca.' The Oz rooms have tasseled green drapes, emerald-green rugs and upholstery and wallpaper emblazoned with silver and gold stars. The Hollywood rooms feature gold-flecked walls hung with prints of Marilyn Monroe, Humphrey Bogart and other icons of the silver screen, beds backed by mirrors, lots of gilded moldings and maple-on-cherrywood furniture. The Southern rooms feature faux 18th-century Old South furnishings and faux-silk beige damask walls hung with prints from *Gone With the Wind*. The Casablanca rooms contain satiny fabrics amid earth tones and prints of Morocco market scenes. Large bathrooms with drop-dead-lovely marble tubs are standard. The Luxurious Suites range in size from 675 to 6040 sq feet and include multiple bathrooms and outdoor

The Great Room-Rate Game

It often pays to call the hotel where you'll be staying a week or so in advance to see if the rates you were quoted when you booked a room have changed. If they've fallen, you can keep the difference *if* you ask that your quoted rate be changed. The savings can be substantial: Let's say, for example, that you booked a room at the Flamingo Hilton on July 1 for the first week of August at a cost of $89 a day. On July 21, you call the Flamingo and learn that the rate for a room the first week of August is now $69. If you tell the Flamingo reservations agent that you reserved a room for that week at $89 a night and want your rate changed to $69, the agent will make the adjustment – and you'll save $140. If you don't ask, you will be charged the higher rate.

patios with whirlpool. Rates start at $69 for standard rooms and $99 for suites ($119 for suites with Jacuzzi tubs).

The Mirage (☎ *702-791-7111, 800-627-6667, fax 702-791-7446, www.themirage.com, 3400 S Las Vegas Blvd)* has three 30-story towers containing a total of 3044 rooms, including one- and two-bedroom suites, as well as eight villa apartments and six lanai bungalows, each with a private pool. The standard guestrooms, at 360 sq feet, are smaller than many found elsewhere along The Strip, but all of the rooms at The Mirage are quite attractive. Gone are the original tropical colors; in their place are subtle color schemes of taupe, beige and peach with black accents. All of the standard rooms have marble entryways and a canopy over the headboard. The bathrooms are adorned with plenty of marble but are rather small. If space is a big consideration – if, for example, there are two of you and both of you packed lots of clothes – you could do better elsewhere for the price. On the other hand, The Mirage is centrally located and has a white tiger's share of attractions. And the rooms, though small, *are* elegant. Rates, which vary with great frequency, start at $69 and run to $399 for standard rooms. Suites start at $259.

The ***Monte Carlo*** hotel-casino *(☎ 702-730-7000, 800-311-8999, www.montecarlo.com, 3770 S Las Vegas Blvd)* offers 3014 rooms decorated in traditional European style, with beige wallpaper, cherrywood furnishings, floral-print fabrics and fleur-de-lis friezes. The standard rooms are only standard size (406 sq feet), but they are lovely retreats and the large marble tubs lend themselves extremely well to long, therapeutic soaks. Rates start at $59 and can go as high as $399 for a standard room. Suites, of which there are 259, start at $139.

There's nothing to dislike about ***New York-New York*** *(☎ 702-740-6969, 800-693-6763, www.nynyhotelcasino.com, 3790 S Las Vegas Blvd)*, except the elbow room of some of its standard guestrooms. The standard rooms range in size from 300 to 400 sq feet, and they vary enormously in layout (there are 63 layouts in all, a product of the hotel's peculiar shape). If you happen to get one of the 300-sq-foot rooms, you'll know it; they are terribly small. However, all 2033 of the guestrooms at the New York-New York are done up splendidly in art deco. Even the bathrooms, with their black marble-topped sinks, are impressive. The standard rooms range in price from $69 to $329, depending on availability. But for only $10 above the standard-room rate, you can get a Deluxe Room with a minimum of at least 450 sq feet of space. The hotel's Marquee Rooms range in size from 500 to 600 sq feet and cost $30 over the current price of a standard room. For $70 above the standard rate, you can get (if available) a Jacuzzi Room, which spreads over 600 to 700 sq feet. There are no suites to be had, unless you're a big spender; those that exist – and plenty *are* located in the towers – are comped to high rollers.

The 2075 guestrooms at the **Riviera** (☎ 702-734-5110, 800-634-6753, fax 702-794-9451, 2901 S Las Vegas Blvd) include 156 suites and 37 rooms that are specially equipped to accommodate wheelchair patrons. The rooms are typical hotel fare – soft floral decor, cable TV, in-room safes, nothing fancy – but then there's usually nothing fancy about the rates, either: during a very quiet time (the first week of August, for example), it's often possible to obtain a standard room at the Riviera for as little as $40 a night. That same room will rocket up to $159 or more during a hotel-filling event or convention. Suites, which are considerably bigger and have a living room that's completely shut off from the bedroom, start at $250 and range to $375.

The 2100 rooms at the **Stardust** (☎ 702-732-6111, 800-634-6757, fax 702-732-6257, www.stardustlv.com, 3000 S Las Vegas Blvd) aren't going to appear in *Architectural Digest* anytime soon. There's nothing terribly wrong with them; they just seem to have been stamped from the same inexpensive mold. However, in the same way that a cheap dress with a floral design can be pretty, so too are these rooms. The general color scheme is peach carpeting with light-colored walls with black accents and floral-print bedspreads. There's little attention to detail, and the hotel staff, perhaps cognizant that their

The Riviera often offers reasonable rates.

rooms don't measure up, won't divulge square footages. However, the dimensions of the bedroom measure a mere 308 sq feet (14 foot by 22 foot); if you add another 40 sq feet for the bathroom and 16 more for the closet, the estimated square footage of a standard room at Stardust is 364 – or well below the norm. Rates for these rooms start at $60. Bigger, nicer, newer suites begin at $175. The Stardust's on-site Motor Inn rooms, which had been a bargain at $39 most nights, were taken off the market in April 1999.

The 1500 rooms at **Stratosphere** (☎ 702-380-7777, 800-998-6937, fax 702-383-5334, www.grandcasinos.com, 2000 S Las Vegas Blvd) are not in the neck-craning tower, but rather in a much smaller building at the base of the spire. The rooms are standard size but more handsome than most, containing cherrywood furniture with black lacquer accents, matching carpet and drapes and abstract paintings. In-room safes, large-screen TVs, phones with data ports and hair dryers are standard. The main drawback to staying at

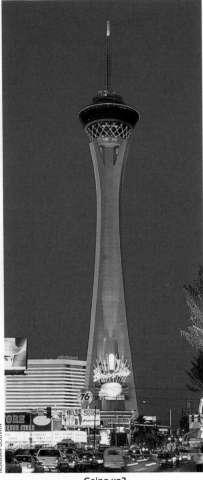

NORMAN GODWIN

Going up?

elegant Caribbean hideaway, including the hotel-casino's three 36-story towers with a total of 2900 rooms, including 212 suites. All of the rooms and suites are decorated with light-colored carpeting, white-washed wood furnishings, brass fixtures and copies of 18th-century nautical paintings. Floor-to-ceiling windows make the average-size rooms seem more expansive than they really are. Rates start at $69 for a standard room, and $149 for a suite.

World famous from the day it opened on April 4, 1957, the ***Tropicana*** (☎ *702-739-2222, 800-634-4000, fax 702-739-2469, www.tropicana.lv.com, 3801 S Las Vegas Blvd*) contains a total of 1884 guestrooms in twin towers, including 120 suites and 80 min-isuites. Those rooms in the Island Tower conform to a Polynesian theme (wood-and-bamboo furnishings, tropical pastel pinks and greens, colorfully pleasing bedspreads). The rooms in the Paradise Tower, far from adhering to a tropical theme, are decorated in French provincial; these rooms were completely renovated in 1998 and, unlike the rooms in the Island Tower, contain refrigerators, hair dryers, irons and ironing boards. The drawback to all of the standard rooms at the Trop is size: the Island Tower rooms are only 350 sq feet; those in the Paradise Tower only 360 sq feet. Mostly, the bedrooms are decent size but the bathrooms are a bit cramped. Suites start at 600 sq feet. The rates are quite agreeable: $49 on up for a standard room, $139 on up for a suite. Most of the rooms have floor-to-ceiling windows.

Places to Stay – Top End

A new ***Aladdin*** (☎ *702-736-0111, 800-634-3424, fax 702-734-3583, 3667 S Las Vegas Blvd*), built on the site of the old one, was under construction at the time of writing and scheduled to open in the spring of 2000. Planned for its 34 acres were two theme hotels: a 2600-room Aladdin Hotel & Casino decked out in a desert motif, and a 1000-room Sound Republic Hotel & Casino with 'a multimedia tribute to live music.' No room rates were available at the time this went to press, but it's likely they will start around $80 to $100 a night.

Stratosphere is the fact that it's far from most of the rest of The Strip's megaresorts. The nearest hotel-casino is Sahara, and even that is a good walk and a major busy intersection away. Rates start at $69.

All public areas of ***Treasure Island*** (☎ *702-894-7111, 800-944-7444, fax 702-894-7446, www.treasureislandlasvegas.com, 3300 S Las Vegas Blvd*) maintain the theme of an

Bally's Las Vegas (☎ 702-739-4111, 800-634-3434, fax 702-794-2413, www.ballyslv.com, 3645 S Las Vegas Blvd) has two 26-story towers containing a total of 2814 guestrooms, including 265 suites. The standard guestrooms measure 450 sq feet, which is larger than average, while the suites range from 900 sq feet to 2600 sq feet. All of the rooms are pleasantly decorated in earth tones, and all contain sofas and TVs with video checkout. Rates start at $99 for a standard room and $300 for a suite. Special guest offerings include a full-service health club, private poolside cabañas and eight tennis courts.

The accommodations at the spectacular **Bellagio** hotel-casino (☎ 702-693-7111, 888-987-6667, fax 702-693-8546, www.bellagio lasvegas.com, 3600 S Las Vegas Blvd) range from 510 sq foot standard guestrooms to 2055-sq-foot penthouse suites. Rates for guestrooms start at $159, and rates for suites start at $1155. Surprisingly, while the guestrooms are tastefully appointed with custom European-style furnishings and soothing earth tones, they actually appear smaller than, say, the 333-sq-foot guestrooms at the

much less expensive Flamingo. That's because the bathrooms and closets in Bellagio guestrooms are oversize, and the guestrooms contain more furniture than most. The bathrooms are also luxurious, featuring Italian marble floors and surfaces, plush robes and soaking tubs. If 'soaking tubs' sounds good to you, be sure to investigate Bellagio's fabulous spa; it offers luxurious body-care treatments in the European tradition.

Caesars Palace (☎ 702-731-7110, 800-634-6661, fax 702-731-6636, www.caesars.com, 3570 S Las Vegas Blvd) offers the most luxurious standard guestrooms in town. The vast majority (1134 out of a total of 2471) are in the 29-story Palace Tower, which opened in late 1997. There are five floor plans in all, ranging in size from 550 to 750 sq feet. All have 9-foot ceilings, which enhance the feeling of spaciousness, and all have subtle design elements such as wall mirrors framed in ancient coin patterns, wood cabinets trimmed in Greek key designs and wall treatments inspired by Pompeian murals. All feature whirlpool tubs, superior custom furnishings, two-line telephones with data ports, ironing boards,

Steve Wynn's European fantasia: Bellagio

NORMAN GODWIN

A holdover from Roman times, Caesars continues to provide luxury.

irons, hair dryers, safes, small refrigerators, TVs with video checkout services and generous closets. The older rooms in the three smaller towers are just as lovely and include even more Greco-Roman touches, such as Roman columns, pilasters and (occasionally) classical sculptures in niches. Rates start at $99 for a standard room and $450 for a suite; be advised that suites are not available on Friday and Saturday nights (when the casino sets them aside for high rollers and other VIPs).

The *Desert Inn* (☎ 702-733-4444, 800-634-6909, fax 702-733-4437, www.thedesertinn .com, 3145 S Las Vegas Blvd) houses 715 elegant rooms and suites in five buildings. All of the rooms were redone during the mid-1990s in light golds and greens and feature armchairs, firm beds and views of either the golf course (preferable) or The Strip. Standard amenities include hair dryers, irons, ironing boards, three telephones (two of which are modem-accessible) and express hotel check-out via in-room television. The least expensive accommodations are the 400-sq-foot deluxe guestrooms, which start at $110. The superior rooms start at $160 and feature sitting areas and oversize bath-

tubs in 490 to 510 sq feet of opulent space. In the next category, each modern contemporary minisuite contains a Jacuzzi tub, beautiful views and increased space ($390 and up). The two-bedroom suites have private parlors and range in size from 812 to 2440 sq feet ($480 and up). There are three magnificent bi-level garden suites, each with a private swimming pool and patio, and up to four bedrooms, all overlooking a lagoon ($3000 and up). For the millionaires among us there are three Casa Grande penthouses, each encompassing 7000 to 9000 sq feet and featuring an elongated marble hallway, European decor, luxurious bathrooms, a private dining room, a bar and entertainment room, a sitting room, an exercise room and a decorative fountain. Did I mention the private pools and Jacuzzis? Each has one. The Casa Grandes rent for a minimum of $10,000 a night.

The *Four Seasons Hotel* (☎ 702-632-5000, 800-332-3442, fax 702-632-5222, www .four seasons.com, inside Mandalay Bay, 3950 S Las Vegas Blvd) is a service-oriented, non-gaming hotel occupying the 35th through 39th floors of the Mandalay Bay hotel-casino. It contains 424 rooms, all of which are spacious, tastefully appointed and filled with the usual amenities. The standard rooms have an average size of 500 sq feet and feature lovely views and oversize marble bathrooms replete with a large vanity, a deep-soaking tub, a glass-enclosed shower stall and a toilet with telephone. These rooms rent from $200 to $400, depending on dates. Also available are 810-sq-feet executive suites, one-bedroom suites that range in size from 1100 to 2170 sq feet, two-bedroom suites (1750 to 2750 sq feet), special suites (2255 to 3255 sq feet) and presidential suites (3400 to 4400 sq feet). These suites start at $360, $500, $1550, $2000 and $3000 a night, respectively. The Four Seasons emphasizes comfort, quiet and service; services include a 24-hour business center, a 24-hour concierge, voice mail and multi-line telephones, complimentary use of the extensive health and fitness facilities, a full-service spa and a free-form swimming pool. There's also 24-hour dining service, an all-day restaurant, express check-in and check-out, an early-arrival and late-departure lounge, no-smoking rooms and a twice-daily housekeeping service. In case you were wondering, Four Seasons guests are whisked to their hotel via three private elevators; they do not have to share elevators with Mandalay Bay guests.

There are 2699 guestrooms, including 108 suites, at **Harrah's** (☎ 702-369-5000, 800-634-6765, fax 702-369-5500, http://harrahs.lv.com, 3475 S Las Vegas Blvd), and all are done up in a pleasing color scheme that evokes the ambiance of Mardi Gras. All contain a table with two chairs, a full-size armoire with his-and-her chests, a large-screen TV with Nintendo and pay-per-view movies, and either one king bed or two other beds: standard-room guests have the choice of two double beds, while superior-room guests have the choice of two queen-size beds; the suites mostly come with one king-size bed, although a few suites have two queen-size beds. The standard room is a typical 336 sq feet, while the superior room is 372 sq feet and also comes with a hair dryer, a work desk, a larger TV, two telephone lines, an iron and ironing board and a bathroom with

a marble countertop and marble floor. The neatest thing about the superior rooms is that they are located in the Carnival Tower, which opened in 1997 and overlooks The Mirage and its erupting volcano; watching the volcano at night from the comfort of your cozy hotel room is very cool. The junior suite is a very spacious 558 sq feet and has a separate seating and work area and a couch that can fold out into a bed, but it does not have a separate bedroom. The executive suite provides 800 sq feet of living space, including a bedroom with walk-in closet that's completely separate from the seating and work area. The rates range from $85 to $165 for a standard room, $105 to $185 for a superior room, $135 to $215 for a junior suite, and $250 to $450 for an executive suite. Guests have free access to a swimming pool, Jacuzzi, health club and arcade.

The standard guestrooms at **Mandalay Bay** (☎ 702-632-7777, 877-632-7000, fax 702-632-7013, www.mandalaybay.com, 3950 S Las Vegas Blvd) are large (515 sq feet) and

Mandalay Bay has its own beach.

ornately appointed by award-winning interior designer Anita Brooks (who also decorated the rooms at the Monte Carlo; see Places to Stay – Mid-Range, above). Each room is done in a tasteful tropical motif and features a floor-to-ceiling window, a 27-inch TV in an armoire, a lighted closet and a desk. Both bedroom phones have data ports. Standard bathrooms include separate tub and shower, twin vanities, a makeup mirror, a third telephone, blow dryer, imported stone floors and surfaces and an enclosed toilet. Suites, in addition to the amenities found in the standard guestrooms, include an imported stone entry, wet bar with refrigerator, spa tub, powder room, big-screen TV, an assortment of brand-name spa products and a dining set in one-bedroom suites and above. Rates range from $99 to $139 for a standard guestroom; suites begin at $149 and range to $649.

The new-in-1999 *Paris-Las Vegas* (☎ 702-739-4111, 888-266-5687, fax 702-967-3836, www.paris-lv.com, 3645 S Las Vegas Blvd) opened with 2916 guestrooms, every one of which is a very comfortable 450 sq feet. All of the rooms are elegantly appointed and are in a 34-story building modeled after the famous Hotel de Ville. The guestrooms feature custom-designed furnishings, crown moldings and rich French fabrics. As in France, the stately armoire serves as the closet, enhancing the European feel of each guestroom. The bathrooms are spacious and contain lots of elegant marble, a separate bathtub and shower with authentic European fixtures, linen hand towels, a large vanity with shelves, hair dryers and a makeup mirror. Like everywhere else in Las Vegas, the room rate varies with availability. Unlike everywhere else in Las Vegas, prices also fluctuate depending on which floor you're on. Rates for rooms up to and including the 16th floor start at $119. Rates for Deluxe Rooms (floors 17 through 23) begin at $139. A Superior Room (floors 24 through 29) goes for $159 or more. And the rate for a Premier Room (floors 30 through 34) will set you back no less than $219; those facing the half-scale Eiffel Tower and the dancing fountains of Bellagio across the street cost more than those facing the back of Paris-Las Vegas' property.

When *The Venetian* (☎ 702-733-5539, 888-283-6423, fax 702-733-5190, www.venetian.com, 3355 S Las Vegas Blvd) opened in 1999, it left a spectacular impression upon the throngs of visitors who crossed its graceful arched bridges and flowing canals. Few of the visitors had the occasion to see one of the hotel-casino's guestrooms; The Venetian was sold-out months before opening day. What the visitors missed were 3036 'standard' guestrooms that are anything but standard. Every one of those rooms is a 700-sq-foot suite, with crown molding, wrought-iron railings, baseboards and a marble foyer entrance. Other features include a 130-sq-foot bathroom finished in fine Italian marble and appointed with a lighted, magnified makeup mirror, hair dryer and telephone; a canopy-draped bedchamber with a spacious closet and a Venetian floral armoire containing a safe and a 27-inch TV; a sunken living room salon; an entertainment center with a second 27-inch TV; a minibar; a fax machine with copier and computer printer capabilities as well as a separate dedicated phone line; a convertible sofa opening to a queen-size bed; two upholstered chairs; and a coffee table, writing desk and game table. These hardly standard rooms rent from $169. The Venetian also offers 318 Piazza, Renaissance, Doge and Penthouse suites ranging in size from 1330 to 5000 sq feet and in price from $650, $1500, $5000 and $10,000 a night, respectively.

Places to Stay – Long-Term Rentals

The *Warren Motel Apartments* (☎ 702-736-6235, 3965 S Las Vegas Blvd) feature 55 rooms with kitchenettes, cable TV and telephones for $146 to $172 a week. A swimming pool and laundry room are on the premises.

EAST OF THE STRIP
Places to Stay – Budget

One of the great budget bargains in Las Vegas is the *Motel 6 Tropicana* (☎ 702-798-0728,

The Often-Overlooked Housing Option

If you're going to be in Las Vegas for a week or more, consider staying at a place that specializes in extended-stay accommodations. The benefits are many: the rates don't tend to fluctuate like those of hotels and motels, long-term rentals are generally more spacious than rooms at hotels and motels, extended-stay rentals come with kitchens or kitchenettes, there are usually laundry facilities, and pets are often allowed.

The drawbacks to extended-stay accommodations: there's a bit more paperwork involved, a nonrefundable cleaning deposit of $50 is usually required, and a minimum stay of one week is often required. After completing an application, the business will conduct a quick background check to determine if you've ever been evicted. If you've been evicted in the US or Canada, you can forget about staying at one of the places here. They won't take you.

Even with the loss of the $50 cleaning deposit, the daily average cost of staying at an extended-stay facility (or long-term rental) is generally much less than spending a week in a Las Vegas hotel or motel – especially during a major convention or event that can push standard-room rates through the roof. See the various Long-Term Rental sections in this chapter for locations.

800-466-8356, fax 702-798-5657, www .motel6.com, 195 E Tropicana Ave), which with 608 rooms is the largest Motel 6 in the world. It's also less than a half mile from The Strip and easily reached by bus (just hop on any westbound CAT No 201 bus). The rooms are nothing spectacular, just quite comfortable in a mostly pink-and-gray color scheme. Each room contains a table and chairs, a large TV (free HBO), a dresser, a queen-size bed (two doubles are also available) and a shower (some have tub as well). There are two swimming pools on the premises (but no Jacuzzi), free parking outside your door and local calls are free. Rates start at $34 for one person, $40 for two.

Places to Stay – Mid-Range

Just outside the budget category – at $44 a night Sunday through Thursday for one bed and $49 for two (weekend rates fluctuate) – is the **Super 8 Motel** (☎ 702-794-0888, 800-800-8000, fax 702-794-3504, www.super 8motel.com, 4250 Koval Lane), which is the world's largest Super 8 with 288 guestrooms. The decor differs among the rooms, but most have blue carpet and white walls. They're cheerful, the HBO is free and there's a free airport shuttle. Some of the rooms

have safes; ask if it's important to have one. There's a pool and a Jacuzzi on the premises. Access to The Strip is easy enough. If you don't have a vehicle and don't want to walk (it's about half a mile), you can take a taxi or walk to nearby Flamingo Rd and catch any westbound CAT No 202 bus.

The decor of the 3479 guestrooms at **Las Vegas Hilton** (☎ 702-732-7111, 800-732-7117, fax 702-732-5790, www.lvhilton.com, 3000 Paradise Rd) consists of earth tones, mostly greens and tan. The furnishings may be described as 'upscale-contemporary

Notable Numbers

The Las Vegas Hilton

- has 5290 telephones and 603 computers.
- uses 153,000 decks of cards and 8357 dice annually.
- has 101,562 lightbulbs and 4552 parking spaces.
- cleans 29.8 million pieces of laundry annually.
- has 224,936 sq feet of windows.

American hotel'; there's nothing particularly memorable about it, but it isn't cheap. It's functional and attractive, and inoffensive in its banality. Rates start at $69 for a standard room; expect to pay three times that for a suite. Very high rollers are offered luxurious Sky Villas, which range in size from 12,600 to 15,400 sq feet. The standard rooms are spacious and include a number of pleasant amenities such as automated drapes (push a button and a machine opens and closes them for you), marble-topped dressing tables, deeper-than-usual bathtubs and deep closets with ironing board and iron. If the rooms have a drawback, it's that none of the views are special. See the Things to See & Do chapter for additional details.

The **San Remo** hotel-casino (☎ *702-739-9000, 800-522-7366, fax 702-736-1120, www .sanremolasvegas.com, 115 E Tropicana Ave*) has 711 guestrooms in all (including Jacuzzi and International suites), most of which are in two towers. The standard rooms ($39 in the garden and $59 in the towers) are nothing special; at 360 sq feet, they are on the small side, and their green-blue carpet, green-blue sofa and bold floral-print bedcover appear cheap and tacky. The walls are off-white and adorned with low-brow art of rivers painted in unnatural colors. The decor in the suites is no better. The smallest of the suites is a mere 400 sq feet and costs $20 above the going rate of a standard room.

No Ordinary Cactus

On the grounds of the San Remo is a very statuesque Saguaro *(Carnegiea gigantea)* cactus. The Hakusui Chemical Company of Japan donated the plant to the hotel-casino as a thank-you for the service it provided Hakusui officials during a stay in 1997. The cactus is more than 60 years old. The Saguaro cactus, which is naturally found in Arizona and Mexico, can reach a height of 50 feet, a width of 2 feet and a weight of many thousands of pounds.

The International and Jacuzzi suites are a full 800 sq feet and cost a reasonable $60 and $80 above the going rate of a standard room, respectively. Both suites feature a wet bar, a refrigerator, an intimate dining area and a marble entryway. Whereas the Jacuzzi suite also features a Jacuzzi, it contains only one bathroom with a separate vanity stall. The International suite features two full bathrooms. Given their price and location near The Strip, the rooms at the San Remo are a good value, particularly the suites. See the Things to See & Do chapter for additional details.

Places to Stay – Top End

The guestrooms at the **Hard Rock Café & Hotel** (☎ *702-693-5000, 800-693-7625, fax 702-693-5010, 800-473-7625, www.hardrock hotel.com, 4455 Paradise Rd*) are as smart as the rest of the glorious shrine to rock 'n' roll. Each of the 668 rooms, including 57 suites, is oversize and European-style in design and furnishings. French doors and tasteful paintings and/or prints of rock stars adorn all rooms. Suites also come with state-of-the-art music systems, large-screen Sony TV, marble bathrooms and wet bar. Guests are entitled to use a swimming pool with a sandy beach, private poolside cabañas, whirlpools and spas, all set in a lush tropical setting. Wondering about the Hard Rock's relative isolation? The hotel provides free transport to and from The Strip. Standard rooms start at $75; suites start at $250. See the Things to See & Do chapter for additional details.

Places to Stay – Long-Term Rentals

The **Brooks Residential Motel** (☎ *702-735-2239, 2112 Paradise Rd*) features 22 suites, each fully furnished and containing a kitchenette, telephones and a TV. On the premises are laundry facilities and a swimming pool. Utilities are included in the weekly rate of $155 to $200.

The **Budget Suites** (☎ *702-699-7000, 3684 Paradise Rd*) has 360 furnished rooms with kitchens ranging in cost from $180 to $200 a week. Features include a heated pool, Jacuzzi, laundry room, cable TV, free local calls, some covered parking and a conference room.

Harbor Island (☎ *702-732-9111, 370 E Harmon Ave*) rents studio and one-bedroom apartments for $150 to $160 and $160 to $170 weekly, respectively. The Harbor Island features kitchenettes, all utilities paid, laundry room, cable TV, two indoor Jacuzzis, exercise room, pets allowed, some covered parking, a tennis court and a clubhouse.

The ***Village Green*** (☎ *702-735-3143, 800-888-0808, 600 Oakmont Drive*) contains 551 furnished and unfurnished apartments in a gated community within the grounds of Las Vegas Country Club. Rates range from $580 to $630 weekly for a studio; a one-bedroom apartment rents for $625 a week; and a two-bedroom rents for $835 to $1600 each week. Features include five swimming pools, a fitness center, two laundry rooms and a clubhouse, and cats are allowed.

The ***Woodbridge Inn Apartments*** (☎ *702-732-7678, 700 E Flamingo Rd*) offers 320 short-term rental units with kitchens and cable TV for $157 a week. Features include a heated pool, Jacuzzi and laundry room, and pets are allowed.

WEST OF THE STRIP
Places to Stay – Budget
The ***Gold Coast*** hotel-casino (☎ *702-367-7111, 888-402-6278, fax 702-365-7505, www.goldcoastcasino.com, 4000 W Flamingo Rd*) possesses 750 rooms, including 18 suites, in two buildings: the original structure, which was built in 1986 and houses 300 guestrooms, and a 10-story tower built four years later and containing 450 guestrooms. The rooms are absolutely nothing special; their blue carpeting and furnishings are similar to what you'd find at any quality American motel. At 355 sq feet apiece, the rooms won't leave you feeling cramped, but that's also because the guestrooms don't have a lot of furniture (there's no room for a sofa, for example). A room with a view, with a floor-to-ceiling window? No, there's not much of a view from any of the rooms at the Gold Coast, and the window doesn't occupy even a third of the narrow wall. But starting at just $29, the standard guestrooms are

perfectly fine. The suites are much larger (576 sq feet), and include one king-size bed (as opposed to two queens), a separate sitting and dining area, and a wet bar. But for $175 or more, a person could do better on The Strip. The Gold Coast provides free shuttle service to and from The Strip. See the Things to See & Do chapter for additional details.

Places to Stay – Mid-Range
The 840 guestrooms at ***The Orleans*** hotel-casino (☎ *702-365-7111, 800-675-3267, fax 702-365-7535, www.orleanscasino.com, 4500 W Tropicana Ave*) are all petite suites – a generous 450 sq feet with a living room containing sitting and dining areas; a bedroom containing either a king-size bed or two queens; and a bathroom containing an oversize tub. All of the rooms are tastefully appointed in a variety of French-style wallpapers, numerous brass fixtures, bed covers in French-provincial style and (generally) French-provincial-style furnishings. The guestrooms are in a 22-story structure and face either The Strip or the mountains. Rates range from $39 to $179, with price varying with availability. These rooms are a very good value. The Orleans provides free shuttle service to and from The Strip and the airport. See the Things to See & Do chapter for additional details.

Places to Stay – Top End
The ***Rio*** (☎ *702-252-7777, 800-752-9746, www.playrio.com, 3700 W Flamingo Rd*) offers only suites, and most are a great deal. The Rio has 2563 'standard' rooms, each 600 sq feet in size and most boasting a floor-to-ceiling window, drip coffee maker, fridge, iron and ironing board, safe, hair dryer, 27-inch TV, cocktail table, separate dressing areas, fully-detailed bathroom and a king-size bed or two queen-size beds. And who could forget the crescent-shaped couch in every room? The lowest nonspecial rate you'll come across for these rooms, which have an occupancy level in excess of 90%, is $70. Beware that some of these guestrooms are windowless; be sure to specify that you want a room with a view if that's important to you. In addition to the regular suites,

there are a number of Masquerade Suites that spread out over 1600 sq feet and contain everything you'd find in one of the regular suites plus a Jacuzzi tub and 180-degree views of the mountains and The Strip. The Masquerade Suites start at $250. The Rio provides free shuttle service to and from The Strip. See the Things to See & Do chapter for additional details.

Places to Stay – Long-Term Rentals

The *Budget Suites* are a chain with comparable amenities and prices. All offer furnished one-bedroom apartments with a kitchen, telephone and cable TV. All have at least one heated pool, Jacuzzi and laundry room. The Budget Suites at 1500 Stardust Rd (☎ 702-732-1500, 800-752-1501) offers 639 furnished apartments. Also on the premises are a conference room and a tennis court. Weekly rates range from $170 to $190.

The *Budget Suites* at 3655 W Tropicana Ave (☎ 702-739-1000) offers 480 furnished suites. Features also include free local calls and some covered parking. Weekly rates range from $180 to $200.

The *Budget Suites* at 4205 W Tropicana Ave (☎ 702-889-1700) offers 414 suites. Features also include some covered parking. Weekly rates range from $190 to $210.

Extended Stay America (☎ 702-221-7600, 800-362-4040, 4270 S Valley View Blvd) offers furnished one-bedroom deluxe suites with kitchenettes. Amenities include exercise facilities, heated pool, laundry room and free local calls. Weekly rates start at $239. A $100 refundable deposit is required.

DOWNTOWN

Note that you can find further descriptions of the Downtown hotel-casinos listed below in the Things to See & Do chapter.

Places to Stay – Budget

Unless you're able to receive a discounted rate, you won't find a place on The Strip with rooms for less than $39 a night. However, just four blocks north of The Strip is the no-frills *Las Vegas International Hostel* (☎ 702-385-9955, lasvegashostel@yahoo.com, www.lasvegashostel.com, 1208 S Las Vegas Blvd), which offers space in four-bed dormitories for $12 to $14. Private rooms run $26/28, single/double. You'll save $2 per night with an HI/AYH card. There's a heater in each room, but no air con. Free access to a nearby pool and tours to the Grand Canyon and other national parks are available. There's a kitchen and a laundry for guests' use, and Internet access may be available by the time you read this. Local calls are permitted, and there's a pay phone just around the corner for long-distance calls. There are three markets and two Cuban restaurants within a short walk. This place is popular with international backpackers.

Nine city blocks east of the Fremont Street Experience sits the *Las Vegas Backpackers Hostel* (☎ 702-385-1150, 800-550-8958, fax 702-385-4940, vegasbackpackers@hotmail.com, www.hostels.com/lvbackpacker, 1322 Fremont St), which has excellent facilities, caring management and low rates: dorm beds go for $12 Monday through Thursday, $15 Friday, Saturday and Sunday; singles are $30 Monday through Thursday, $35 Friday, Saturday and Sunday; doubles rent for $40 Monday through Thursday, $45 Friday, Saturday and Sunday. Rates include breakfast. Facilities include a swimming pool, a Jacuzzi, laundry machines, a kitchen for guests' use and even Internet access ($5 per hour). The rooms are nothing special, but they do have air con and heating and are nonsmoking, and there's 24-hour access. Keg parties and barbecues are often held during the summer. Cheap tours to the Grand Canyon and area national parks can be arranged from the hostel. A shuttle from the hostel to Los Angeles leaves three times a week ($35 each way). Safe deposit boxes are available for rent ($5 for the length of your stay). Six free shuttle trips are provided to/from the Sahara daily. There's also free pick up from the Greyhound bus depot ($2 return) and transportation to/from the airport *in a limousine* for a mere $4.75 each way (two person minimum). Also available are three public phones, special car-rental rates, free passes to The Beach dance club and discount prices at the decent Mexican/

Cuban restaurant next door. This hostel is so excellent (nevermind its location in a crappy part of town) that the management is somewhat strict about who it's willing to let stay there. American guests must have a hostel card or a student ID. Foreigners need to show only an ID. You must be at least 18 years old or accompanied by a parent.

The ***Budget Inn*** (☎ 702-385-5560, 800-959-9062, fax 702-382-9273, 301 S Main St) offers 81 pleasant rooms with air con, heating and satellite TV in a four-story building 75m or so from the Greyhound bus depot. There's no laundry room, nor is there a swimming pool or a slot machine, but if all you're looking for is a quiet place to stay in downtown, this may be for you. Rates start at $29.

The hotel-casino ***California*** (☎ 702-385-1222, 800-634-6255, fax 702-388-2610, www.thecal.com, 12 E Ogden Ave) has a total of 781 guestrooms, including 74 suites, in an 11-story tower and a newer nine-story tower. The rooms in the newer, West Tower are slightly larger than those in the East Tower (which was being renovated at the time of writing), but the Cal doesn't divulge square-footage figures. The towers share a consistent decor, though it's neither particularly Californian nor particularly Hawaiian (the Cal receives many Hawaiian guests and dresses appropriately, as it were). The decor may be described at American contemporary hotel, with handsome mahogany furnishings, attractive marble baths and color schemes that tend to be either apricot/teal or mauve/burgundy. If views are important to you, stay elsewhere; the views from the rooms here are generally unappealing. Rates start at a very appealing $35, twice that on weekends.

The recently remodeled 447 rooms at the ***Fremont*** hotel-casino (☎ 702-385-3232, 800-634-6182, fax 702-385-6229, www.boydgaming.com, 200 E Fremont St) are noticeably smaller than most in town (hotel staff won't divulge figures), but they are also attractive and reasonably priced. Most of the rooms have beige carpeting, low-profile wallpaper and gold bedspreads with a mild floral pattern overlay. There's little in the way of a view from Fremont rooms. Be advised that a

guestroom with two double beds is much more cramped than the same room with just one king-size bed; at the Fremont you have your choice. Kids under 12 stay free with parents, but the Fremont limits the number of guests per room to three – no exceptions. Rates start at $35. There are suites, but they are reserved for players' club cardholders. If you intend to be doing some serious gambling, you'd be wise to enroll in the Fremont's players' club (it's free) and ask to be rated. Then, as you gamble, the amount you gamble will be tallied. You don't need to gamble that much before the hotel will upgrade you to a suite or offer you a very discounted rate on your standard room.

If you're looking for a big inexpensive downtown hotel-casino that's within easy walking distance of other hotel-casinos, look no farther than ***Jackie Gaughan's Plaza*** (☎ 702-386-2110, 800-634-6575, fax 702-382-8281, www.plazahotelcasino.com, 1 Main St). Built in 1971, the Plaza has two towers, one with 21 floors and the other with 25 floors. The rooms overlook either downtown Las Vegas or freeway spaghetti; neither sight is lovely, and the rooms facing downtown catch a lot of noise coming up from the Fremont Street Experience. But with standard room rates starting at $25 and suite rates starting at $60, and one- and two-bedroom apartments starting at $80 and $120, respectively, guests are getting very good value for the money. (Bring a pair of earplugs if you're particularly sensitive to noise when you're trying to sleep.) At 378 sq feet, the standard rooms are average in size. But they're attractively decorated, and all of the 1034 rooms (including the 136 suites and apartments) have balconies, which you'll appreciate if you've just got to have fresh air.

The ***Showboat*** (☎ 702-385-9123, 800-826-2800, fax 702-383-9238, www.showboatlv.com, 2800 E Fremont St) has 456 standard rooms and suites that maintain the Mardi Gras and old-time Louisiana theme happening throughout the rest of the hotel-casino. The rooms are pleasant enough, but their amenities are limited to hair dryers, cosmetic mirrors and a bathroom telephone (do people really use them?). Given their distance from The Strip and from downtown proper, there's no reason to stay here unless there are no vacancies anywhere else or unless you are attending a function at the Showboat. Be forewarned that the Showboat's reservations agents tend to be more quick-tempered or less friendly than at other Las Vegas hotel-casinos. Most megaresorts 'monitor' their reservations lines for quality control, but you'll hear no such warning message when you call the Showboat because no one monitors the calls there. This has had an obvious result. Rates start at $29 for a standard room, and $149 for a suite.

Las Vegas' oldest hotel is the *Victory Hotel* (☎ 702-387-9257, 307 S Main St). The hotel, which opened in 1908, offers 32 clean and comfortable rooms with central air con, heating and private hot-water bathrooms for $28 most nights. The Victory features laundry facilities and gated parking, and it makes lockers available to its guests. This is a very good budget hotel, a fine option for people considering either of the hostels appearing in this chapter but who want to be closer to the action.

Places to Stay – Mid-Range

A lot of people like the guestsrooms at the *Golden Nugget* (☎ 702-385-7111, 800-634-3454, fax 702-386-8362, www.mirageresorts .com, 129 E Fremont St), which was gaming tycoon Steve Wynn's first major project in Las Vegas (he's now better known for The Mirage and Bellagio). In fact, the 1907 renovated rooms at the Golden Nugget closely resemble those of The Mirage, only the rooms at the Golden Nugget are gold and brown in color (as opposed to beige). All the standard rooms are a generous 425 sq feet in size and include half-canopy beds, marble entryways, vanity tables with magnifying makeup mirrors and marble bathrooms with hair dryers. There are also one- and two-bedroom luxury apartments that are unlike any others found in Las Vegas megaresorts. Each features a spiral staircase that leads from a spacious living room to the bedroom area. Floor-to-ceiling windows span the

NORMAN GODWIN

Behind the neon are comfortable rooms.

length of the room, providing guests with a captivating view of Las Vegas. Each of these suites contains two bathrooms, one designed for men, the other (with potpourri and a Jacuzzi tub) for women. And each bathroom contains a TV, just in case. The standard rooms start at $49 and are a particularly good deal. The suites start at $275. The Golden Nugget's casino clings to its Victorian-era theme, just as it has since the hotel-casino opened on August 30, 1946, only now – since Wynn took charge in 1973 – it's fairly classy. There's no shortage of brass or cut class, and the entire casino, once dimly lit and a bit depressing, is bright and cheerful. Also on the premises are a lavish spa, a salon, five restaurants, a swimming pool and whirlpool, a fitness center and the requisite gift shop.

The 406 guestrooms at *Main Street Station* (☎ 702-387-1896, 800-713-8933, fax 702-386-4466, www.mainstreetcasino.com, 200 N Main St) are as handsome as the rest of the hotel-casino and are in a 17-floor tower that features marble tile foyers, Victorian sconces and marble-trimmed hallways. The recently refurbished, spacious rooms are elegant, bright and cheerful, with large plantation shutters instead of drapes, soft home-style fabrics and upholstery, rich wood tones, white-embossed wall coverings and wall sconces and tasteful framed art. These are among the loveliest rooms in all of Las Vegas, yet the prices are extremely agreeable, with rates starting at only $40 (usually twice that on weekends). There are suites, but the casino controls them; they are available mostly to members of the players' club (which operates the same way as the Fremont's players' club). However, suites are occasionally available on a walk-in basis; if you've just got to have one, say so when you reach the reception desk and vow to gamble like a crazed human money-dispensing machine. They've heard it all before, but it never hurts to try. If you're set on staying in the downtown area but haven't yet developed an intimate relationship with another downtown hotel, you'd be wise to call Main Street Station to see if it's got a room at a price you like.

Main Street Station has classy 'standard rooms.'

Places to Stay – Top End

There are no places in the downtown area with a midweek, low-season rate in excess of $70. However, you can find many places charging well over that sum for a standard room if you're in town during a huge convention or if New Year's Eve lands midweek. Otherwise, standard rooms don't top $70 except on the weekends, and you'll find many of them then.

Places to Stay – Long-Term Rentals

The *Peter Pan Motel* (☎ 702-384-8422, 110 N 13th St) has 38 rooms with refrigerators and cable TVs for a mere $85 to $95 a week. Monthly rates of $380 to $420 are available.

Places to Eat

Excluding the city's 1345 fast-food joints, its 49 ice cream and candy shops and its 57 bakeries and 70 buffets, there is an impressive total of 722 restaurants in Las Vegas serving more than 30 ethnic varieties of cuisine. Las Vegas has, as Sin City's perspicacious spin doctors like to say, many places at which to dine.

With so many restaurants – and so many really fantastic ones – within only 10 sq miles, deciding where in Las Vegas to don a bib and unsheathe the fork can pose a problem. Trouble is, who can think on an empty stomach?!

If the prospect of making a meal decision becomes so daunting that you feel the need to toss back a few vodka martinis before committing yourself, you might like to know that many of Las Vegas' 412 bars and cocktail lounges offer full dinners – which, of course, only complicates matters.

Decisions, decisions. If you can at least decide on what type of food you want, you've won half the battle, because the Killer

Killer Vegas Eateries

Best Bakery
Freed's Bakery

Best Barbecue
Fireside at Carollo's

Best Brazilian
Yolie's Brazilian Steak House

Best Cheesesteak Sandwich
Straight From Philly Steakhouse

Best Chinese
Chin Chin

Best Deli
Celebrity Deli & Restaurant

Best Doughnuts
Krispy Kreme Doughnuts

Best Family Eatery
Applebee's Neighborhood Grill & Bar

Best French
Bistro Le Montrachet

Best Gourmet
Pamplemousse

Best Hamburgers
Kilroy's

Best Indian
Gandhi India's Cuisine

Best Italian
Ristorante Italiano

Best Japanese
Hyakumi

Best Late-Night Dining
Ruth's Chris Steak House

Best Mediterranean
Mediterranean Café & Market

Best Mexican
La Barca Mexican Seafood Restaurant

Best Patio Dining
Enigma Garden Café

Best Pizza
Pizzeria Uno Chicago Bar & Grill

Best Rotisserie Chicken
Sonia's Café & Rotisserie

Best Salad Bar
Sweet Tomatoes

Best Seafood
The Tillerman

Best Steakhouse
Hungry Hunter

Best Sushi
Nippon

Best Takeout
Pick Up Stix

Best Thai
Prommare's Thai Food

Best Vegetarian
Wild Oats Community Market

Vegas Eateries boxed text lists the city's best restaurants by cuisine and specialty. Below, the restaurant descriptions are arranged geographically and listed alphabetically within price categories. Note that not every restaurant in town is mentioned here, just many of the noteworthy ones. A complete restaurant guide to Las Vegas would be so unwieldy it would pose a hazard to your health.

Speaking of health hazards, there's one more dining option to consider: buffets. For the skinny on these Rabelaisian feasts, see the buffet boxed text in this chapter. But remember, just because Vegas buffets are always 'all you can eat,' don't feel you have to eat all you possibly can. As author Anthelme Brillant-Savarin once wrote, "Tell me what you eat, and I will tell you what you are."

Then again, Virginia Woolf once noted in her immortal *A Room of One's Own*, 'One cannot think well, love well, sleep well, if one has not dined well.' Now *that's* more like it. To hell with Anthelme!

THE STRIP

Most of the restaurants on The Strip are nestled inside the huge hotel-casinos that flank both sides of Las Vegas Boulevard from the Stratosphere to Mandalay Bay. These get the lion's share of the restaurant business, but some of the independents (GameWorks Grill and Harley-Davidson Café among them) are crowd-pleasers too and warrant consideration.

One of the neat things about the restaurant options on The Strip is that so many are actual attractions in themselves. It's not simply that they have *ambience*; on the most basic level, so does a Pizza Hut. Rather, many of these places qualify as bona fide entertainment. The Rain Forest Café, for example, creates a dining experience that rivals a theme park ride, with animatronic jungle animals and simulated thunderstorms with lightning and rain.

Not only that, amid all the restaurant-attractions are some great culinary choices. Emeril Lagasse's New Orleans Fish House and Gatsby's would receive rave reviews in

Locating Resort Restaurants

If you want to find all of the recommended restaurants in a particular casino-resort, check the Lonely Planet map on which the resort appears. Under the Places to Eat key, all of the recommended restaurants in that resort are listed together under the same key number. You can then find their descriptions – which are distinguished by budget and alphabetized by restaurant name – in this chapter more quickly.

New York. Aureole's, which *is* one of New York's finest restaurants, now has an identical twin at Mandalay Bay. Another of New York's best, Le Cirque, is also now represented in Las Vegas (at Bellagio).

There's some great dining to be had in Las Vegas. As they say in parts of Canada, bon appetit!

Places to Eat – Budget

Coyote Café & Grill Room (☎ 702-891-7777, inside the MGM Grand) is two establishments in one, both serving spicy Southwestern cuisine. The popular café, which opens early and closes late, offers lots of fun food such as jerk chicken tacos and blue-corn pancakes with toasted pine nuts in an inviting room featuring colorful terra-cotta walls adorned with Southwestern art. Most entrées are under $10. Open daily. See Places to Eat – Top End for the grill room.

GameWorks Grill (☎ 702-597-3122, 3769 S Las Vegas Blvd) is a very popular and casual restaurant located amid the high-tech video games and virtual-reality experiences of GameWorks. A fair variety of sandwiches, salads, pastas and pizzas are offered. Most entrées are between $7 and $9. Open daily for lunch and dinner.

Holy Cow! (☎ 702-732-2697, 2423 S Las Vegas Blvd) is a microbrewery and a 24-hour restaurant with very bovine decor – cow photos, cow graphic art, cow-patterned lamps, etc – with some award-winning home

An udder delight

brews, baby back ribs, steak sandwiches, burgers and the like. Few entrées are over $10.

La Piazza Food Court (☎ *702-731-7110, in the casino at Caesars Palace*) offers lunch and dinner selections that spotlight a variety of the world's most popular cuisines, including Chinese stir-fry, Italian pasta and pizza, Mexican favorites, American deli fixtures and Japanese ramen soups and teriyaki. Most entrées are under $10. Open daily.

Liberty Café (☎ *702-383-0101, 1700 S Las Vegas Blvd, inside White Cross Rexall Drugs*) features an old-fashioned drugstore counter where generous breakfasts, fatty-but-delicious burgers, biscuits and cream, and awesome malts are served 24 hours a day. With few items over $6, this place is a great budget find.

Places to Eat – Mid-Range

All-Star Café (☎ *702-795-8326, 3785 S Las Vegas Blvd*) is a sport-themed eatery with lots of sports memorabilia, much of it from owners Andre Agassi, Monica Seles, Shaquille O'Neal, Joe Montana et al. Pastas, burgers and the like – the usual all-American standbys – fill the menu. Most entrées are around $12. Open daily for lunch and dinner.

Chin Chin (☎ *702-740-6969, inside New York-New York*) serves wonderful traditional Chinese food in a cheerful café setting. Among the wide range of sumptuous dishes prepared in the open kitchen is Chin Chin's signature classic shredded chicken salad. Also available are an assortment of dim sum items. Entrées run from $5 to $12. Open daily for lunch and dinner. Closes late.

Country Star American Music Grill (☎ *702-740-8400, 3724 S Las Vegas Blvd*) exists for country music fans. TV monitors playing country music videos are everywhere. Country music memorabilia, includ-

Join the all-stars at the All-Star Café.

ing Dolly Parton's wedding dress, abound. The house specialties are ribs, steaks and hickory chicken. Most entrées are under $14. Open daily for lunch and dinner.

Dive! (☎ *702-369-3483, inside the Fashion Show Mall*) is Steven Spielberg's nautical-themed restaurant. Inside, you feel like you're in a submarine far beneath the ocean surface. Replete with periscopes, sonar screens and the like, Dive! is a big splash with kids and an amusing plunge from the norm for most adults. The menu's submerged in salads, burgers, pizzas and submarine sandwiches. Entrées range from $7 to $14. Open daily for lunch and dinner.

Dragon Noodle Company (☎ *702-730-7777, in the casino area of the Monte Carlo*) feels like an authentic Hong Kong eatery dropped into Las Vegas. Many of the meals are displayed for diners' inspection, the food is cooked on grills in plain sight, and there's a tea bar where many brands can be sampled. Try the air-dried roast duck (all the flavor, half the fat). Entrées range from $6 to $18. Open for lunch and dinner. Closed Monday.

Harley-Davidson Café (☎ *702-740-4555, 3725 S Las Vegas Blvd*) is more a tourist attraction than a biker joint, with a dozen shiny hogs, lots of celebrity-autographed gas tanks and plenty of Harley racing photos on display. American roadside cuisine (mostly burgers and barbecue meats) is the specialty here. Entrées run from $7 to $17; burgers and sandwiches around $9, barbecue ribs $16. Open daily for lunch and dinner.

Montana's Café & Grill (☎ *702-380-7711, 800-998-6937, in the casino area of the Stratosphere*) is a casual, Old West-themed restaurant specializing in prime rib and a variety of barbecued meats. Typical side dishes include coleslaw, corn on the cob and baked beans. Entrées range from $10 to $15. Open daily for breakfast, lunch and dinner.

Noodle Kitchen (☎ *702-791-7111, in the casino area of The Mirage*) serves authentic Chinese fare and is easy to miss as it's actually located within another restaurant – The Mirage's heavily foliaged Caribe Café. Among the Noodle Kitchen's tasty offerings: soy chicken slices, roast duck with

You won't get wet at Dive!

NORMAN GODWIN

plum sauce and steamed vegetables in oyster sauce. Most entrées are under $12. Open from 11 am till 4 am daily.

Planet Hollywood (☎ *702-791-7827, inside the Forum Shops at Caesars Palace*) is a shrine to legends of the big screen. It's packed with well-displayed Hollywood memorabilia and video monitors showing films. The food is predictable and popular: burgers, pasta, gourmet pizzas, sandwiches and salads. Entrées range from $8 to $20. Open daily for lunch and dinner.

Rain Forest Café (☎ *702-891-1111, in the casino area of the MGM Grand*) is a jungle-themed restaurant where the selection of pasta, burgers, sandwiches and salads is secondary to the lush faux-forest setting, a host of mechanized exotic animals and simulated tropical downpours. The fruit smoothies are divine. Main courses typically run $15. Open daily for lunch and dinner.

Ristorante Italiano (☎ *702-794-9363, in the casino area of the Riviera*) is a quiet, elegant restaurant with superb service and great food (the lasagna is especially delicious). It's easy to overlook the restaurant's door inside the casino, and if you have trouble finding it, keep looking; one bite into your meal and you'll be glad you did. Most entrées are around $14. Open for dinner only; closed Wednesday and Thursday.

Stage Deli of Las Vegas (☎ *702-893-4045, inside the Forum Shops at Caesars Palace*) is the twin of the legendary Stage Deli of New York, with more than 300 items on its terrific menu. Typical items include oven-roasted prime brisket of beef, stuffed cabbage and an assortment of sky-high sandwiches. Entrées are from $6 to $14. Opens early, closes late, daily.

Tony Roma's: A Place for Ribs (☎ 702-732-6111, *in the casino area of the Stardust*) is an informal, very popular restaurant specializing in barbecued baby back ribs, ribs served with a variety of sauces and barbecued shrimp and broiled chicken. Entrées range from $7 to $27, with most around $11. Open daily for dinner only.

Places to Eat – Top End

Aqua (☎ 702-693-7111, 888-987-6667, *in the Bellagio*) features the acclaimed seafood preparations of chef Mark Lo Russo, former sous chef of San Francisco's famous Aqua. House specialties include Hawaiian swordfish and medallions of ahi tuna. Entrées typically cost $30 to $35, first courses half that. Open daily for dinner only.

Aureole (☎ 702-632-7777, *inside Mandalay Bay*) is a sibling of the famous New York Aureole. The menu features seasonal American dishes, which could include a sea scallop sandwich, smoked capon ravioli and pan-seared veal T-bone. At the heart of the elegant restaurant is a four-story wine tower. The prix-fixe menu runs $65; a la carte entrées start at $22. Open daily for dinner.

Chin's (☎ 702-733-8899, *inside the Fashion Show Mall*) is a fairly formal favorite with

A Few Words about the Buffets

The old axiom *You get what you pay for* applies to Las Vegas hotel buffets. Circus Circus boasts one of the cheapest buffets in town, but unless you don't mind eating fat-filled cafeteria fare, you wouldn't touch CC's buffet food with a ten-foot fork. For the really good stuff you usually have to pay nearly twice as much, but the difference in quality is as apparent as the difference between a filet mignon and an overcooked meatball.

Generally, you can predict which hotel-casinos will have killer buffets. Circus Circus and Excalibur, for example, are geared for families and thus charge prices that are family friendly. Their buffet food tends to be cheap as well: heavy on spaghetti and low-grade meats. Bellagio, Luxor and Mandalay Bay are competing for top honors in the Class Act category; you won't find a lot of spaghetti and other typical Food for the Masses at their buffet counters.

What you will tend to find at the buffets in the better hotel-casinos are various food stations specializing in sushi, seafood, pasta, stir-fry, carved meats and so on. Among the standard entrées at the upscale megaresorts: mounds of fresh shrimp, lobster claws, red snapper, pasta and antipasti, beef tenderloin, roast meats carved to order, bowls of fresh fruits, various soups and lots of salad material.

locals and tourists alike serving delicious gourmet Chinese food. Offerings include orange-peel shrimp, strawberry chicken and dim sum. There's a separate piano bar on the premises. Entrées range from $10 to $28. Open daily for lunch and dinner.

Coyote Café & Grill Room *(☎ 702-891-7777, inside the MGM Grand)* serves spicy Southwestern cuisine. The Grill Room, which opens for dinner only, features more substantial dishes than the café (mentioned above), such as grilled rack of lamb, wild venison and a garlicky black bean soup. Entrées range from $15 to $35. Casual attire is fine. Open daily.

Emeril Lagasse's New Orleans Fish House *(☎ 702-891-7374, inside the MGM Grand)* features the famous Crescent City chef's creative Creole and Cajun dishes, including lobster cheesecake, barbecued shrimp and oysters on the half shell with a tangy sauce. Not to be missed is the banana cream pie with banana crust and caramel. Entrées range from $20 to $40. Open daily for lunch and dinner.

Gatsby's *(☎ 702-891-7337, inside the MGM Grand)* features Continental cuisine with California accents. Among the house specialties are ostrich with wild mushroom risotto, seared ahi tuna and poached seafood ravioli. The restaurant also has a superb wine list. Entrées range from $55 to $70. Open for dinner only; closed Sunday and Monday. Reservations required.

A Few Words about the Buffets

Buffet prices, like hotel rates, fluctuate in Las Vegas. When there's a big convention in town, they're set a little higher than usual. Generally, at the memorable buffet restaurants you can expect to pay around $6 for breakfast, $7 to $10 for lunch, and $10 to $15 for dinner. Breakfast prices usually are in effect from 7 till 11 am, lunch prices from 11 am till 4 pm and dinner from 4 pm till closing (10 pm generally).

The best daily buffets can be found at Rio and Main Street Station. The Garden Court buffet at Main Street Station features no fewer than 10 stations where food is prepared right before your eyes; it doesn't get any fresher than that. Among the items available there: wood-fired pizza, a slew of fresh salsas to accompany delicious Mexican fare and specialties from Hawaii, China and the American Southwest.

The Rio has two buffet restaurants. Its Carnival World Buffet features dishes from China, Brazil, Mexico, Italy and around the US. Many people view Carnival World as the best buffet in town, and it's hard to dispute that – unless you're a seafood fiend. Then, the choice is simple: Rio's Village Seafood Buffet. It features lots of fresh seafood flown in daily. The seafood buffet is expensive (generally $18 for lunch, $22 for dinner), but it's worth it.

Other excellent buffets can be found at Bellagio, Mandalay Bay, Bally's, Caesars Palace, Luxor, Mirage, Golden Nugget, Fremont and the Las Vegas Hilton. In addition to the unhealthy buffets at Circus Circus and Excalibur, other relatively low-quality (and less expensive) buffets can be found at Sahara, Stardust, Stratosphere, Showboat and Lady Luck.

If you had tremendous luck at the gaming tables Saturday night and want to spend Sunday morning celebrating, head to Bally's, home of the best Sunday brunch in town. Bally's Sterling Sunday Brunch will set you back $40, but it's so impressive you'll forget about the money right away. Ice sculptures and lavish flower arrangements abound, as do food stations laying out roast duckling, steak Diane, seared salmon with beet butter sauce – you get the idea. There's even a sushi and salmon bar. Reservations recommended (☎ 702-739-4111).

Hamada of Japan (☎ 702-733-3333, inside the Flamingo Hilton) features a Teppan grill, a sushi bar and a sukiyaki dining room that has the feel of an authentic Japanese home. Specialties include tenzura, donburi and beef sukiyaki. Entrées range from $12 to $42. Dress is informal and reservations are not needed. Open daily for dinner only.

Hyakumi (☎ 702-731-7731, inside Caesars Palace) is the top Japanese restaurant in Las Vegas and offers visitors a choice of sushi bar or seating at a Teppan table. Hyakumi's chef, Hiroji Obayashi, has won many awards. Reservations are required at this dinner-only eatery, which is done up to resemble an old Japanese village. Entrées run $30 to $65. Closed Sunday and Monday.

Le Cirque (☎ 702-693-7111, in the Bellagio) features haute cuisine and world-class wines in an intimate and opulent setting. The chef is Marc Poidevin, formerly the chef de cuisine at New York's legendary Le Cirque 2000. The restaurant is known for its varieties of foie gras and its signature black-tie scallops. Entrées range from $32 to $42. Open daily for dinner only.

Mizuno's (☎ 702-739-2713, at the Tropicana) features chefs preparing tempura, shrimp, lobster, chicken and steak with swordsmenlike moves on a grill in front of you. The restaurant is itself a work of art, with gorgeous marble floors and many Japanese antiques. Standard dinners range from $15 to $20, superior dinners run twice that. Open daily for dinner only.

Monte Carlo Room (☎ 702-733-4444, on the mezzanine level of the Desert Inn) features fine French cuisine in an elegant room with garden views. Specialties include boneless roasted duck, Cornish game hen and duck à l'orange served with apple- and pine-nut-studded wild rice. Entrées range from $30 to $80. Jackets required for men. Open for dinner only; closed Tuesday and Wednesday.

Morton's of Chicago (☎ 702-893-0703, inside the Fashion Show Mall) is one of America's great steak and lobster chains, serving succulent Midwestern steaks, whole baked Maine lobster, Sicilian veal and prime rib in a room lined with mahogany and adorned with LeRoy Neiman prints. Entrées range from $18 to $30. Open daily for dinner only.

Palace Court (☎ 702-731-7731, inside Caesars Palace) is one of the top French restaurants in Las Vegas. Specialties include terrine of fresh duck liver with smoked duck breast salad and baked Burgundy snails in garlic and herb butter. Entrées range from $13.50 for the cured carpaccio of beef to $110 for the caviar on ice. Open for dinner only; closed Tuesday and Wednesday.

The Palm (☎ 702-732-7256, inside the Forum Shops at Caesars Palace) is one of the best restaurants in town for lobster, but expect to be clawed by the prices. Among the entrées is a 7lb lobster for $140. The shrimp cocktails and prime steaks are also fantastic. Entrées range from $16 to $150. Open daily for lunch and dinner.

Picasso (☎ 702-693-7111, 888-987-6667, in the Bellagio) features the memorable Mediterranean cooking of chef Julian Serrano. Serrano's cuisine is inspired by the regional cuisine of France and Spain where Pablo Picasso spent much of his life. Guests have a choice of a four-course meal ($70) or a five-course meal ($80), with two or three selections for each. Among Serrano's signature dishes are a lobster salad served with a saffron sauce and fried leeks and a seared foie gras served with a balsamic vinaigrette and sliced cucumber. Several original Picasso masterpieces as well as a large collection of his charming ceramic pieces further delight the senses. Dinner only; closed Wednesday.

Prime (☎ 702-693-7111, in the Bellagio) is another excellent steakhouse. Prime's signature dishes include garlic soup with frog legs, rib-eye steak for two with wild mushrooms and roasted garlic and live Maine lobster. Entrées range from $18 to $54. Open daily for dinner only.

The Range (☎ 702-369-5000, inside Harrah's) is as notable for its view of The Strip as it is for steak, both of which are spectacular. The short menu in this semiformal restaurant features various cuts of beef, a few chicken dishes and salads. The prices are a bit on the high side, but the beef is superior grade, all entrées come with sides and the elevated view *is* stunning. Entrées range from $20 to $29. Open daily for dinner only.

Spago (☎ 702-369-6300, *inside the Forum Shops at Caesars Palace*) features California-style cuisine made famous by chef Wolfgang Puck's landmark Los Angeles restaurant of the same name. Specialties include Puck's signature Chinois chicken salad and pizza topped with salmon. Spago is well known for its rich desserts. Entrées range from $15 to $30. Open daily for lunch and dinner.

Top of the World (☎ 702-380-7711, 800-998-6937, *Stratosphere*) is a dressy, revolving restaurant perched high atop the Stratosphere Tower. While taking in cloud-level views of Las Vegas Valley, patrons enjoy impeccable service and delicious though overpriced entrées such as veal, lobster and almond-crusted salmon. Entrées range from $21 to $33. Open daily for dinner only.

EAST OF THE STRIP
Places to Eat – Budget

Celebrity Deli & Restaurant (☎ 702-733-7827, *4055 S Maryland Parkway*) is a classic New York-style delicatessen with lots of corned beef, pastrami and salami. Dinner entrées include smoked fish, brisket of beef and stuffed cabbage. The Vegas characters who frequent Celebrity are as colorful as the eatery's pink and lavender walls. Entrées run $7 to $12. Open for lunch and dinner Monday through Saturday and until 3 pm on Sunday.

Drink! (☎ 702-796-5519, *200 E Harmon Ave*) is a super-popular nightclub from about 10 pm on, but it's also a fine place to grab some reasonably priced but exotic Italian food such as seafood Belmonti and wild mushroom pasta. Don't worry; chicken ravioli and other standard fare is also available. Entrées range from $6 to $11. Open for dinner only; closed Monday.

Einstein Bros Bagels (☎ 702-795-7800, *4624 Maryland Parkway*) produces 17 varieties of bagels fresh every morning, and it offers 10 flavors of cream cheese to accompany them (even jalapeno!). Wash it down

with one of their quality blended coffees. All items are less than $6. Open from dawn till dusk daily.

Fireside at Carollo's (☎ 702-270-3700, *2301 E Sunset Rd*) creates incredible barbecue ribs. The meat, always made sweet and tangy with a secret sauce, is so tender you needn't use a fork. The steakhouse-style restaurant has won local rib contests time and again. Entrées run $13 to $18. Open for lunch Monday through Saturday and dinner daily.

Freed's Bakery (☎ 702-456-7762, *4780 S Eastern Ave*) has been a Las Vegas favorite since it opened in 1959. Despite a recent explosion in bakeries with great buns, time and again local surveys pick Freed's as tops among the yeast-driven businesses. You've just got to like a place that advertises same-day made-to-order wedding and birthday cakes. Opens at 7 am daily.

Freed's has The Strip's best buns.

La Barca Mexican Seafood Restaurant *(☎ 702-657-9700, 953 E Sahara Ave)* offers a full menu of excellent, authentic Mexican seafood dishes. Among the restaurant's popular specialties are a 45oz shrimp cocktail and a chopped clam tostada that's to die for. Film buffs might like to know that the restaurant scene in *Leaving Las Vegas* was shot here. Entrées range from $5 to $25, with many items under $10. Open from 10 am to 10 pm Friday through Sunday.

Mediterranean Café & Market *(☎ 702-731-6030, 4147 S Maryland Parkway)* is a great find for vegetarian items such as baked eggplant with fresh garlic, baba ganoush, tabouli and hummus. Carnivores may prefer the kabob sandwich, the gyros salad or rotisserie lamb. Entrées range from $4 to $13, with most sandwiches under $5. Open for lunch and dinner Monday through Saturday and until 5 pm Sunday.

Toto's *(☎ 702-895-7923, 2055 E Tropicana Ave)* is where locals go when they want enormous quantities of Mexican food at reasonable prices. Toto's burritos are just a tad smaller than a zeppelin. A shark could live comfortably in a Toto's margarita. The chips are grease-free, and there is plenty of seafood to choose from. Entrées run $7 to $15, with many under $10. Open from 11 am to 10 pm daily.

Wild Oats Community Market *(☎ 702-434-8115, 3455 E Flamingo Rd)* has a small café inside it, and it is at this café that you'll find the best vegetarian food in town. 'Super natural' sandwiches, meatless burritos, vegetarian chili and homemade soups are just a few of the items on Wild Oats' fairly extensive menu. Few items are over $6. Café hours are 10 am to 8 pm daily.

Places to Eat – Mid-Range

Allie's American Grille *(☎ 702-650-2000, in the Marriott Suites at 325 Convention Center Drive)* is a café featuring nouveau Southwestern cuisine. The more popular items include the salmon BLT (a seared salmon steak served on a toasted brioche with pepper bacon, a mustard sauce and fresh lettuce) and a tuna salad consisting of delicious chunks of yellowfin tuna served on a bed of crispy Asian vegetables. Entrées range from $6.50 to $15. Open daily, early till late.

Cozymel's *(☎ 702-732-4833, 355 Hughes Center Drive)* features Mexican coastal fare in a delightful setting. Lunch specials, served weekdays till 4 pm, include fresh fish of the day, chicken or beef fajitas and Cozy Combo (a pork tamale, chicken enchilada, soft beef taco and rice and beans); most items are $7 or less. Dinner items include grilled salmon topped with a delicious cream sauce, and plump shrimp sautéed in garlic lime butter and julienne ancho chilies. Entrées range from $9 to $16. Open 11 am till late daily.

Gordon-Biersch Brewing Company *(☎ 702-312-5247, 3987 Paradise Rd)* is both a brewpub and a popular restaurant featuring good California cuisine. Among the tasty dishes on its extensive menu are peppered ahi tuna, spit-roasted porkloin chops with Creole bread pudding and Moroccan spiced grilled lamb sirloin. The food is as delicious as it sounds. Also available are exotic pizzas cooked in a wood-burning oven. Open daily for lunch and dinner.

Hard Rock Café *(☎ 702-733-8400, 4475 Paradise Rd)* is, like the adjacent Hard Rock Hotel, dripping with rock memorabilia, and the piped-in music ain't classical, unless it's classic Zeppelin, Clapton or Hendrix. The cuisine is predictable (burger, sandwiches, ribs) with a few surprises (among the better ones: the lime barbecued chicken). Entrées range from $6 to $16. Open from 11 am till midnight daily. There's a kids' menu to boot. Rock on!

Kabuki *(☎ 702-733-0066, 1150 E Twain Ave)* is one of the top Japanese restaurants in town. The decor is authentic Japanese, as are most of the clientele, and most of the dishes are fantastic (although the sushi is nothing special). Among the popular choices: Tatsuta Age (marinated chicken) and Zarusoba (cold buckwheat noodles). The potstickers are wonderful. Entrées range from $7.50 to $18. Open for lunch and dinner; closed Sunday.

Komol *(☎ 702-731-6542, 953 E Sahara Ave)* is in a commercial center and easy to write off because of its location, but its Thai and Chinese fare is very good. The dishes are traditional and familiar (Thai beef salad, tom yum goong, beef panang), and they're done just the way you like them. Lovely hand paintings cover the walls, and the service is prompt and friendly. Entrées range from $6 to $16. Open for lunch and dinner daily.

Ricardo's (☎ 702-798-4515, 2380 E Tropicana Ave) is a hacienda-style restaurant featuring roving mariachis, pool-size margaritas and a large offering of traditional Mexican specialties. Ricardo's is known for its sizzling fajitas, but its chili rellenos and carne asada are also divine. If you're really hungry, order one of the combo platters. Entrées run from $6 to $16. Open daily for lunch and dinner.

Shalimar (☎ 702-796-0302, 3900 S Paradise Rd) is known throughout Las Vegas for its terrific North Indian cuisine. Lunch is served buffet-style and is a bargain at $8. The same dishes appear a la carte for dinner. The marinated tandoori chicken is particularly good, and the spicy vindaloo chicken curry is likewise exceptional. Entrées range from $11 to $16. Open for lunch and dinner weekdays, and dinner only on Saturday and Sunday.

Z'Tejas Grill (☎ 702-732-1660, 3824 S Paradise Rd) is a Texas-based restaurant with a real friendly atmosphere and imaginative Southwestern cuisine. Typical entrées include blackened catfish tacos, king salmon brushed with miso glaze and blackened tuna served with a spicy soy sauce. The red-tufted leather and cowhide bar is a good place to be during happy hour (4 to 7 pm weeknights). Entrées range from $8 to $18. Open daily from 11 am to 11 pm.

Places to Eat – Top End

Bistro Le Montrachet (☎ 702-732-5111, in the Las Vegas Hilton) is an elegant restaurant where award-winning contemporary French cuisine is served in a room that's as lovely as a Renoir. In 1995 Bistro Le Montrachet was voted one of the country's top 10 restaurants by the American Academy of Restaurant Sciences. Specialties include medallions of veal, rack of lamb, roast duck, breast of pheasant, all prepared in glorious

sauces. Entrées range from $25 to $35, a la carte. Dinner only; closed Monday and Tuesday.

Gandhi India's Cuisine (☎ 702-734-0094, 4080 Paradise Rd) features excellent Indian food in a colorful and charming atmosphere. Specialties include tandoori chicken, lamb and chicken curries and a host of vegetarian dishes. Big eaters should consider Gandhi's superb lunch buffet, available daily from 11 am till 2:30 pm. Dinner is served daily from 5 to 10:30 pm. Entrées range from $13 to $19. A children's menu is available.

Lawry's The Prime Rib (☎ 702-893-2223, 4043 Howard Hughes Parkway) is king of the Vegas prime rib scene. Although Lawry's also offers fresh fish and lobster, it's the prime rib and accompanying spinning-bowl salad, Yorkshire pudding, mashed potatoes and whipped cream horseradish that has made Lawry's a meat-lover's magnet since the original opened in Los Angeles in 1938. Diners have the option of four cuts, which range in price from $20 to $28. Open daily for dinner only.

McCormick & Schmick's (☎ 702-836-9000, 335 Hughes Center Drive) is an excellent seafood house, perhaps the best in Las Vegas dollar for dollar. McCormick's long list of specialties includes grilled Hawaiian mahi mahi served with a spicy tomato sauce, Oregon dungeness crab cakes served with red pepper aioli and sautéed seafood with Asian vegetables. Entrées range from $14 to $20. Open for lunch and dinner weekdays, dinner only on weekends.

Nippon (☎ 702-735-5565, 101 Convention Center Drive) is the name of the best sushi restaurant in Las Vegas. Here, diners can feast on more than 30 varieties of raw fish or treat themselves to beef sukiyaki or shrimp tempura. The restaurant also makes a mean nabe yaki udon, which consists of shrimp tempura, green onion, Japanese mushrooms, cabbage and a fish cake served in an iron kettle with udon noodles. Entrées run from $15 to $20. Lunch and dinner. Closed Sunday.

Pamplemousse (☎ 702-733-2066, 400 E Sahara Ave) is one of Las Vegas' landmark restaurants, featuring a French Riviera-style

Get pampered at Pamplemousse.

salad (a basket of fresh veggies and vinaigrette house dip), appetizers such as escargots and soft-shell clams, and entrées such as Wisconsin duckling with orange curry sauce. Semiformal to formal attire is required at this romantic hideaway. Entrées range from $18 to $30. Dinner only; closed Monday.

P. F. Chang's (☎ 702-792-2207, 4165 Paradise Rd) is a classy and modern Chinese bistro with lots of artistic touches, from an enormous mural that recreates a mid-12th century narrative screen painting to the inviting menu items. Among Chang's top sellers are lemon pepper shrimp, Cantonese duck and orange peel beef (Szechwan-style beef tossed with red chilies and fresh orange peel). Entrées range from $8 to $13. Open daily for lunch and dinner.

The Tillerman (☎ 702-731-4036, 2245 E Flamingo Rd) is the best seafood restaurant in Las Vegas, with prices to match. Specialties include farm-raised salmon from Norway, Florida red snapper, Australian whole lobster and blackened yellowfin tuna served almost rare in a tangy mustard sauce. Entrées, which range from $20 to $40, include a Lazy Susan salad bar. Open daily for dinner only.

Yolie's Brazilian Steak House (☎ 702-794-0700, 3900 Paradise Rd) is a Brazilian-style steakhouse featuring daily lunch specials from $5 to $13 and fixed-price dinners for $25, which includes your choice of soup or salad followed by a procession of waiters carrying trays of New York sirloin, sausage Ipanema, turkey breast wrapped in bacon and on and on. This is a meat-lover's paradise. Open from 11 am to 11 pm weekdays, and 5 to 11 pm weekends.

WEST OF THE STRIP
Places to Eat – Budget

Applebee's Neighborhood Grill & Bar (☎ 702-878-3399, 4760 W Sahara Ave) offers both a healthy family atmosphere and a substantial pickup bar. Moms and Dads enjoy the affordable prices and kids' menus to keep Johnny and Suzy occupied. Yet unlike some family restaurants, Applebee's food (such as the gourmet burgers and salads) is first rate. Entrées range from $6.50 to $9.50. Open daily for lunch and dinner; Sunday brunch till 3 pm.

Dragon Sushi (☎ 702-368-4336, 4115 Spring Mountain Rd) offers better-than-average sushi at lower-than-average prices. What's also neat about this place is you can rent tatami rooms – private rooms with paper sliding doors, mat-covered floors and a stout table in the center for a mere $10 for groups ranging from two to 20 people. The rooms create a special atmosphere at low cost. Sushi items range from $3.50 to $6 per person. Open daily from 10:30 am till late.

Kilroy's (☎ 702-259-6400, 310 S Decatur Blvd) makes killer burgers. Their hand-formed hamburgers are the kind of dreams: huge, smothered with fresh toppings and very, very tasty. If you find yourself staring at the menu, unable to decide, try the three-cheese mushroom burger; it's awesome. Prices range from $5 to $8. Take note: The kitchen is only open from 11 am to 4 pm. Closed Sunday.

Krispy Kreme (☎ 702-222-2320, 7015 W Spring Mountain Rd) is a doughnut chain – a *really good* doughnut chain. At the heart of Krispy Kreme's operation are melt-in-your-mouth glazed doughnuts. Also heavenly are KK's raspberry- and blueberry-filled doughnuts. Seating is available early till late every day, and there's 24-hour drive-thru service. A box of 12 glazed doughnuts costs $4.50.

Pick Up Stix (☎ 702-636-6600, 2101 N Rainbow Blvd) is a great place to keep in mind if you're on a budget and want to pick up a meal or two to go. Pick Up Stix prepares Chinese wok food to order, and for what you'd pay most anywhere else for one meal you could take home two from Pick Up Stix. Entrées typically run about $5. Open from 11 am to 9 pm daily.

Pizzeria Uno Chicago Bar & Grill (☎ 702-876-8667, 2540 S Decatur Blvd) features original Chicago-style pizza (deep dish, heavy on the sauce), sandwiches, pasta, steak fajitas and chicken entrées. Yes, it's a diverse menu, and a good one. The pizza is available by the slice, which permits low-cost sampling. Entrées range from $6 to $9, with daily lunch specials. Open daily from 11 am till midnight.

Sonia's Café & Rotisserie (☎ 702-870-5090, 3900 W Charleston Blvd) is one of those places that's just plain habit forming. Not only is Sonia's rotisserie chicken the best in town, but her pasta salad and roasted potatoes are fine. And Sonia offers some excellent Mexican specialties to boot. All entrées are well under $10. It's open 11 am to 7:30 pm weekdays, and 11 am to 4 pm Saturday.

Straight From Philly Steakhouse (☎ 702-878-6444, 425 S Decatur Blvd) makes superb cheesesteak sandwiches. All contain the tender meat, gloppy cheese, zesty toppings and firm yet manageable roll you want in a cheesesteak sandwich. Other accomplishments at this none-too-fancy 24-hour diner include delicious meatballs and tasty Italian sausage. Entrées run $5 to $8.

Sweet Tomatoes (☎ 702-648-1957, 2080 N Rainbow Blvd) is a salad and soup establishment that is thriving in a city filled with salad

A glazed slice of heaven

bars. That's because its dressings go well beyond the regular ranch/Italian/thousand island selection, and because the produce is always crispy fresh. The cream of broccoli soup and the chili are delicious as well. The all-you-can-eat salad bar costs $7. Open from 11 am to 9 pm daily.

Places to Eat – Mid-Range

All American Steak House (☎ 702-252-7767, inside the Rio) is a bar and grill specializing in steaks, seafood and pork ribs, which are cooked to order on a mesquite grill at the entrance of a handsome dining room. All entrées come with salad, sourdough bread and vegetables. Burgers and sandwiches are also available. Lunch entrées range from $5 to $8, while dinner entrées run $12 to $26. Open from 11 am to 11 pm daily.

Café Nicolle (☎ 702-870-7675, 4760 W Sahara Ave) offers a yummy variety of entrées including lamb chops, filet mignon with béarnaise sauce and veal piccata. Seating is available inside at black-and-gray Lucite tables accented with brass fixtures, or outside amid swaying palm trees and lovely flower boxes on a variously mist-cooled or heated patio. Entrées, which come with a choice of salad, range from $9 to $19. Open for lunch and dinner. Closed Sunday.

Fiore (☎ 702-252-7777, *inside the Rio*) is a semiformal restaurant with superb cuisine in a dining room that boasts an exhibition kitchen and dramatic windows overlooking a lush pool area. Although the menu changes seasonally, expect to see creative presentations of beef, veal, pork, ostrich and buffalo. Seafood offerings might include pan-seared striped bass with lobster sauce or grilled Maine lobster stuffed with wild mushroom risotto. Entrées range from $26 to $50. Open daily for dinner only.

Joe's Crab Shack (☎ 702-646-3996, *1991 N Rainbow Blvd*) is a great find for seafood lovers on a budget. Specialties include coconut shrimp, king crab legs, blue and Alaskan snow crabs, red lobster and even fish and chips. The atmosphere is fun – the setting resembles a fishing shack and the servers are rather entertaining. Entrées range from $10 to $20. Open daily for lunch and dinner.

Petite Provence (☎ 702-248-7272, *3715 S Decatur Blvd*) is a semiformal family restaurant serving authentic Provence cuisine such as rack of lamb and coq au vin at reasonable prices. All of the furnishings were imported from France, and the staff treats diners with a degree of friendliness not often found at French restaurants. Entrées range from $10 to $28, with most around $15. Open for lunch and dinner. Closed Sunday.

Prommare's Thai Food (☎ 702-221-9644, *6362 W Sahara Ave*) serves some of the best Thai food in Nevada, but you do pay handsomely for it. House specialties include catfish smothered in a tangy sauce, crab, squid and a variety of curries. Entrées start at $10. Open 11 am to 10 pm Monday and Wednesday through Saturday, and 5 to 10 pm Sunday. Closed Tuesday.

Thai Spice (☎ 702-362-5308, *4433 W Flamingo Rd*) is a favorite among locals, who generally come in for the excellent pad thai noodle, Siamese duckling and the lemon chicken. Specialties can be ordered on a heat scale from 1 to 10. The lunch special, which includes salad, soup, spring rolls and steamed rice with a choice of entrée, runs $6. Dinner entrées range from $7.50 to $15. Closed Sunday.

Viva Mercados (☎ 702-871-8826, *6182 W Flamingo Rd*) serves traditional homemade Mexican food without all the artery-clogging lard used south of the border. Only heart-friendly canola oil is used here, and the chili rellenos, steak asada and enchiladas poblanos taste great all the same. The portions are large, the food is fresh and tasty and the service friendly. Entrées range from $8 to $18. Open for lunch and dinner daily.

Places to Eat – Top End

Antonio's (☎ 702-252-7737, *inside the Rio*) serves sumptuous Northern Italian cuisine in a stylish Mediterranean atmosphere replete with inlaid marble floors and pillars and a domed faux sky. Appetizers include a paper-thin carpaccio with shaved parmesan cheese and a five-onion soup served in a hollowed-out onion. There are plenty of pastas available. Veal lovers will want to sample the fork-tender osso bucco, served on a bed of saffron-infused risotto. Entrées range from $18 to $50. Open daily for dinner only.

Garlic Café (☎ 702-221-0266, *3650 S Decatur Blvd*) features dishes from around the world that contain varying amounts of its namesake herb, which is grown for its glorious pungent bulbs. How much garlic is up to you; the scale ranges from 1 (for one head of garlic) to 5 (for five heads). The food is about average in quality, quantity and price, but the experience is altogether fun. Don't forget to try the garlic ice cream for dessert. Entrées run from $10 to $30. Open daily for dinner only.

Hungry Hunter (☎ 702-873-0433, *2380 S Rainbow Blvd*) is the local favorite for steaks, such as the restaurant's signature Whiskey Peppercorn Filet. But Hungry Hunter also offers a fine rack of lamb, grilled swordfish and even pressed duck. There's a children's menu to help keep family costs down, and dress is casual. Entrées range from $13 to $33. Open for lunch and dinner weekdays, dinner only on weekends.

Ruth's Chris Steak House (☎ 702-248-7011, *4561 W Flamingo Rd*) is *the* place to go when you're looking for high-quality beef, especially in the wee hours of the night.

Served amid elegant brass and etched glass, Ruth's Chris steaks come only from selected Midwestern corn-fed beef. Entrées range from $19 to $34. A special late-night menu featuring a selection of lighter choices, including pasta, is available after 11 pm. Open from 4:30 pm to 3 am daily.

DOWNTOWN
Places to Eat – Budget
Binion's Horseshoe Coffee Shop (☎ 702-382-1600, inside Binion's Horseshoe, 128 E Fremont St) is the Las Vegas coffee shop of yesteryear – a place where it's still possible to get a hearty breakfast for under $5 and a 16oz T-bone steak for under $8. In fact, very little at the coffee shop sells for more than $10, which is one reason it's so popular with locals. Open 24 hours.

Old-fashioned prices rule at Binion's.

Carson Street Café (☎ 702-385-1111, inside the Golden Nugget) is a semi-elegant coffee shop with surprisingly good food. Although a tad pricier than Binion's coffee shop, the café produces superior sandwiches, Mexican fare, filet mignon and prime rib. And for dessert Carson Street features a slew of delectable sundaes. All bar drinks

are available (the same can be said for Binion's), and the café never closes.

Center Stage (☎ 702-386-2110, inside Jackie Gaughan's Plaza) offers diners mediocre food but semicircular booths that overlook the Fremont Street Experience and afford excellent people watching. Center Stage is a particularly good place to be when the crowds are thick, since from its second-story position overlooking the pedestrian mall it's hard not to feel you're on top of the world. However, the typical coffee-shop food is nothing special and the entrées are overpriced at $6 to $16. Open daily for dinner only.

Dona Maria Tamales (☎ 702-382-6538, 910 S Las Vegas Blvd) is a pleasant, family-run cantina specializing in a variety of tasty chicken, cheese, beef and pork tamales. Also available are made-to-order enchiladas, burritos, tacos and chimichangas. Entrées range from $5.50 to $8.50. Open daily for breakfast, lunch and dinner.

Enigma Garden Café (☎ 702-386-0999, 918 4th St) features a 24-hour menu of health-oriented egg dishes, sandwiches, salads and Middle Eastern specialties served in the patio of a converted house turned hippie pad. Expect poetry readings or live music between 7 and 10 pm. Most everything is well under $10. There's a cappuccino machine on the grounds.

Rincon Criollo (☎ 702-388-1906, 1145 S Las Vegas Blvd) is a no-frills locals hangout with some very tasty Cuban offerings; among the better ones are the Cuban sandwich (mostly ham, roast pork and cheese on bread toasted and pressed flat), marinated pork leg and chorizo (spicy sausage). Many items are under $5. Open for lunch and dinner. Closed Monday.

Places to Eat – Mid-Range
Tony Roma's: A Place for Ribs (☎ 702-385-3232, in the casino area of the Fremont) is an informal, very popular restaurant specializing in barbecued baby back ribs, ribs served with a variety of sauces, and barbecued shrimp and broiled chicken. Entrées range from $7 to $14, with most around $10. Dinner only daily.

Places to Eat – Top End

Andre's (☎ 702-385-5016, 401 S 6th St) is yet more proof that you don't have to go to one of the megaresorts on The Strip to enjoy superb cuisine in Las Vegas. Inside this converted 1930s house you can enjoy excellent Dover sole served à la facon du chef, stuffed pork tenderloin with apple and walnuts, marinated salmon tartare and Maryland blue crab cakes, to name a few of the many French entrées that are offered. Entrée prices range from $20 to $28. Open daily for dinner only.

Hugo's Cellar (☎ 702-385-4011, inside the Four Queens, 202 E Fremont St) is an elegant brick-and-brass restaurant where each female diner is presented a red rose, and the salads, which are included in the price of the entrées, are prepared tableside. Specialties include tournedos Hugo, roast rack of lamb, broiled swordfish and veal. For dessert, say yes to the chocolate-dipped fruits served with whipped cream. Entrée prices range from $25 to $50. Open daily for dinner only.

Limerick's (☎ 702-388-2460, inside Fitzgerald's, 301 E Fremont St) is the product of a 1996 renovation that transformed a forgotten diner into a posh steakhouse decked out like a British gentlemen's club. Meat is the mainstay, and it comes big and tender.

Particularly good is the beef Wellington and the filet mignon. The apricot chicken is likewise memorable. Entrées range from $7 to $17, which is quite competitive considering the portions and the quality. Open daily for dinner only.

The Pullman Grille (☎ 702-387-1896, at Main Street Station) is a well-kept secret. The restaurant features the finest Black Angus beef and seafood specialties in addition to an extensive wine list. The food is excellent, but equally memorable is the setting. Most of the gorgeous carved wood paneling that surrounds patrons was originally from the Prestwick Castle in Scotland. The centerpiece of the restaurant is a Pullman train car built in 1926 for Louisa Alcott; it was one of only four car series named after famous women authors. Entrées range from $14 to $18 for meat dishes, and $18 to $40 for seafood. Dinner only; closed Monday and Tuesday.

Second Street Grille (☎ 702-385-3232, inside the Fremont) is a great find, an intimate, semiformal and generally overlooked restaurant with wonderful international cuisine with a Hawaiian influence. Specialties include wok-charred salmon, lobster, ahi tuna and filet mignon. Veal, chicken and beef dishes are also available. Entrées range from $18 to $35. Open daily for dinner only.

Entertainment

Las Vegas isn't widely regarded as the entertainment capital of the world for nothing. The city is famous for its showgirls, its lounge acts, its illusionists, its championship fights, its headliner performances by some of today's biggest stars and, of course, for its standard-setting gaming houses.

But in recent years Las Vegas has also become a major venue for music concerts, amusement rides, nightclubbing, acrobatic performances, virtual-reality arcades, circus acts and impressive outdoor attractions – for want of a better name – such as the regularly erupting volcano at The Mirage, the light shows on Fremont Street and the pirate battles outside Treasure Island.

A person can go broke seeing and doing all there is to see and do in Las Vegas, but a person can also see and do a lot in Sin City at little or no cost. The choices seem almost infinite, with new shows, new venues and new sites opening all the time. In the Things To See & Do chapter, you'll find information on casinos, museums, arcades and rides, outdoor attractions and other sites. Here you'll find information on the more typical forms of nighttime entertainment – dance clubs, bars, music venues, production shows, performances and cinema – as well as all of the spectator sports available in Las Vegas.

Most of Las Vegas' bars are open round the clock. The hours of the dance clubs vary from club to club and season to season, with most closed Sunday and Monday. It's best to call ahead, not only for times but for music news as well. A club that was featuring rock 'n' roll when this was written may have turned to hip-hop or something else by the time these words reach you. Nothing remains the same for very long in Las Vegas.

Biggest Bangs for the Buck

Dance Clubs	The Beach
	Drink!
	Ra
Straight Bars	The Bar at Times Square
	Double Down Saloon
Gay Bars	The Gipsy
	Angles
Bars with a View	Top of the World Lounge
	VooDoo Lounge
Sports Bars	All-Star Café
	Sneakers
Production Shows	Cirque du Soleil's O
	Cirque du Soleil's Mystère
Rock Venues	The Joint
	House of Blues
Jazz Venue	Rum Jungle
Blues Venue	Sand Dollar Blues Lounge
Cinemas	Caesars Omnimax Theater
	Century Orleans

The view from the VooDoo Lounge

THE STRIP
Dance Clubs

The dance clubs found inside the megaresorts along the spectacular Las Vegas Strip are a Hollywood set designer's dream. Seemingly no expense has been spared to bring Las Vegas on par with New York and Los Angeles in the area of wildly extravagant and exceedingly hot dance clubs.

One of the most unusual dance clubs in Las Vegas is *Cleopatra's Barge Nightclub* (☎ *702-731-7110, inside Caesars Palace)*, which is an imposing floating cocktail lounge that is a replica of one of the majestic ships that sailed the Nile in ancient Egypt. A hydraulics system constantly raises and lowers the boat to mimic sailing. The ornate vessel is replete with oars, furled sails and a canopied bow. Out front of the stationary rock 'n' roll boat is a bare-breasted figurehead that could use a little touching up on account of all the dirty old passers-by who've copped a feel (life as a bare-breasted figurehead isn't all that it's cracked up to

be). There's no cost to board Cleopatra's Barge, but there is a two-drink minimum. Due to the relatively small size of the vessel – after all, this isn't a replica of the Titanic (hey, Mr Wynn, there's an idea!) – there are few places to sit aboard the swaying nightclub, although there are a few more tables set around the boat on terra firma. Even so, if you were hoping to chat at CB's, forget it; the music's turned up for dancing.

While most of the dance clubs along The Strip cater strictly to tourists, the industrial-size *Monte Carlo Pub & Brewery* (☎ *702-730-7777, inside the Monte Carlo)* is popular mostly with twenty- and thirtysomething locals – after sundown, that is. As its name suggests, the Monte Carlo is mostly a pub and brewery. The warehouselike establishment is, by day, a restaurant serving pizzas, salads, sandwiches, steaks and its own beers, brewed in huge copper barrels; at night, the creature transforms into a heaving, pulsating dance club. The blaring music is variously live or spun, but there's always something to dance to starting around 10 pm. More of a couch potato than a Fred Astaire? Well, for you, there are three dozen TV monitors and one big-screen TV on the premises that are tuned to sports during the day and rock vids after dark. There's no cover charge or drink minimum, but a dress code (no strategically ripped clothing, T-shirts or gangsta pants) is enforced.

The most spectacular dance club in Las Vegas is *Ra* (☎ *702-262-4000, inside Luxor)*, which takes its name from the ancient Egyptian god of the sun, who was said to travel through the heavens by day and rage in the underworld at night. Today, a possible likeness of this winged, radiating god towers over the nightclub's primary bar: Ra sits upon a golden throne, has a 30-foot wingspan and lights up the club with a dozen fire-green lasers that beam from its sunken eye sockets. The Old Egypt theme is heavily applied throughout the club, beginning with the entryway – a stunning marble-and-sandstone corridor lined with statues of Egyptian gods and guards. The interior is rectangular, with the main bar at one end, a bandstand built into one of the long walls

DAVID PEEVERS

It's not Sin City for nothing.

and the dance floor in front of the stage. Flanking the bandstand are cages containing go-go girls in red-velvet bikinis. Scattered about the club are VIP booths and cigar lounges. Although the music at Ra is mostly furnished by disc jockeys, it occasionally hosts big-name bands. Blue jeans, ripped trousers and collarless shirts aren't allowed. Admission is generally $10.

Like a bad remake of a great film, **Studio 54** (☎ 702-895-1111, inside the MGM Grand) doesn't capture the magic that existed at New York's legendary Studio 54. For one thing, the original attracted a classy clientele – or at least a well-dressed one. No matter how the people inside behaved, they weren't kicking around in blue jeans and looking like they'd spent the day slumped over slot machines. This Studio 54 does have a dress code – no T-shirts, no gangsta-baggy pants, no tank tops, no work boots and no sandals – but in reality it rarely denies admission to anyone. Which makes the club's red-rope practice a tad ridiculous. What you find inside are mostly casually dressed tourists wondering where the glamorous people went. The club, by the way, is huge – three stories, with four dance floors, four bars, semiprivate lounges and a gallery of celebrity photos taken at the original Studio 54. The decor is black, silver and industrial; the music always DJ-driven chart toppers. Women get in free, men pay $10.

With the name **Utopia** (☎ 702-736-3105, 3765 S Las Vegas Blvd), this place had better be good, and most nights it's *very* good. Generally open Tuesday through Saturday from 11 pm on, Utopia features something different every night. On Tuesday, it's canned rhythm & blues or hip-hop, Wednesday night is ladies night (women drink free and get in free), Thursday it's progressive house music, and Friday and Saturday it's live music (usually hip-hop, hard rock and/or funk). As you might have guessed, Utopia caters to Generation Xers. If you haven't yet been appropriately pierced, tattooed or branded – and know no one else who has been either – you'll probably feel as comfortable here as a soda jerk in an English gentlemen's club. Cover charge ranges from $5 to $10.

Bars

Every megaresort on The Strip has several bars in addition to numerous restaurants that offer a full palette of alcoholic beverages. Drinks are available in casinos to persons 21 and older at all hours, due to Nevada's liberal drinking laws. Most of the bars boast 2-for-1 happy hours, which generally run from 4 to 6 pm or 5 to 7 pm, with times varying from one establishment to another.

The vast majority of Sin City's bars are smoke filled; the antismoking laws in neighboring California banning cigarette, pipe and cigar smoking in all public facilities are viewed with heartfelt disgust, disdain and indignation in Las Vegas and won't likely be adopted by the city any time soon. If smoke doesn't bother you or you can at least cope with it, you'll likely enjoy your time in the bars mentioned here.

The **Bar at Times Square** (☎ 702-796-6969, inside New York-New York) is possibly the liveliest bar in Las Vegas. Every night the pub fills to overflowing as not one but two singing pianists lead a raucous crowd through old favorites. This is the kind of place where young and old alike raise their steins and their voices in camaraderie, where they dance between the tables, and where latecomers press their faces against the windows to catch a glimpse of the festivities taking place inside. There's never a cover charge or a drink minimum at the Bar at Times Square, but you've got to arrive early if you want to get inside. Arrive late and you'll have to wait for someone to leave before you can enter. And at this fun place, that could be a while.

The **Glass Pool Lounge** (☎ 702-739-6800, 4611 S Las Vegas Blvd) could be better named (the pool isn't glass-sided or glass-bottomed), but there *is* a swimming pool involved (ah, nothing like mixing drinking and swimming to test one's luck!). The object after which the bar takes its name is a raised, concrete-sided outdoor swimming pool. All around it are porthole windows that permit total strangers to gape at your mostly naked body as you splash around. Hey, as they say in Vegas, if you've got it, baby, flaunt it. The pool is open during the spring and summer. Inside the Glass Pool Lounge, the walls are covered with photos of celebrities wearing bikinis, and during the day the cocktail waitresses show a lot of cheek and make their rounds in – you got it – bikinis. For this reason, the lounge is also known locally as the Bikini Café. If you're hungry for a burrito at 3 am, remember this place: burritos, breakfast, tacos, burgers, even kosher sandwiches are served round the clock.

Holy Cow! (☎ *702-732-2697, 2423 S Las Vegas Blvd)* is a microbrewery and a restaurant, and it's what you might say when you enter the establishment. Holy Cow! is a shrine to all things bovine – exalting Herefords, Holsteins and Brafords and awash in cow photos, cow graphic art, tacky cow sayings ('Bucky sez ... moo for a brew'), cow-patterned lamps, cow-shaped statues and giant cow cutouts. The menu has even more cow, with the patty melt, beef-dip sandwich and burgers coming recommended. It's udderly fantastic! You can bet your ear tag on that. But amid the rodeo of things cowlike don't overlook the Amber Gambler pale ale or the Vegas Gold wheat beer, both of which have taken top honors at major beer competitions. Open 24 hours.

For a very romantic atmosphere, settle into the *Fireside Lounge at the Peppermill* (☎ *702-735-7635, 2985 S Las Vegas Blvd)*, where couples can get cozy and have intimate conversations in plush, dimly lit red-velvet booths. Most of the dozen or so booths are separated by plants, which increase privacy in a subtle and soothing way. The carpet is jet black, as are the form-fitting dresses of the cocktail waitresses who serve the lounge (it's a tradition). The Fireside Lounge is also known for its circular fire-on-water fireplace; gas rising from the depths of a Jacuzzi-resembling tub ignite at the water's surface, creating flames that are simply spellbinding after a couple of piña coladas and several fistfuls of honey-sweetened peanuts (they're free and generously provided). The lounge serves lots of tropical concoctions such as blue Hawaiians, tequila sunrises and mai tais, and all are rea-

sonably priced and arrive in bowl-glasses large enough for gold fish. The background music is unintrusive and easy listening. Tasty appetizers such as nachos and deep-fried potato skins are also available.

Whereas the Fireside Lounge is a favorite with locals, the bar at *Planet Hollywood* (☎ *702-791-7827, inside The Forum Shops at Caesars Palace)* is almost exclusively patronized by tourists. Yeah, okay, it *is* pretty cool, for guys anyway – guys who like macho killing-machine cyborgs from the future. At every turn there's a prop from an Arnold Schwarzenegger movie, and we're not talking about those 'family movies' in which the 64-time Mr Galaxy plays a lovable kindergarten teacher or the larger, near-identical twin of Danny DeVito. As Dennis Hopper might say, '*Terminator*, man, *Terminator*.' If you're a fan of the Big Bad Arnold and would like to tip a cold one in the shadow of a violence-prone robot who cannot be stopped, there's a seat in the bar just waiting for you.

A not-so-lonely Planet

A bar that's considerably more sedate is *The Polo Lounge* (☎ 702-261-1000, 3745 S Las Vegas Blvd, atop the Polo Towers). The lounge is mid-Strip and offers captivating views of Las Vegas Boulevard even though it's only 19 floors up – or a full 88 floors lower than the sky-high bar inside the Stratosphere Tower. Its decorator went way overboard with the black paint; the entire place is jet black, which perhaps makes it look thinner. Who knows what the decorator was thinking!? A duet performs easy-listening music Thursday through Sunday nights, and there's rarely a cover charge. Now, if only they would flush some of the cigarette smoke out of the air. Ventilation is not one of the lounge's strong suits. You've been warned.

Like to listen to music and get high? There's no place in Las Vegas where you can get higher without the approval of an air traffic controller than the Stratosphere's *Top of the World Lounge* (☎ 702-380-7711, on the 107th floor of the Stratosphere). Every night beginning about sundown a pianist provides easy listening music in the 220-seat cocktail lounge that overlooks the revolving restaurant on the 106th floor and, beyond the restaurant, Las Vegas from an eagle's point of view. There's rarely a cover (New Year's Eve being an exception), but there is a $6 fee to take the elevator to the lounge. The lounge is generally open till midnight or thereabouts.

Production Shows

Las Vegas offers the visitor more production shows – that is, shows typically including a variety of song, dance and magic numbers that don't follow a story line – than any other city in the world. Leaving Sin City without seeing one is like leaving Paris without seeing Notre Dame – it's surely some kind of crime. But don't just see any show. Las Vegas has got some great ones, some terrible ones and lots that fall somewhere in between.

American Superstars (☎ 702-380-7777, 800-998-6937, at Stratosphere) is one of the many Vegas shows featuring celebrity impersonators, in this case five performers

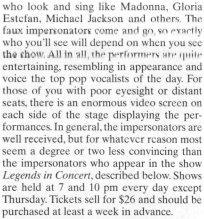

The Money in Magic

Ever wonder how much a big-name magician is paid? In 1998, world-renowned illusionist David Copperfield, who occasionally performs in Las Vegas, earned $49.5 million. That placed him at No 20 on the list of best-paid celebrities in the US for that year.

Among the rich and famous whose names appeared beneath Copperfield's were actors Eddie Murphy ($47.5 million), John Travolta ($47 million) and Tom Hanks ($44 million); author and director Stephen King ($40 million); race car driver Michael Schumacher ($38 million); hockey player Sergei Federov ($29.8 million); golfer Tiger Woods ($26.8 million); basketball player Grant Hill ($21.6 million); TV and radio host Howard Stern ($20 million); and boxer Oscar de la Hoya ($18.5 million).

who look and sing like Madonna, Gloria Estefan, Michael Jackson and others. The faux impersonators come and go, so exactly who you'll see will depend on when you see the show. All in all, the performers are quite entertaining, resembling in appearance and voice the top pop vocalists of the day. For those of you with poor eyesight or distant seats, there is an enormous video screen on each side of the stage displaying the performances. In general, the impersonators are well received, but for whatever reason most seem a degree or two less convincing than the impersonators who appear in the show *Legends in Concert*, described below. Shows are held at 7 and 10 pm every day except Thursday. Tickets sell for $26 and should be purchased at least a week in advance.

Not content to bring yet another topless revue or magic show to Vegas, Mandalay Bay presents the six-time Tony Award-winning musical *Chicago* (☎ 702-632-7580, 877-632-7400, at Mandalay Bay). The show's run in the resort's 1700-seat theater heralds the arrival of a top-tier Broadway production committed to a lengthy engagement in Sin City. The musical is based on the 1926 play by Maurine Dallas Watkins, but with a plot that could be ripped from today's headlines. Two-time Tony Award-winner Chita Rivera plays a nightclub dancer who kills her lover and then hires Chicago's shrewdest lawyer, who ultimately turns her crime into celebrity headlines and gets his client acquitted. Also starring with Rivera is Tony- and Emmy-winner Ben Vereen. Tickets run $65, $75 and $90. Performances are held at 7:30 pm on Tuesday, Thursday and Friday. Shows are 7 and 10:30 pm on Wednesday and Saturday. Dark Sunday and Monday. Buy your tickets in advance.

To call **Crazy Girls** (☎ *702-794-9433, 800-634-6753, at the Riviera*) nothing but a titty show gussied up with costumes, props and sets to pass as something of value would be wrong; after all, between the lip-synched tits-and-ass numbers there *is* a stand-up comedian who comes out and tells funny jokes. These showgirls can't dance or sing, but five minutes into the show, it's clear that's not why they were hired. There isn't much to recommend this show. On the one hand, if you want a little actual entertainment mixed in with your procession of showgirls, there are several other much better revues; on the other, if all you want is to look at naked women, you'll get much better value for the money at one of the city's many strip joints. Shows are held at 8:30 and 10:30 pm every day but Monday. Tickets sell for $24 and include two beverages.

Nine-time Tony Award-winner Tommy Tune is the star around which **EFX** (☎ *702-891-7777, 800-929-1111, at the MGM Grand*) revolves, and his abilities as an actor-singer-dancer are astounding. Supporting him is a talented and superbly choreographed cast, as well as $40 million in truly spectacular props, sets and special effects ('EFX' is a film industry term for special effects). *EFX* takes the audience on a musical journey through space and time during which Tune, a regular Joe who's lost his imagination, is able to assume the personas of Harry Houdini, H.G. Wells and King Arthur in order to rediscover his powers of imagination. The story line allows the seamless inclusion of wonderful special effects while introducing one well-delivered song, dance, acrobatic and magical number after another. This is a show everyone enjoys. Tickets sell

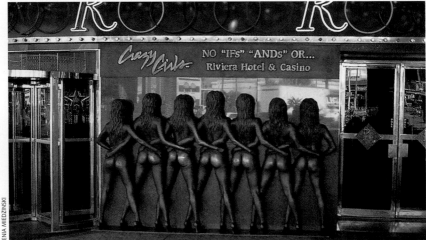

That's one way to keep your brass polished.

for $51 or $72. Shows are at 7:30 and 10:30 pm, Tuesday through Saturday; dark Sunday and Monday. Reserve your seat in advance.

There's more or less one thought on everyone's mind as they leave the variety show *Enter the Night* (☎ 702-732-6325, 800-824-6033, at the Stardust): *That* was weird, but fun. With uncanny clumsiness, the show moves from one topless routine to another, occasionally injecting into the show acts that actually require some semblance of skill. Fortunately, *Night's* many talent-lacking topless numbers are overshadowed by powerful vocals from Jennifer Page, a humorous and captivating performance by an Argentinean folk-dance troupe and thrilling and daring moves by former champion ice skaters Cindy Landry and Burt Lancon on what has to be the world's smallest rink. All in all, it's a pretty good show for the money ($35 for regular seats, $40 for slightly better seats, $50 for the best; the price includes two drinks). Shows begin at 7:30 and 10:30 pm Tuesday, Wednesday, Thursday and Saturday, and at 8 pm Sunday and Monday. There's no show on Friday. Buy your ticket at least three days in advance.

If you haven't been to a female-impersonator revue yet, *An Evening at La Cage* (☎ 702-794-9433, 800 634 6753, at the Riviera) will be a pleasant surprise. The show features an extremely likeable Frank Marino as a catty Joan Rivers, who dispenses naughty jokes and remarks between mostly lip-synched impersonations of Madonna, Diana Ross, Cher, Judy Garland and others. The show has the potential to flop big-time, but instead it rides to a well-deserved standing ovation on the basis of rock-solid choreography, very believable performances by the drag queens and some top-notch work by supporting female dancers (at times it's difficult differentiating the men from the women). A Las Vegas revue featuring drag queens may not appeal to everyone, but few people leave *An Evening at La Cage* without a smile on their face. The ticket prices of $30 or $35 include two drinks. Shows begin at 7:30 and 9:30 pm, Wednesday through Monday, with a third show at 11:15 pm Wednesday and Saturday. There's no show on Tuesday. Buy your tickets at least three days in advance.

Las Vegas' longest-running production show, *Folies Bergère* (☎ 702-739-2411, 800-468-9494, at the Tropicana), is a tribute to the Parisian Music Hall. Appropriately, it contains the most beautiful showgirls in town. So far so good. The story line consists of presenting a 'France through the years,' from the end of the 19th century to Y2K; among the numbers are a French fashion show, a royal ballroom number and the inevitable can-can routine. The show is entertaining for the most part, but the obviously forced introduction of bare breasts – they appear when they're least appropriate, such as during an en-pointe ballet sequence – doesn't have the effect that's intended. Instead, like *Enter the Night*, you start feeling that the director thinks so little of the audience that with just the right number of breasts the show will be a real crowd pleaser. Still, the show has its moments, quite a few in fact, and the finale is definitely worth sticking around for. Tickets are available for $50 and $60. Showtimes are 8 and 10:30 pm, Friday through Wednesday. Closed Thursday.

In *The Great Radio City Music Spectacular* (☎ 702 733 3333, 800 221 7299, at the Flamingo Hilton), the Radio City Rockettes pay tribute to New York's Radio City Music Hall with numerous high-kicking numbers. Accompanying this world-famous chorus line is Paige O'Hara, who provided the lovable voice of Belle in Disney's animated classic *Beauty and the Beast*. If O'Hara is still performing in the show when you're in town, don't miss her. However, regardless of who the headliner is at the center of this high-kicking storm (and it changes fairly frequently), the dance numbers performed by the Rockettes are so strong you're bound to see a good show. In addition to the ladies and the headliner, there are several amusing variety acts, including a juggler, a magician and a trained-dog act that everyone warms to. Tickets for the 7:45 pm dinner show start at $56; tickets for the 10:30 pm cocktail show (Saturday and Monday only) cost $49 each and include two drinks. The show is dark on Friday.

There's never a dull moment at *Imagine: A Theatrical Odyssey* (☎ *702-262-4400, 800-288-1000, at Luxor*). The show doesn't have much of a plot; instead it consists of a combination of dancing, illusions, clowns, acrobats, Chinese jugglers and a hodgepodge of others in a fast-paced show with a fairly big wow factor. The music is heart-thumping, constantly shifting among different styles. Though similar to Cirque du Soleil's *Mystére* in many ways, *Imagine* isn't nearly as good. However, at $40 *Imagine* is about half the price and an excellent value. Shows start at 7 pm Sunday, 7:30 and 9:30 pm Tuesday and Saturday, and 8:30 pm Wednesday through Friday; dark Monday. Get your tickets early.

Vegas wouldn't be Vegas without *Jubilee!* (☎ *702-739-4567, 800-237-7469, at Bally's*). The long-running show opens with a huge topless routine with the showgirls in classic showgirl attire (the huge, feathered headdresses, the sequined bikini bottoms) and the men in tuxedos and later in G-strings. Each number is quite visually appealing, with tremendously colorful outfits and marvelous sets. The voices, by and large, are so-so, and the dancers aren't always in step. Clearly the audience is supposed to be so dazzled by the spectacular costumes and sets and the sheer number of people on stage that it's not supposed to notice the mediocre singing or dancing. Instead, we're supposed to look on in total awe as the *Titanic* sinks and other impressive props come and go. And as it started, so does it end: with lots of nipples and twinkling rhinestones on display. If you're of the opinion that big is always beautiful, you'll love this show, since every number's a big one. But a little less quantity and a little more quality in the talent department wouldn't hurt. Tickets go for $50 to $66. Shows begin at 7:30 pm Tuesday and Sunday, and at 7:30 and 10:30 pm Monday, Wednesday, Thursday and Saturday. Closed Friday.

You've got to be wired a certain kind of way to appreciate *King Arthur's Tournament* (☎ *702-597-7600, 800-933-1334, at Excalibur*). First off, it's not a cocktail show

COMPLIMENTS *JUBILEE!*

Jubilee! puts on a really BIG show.

but a dinner show where guests are expected to eat the medieval way – with their fingers. Second, the show demands audience participation. Armor-clad knights joust and battle with swords in the arena before you, and you're encouraged time and again to pound on the table and shout words of support to your designated knight. The constant encouragement to shout aloud and pound on the table is popular with kids, but it gets stale quickly for everyone else. There are magic acts and singing as well, but for the money, you can do better. Tickets run $42. The show starts at 6 and 8:30 pm every night. Buy your tickets at least three days in advance.

There are lots of illusionists in Las Vegas, but few are as engaging and talented as *Lance Burton: Master Magician* (*702-730-7160, 800-311-8999, at Monte Carlo*). He has several grand illusions, including his signature 'flying' white Corvette. But Burton differs from Siegfried and Roy and others by emphasizing sleight-of-hand tricks and other close-up magic involving disappearing birds and whatnot. And instead of moving about the stage in a heightened state of alert like most magicians, Kentucky-raised Burton is attractively low-key in his delivery. The juxtaposition of his mellow manner with his mind-boggling feats makes what he's doing all the more enjoyable. Adding excitement and laughs to Burton's show is Michael Goudeau, who juggles the most unusual objects. At $35 or $40 apiece ($40 for slightly better seats), Burton's tickets are a great value, and the $27-million theater built for the magician hasn't a bad seat – just what you'd expect from the people behind Circus Circus and Bellagio. Burton performs at 7 and 10 pm Tuesday through Saturday; dark Sunday and Monday. Purchase your tickets early.

The best of the impersonator shows is **Legends in Concert** (☎ 702-794-3261, 800-634-6441, *at Imperial Palace*), which has been around since 1983 and will likely be around for years to come. The award-winning cocktail show features performers who must not only look like famous vocalists such as Elton John, Neil Diamond, Prince and Dolly Parton, but they must sound like them as well; no lip-synching is allowed. The acts frequently change, but the quality doesn't. Adding to the show's appeal are well-choreographed male and female dancers, who appear in most of the acts. On one particular night, the evening started with a con-

vincing Gloria Estefan getting the crowd in the mood with several hits, then it segued into a very likeable Rod Stewart who upped the heat with a scalding rendition of 'Hot Legs,' and then it progressed to Diana Ross, Garth Brooks, Tina Turner and the Four Tops. While the impersonators sing former chart toppers and do it amazingly well, large video screens on both sides of the stage show not only the live action but also clips of the real performers in concert; the screens add a lot to the entertainment value of *Legends*, which is already one of the biggest crowd pleasers in town. Capping the series of acts most nights is a trim young Elvis (not the fat older one of the 1970s), who brings back fond memories and is among the town's best Elvis impersonators. An almost tangible, collective heartbreak occurs in the hotel every time the curtain closes on Elvis. Tickets cost $35 and include two drinks. Shows start at 7:30 and 10:30 pm Monday through Saturday. Buy your tickets early.

Franco Dragone, director of the Cirque du Soleil production **Mystère** (☎ 702-894-7722, 800-944-7444, *at Treasure Island*), describes his show as a celebration of life. It begins with a pair of babies making their way in a world filled with strange creatures and brilliant colors, a misguided clown who can bring this smooth running production

Legends in Concert at Imperial Palace

COMPLIMENTS IMPERIAL PALACE

COMPLIMENTS AL SEIB

Cirque du Soleil's *Mystère*

to a halt with his humorous antics, and acro-bats, dancers and musicians who display remarkable and at times nearly unbelievable talent. *Mystère* features one spectacular feat of human strength and agility after another, often suspended over the audience and per-formed by people in costumes like you've never seen before. The show is entertain-ment at its finest. Tickets are pricey at $70 for adults and half that for children under 11, but they're worth every penny. Shows begin at 7:30 and 10:30 pm Wednesday through Sunday. Purchase your ticket in advance, as the shows are usually sold out.

Steve Wynn, chairman of the company that owns Bellagio, is quoted in a media guide about the resort as saying, 'We had to produce an entertainment experience that people would talk about in Singapore, Rome, Hong Kong, London, New York and Buenos Aires.' After searching the globe, Wynn and company approached Montreal-based Cirque du Soleil about producing a show worthy of the most expensive hotel on Earth. The result was *O* (☎ *702-693-7722, 888-987-6667, at Bellagio)*, which, phoneti-cally speaking, is the French word for water (spelled 'eau'). With an international cast of

74, performing in, on and above water, *O* tells the tale of theater through the ages. The show features daring displays of aerial acrobatics and synchronized swimming. Cirque du Soleil's first venture into aquatic theater is a spectacular feat of imagination and engineering. It is indeed the kind of entertainment that has people talking about it in cities around the planet. Tickets sell for $90 and $100, and are a great value at that. Performances are at 7:30 and 10:30 pm Friday through Tuesday; dark Wednesday and Thursday. Buy your tickets early. Every show is sold out.

The illusionists *Siegfried & Roy* (☎ *702-792-7777, 800-627-6667, at The Mirage)* have been performing sold-out shows in Las Vegas for more than two decades, and they remain the hottest ticket in town – though they aren't the best ticket in town. The Aus-trians made a name for themselves with their charm, their illusions and their white tigers, but today's *Siegfried & Roy* contains so many special effects and showgirls and props, usually simultaneously, that it's a bit overwhelming. Instead of feeling thoroughly impressed by the magic, one cannot help but feel somewhat distracted by what the show's become. The illusions are mixed into the collage of light and smoke and fire to the point that they become easy to miss. Too much smoke, not enough mirrors, as it were. For $90 a ticket, there are better shows around town (*O* and *Mystère* among them).

DAVID PEEVERS

The dynamic duo of illusions – suitably at Mirage

And Now, Our Very Special Guest . . .

To many people in Las Vegas, Frank Sinatra and his Rat Pack pals *built* this town. For years, they weren't merely legendary headliners; they were the darlings of gossip columnists from Los Angeles to New York, and their all-night partying and tumultuous lives entertained millions of readers daily. Their antics in Vegas brought adoring fans by the planeload.

Today, there's only one surviving member of the Rat Pack, and most of the other legendary headliners who 'built Las Vegas' – Elvis among them – are no longer entertaining crowds here on Earth. But Las Vegas continues to book top entertainers such as Dennis Miller, David Copperfield and Rich Little for two- and three-night engagements.

These brief engagements are often overlooked by visitors, due to the fact that the performances are fleeting and information about them can't be found in any guidebook. The easiest way to get the lowdown on upcoming headliners is to call the Las Vegas Entertainment Guide (☎ 702-225-5554), which has tape-recorded information about who will be performing during the current month and the next.

If you prefer, you can also call the hotel-casinos that have showrooms designated for special guests. These include Bally's (☎ 702-739-4111), Desert Inn (☎ 702-733-4444), Flamingo Hilton (☎ 702-733-3111), Gold Coast (☎ 702-367-7111), Golden Nugget (☎ 702-385-7111), Las Vegas Hilton (☎ 702-732-5111), Mandalay Bay (☎ 702-632-7580), Riviera (☎ 702-794-9433), Sahara (☎ 702-737-2515), Showboat (☎ 702-385-9123) and Stardust (☎ 702-732-6111).

Ol' Blue Eyes

Shows start at 7:30 and 11 pm Friday through Tuesday; dark Wednesday and Thursday. Purchase your tickets in advance.

If you haven't seen someone of Lance Burton's calibre, you might find the illusionist at the heart of **Spellbound** (☎ 702-369-5111, 800-392-9002, at Harrah's) to be extremely impressive. But Mexico's Joaquin Ayala is no Lance Burton, nor even a Siegfried or Roy for that matter. The execution of his tricks is at times clumsy, and Ayala tends to overdramatize his feats. Unfortunately for him, the Spellbound Theater places seats so close to the action that attentive audience members will see things they aren't supposed to – tricks of the trick trade, you might say. All this is to say that while Ayala is spellbinding at times, he's not in the same class as some of his colleagues down the road. The same cannot be said about the dancers who perform between illusions; they are a pure delight to watch, executing their moves with precision and beauty. Also adding a great deal to

Spellbound is a humorous juggler and an apparently boneless contortionist. Tickets go for $35. Shows are at 7:30 and 10 pm Monday through Saturday; dark Sunday.

One of the realities about shows with a variety of unrelated production numbers is that some are always better than others, and that's certainly the case with **Splash** (☎ 702-794-9433, 800-634-6753, at the Riviera). In the show's current incarnation, hope that good taste moves the producers to pull the plug on the truly stupid number featuring a topless singing biker chick on a motorcycle. Also entirely forgettable is a weak John Travolta impersonator who performs two hits from John's *Saturday Night Fever* days. Fortunately, most of the acts are excellent. There's a contortionist whose feats of strength and balance are scarcely believable. There's a magician whose close-up illusions are good plain fun. And the showstopper: four daredevil motorcyclists who enter a round cage and execute 360°, upside-down moves that require split-second timing to avoid a horrific accident. All things considered, *Splash* is a very entertaining show. Tickets go for $45 and $57. Shows start at 7:30 and 10:30 pm daily.

Viva Las Vegas (☎ *702-380-7777, 800-998-6937, at the Stratosphere*) is the only daytime production show in Las Vegas, and the free trade publications *What's On* and *Showbiz Weekly* (found in most Vegas hotel rooms) usually contain coupons offering 'Free Admission for 2.' The coupon's fine print states that each person must purchase one drink ($4.25 minimum), but for that price *Viva Las Vegas* offers tremendous value. It's a variety show, with beautiful showgirls, an entertaining magician, a comedian-emcee and two other very funny men. It's fun for the whole family (yes, the women keep their tops on), but beware: the jokes are intended for adults. If you're wondering what a Vegas production show is like but are traveling on a tight budget, *Viva Las Vegas* (and a coupon) will entertain and educate at very low cost. Even without a coupon, the price of a ticket is only $11. Showtimes are 2 and 4 pm Monday through Saturday; dark Sunday.

Gay & Lesbian Venues

There are quite a few gay and lesbian bars and dance clubs in Las Vegas, but none was located on The Strip at the time of writing.

Rock

The premier venue for live rock 'n' roll on the Las Vegas Strip is the **House of Blues** (☎ *702-736-7470, at Mandalay Bay*). The House, which opened in March 1999 with a performance by Blues Brothers Dan Ackroyd, Jim Belushi and John Goodman, features live music in a venue that can accommodate 2000 people along with a 600-seat restaurant just off Mandalay Bay's casino floor. The decor is Mississippi Delta juke joint, and the deep purple lighting casts an ethereal glow on everything and everyone, which is all the more striking against the bright, brassy backdrop of the resort's elegant casino. Despite its name, the House of Blues provides a fairly wide variety of

It looks like Mississippi, but Tom Jones sometimes performs at House of Blues.

quality live music that includes blues, soul, pop and rock (mostly the latter). Acts range from such living legends as Tom Jones, Chuck Berry and BB King to the Crash Test Dummies. Ticket prices vary with performers. Be advised that the number of tickets sold usually exceeds the number of available seats; if being seated is important to you, arrive early or you'll end up standing during the show. For a look at the House of Blues' entertainment schedule, call the number above or visit the club's website (www.hob.com).

Jazz

Live Latin jazz can be heard at ***Rum Jungle*** (☎ *702-632-7000, at Mandalay Bay*), a tropical-themed bar/restaurant/dance club that actually spells its name *rumjungle* to the annoyance of writers and editors alike. Rum Jungle is notable for the wall of fire at its entrance, the tumbling ceiling-to-floor cascades inside the bar and its dance floor, which really heats up on weekend nights. Also remarkable about Rum Jungle is its selection of rums – more than a hundred at last count. If you're wondering which brands are offered, just read the labels on the tower of rum bottles behind the bar. Yes, an actual tower of rum bottles. You read it here first. There's a restaurant attached to the bar, and it has its own attraction: a window into the kitchen. Indeed, the Rum Jungle's chefs are a fairly animated group. Admission is free unless there's live music (usually Tuesday through Saturday), then there's a $10 cover charge. No athletic wear, baggy pants, bell bottoms, hats or T-shirts are allowed.

Cinemas

The best movie theater in town is the Omnimax theater at Caesars Palace (see the Caesars Omnimax Theater entry in the Things to See & Do chapter for details). Here, images are projected against the walls and domed ceiling of the theater, and the movie seems to envelope you.

Elsewhere on The Strip, movie buffs have the opportunity to watch films shown the traditional way: on a flat screen that's perpendicular to the floor. First-run films can be seen at the ***United Artists Showcase*** (☎ *702-740-4911, 3785 S Las Vegas Blvd*). The UA Showcase and Caesars Omnimax Theater are the only cinemas on The Strip showing feature-length films. Admission is $7 for adults and $4 for children.

EAST OF THE STRIP
Dance Clubs

The club with the greatest level of palpable sexual tension has got to be ***Drink!*** (☎ *702-796-5519, 200 E Harmon Ave*), which is a hit with locals and tourists alike. On any given Friday or Saturday night Drink! is simply swarming with good-looking, fashion-conscious and uncommonly friendly people searching for other good-looking, fashion-conscious and uncommonly friendly people. The club itself consists of one big central room with a wall-to-wall bar, a dance floor and a bandstand, flanked by two smaller rooms that each contain a dimly lit bar, chairs and tables. The decor is a strange brew of industrial warehouse and designer orange-brown peeling plaster and exposed brick; it's got the gritty feel of downtown Los Angeles and the charm of San Francisco. The crowd principally runs from twentysomething to twentysomething, and the music's always live and pounding. Drink! is generally open from 10 pm to 4 am Tuesday through Thursday, and 8 pm to 5 am Friday and Saturday. Admission is typically $10.

Ask any Vegas hipster to name the hottest straight dance clubs in town and ***The Beach*** (☎ *702-731-9298, 365 Convention Center Drive*) will undoubtedly be the first or second place mentioned. The Beach is the only dance club in Las Vegas open 24 hours, although sparks don't usually start flying much before midnight. It's then that this roomy, rectangular, two-story club with heavy Southern California surfer-bar overtones is hanging ten. It's then that throngs of mostly twentysomethings burn up the dance floor under lots of blacklight and a suspended Corvette, bumping the night away to hip hop, R&B and rock from the 1950s. It's then that booze is pouring at all five of the club's lengthy bars. And it's then that hard-bodied bikini-clad women roam the club

NORMAN GODWIN

Wear your bikini to The Beach.

with shot belts trying to keep up with the demand for their breath-taking libations. The cover charge is typically $10.

For those of us closer to 50 than 20 there's **The Nightclub** (☎ *702-732-5111, inside the Las Vegas Hilton)*, which is done up in classy art deco, has tremendous sound and light systems and features a variety of lounge acts that are continuously changing. Most of the acts are led by male vocalists who belt out soul, funk or soft rock, or by female vocalists who put on 'adult dance shows' featuring 'hot girls, hot music, hot dancing and much more,' to borrow a few words from the club's announcer. There's a one-drink minimum but never a cover at The Nightclub, which opens at 3 pm daily and remains quiet until 9 or 10 pm. There are usually two shows a night; call for details.

Bars

You just gotta love a gin joint that shows midget porn flicks on its TV monitors and whose tangy, blood-red house drink is named 'Ass Juice.' Yes, the **Double Down Saloon** (☎ *702-791-5775, 4640 Paradise Rd)* isn't your typical Vegas bar. For one thing, it has a behavior code: 'You puke, you clean.' For another, the club mostly appeals to the

well-heeled lunatic fringe. Here, the decor is dark and psychedelic, and the jukebox vibrates with New Orleans jazz, British punk, Chicago blues and surfer guitar king Dick Dale. On Wednesday nights, the music is always provided by a local blues band. Regardless, there's never a cover charge at this club, which doesn't accept any credit cards and claims to be 'the happiest place on Earth.'

If your idea of a good time involves being surrounded by rowdy college students in a club where the music's cranked to an ear-damaging level and the dance floor's so small that you're never dancing with one person but actually three or four, then head to **Favorites** (☎ *702-796-1776, 4110 S Maryland Parkway)*. Yes, Favorites is a favorite with the UNLV crowd, which appreciates the establishment's variety of live music, which runs from blues to jazz to swing to rock. There's also bar-top video poker, two pool tables, darts, shuffleboard, a basketball machine and video games. A traditional bar menu is available 24 hours. Cover fees are rarely charged.

You can live a full and rewarding life without ever setting foot in **Gold Mine Bar & Grill** (☎ *702-696-9722, 252 Convention*

Center Drive), but if you just love places with a gold mine theme, you won't want to miss it. Rock walls, mighty beams, a gold cart and a trestle loom above the bar. There's also a jukebox, a sports ticker, keno machines and video poker. Occasionally there's even live entertainment. Burgers, sandwiches, salads and some more substantial items are always available, and there are usually a few food specials.

One of 80 worldwide on a growing list, the Las Vegas *Hard Rock Café* (☎ *702-733-8400, 4475 Paradise Rd*) is just like all the others: walls plastered with memorabilia from rock stars, recorded rock music coming at you from every direction, the usual burgers-sandwiches-salads menu, the requisite Hard Rock sportswear counter. Unlike the Hard Rock casino, about 100 yards away, the café is no big deal. But if you absolutely, positively must have a T-shirt that reads 'Hard Rock Café Las Vegas,' this is where to come for it. Open from 11 am to midnight daily.

If the tables have large buckets of peanuts on them and the patrons are tossing the shells on the floor, you can bet your silver belt buckle you've stumbled into a country bar, and that's exactly what you'll find at the *Lone Star Steakhouse & Saloon* (☎ *702-893-0348, 1290 E Flamingo Rd*). At the Lone Star the waiters and waitresses sing along and dance when their favorite country songs are played, and the walls are decorated with cattle heads and paintings of cowboys bringing home the herd. The Lone Star is a little slice of Texas for all the homesick cowpokes in Vegas.

Can do without the cow heads? Really don't care much for rock stars, gold mines or other gimmicky themes? If all you really want in Sin City is a regular bar – a place with cheap beer and a happy hour that never quits – *PT's Pub* (☎ *702-792-4121, 532 E Sahara Ave*) is your kind of place. You won't find any psychedelic paint jobs here, no Ass Juice, no wet T-shirt contests, no one-man band. PT's Pub has got pool tables that have been around since the time of Moses and dartboards that have seen better days, and you'll be sharing the bar with local college kids, drunks and off-duty cops.

Sneakers (☎ *702-798-0272, 2250 E Tropicana Ave*) is a popular sports bar with college and white-collar singles. It's got a large-screen TV and 10 TV monitors switched to sporting events, and a dining room serving gourmet burgers, sandwiches, salads, tacos, appetizers and desserts. Sneakers has several beers on tap and can produce just about any alcoholic combination you could ask for, but it's known for its fruit margaritas.

It's a quibble, but for those of you who don't know, the 'T.G.I.' in *T.G.I. Friday's* (☎ *702-732-9905, 1800 E Flamingo Rd*) stands for Thank God It's, which means that the inclusion of the apostrophe S at the end of 'Friday' is all wrong. Remember, you read it here first. But what's really important is that if you're single and cruising for Mr or Ms Right – especially if it's Mr or Ms Right Just for One Night – this is a good place to come. It's a veritable meat market most evenings, attended primarily by white-collar singles who can really relate to the name of the place – even when it isn't Friday. Easing their pain are two daily happy hours (from 4 till 7 pm, and from 10 till midnight) and six TV monitors. A chicken wing's toss from the bar is a full-on restaurant with a long menu of fun food. Warning: There are no gambling devices in this establishment.

Production Shows

Talk about bizarre. For starters, *Forever Plaid* (☎ *702-733-3333, 800-221-7299, at the Las Vegas Hilton*) hasn't any showgirls, it hasn't any disappearing tigers or other illusions, and in fact, it hasn't any special effects at all. On top of that, its story line is, well, twisted: Members of an early 1960s harmony quartet called the Plaids are on their way to their first gig when a carload of Catholic schoolgirls en route to the Beatles' debut on the *Ed Sullivan Show* crashes into the Plaids' bus, killing everyone inside. Somehow, the Plaids manage to return to Earth in the present to perform that gig they were on their way to when they were creamed by the parochial-school girls. Strangest of all, the show works, held together by a trip down melody lane – 29 American songs from the 1950s and '60s performed live. Of course, if you aren't a fan of those oldies, these nostalgic songsters won't seem so engaging. Tickets cost $22. Showtimes are 7:30 and 10 pm, Tuesday through Sunday; dark Monday.

Gay & Lesbian Venues

There are many gay and lesbian bars and dance clubs east of The Strip. Among the classiest of the bunch is *Angles (☎ 702-791-0100, 4633 Paradise Rd – same as Lace)*, which features mostly local and fairly well-to-do men in their twenties and thirties. Angles hosts a midnight drag show every Wednesday, and on weekends both male and female strippers perform, beginning about midnight. There's dancing and pool tables, darts and pinball machines. Unlike other gay bars in town, this one has a warm, neighborhood feel. If you've grown tired of the push of other places, you'll find Angles a refreshing change.

The hottest gay club in Las Vegas is *The Gipsy (☎ 702-731-1919, 4605 Paradise Rd)*. The Gipsy features state-of-the-art light and sound systems, two fully stocked bars and a sunken dance floor. The decor can be described as lost jungle temple, replete with faux archaeological pits, crumbling columns and tumbling vines. There's also a lot of polished marble and etched glass – pleasing elegant touches. Also nice is a glassed-off bar area that accommodates conversations at normal decibel levels. There's plenty of entertainment at Gipsy, including amateur strip shows, drag queen shows, a gong show and even a dance show. Call for a schedule of upcoming events. Typically there's a $4 entrance fee. Open from 10 pm to 4 am Tuesday through Sunday; closed Monday.

With the name *Goodtimes Bar & Grill (☎ 702-736-9494, 1775 E Tropicana Ave)*, you might assume this place was pretty wild – but you'd be wrong. Goodtimes is a quiet, mellow men's club that's perfect for intimate conversations. There's a dance floor, of course, as well as pool tables and video poker, but unlike most of the city's gay bars, Goodtimes mostly attracts people who want to talk. To help oil your tongue, there's a

daily happy hour from 5 to 7 pm and a liquor bust (all you can drink from midnight till 3 am for $5) on Monday. There's never a cover charge. Open 24 hours daily.

Adjoining Angles is the sometimes lesbian bar *Lace (☎ 702-791-1947, 4633 Paradise Rd)*. Lace was once the only lesbian bar in Las Vegas. Today it attracts a mix of men and women, straight and gay, on Tuesday, Wednesday, Saturday and Sunday. Thursday and Friday nights remain 'for womyn only.' The club features a dance floor, pinball machines, video poker and occasional shows. There's no cover or minimum drink requirement. Closed Monday.

For all you men out there who look really good in your briefs, there's the *Las Vegas Eagle (☎ 702-458-8662, 3430 E Tropicana Ave)*. The Eagle is locally famous for its Underwear Night on Wednesday, and the men who take U night seriously are generally built like ancient Greek warriors. Be advised that soft-bodied types in worn Jockeys are cut no slack at this 24-hour club on Wednesday night. And the rest of the week? Well, it's still pretty much your leather- and Levi-wearing, firm-bunned crowd.

Rock

Las Vegas occasionally attracted big-name rock bands prior to the mid-1990s, but until then it didn't have a regular venue for such groups. That changed in 1995 with the opening of *The Joint (☎ 702-226-4650, inside the Hard Rock Hotel)*. The Joint not only attracts megabands like The Rolling Stones and U2, but it's so small (a mere 1400 seats, *when* seats are available) that concerts here feel more like private shows. It's a great place to see hugely popular groups in an intimate setting. Unfortunately for non-smokers, smoking *is* permitted at The Joint, even when the chairs are brought out (some shows are 'general admission,' which in Joint parlance means standing room only; the remaining shows are assigned seating). Ticket prices typically start at $20 (though they started at $50 for Billy Joel in March 1999) and can be purchased no more than 30 days in advance. The Eagles were the first

For Music and Dancing, Call . . .

One hundred and thirty-four pages. That's how long the Adult Entertainment section runs in the Las Vegas Yellow Pages. The businesses that advertise there are not fronts for prostitution, run by eight extremely wealthy and influential people, as Las Vegas police officers have testified on numerous occasions. They can't be; prostitution is illegal in Sin City and the rest of Clark County, and it has been for years.

In fact, prostitution has been banned from Las Vegas since the 1940s – when the US Air Force built a base nearby and forced the closure of the city's brothels. Since then an interesting (and probably unrelated) development transpired: The number of the city's entertainment services soared. These services offer, in their own words, adult entertainment for adults only at your private party. But do these off-duty stewardesses, hard-bodied college girls and restless housewives do more than dance, sing, take their clothes off and leave?

Officially, no, but no one would blame you if you got the wrong impression. Before 1997, the Yellow Pages ads contained photographs of scantily clad women who suggested they would indeed be offering sex. That year, however, the police proposed a bill to outlaw escort services; the bill failed, but the services voluntarily toned down their advertisements as a result. Now they only show champagne bottles, strawberries with whipped cream, cheerleading uniforms and so on, but no actual women – because they aren't offering sex (really!). No doubt it's the abundant talents of these women that justify their $300-an-hour rates.

Then again, not everyone is against the idea of prostitutes in Las Vegas. Newly elected mayor Oscar Goodman has gone on record with his 'pro-prostitution' stance, calling prostitution 'great,' though he's said he won't try to legalize it as mayor. And there's George Flint, an ordained minister who is Nevada's only paid lobbyist for the state's legal bordellos. His job is to see that attempts to end legal prostitution in Nevada, where it is permitted in 10 of the state's 17 counties, don't get too far.

The Rev George Flint has been working for the Nevada Brothel Association since 1985, and he seems to like his work. When people ask George to reconcile his theology degree with his job, he says, 'I just remind them that Jesus' best friend, outside his family, was a working girl named Mary from a little town called Magdalen.'

It's true. You can look it up in that other large book found in most Vegas hotel rooms.

group to perform at The Joint, and since then the club has presented lots of big-name talent, including Iggy Pop, Stephen Stills, Duran Duran, Sheryl Crow, Hootie and the Blowfish, Ziggy Marley, Johnny Cash and Bob Dylan.

Cinemas
There is one movie theater within striking distance of Las Vegas Boulevard and east of The Strip – the **Dollar Cinema** (☎ 702-434-8101, at 3330 E Tropicana Ave). Good as its name, it charges only $1 for its second-run English-language films. This is the least

expensive cinema in town and an excellent value.

WEST OF THE STRIP
Dance Clubs
There's only one dance club west of The Strip, and it's enormously popular despite an unforgiving dress code and a steep, $20 admission fee. It's **Club Rio** (☎ 702-252-7777, at the Rio), and it has one of the largest dance floors in Las Vegas. After the resort's evening performance in its main showroom (most nights featuring Danny Gans, described later in this chapter), the

One for the Money, Two for the Show

The Joint at the Hard Rock Café & Casino often loses money on big-name groups, charging less for tickets than the performers demand. But don't mistake the losses for charity; in Vegas, the house always wins.

About 10 steps from the door of The Joint is the Hard Rock's dish-shaped gambling area. For the casino, the concert hall is a way to draw thousands of affluent baby boomers and Gen X music fans within arm's reach of its slot machines and gaming tables.

'The business boost we get from shows like that is quite significant,' the Hard Rock's Gary Selesner said recently after a sold-out Sheryl Crow concert. 'There's the potential for one player to pay for the [show's box-office] loss. Seriously. It's like hosting a Tyson fight, only safer.'

Late rocker Kurt Cobain lives on at the Hard Rock Hotel & Casino.

---

place is reopened as Club Rio at 10:30 pm Wednesday through Saturday – and like most Vegas showrooms, it's got tall ceilings and plenty of seating and intimate booths. However, the lines to get in are often enormous and slow moving, and no allowances are made to the dress code – no uncollared shirts, tennis shoes, gangsta pants or ripped clothing – even if you've waited in line an hour. The music is generally soft rock – you better like Madonna – and the crowd ranges in age from twentysomething to fortysomething. On Friday and Saturday, be sure to arrive at least an hour early to avoid a near-motionless line and to stand a chance of obtaining a booth.

Bars

Today, following the enormous success of the Rio west of The Strip, lots of tourist-oriented businesses are opening in this part of town. Others have been around a long time and are just now feeling the effects of tourism. Among them is *Andy Capz Pub* (☎ 702-647-1178, 1631 N Decatur Blvd), a friendly neighborhood bar that serves food and liquor 24 hours and is the Las Vegas rallying point of Denver Broncos fans. If

there's a Broncos game on when you're in town and if you're a Broncos fan, this is where you want to be. Andy Capz has a big screen TV, pool tables and British draft beer; the pub takes its name from the British comic strip character who spends his days slumped over a beer, opining on subjects of common interest. Unlike the bar the comic strip character frequents, Andy Capz has video poker. Way to go, Andy!

The same folks who brought Holy Cow! (described earlier in this chapter) into the world were behind the birth of *Big Dog's Bar & Grill* (☎ 702-876-3647, 6390 W Sahara Ave). And that should tell you everything you need to know: Big Dog's is filled with photos and memorabilia of – yes – big dogs. Hey, in a town where practically every business owner assumes you must have a theme to survive, why not big dogs? Like Holy Cow!, Big Dog's is a fun establishment that, in addition to all things canine, has 35 video poker machines, a restaurant serving steaks, ribs, chicken, burgers, fajitas and so on, and a daily midnight special of steak and eggs for a mere $3. Open 24 hours.

If Big Dog made you howl and Holy Cow! rattled your neck bell, you'll probably like **Pink E's** (☎ 702-252-4666, 3695 W Flamingo Rd), where everything – including the pool tables (all 57 of them!), the faux leather booths and the bar's lava lamp – is as pink as that mischievous panther of cartoon fame. Beware: There are no pink elephants on the premises; if you see one, switch to coffee! For you athletes, there's shuffleboard, a dartboard and three pink Ping-Pong tables. There's a dance floor, occasional live music (usually late-eighties rock 'n' roll on Friday and Saturday), and food (burgers, Philly cheesesteaks, chicken wings and so on). There's no charge to shoot pool at Pink E's on Sunday and Wednesday, there's an excellent daiquiri bar, and there are seasonal wet T-shirt contests (usually on Monday during the summer). Also, 16oz draft beers are available for only $1.50 weekdays from 11 am till 7 pm. Not so important is the fact that the bar top stretches 250 feet, but now you know. There's generally an admission fee of $5 Thursday through Saturday nights.

For something completely fun and different on a weekend night, steer yourself into **Tommy Rocker's Cantina & Grill** (☎ 702-261-6688, 4275 S Industrial Rd). Tommy Rocker's features live, sing-along rock 'n' roll and dancing every Friday and Saturday night with the one-and-only, truly incomparable Tommy Rocker, with disco dancing before and after the show. Tommy Rocker's also has pool tables, video poker gaming, eight TV monitors and a crystal-clear big screen receiving all major satellite sports. Tommy's menu features burgers, barbecue baby back ribs, Southwest and Mexican favorites, salads, sandwiches and appetizers 24 hours a day. The whole place has a surfer/beach theme going on, an atmosphere that feels thoroughly frat house, and a clientele that's mostly thirtysomething Jimmy Buffet parrothead types. There's never a cover charge or drink minimum.

Production Shows

Danny Gans: The Man of Many Voices (☎ 702-252-7776, 800-752-9746, at the Rio) puts on a super show. As the title suggests, Gans is an impressionist, and perhaps the best one alive. Of course, you have to be fluent in Americanism to enjoy him; if you're unfamiliar with the voices of such American celebrities as Clint Eastwood, Peter Falk, Stevie Wonder, Frank Sinatra and Bill Clinton (among many others), much of the show won't translate. But if you are familiar with these famous Americans, you'll likely join the rest of the house in rising to an enthusiastic standing ovation when Gans bows out. Shows are at 7:30 pm Tuesday, Wednesday and Friday through Sunday; dark Monday and Thursday. Tickets cost $99, including two drinks, and should be purchased at least a week in advance.

Gay & Lesbian Venues

What's nice about **Flex** (☎ 702-385-3539, 4371 W Charleston Blvd) is that it's neither gay nor straight, but both. Flex is known for its friendly atmosphere, its lively dance floor and its occasional live music. Its kitchen is open at all hours, and there are pool tables and video poker machines. There usually isn't a cover charge to get in, but when there is, it rarely exceeds $5.

Blues

Every major US city has got a preeminent blues venue, and in Las Vegas that place is the **Sand Dollar Blues Lounge** (☎ 702-871-6651, 3355 Spring Mountain Rd). Sure, there's the House of Blues at Mandalay Bay, but most nights it doesn't feature blues music. The Sand Dollar is a blues club all of the time, and it books captivating but generally unknown blues musicians, most of whom you haven't heard of unless you really follow the blues scene. There's nothing pretentious about the Sand Dollar: the façade could belong to an accounting office, and the club's 'art' consists mostly of bumper stickers like 'Work is the curse of the drinking class' and posters distributed by beer company reps. Same goes for the clientele, who would look equally at home fixing bikes at the Harley-Davidson repair shop five doors down. It's a friendly place, and there's definitely no dress code; if you want to hear some good blues in a club that's made for it, put on your jeans, a T-shirt and sneakers and come on down. There's live blues almost every night (call ahead), and only a cover when the status of the band warrants a larger fee. Also on the premises are video poker machines and pool tables.

Rock

Looking for that ultrahip rock 'n' roll club with a breathtaking view of The Strip? Look no farther than the 51st floor of the Rio's Masquerade Village, home of the **VooDoo Lounge** (☎ 702-252-7777, at the Rio). Situated at the top of an exhilarating glass-elevator ride, the VooDoo Lounge combines forces late at night with the equally impressive VooDoo Café, one flight below it, to produce a killer nightclub. The walls and ceilings of both sites, painted by artists brought in from New Orleans, depict objects often found in Haitian voodoo ceremonial flags – snakes, crosses, fanciful hearts. The major colors are purple, yellow and red; the furniture is black and modern. You can sit inside or on a patio with sweeping views of Las Vegas. The drinks are as exotic and potent as their names suggest – Witchy Woman, Jamaican Hellfire, Sexual Trance – and often contain Midori, rum and tropical juices. There's live music nightly starting around 9 pm, usually rock but occasionally contemporary jazz or hip-hop (call for the lowdown). There's no cover charge except on special occasions such as Halloween and New Year's Eve, or the night of a big boxing match. Their dress code – banning tank tops, T-shirts, athletic shoes, blue jeans and strategically ripped trousers – is strictly enforced.

Cinemas

There are two movie theaters west of The Strip. The better of the two is the **Century Orleans 12** (☎ 702-227-3456, at The Orleans), which with the Omnimax theater at Caesars features the only stadium-style staggered seating in town. The advantage to this seating is that your line of sight is never obscured by someone's head. Admission is generally $4 before 6 pm and $7 thereafter.

The **Gold Coast Twin** (☎ 702-367-7111, at the Gold Coast) features a mix of little-known but high-quality films and first-run Hollywood blockbusters. This intimate cinema is popular with locals who recall the time when it was the closest thing the city had to an art house. Amazingly, the prices at the snack bar haven't changed much over the years. Admission is generally $4 before 6 pm and $7 thereafter.

DOWNTOWN
Dance Clubs

In the area of dance clubs, what the downtown area lacks in quantity it makes up for in quality. That said, the **Triple 7 BrewPub** (☎ 702-387-1896, at Main Street Station) isn't actually a dance club at all, not in the conventional sense: it doesn't have a dance floor. But the live music heard there three nights a week is generally so profound it moves people to get up and dance between the chairs and tables. Every Tuesday, from 8 pm till midnight, the urge to dance is brought on by a three-piece rhythm & blues band – one of the hottest in town. On Friday and Saturday nights at 8 pm, 10 pm and midnight, the urge is sparked by gorgeous and talented women impersonating the likes of Gloria Estefan, Diana Ross, Patty LaBelle and Donna Summer. Incredibly, all of the performances are free. Not free but certainly worth the money is a beer brewed on the premises; there's also a restaurant menu and even a 'raw bar' featuring fresh sushi and oysters. The pub's decor is supposed to resemble a 1930s warehouse, but the medium-size, high-ceilinged room is so attractive that *warehouse* doesn't exactly apply. The brewery, for example, is visible behind a wall of glass, and every piece of equipment absolutely sparkles. The stately mahogany bars with carved griffins and stained-glass accents originally graced the Schlitz family home in Milwaukee, WI. The Triple 7 makes a superb place to tip back a brew, sink your teeth into a sandwich and then sweat the night away dancing to some excellent music.

Bars

Of course, every casino-hotel in the downtown area has got a bar or two or three inside its main gaming area. Generally, there isn't much more to them than a beverage counter, lots of libations and a bartender named Mac or Barb (except for the Triple 7 BrewPub at Main Street Station, described above).

East of the Fremont Street Experience are quite a few down-and-out bars offering cheap booze and cheap company and little or nothing else. A big exception to this rule is **Bunkhouse Saloon** (☎ 702-384-4536, 124 S 11th St). The Bunkhouse is owned by a judge and is popular with the downtown legal community. As you might have guessed by the name, it's got a cowboy theme and even free barbecues on occasion. Gamewise, there's video poker, pool tables and darts, and occasional live music. If you're looking for a decent bar downtown, give this place a try – unless you've got a problem with saddles, Old West art or lawyers. It's a good find.

South of Fremont St, the **5th Avenue Pub** (☎ 702-385-5000, 906 S 6th St) also has video poker machines (some with progressives), and it features karaoke every Saturday night from 9 pm till 1 am. There's an ATM inside, and food (breakfast, steak, shrimp, burgers and appetizers) is served from 7 am till 9 pm daily.

Production Shows

Longtime female impersonator Kenny Kerr is the star of **Boy-lesque** (☎ 702-386-2444, 800-674-6575, at Jackie Gaughan's Plaza), an amusing drag-queen show featuring his 'Women of Hollywood' – that is, guys who look and sound like Cher, Diana Ross, Marilyn Monroe and others. These aren't your usual nice-talking transvestites; no, these queens let loose with their nasty-talking alter egos. Due to the very adult nature of the comments, no one under 18 is admitted. Tickets go for $24. Showtimes are 8 and 10 pm Tuesday through Saturday. Purchase your tickets in advance.

Gay & Lesbian Venues

There are several men's bars in the downtown area, but no women's clubs to speak of. All of the gay bars appearing here are open 24 hours.

The **Backdoor Lounge** (☎ 702-385-2018, 1415 E Charleston Blvd) claims to have the friendliest bartenders in town, and they certainly are pleasant. On top of that, they offer lots of drink specials, and on all major holidays they serve free home-cooked buffet meals. When you've had enough of the aggressive atmosphere at the cruising bars, try this more relaxed neighborhood spot.

Then again, if you're ready for a little action, head to **Choices** (☎ 702-382-4791, 1729 E Charleston Blvd), which is one of those traditional cruising bars. Any night is a good time to roam the room, checking out and being checked out, but from midnight till 3 am on Sunday, Choices offers all-you-can-drink beer for only $5. You know what they say, everyone looks better after a pitcher of Budweiser.

The oldest gay bar in Las Vegas is **Snick's Place** (☎ 702-385-9298, 1402 S Third St), which primarily offers friendly faces. If you're in the area, drop by and say hi. This is the kind of place where people always say hi back.

SPECTATOR SPORTS

Las Vegas offers the fan a plethora of spectator sports, from baseball, basketball and bowling to rodeos, rugby and volleyball. In between there's boxing, football, golf, ice hockey, ice skating, marathon running, motor sports and tournament poker. If you thought Las Vegas was just eating, drinking, gambling and shows, think again.

Baseball

The Las Vegas Stars, the AAA franchise of the San Diego Padres, play a 70-game home schedule at Cashman Field (☎ 702-386-7200, 850 N Las Vegas Blvd). Triple-A ball is just one step down from Major League Baseball, so the level of play is extremely high quality. Tickets generally range from $4 to $8, which is an excellent value. The season runs from early April through August. Call for game dates.

Basketball

The Runnin' Rebels of the University of Nevada, Las Vegas, won the national collegiate basketball title in 1990, and UNLV has sent many players to the pros since the Rebels played their first game in 1958. The quality of play is outstanding. The Rebels hold their home games at Thomas and Mack Center (☎ 702-895-3900, at the corner of Tropicana Ave and Swenson St). The season runs from November till March. Tickets cost $12 to $50.

Bowling

Top-notch amateur bowlers compete for big prize money four times a year at the Showboat Hotel (☎ 702-385-9150, 800-257-6179, 2800 Fremont St). Bleacher seating accommodates about 500 spectators, and there's no fee to watch. The Super Bowl High Roller Tournament runs for a week in late January (the entry fee is $750; the purse tops $1 million). The Easter and Thanksgiving Senior High Roller tournaments run for five days around those holidays, which are held in early April and late November, respectively (the entry fee is $400 per event; the purse for each competition tops $500,000). The richest high roller tournament of the four is held in early July (the entry fee is $1100; the purse tops $2.5 million).

Boxing

Las Vegas has hosted more championship fights than any other city in the world. These bouts are variously held at Caesars Palace (☎ 702-731-7110, 800-634-6698), the MGM Grand (☎ 702-891-7777, 800-929-1111) and The Mirage (☎ 702-791-7111, 800-627-6667). Big fights generally take place in September and November, but they can be held anytime. Call the megaresorts for schedules and ticket prices. Tickets for major bouts typically sell for between $200 and $1500.

Football

The UNLV Runnin' Rebels have never been ranked No 1 in the country, and in fact the team has lost more games than it's won in recent years. But because they've been losers, it's easy to obtain good seats to their six annual home games. Ticket prices start at $10. The team opens its season in September and plays until December. The Rebels play their home games at 32,000-seat Sam Boyd Stadium (☎ 702-895-3900, at the end of E Russell Rd, past Boulder Hwy).

Golf

There are two major professional competitions in Las Vegas every year. The Las Vegas Senior Classic is held every April at Tournament Players Club at The Canyons (☎ 702-242-3000, 1951 Canyon Run Drive), which is in the western foothills of the city, off the Summerlin Parkway. Top players from the

NORMAN GODWIN

Like everything in Vegas, bowling is BIG.

senior tour compete for $1 million at this event. Ticket prices start at $15 per day for the four-day event. Incidentally, Raymond Floyd, who often competes in the Classic, designed the course at TPC.

The other major professional competition held in Las Vegas each year is the ITT-LPGA Tour Championship, which takes place in November at the Desert Inn Country Club (☎ 702-733-4653, 3145 S Las Vegas Blvd). This event features the 30 top money winners on the women's golf circuit, who tee up for $800,000 in prize money. Tickets for the four-day event range from $10 to $15 per day.

Ice Hockey

You've probably never heard of the Las Vegas Thunder of the International Hockey League, but some of its players have gone on to the National Hockey League – the really big show – in years past. The Thunder play 41 regular-season home games from October through April at Thomas and Mack Center (☎ 702-895-3900, at the corner of Tropicana Ave and Swenson St). Tickets run $4 to $8.

Ice Skating

Olympic medalists and national champions always compete in the Tour of World Figure

Skating Champions sponsored by Campbell Soups and held at the Thomas and Mack Center (☎ 702-895-3900, at the corner of Tropicana Ave and Swenson St) every July. Tickets generally run from $20 to $45. Be advised that the event is often held on Independence Day (July 4), which means you'll want to reserve a hotel room and purchase your ticket as far in advance as possible.

Marathon Running

The Las Vegas International Marathon (☎ 702-876-3870), held in early February, attracts long-distance runners from all corners of the globe. The 26.2-mile race begins in the Nevada town of Sloan and ends at the south end of The Strip. The event usually draws in excess of 6000 competitors from more than 40 countries. It's quite an event to be a part of as a competitor or a spectator. The entry fee is $40. There's no fee for viewing.

Motor Sports

The Las Vegas Motor Speedway (☎ 702-644-4444, 800-644-4444, 7000 N Las Vegas Blvd) is a 1500-acre complex featuring a 1.5 mile superspeedway, a 2.5-mile road track, a drag strip, a half-mile dirt track, go-cart tracks and a racing school. Events are held nearly every day. Call for information. The Richard Petty School (☎ 702-643-4343, 800-237-3889) features one-on-one training and, of course, high-speed trips around the superspeedway. Packages start at $330.

Rodeos

There are three main rodeo events in Las Vegas each year, all held at the Thomas and Mack Center (☎ 702-895-3900, at the corner of Tropicana Ave and Swenson St). The most spectacular of the three is the National Finals Rodeo, which ropes in the top 126 money winners in the Professional Rodeo Cowboys Association, who compete for $3 million in prize money. The event spans 10 days and is held in December. Tickets, which are very difficult to come by, start at $25 per competition.

The Wrangler Bull Riders Only World Championships is a three-day event in early

April that attracts the world's best bull riders. The action is fast, furious and frightening as these men compete for $1 million in title money. Daily tickets start at $30.

Helldorado Days is the name of a four-day hoedown held in early June that features three nights of professionally sanctioned rodeo activity and one night of bull riding. Tickets for bull-riding night generally go for $12, while admission the remaining nights is usually $11 per night.

Rugby

More than 70 teams from around the world compete for prize money and trophies during the first weekend of December at the Las Vegas Rugby Challenge held in Freedom Park (☎ 702-656-7401, at the corner of E Washington Ave and Mojave Rd). Entry fees go to local charities. There is no charge to view the two days of fast-paced action.

Volleyball

The Hard Rock Hotel (☎ 702-693-5000, 800-693-7625, www.hardrockhotel.com, 4455 Paradise Rd) is the site of a Miller Lite King of the Beach Invitational each March. The three-day event features two-person teams playing in round-robin style and competing for $250,000 in prize money. Tickets range from $10 to $30 per day. The competition takes place on 350 tons of sand in the hotel's parking lot. It seems that Las Vegas still doesn't have an ocean – yet.

Shopping

Las Vegas is a shopper's paradise, and not just for one socioeconomic group. Sin City will please you if you're seeking everyday bargains, such as designer clothes at greatly reduced prices. It'll delight you if you're looking for a special gift, such as an excellent bottle of wine or a basketball signed by Michael Jordan. And if you're looking for something truly spectacular, such as a piece of jewelry with history, Las Vegas has plenty to offer. Among the pieces for sale – and not likely to be sold any time soon – are the 17th-century, 430-carat Carved Moghul Indian Emerald (the world's largest carved emerald) and Ginger Rogers' engagement ring with a marquis diamond of 7.02 carats (see Fred Leighton under Jewelry, below).

WHAT TO BUY

Las Vegas isn't a city like Istanbul, where a full 80% of foreign visitors purchase at least one handmade carpet before they head home. Las Vegas is famous for many things, but it isn't known for any particular souvenir. Rather, it's a place where you can buy almost anything if you have the money. And because so much merchandise in Las Vegas is sold to visitors, most merchants can arrange to have your purchase shipped home if you don't want to take it with you.

Clothing

America's largest factory outlet mall is Belz Factory Outlet World (☎ 702-896-5599, at the intersection of S Las Vegas Blvd and Warm Springs Rd), a short drive south of Mandalay Bay. At Belz, you're able to buy direct from the manufacturer at 145 outlets. At some stores it's possible to get up to 75% off regular prices because there are no middlemen involved. Among the clothing manufacturers with outlets at Belz: Adolfo II, Bugle Boy, Burlington Brands, Danskin, Esprit, Geoffrey Beene, Jockey, Levi's, Nautica, Reebok and Van Heusen. The mall is open from 10 am to 9 pm Monday through Saturday, and from 10 am to 6 pm Sunday.

Nevada's largest mall is The Boulevard (☎ 702-732-8949, at the intersection of S Maryland Parkway and E Desert Inn Rd). Like Belz, this mall is only minutes by car or bus from The Strip. Among the dozens of clothing stores at The Boulevard are The Gap, Sports Logo, Casual Corner, Lane Bryant, Modern Woman and Victoria's Secret. There are also five department stores at the mall: Dillard's, JC Penney, Macy's, Marshall's and Sears. The Boulevard is open from 10 am to 9 pm Monday through Friday, 10 am to 8 pm Saturday, and 11 am to 6 pm Sunday.

The Forum Shops (☎ 702-893-4800, at Caesars Palace) is the most successful shopping center in the US, with average annual sales of more than $1200 per sq foot (the industry average is $300). One stroll through this mall and you'll understand why it's so successful; not only does it contain upscale restaurants, shops, services and even a motion-simulator ride, but it also contains two groups of robots that perform throughout the day. There are other attractions as well, and the location can't be beat. Among the stores at The Forum Shops specializing in women's apparel are Ann Taylor, bebe, DKNY, Max Mara and Shauna Stein. For men's apparel, seek out Bernini, Hugo Ross,

The Forum Shops at Caesars

Kerkorian and Vasari. The mall is open from 10 am to 11 pm Sunday through Thursday, and 10 am to midnight Friday and Saturday.

Located mid-Strip, the Fashion Show Mall (☎ 702-369-0704, 3200 S Las Vegas Blvd) is home to over a hundred specialized shops and stores, as well as Macy's, Dillard's, Saks Fifth Avenue, Robinsons-May and Neiman Marcus department stores. Among the boutiques featuring men's and/or women's apparel: Abercrombie & Fitch, Ann Taylor, Bally, Banana Republic, The Gap, Liz Claiborne, Millers Outpost and Uomo. The Fashion Show Mall is open from 10 am to 9 pm Monday through Friday, 10 am to 7 pm Saturday, and noon to 6 pm Sunday.

The least remarkable of Las Vegas' five malls is Meadows Mall (☎ 702-878-4849, 4300 Meadows Lane), but with 140 tenants this shopping center would be a big deal most anywhere else. Among the mall's many clothing stores are Coda, Casual Corner, Charlotte Russe, Frederick's of Hollywood, Lane Bryant, The Limited, Motherhood Maternity, Petite Sophisticate and Victoria's Secret. There are also four department stores: Macy's, JC Penney, Dillard's and Sears. Meadows Mall is open from 10 am to 9 pm Monday through Friday, and 10 am to 6 pm Saturday and Sunday.

Leather Jackets

An item many visitors leave Sin City with is a leather jacket boldly emblazoned with 'Las Vegas' on the back. These pricey souvenirs usually sell for $200 to $300. The ones found at the three sites mentioned here are high quality and good looking. They won't fall apart on you, and they *will* turn some heads.

The Hard Rock Hotel Store (☎ 702-693-5000, 800-693-7625, inside the Hard Rock Hotel) has lots of spiffy leather jackets with the hotel's logo stitched on the back and a tastefully muted 'Las Vegas' appearing underneath it. These jackets can be viewed and purchased via the Internet as well (www.hardrockhotel.com). Store hours are 8 am to 1 am Sunday through Thursday, and 8 am to 2 am Friday and Saturday.

The World of Coca-Cola (☎ 702-597-3122, 800-720-2653, 3769 S Las Vegas Blvd) has several bomber-style leather jackets with 'Coca-Cola' and 'Las Vegas' displayed in an attractive design on the backs. Hours are 10 am to midnight Sunday through Thursday, and 10 am to 1 am Friday and Saturday.

There are three Harley-Davidson merchandise stores in town (☎ 702-795-7073, inside the MGM Grand; ☎ 702-383-1010, corner of 4th St and Fremont St; ☎ 702-736-9493, inside Concourse B at McCarran International Airport), and all carry a large selection of motorcycle and bomber jackets, some bearing 'Las Vegas' and some *sans* Sin City markings. Call for store hours.

Stripper Apparel

In a town with as many strip clubs as McDonald's, it should come as little surprise that the stripper-apparel business is ba-booming. All those beefy guys and sultry women don't make their own G-strings, tasseled undies or dominatrix wear. They buy it at stores that differ little from regular apparel stores, except that these feature dancer wear, fetish gear, theme wear – well, you get the idea. So if you were hoping to find something sexy they don't sell in Kansas – or you want to surprise a loved one with a truly memorable Vegas souvenir – head for one of these two very comprehensive stores.

For their business attire, many professional dancers turn to Bare Essentials (☎ 702-247-4711, 4029 W Sahara Ave). It's got everything you could possibly want, and a lot of things you don't need. The store features merchandise for men as well as women, and offers many items in plus sizes. This place is heavily into theme wear – lots of cheerleader, nurse and schoolgirl outfits, though possibly not as much zookeeper attire as we'd like to see. It's open from 10 am to 7 pm Monday through Saturday, and from noon to 5 pm Sunday.

On the same stage with Bare Essentials is A Slightly Sinful Adventure (☎ 702-387-1006, 1232 S Las Vegas Blvd), which sells some really mischievous outfits. Many of the outfits are layered: there's a tiny outer garment, followed by much tinier undergarments. Just admiring the goods in the presence of the attractive sales staff and professional clientele can make the visit worth the trouble. The store's hours are 10 am to 10 pm Sunday through Thursday, and 10 am to midnight Friday and Saturday.

Jewelry

There is a jeweler inside all of the megaresorts. Most, such as the Cartier boutique inside Caesars Palace, sell lovely adornments. One store that's definitely worth a look even if you aren't in the market is Fred Leighton: Rare Collectible Jewels (☎ 702-693-7050, inside the Bellagio). Fred's been a busy man since he entered the jewelry business 25 years ago, building the world's largest and most prestigious collection of estate and antique jewelry. Many of the necklaces and earrings worn by stars on Academy Awards night are on loan from Fred. Among the celebrities who've worn his jewelry to the Oscars are Sharon Stone, Melanie Griffith, Madonna, Cameron Diaz and even Antonio Banderas (a ruby and diamond stud, for a stud; how fitting). At Fred Leighton you can find jewelry that once belonged to royalty. Prices run from about $100 for a tiny but exquisite pin to

Fred Leighton ain't running no pawn shop.

well over $1 million for jewelry that's simply incredible.

Coming back down to earth, The Jewelers (☎ 702-893-9979, inside the Las Vegas Hilton; ☎ 702-796-6000, inside the Boulevard Mall; ☎ 702-731-3700, inside the Flamingo Hilton; and several other locations) is Nevada's largest chain of discount-jewelry stores. These stores offer a wide selection of rings and necklaces at affordable prices. The store at the Las Vegas Hilton is open 24 hours to accommodate any middle-of-the-night urge to buy a solid gold rope chain. The store at the Boulevard Mall is open from 10 am to 9 pm weekdays, 10 am to 8 pm Saturday, and 11 am to 6 pm Sunday. The store at the Flamingo is open from 9 am to 1 am daily.

Memorabilia

There's really only one name in sports and celebrity memorabilia in Las Vegas, and it's Field of Dreams (☎ 702-221-9144, inside Masquerade Village at the Rio). Like the Fred Leighton store at the Bellagio, this store deserves a look whether you're buying or not. Among the items on sale recently were a thank-you note signed by John F Kennedy, a poster of The Beatles signed by all four band members, a football jersey with Dan Marino's autograph, and a basketball signed by Michael Jordan. (Do you think Jordan, the one-time baseball farm-club player, is signing any baseball bats? Probably not.) If you've been meaning to buy a framed electric guitar with Carlos Santana's signature on it, there's a good chance Field of Dreams has got one or can locate one for you. How about an autographed photo of Jack Nicholson? Usually not a problem. The John Hancock of John Travolta? No big deal. But a blue dress with the president's personal mark of approval? That could be more difficult. Field of Dreams is open from 11 am to midnight Tuesday through Friday, and 10 am to midnight Saturday through Monday.

Wine

With all the money that enters Las Vegas on any given day, it's no surprise that many of the city's premier restaurants possess some very impressive wine lists. What *is* surprising is that Las Vegas is home to the largest public collection of fine wines in the world. At The Wine Cellar tasting room and retail shop (☎ 702-252-7718, 800-752-9746, inside Masquerade Village at the Rio), there is in

---

Bright Lights, Big City, High Costs

The cost of living in Las Vegas does not compare favorably to the cost of living in other large cities in the United States. The cost of having a man's two-piece suit dry-cleaned in Las Vegas runs $7.83 on average, compared to just $6.05 in Los Angeles and $6.68 in Atlanta. And despite all its steak houses, the per-pound price of a T-bone steak in Sin City runs $6.91, versus $5.50 in Phoenix, $5.30 in Denver and $5.58 in St Louis.

On the other hand, when it comes to food that's bad for you, Las Vegas holds its own. A 750ml bottle of J&B scotch, on average, will only set you back $17.21 in Sin City, compared to $18.75 in Atlanta, $19.24 in Dallas and $20.95 in Portland, Oregon. A 12-inch pizza at a Las Vegas Pizza Hut costs $8.49, or a full 50¢ less than the same pizza in New York City, Boston, Phoenix or Atlanta. In Portland, you'd pay a whopping $10.59.

But, generally, you pay more in Las Vegas. A 20oz loaf of white bread in Sin City typically costs $1.11, which is more than you'd hand over in Denver (80¢), Minneapolis (85¢), Dallas (84¢) and even Portland (75¢). And in Las Vegas a woman getting her hair washed, cut and blow-dried at the Average Beauty Salon could expect to pay $24.60, versus $22.40 in Los Angeles and $21.50 in Minneapolis.

excess of 65,000 bottles of wine worth more than $8 million. The wines have been collected from the world's top wine-producing regions, with no shortage of superb grape juices from the Bordeaux area of France and California's Napa Valley. Every bottle is available for sale.

The cellar contains scores of wines that are extremely difficult to find. Some of the bottles are sold 'as a set,' as it were; such is the case with the cellar's $1-million Chateau d'Yequem collection, with bottles from every vintage produced between 1855 and 1990. Assisting customers with their purchases and/or sampling of wines are a dozen stewards, every one of whom has at least one wine qualification, and some have as many as 20. Directing the entire operation, and continuing the education of its staff, is the Rio's master sommelier Darrie Larvin, former president of the International Court of Master Sommeliers. Not only does the cellar sell great wines, but its staff can discuss them intelligently and make informed recommendations.

There are always specials on selected wines (typical of them are the '$3 specials' – wines for $3 that regularly sell for $20 or more), and custom glass etching is available. Shipping is not a problem. This is a great place to pick up a special gift for a wine lover. It's also a super place to sample wines; the price of three 1oz tastings generally runs from $8 to $30, depending on the quality of the wines selected for sampling. Tasting is available during shop hours, which are 11 am to midnight Monday through Thursday, and 10 am to 1:30 am Friday through Sunday.

Antiques

Antiques in Las Vegas? Yes, indeed, and lots of them, ranging from many objects that must have been regarded as junk when they were created and haven't appreciated with age to fancy crystal and china and lovely grandfather clocks. There's a dizzying array of older, unusual furniture, as well as a seemingly infinite number of items that could easily fit in a suitcase. If you've got a hankering to get something for someone who's

'impossible to shop for,' you might want to give the following sites the once-over twice.

Most of the antique dealers in Las Vegas are along E Charleston Blvd between Maryland Parkway and Eastern Ave. The Antique Square Shopping Center (☎ 702-386-0238, 2014-2026 E Charleston Blvd) is home to a dozen or so antique stores. Here, you'll find a very diverse selection of stuff, such as sterling silver dinnerware, hand-crank ice cream makers, marble-top washstands, unique letter-openers, panels of stained glass, tiny clocks, hat pins and even (occasionally) a Civil War flag. Hours vary from store to store.

An even bigger market exists at The Sampler Shops (☎ 702-368-1170, 6115 W Tropicana Ave), where scores of antiques dealers sell their goods in a mall-like setting. The shops feature lots of clothing, shoes, lamps and silver from the 19th century, as well as many quirky things that most people would view as unnecessary, to put it diplomatically. The shops are open from 10 am to 6 pm Monday through Saturday, and noon to 6 pm Sunday.

Next door to the Antique Square Shopping Center is Toys of Yesteryear (☎ 702-598-4030, 2028 E Charleston Blvd), which is a fun little place specializing in toys of the not so distant past. The store's inventory is constantly changing, as are the inventories of all of the sites mentioned here, but generally it includes several lovely old train sets, carnival dolls and wind-up toys. Open 11 am to 4:30 pm Monday through Saturday; closed Sunday.

Art

Got $1 million lying around and don't know what to do with it? Every painting on display at Bellagio Gallery of Fine Art (☎ 702-693-7111, 888-987-6667, at the Bellagio) is available for purchase. For further details, see the Things to See & Do chapter. For prices, contact the gallery. It may interest you to know that the price-to-earnings ratio of art by men whose last names were Van Gogh, Picasso or Pissarro is about 7000 times greater than some Internet stocks. At least that was the case at the time of writing.

Except for the Bellagio Gallery, the art bearing price tags in Las Vegas is typically of low quality. But if you're determined to buy artwork in Sin City, start your search at Galerie Lassen (☎ 702-731-6900) or Galleria di Sorrento (☎ 702-369-8000), both of which are in The Forum Shops at Caesars Palace. They are two of the best galleries in town. Still, when a sales rep at Galerie Lassen was asked recently if she had any Robert Batemans or Carl Brenders, she replied: 'Who are they?' Answer: Only the top wildlife painters in the country. In other words, when it comes to art world sophistication, Las Vegas still isn't Los Angeles or New York.

Gambling Merchandise

If you fancy shoving coins into a slot machine, consider buying one. There are many places in Las Vegas selling new and reconditioned electronic slot and video poker machines (they generally cost between $600 and $1000, although some games are priced much higher), and putting coins in a machine that you own will ultimately cost you less than putting money into a casino-owned machine.

A great place to check out even if you're only a tiny bit tempted to buy a gambling device is Gamblers General Store (☎ 702-382-9903, 800 S Main St). Gamblers has one of the largest inventories of slot machines in Nevada. Here, you'll find the latest models as well as beautiful vintage machines. Also available are roulette, craps and blackjack tables identical to those found in casinos around town. You can also find just about every book ever written on gambling, and loads of gambling paraphernalia such as coin changers, dice, customized poker chips, dealer aprons and even dice-inlaid toilet seats. Yes, even something for grandpa. Open 9 am to 5 pm daily.

Souvenirs

If all you really want is a T-shirt, a snow dome or a coffee mug that announces that you've been to Las Vegas or know someone who has, you'll find such things everywhere you turn in Sin City. Every megaresort on The Strip has gift shops that are chockful of mementos and souvenirs, and some of these places carry entire lines of clothing and other items.

For instance, the Flamingo Hilton sells lots of toys with 'Flamingo' on them, and there's even a Flamingo Apparel store brimming with 'Flamingo' clothing. O'Shea's Casino put thousands of hours of thought into their product line and came up with a design that – are you seated? – features a green four-leaf clover. If you want to announce to the world that O'Shea's is your kind of place, you'll be glad to know that shirts and caps with their 'unique' design are for sale at the casino. Excalibur features wizard sculptures, pewter axes and assorted other disturbing things. At Luxor you'll find lots of Egyptian handicrafts, some of which are actually quite lovely. And so on, and so on . . .

Books

If you came to Las Vegas intending to shop for books, the city won't likely disappoint you. There is at least one bookstore in all five malls (see below), and there are many others scattered about. All of the big chains – B Dalton Bookseller, Barnes & Noble Booksellers, Bookstar, Book Warehouse, Borders Book Shop and Waldenbooks – have stores here, most more than one.

In addition, there are lots of specialty bookstores in Las Vegas, such as the Psychic Eye Bookshop (☎ 702-369-6622, 953 E Sahara Ave), which features books on the occult, astrology and self-help. It also offers psychic readings.

Of course, Las Vegas wouldn't be complete without a slew of stores selling books on gambling. The best of the bunch is Gambler's Book Club (☎ 702-382-7555, 800-522-1777, 630 S 11th St), where owner Edna Luckman (great name, huh?) carries more than 4000 gambling-related titles, including lots of out-of-print titles. The store is open from 9 am to 5 pm Monday through Saturday.

WHERE TO SHOP

The metropolitan Las Vegas area has more than 30 million sq feet of retail space, and that staggering number is growing all the time. It's almost reached the point where one can say that if it isn't available in Las Vegas, it simply isn't available. That said, you still need to know where to look for what you're after. Those places tend to be the malls, although many of the hotel-casinos such as the MGM Grand, Bellagio, the Rio and Luxor also contain specialty stores offering good value.

Malls

There are no fewer than five major malls in the city; all of them are described in some detail under Clothing, earlier in this chapter. For information on what you can find at these malls in addition to clothing (for one thing, lots of ATM machines), read on.

Adjacent to the casino at Caesars Palace are The Forum Shops (☎ 702-893-4800), which are a visual as well as a retailing attraction. Storefront façades and common areas resemble an ancient Roman streetscape, with Corinthian columns and triumphant arches, grandiose fountains, delightful piazzas and classic statuary. Overhead, on a barrel-vaulted ceiling, a painted sky emulates a changing Mediterranean day; as the day progresses, the sky magically transforms from rosy-tinted dawn to cloud-laced picture blue to twinkling evening stars. Elsewhere visitors are treated to two sensational shows performed by faux-marble Animatronic statues of Roman gods that come to life every hour, on the hour, amid dancing waters and laser-light effects. New in 1998 is a giant Roman Hall, at the center of which is a 50,000-gallon circular aquarium and a fountain that shoots fire instead of water. Amid all of the free entertainment it's easy to overlook the more than one hundred prestigious emporia, which carry not only clothing and accessories produced by the world's top designers but also highly unusual objects, such as big-name sports memorabilia, 16th-century hand-painted Turkish boxes and high-quality Native American jewelry. There's even a half-court basketball arena and treadmill machines in an athletic-shoe store where prospective customers can test run potential purchases. The Forum Shops is much more than simply a grouping of retail stores under one roof;

it's an excursion. The mall is open from 10 am to 11 pm Sunday through Thursday, and 10 am to midnight Friday and Saturday.

Also conveniently located on The Strip is the Fashion Show Mall (☎ 702-369-0704, 3200 S Las Vegas Blvd), which has lots of tenants that aren't particularly fashion conscious. There are, for example, seven art galleries and four full-service restaurants, including the excellent Morton's of Chicago. There are dozens of specialty stores selling sunglasses, skin and health products, electronic devices and coffee beans, compact discs and wrist watches, cookies and chocolates, jewelry and fast food, and shoes, shoes, shoes. Among some of the clothing stores not previously mentioned are Abercrombie & Fitch, Banana Republic, Diane's Swimwear, North Beach Leather, Private Collections, Schwartz Big & Tall and Victoria's Secret. The Fashion Show Mall is open

Fashion Show Mall on The Strip

from 10 am to 9 pm Monday through Friday, 10 am to 7 pm Saturday, and noon to 6 pm Sunday.

If you're unable to find what you're looking for at The Fashion Show, pay a visit to The Boulevard (☎ 702-732-8949, 3528 Maryland Parkway), a 1.25-million-sq-foot mall with more than 150 tenants. Natural lighting and lush landscaping add to the pleasure of shopping here. In addition to a tremendous variety of stores featuring men's, women's and children's apparel, there are lots of stores specializing in other merchandise, among them: cards and gifts stores (African

& World Imports, Bath & Body Works, The Disney Store and The Nature Company, to name a few), food (Ethel M Chocolates, General Nutrition Center, Mrs Fields Cookies, Pretzel Time and many more), hobby and electronics (The Good Guys, Nordic Trak, Ritz Camera, Software Etc and others), jewelry (11 jewelers in all) and shoes (12 shoe stores). However, for bargains in footwear you're better off shopping at Belz. The Boulevard is open from 10 am to 9 pm Monday through Friday, 10 am to 8 pm Saturday, and 11 am to 6 pm Sunday.

The largest factory outlet mall in the US is Belz Factory Outlet World (☎ 702-896-5599, at the intersection of S Las Vegas Blvd and Warm Springs Rd). At Belz, you can buy direct from the manufacturer at 145 outlets. In addition to nearly a hundred factory apparel outlets, Belz is home to dozens of outlets specializing in accessories (luggage, hats, bags, sunglasses, etc), cameras and electronics (power tools, watches, video cameras, etc), health and beauty aids (with an emphasis on perfumes), housewares and linens (including Corning-Revere), jewelry (seven discount jewelers in all), lingerie (Jockey, Leggs, Haines, Bali, Playtex, Maidenform, Olga and Warner), sportswear (Nike, Reebok, Nautica and Danskin, among others) and toys and gifts. The mall is open from 10 am to 9 pm Monday through Saturday, and 10 am to 6 pm Sunday.

If you've been to all of the above and still haven't found what you're looking for, or you just really love to shop, Meadows Mall (☎ 702-878-4849, 4300 Meadows Lane) is your next best bet. It's got many of the same stores as the other malls, plus a few new ones. The mall is home to no fewer than 12 shoe stores, 15 hobby and leisure stores, eight stores specializing in home furnishings and exactly 20 stores that do business in jewelry and gifts. Meadows Mall is open from 10 am to 9 pm Monday through Friday, and 10 am to 6 pm Saturday and Sunday.

Excursions

Las Vegas is the antithesis of a naturalist's vision of America. It is, however, surprisingly near some of the Southwest's most spectacular attractions. Beautiful Red Rock Canyon is just outside of town, while the forests and snowfields of Charleston Peak are less than an hour away by car. Also within easy striking distance of Sin City are the imposing Hoover Dam, the Lake Mead National Recreation Area and the popular gambling gulch of Laughlin.

The brilliant Valley of Fire State Park northeast of town is just a short, scenic drive away, and for those with more than an afternoon to spare, the most incredible natural wonders await. Longer drives bring you to the Grand Canyon in Arizona and to Zion and Bryce Canyon National Parks in Utah. One option is to view these lovely sights by air, which can be easily done from Las Vegas.

Lonely Planet's *Southwest* extensively covers outdoor recreation in Arizona, Utah

and New Mexico, but the following section provides basic information for getting away from the neon and into this indescribable country.

West of Las Vegas

RED ROCK CANYON
The contrast between the artificial brightness of Las Vegas and the natural splendor of Red Rock Canyon, a mere 20-mile drive west of The Strip, couldn't be greater. The canyon is actually more like a valley, with the steep, rugged red rock escarpment rising 3000 feet on its western edge. It was created about 65 million years ago when tectonic plates collided along the Keystone Thrust fault line, pushing a plate of gray limestone up and over another plate of younger red sandstone. In 1994, President Clinton doubled the conservation area to almost 200,000 acres. Red Rock should be on the

Red Rock Canyon is just 20 miles from the Vegas Strip.

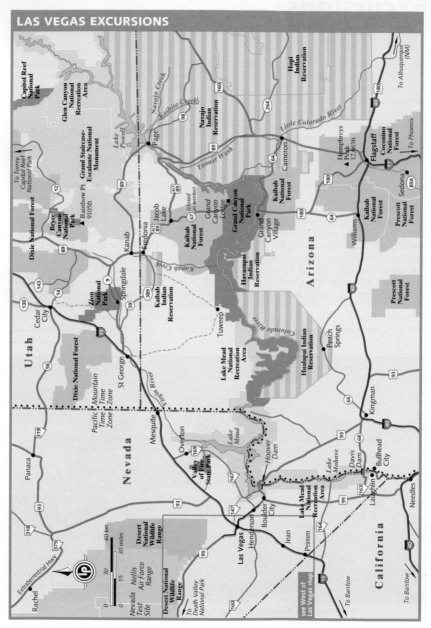

LAS VEGAS EXCURSIONS

must-see list of every visitor to Las Vegas but – perhaps fortunately – it usually isn't.

The canyon rocks make for some of the finest rock climbing in the nation, though not for the inexperienced. Jackson Hole Climbing School (☎ 702-223-2176) offers basic climbing courses for $65 and guided climbs from $80.

Orientation & Information

To get to the canyon from Las Vegas, go west on Charleston Blvd, which turns into SR 159, for about 30 minutes. A 13-mile, one-way scenic loop allows you to drive past some of the area's most striking features and to access the hiking trails.

The excellent visitors' center (☎ 702-363-1921) has maps and information about several short hikes in the area and is open from 8:30 am to 4:30 pm daily. The scenic driving loop is open from 8 am to dusk (sunset and sunrise are the best times for viewing). The park's day-use fee is $5. First-come, first-served camping at the Oak Creek site is available year-round.

SPRING MOUNTAIN RANCH STATE PARK

South of the scenic loop drive, a side road goes off to the west, to Spring Mountain Ranch (☎ 702-875-4141), underneath the steep Wilson Cliffs. The ranch was established in the 1860s and owned by the Wilson family for over 70 years. Then it had various owners, including Vera Krupp (of the German industrialist family) and Howard Hughes, before the state bought it in 1974.

The ranch is amazingly green and lush, with white fences and an old red ranch house, like a farm home from back east. The park is open for visits and picnics from 8 am to dusk daily (there's a $5 day-use fee per car), and you can tour the ranch house from 10 am to 4 pm daily.

OLD NEVADA & BONNIE SPRINGS RANCH

At the south end of Red Rock Canyon, Old Nevada (☎ 702-875-4191) is a touristy reproduction of an 1880s mining town, complete with wooden sidewalks, staged gunfights and hangings, and a Boot Hill cemetery. There's also a restaurant, an ice cream parlor, a saloon and a motel.

The adjacent Bonnie Springs Ranch has various types of farm animals and a petting zoo, and it offers guided horseback riding trips. The ranch is open every day from 10:30 am to 6 pm. Tickets are $6.50 for adults and $4 for children.

TOIYABE NATIONAL FOREST

The Spring Mountains form the western boundary of Las Vegas Valley, with the highest point, Charleston Peak, situated 11,918 feet above sea level. It's an area of pine forests, higher rainfall and lower temperatures, and it swarms with locals on sunny weekends. As an isolated mountain range surrounded by desert, Toiyabe has evolved some distinct plant species unique to the area.

Highways 156 and 157 turn southwest off Hwy 95 north of Las Vegas, climb into the forest, and are later connected by scenic 12-mile Hwy 158; driving the loop is possible unless the roads are closed by snow.

Sixteen miles north of Las Vegas, Hwy 157 follows Kyle Canyon up to the village of **Mt Charleston**, which has a US Forest Service office (☎ 702-386-6899). The trailhead at the end of the road provides access to several hikes, including the demanding nine-mile trail to Charleston Peak. Campgrounds, open from about May to October, are $7. The *Mt Charleston Hotel* (☎ 702-872-5500, 800-794-3456, fax 702-872-5685, on Kyle Canyon Rd) is a comfortable place, with a mountain lodge atmosphere, charging about $50 most nights, though prices can climb up to $140. Also here is the appreciably more rustic *Mt Charleston Lodge* (☎ 702-872-5408, 800-955-1314, fax 702-872-5403), with its lovely cabins with fireplace, double whirlpools and private deck costing $125 midweek and $180 weekends.

About 30 miles north of Las Vegas, Hwy 156 turns southwest from Hwy 95 and goes to **Las Vegas Ski & Snowboard Resort** (☎ 702-645-2754). It's a small, mostly intermediate ski area (there's a mere 1000-foot slope) enjoyed by locals on weekends, with

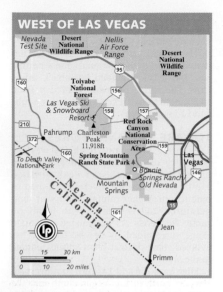

WEST OF LAS VEGAS

good scenery and a season from late-November to April. Lift tickets are $27. Call to find out if the bus service is running from Las Vegas. A couple of nearby campgrounds are open during the warmer months.

PAHRUMP

It might not look like it, but the real estate tracts between the Spring Mountains and the California state line are home to 13,000 people and constitute one of the fastest growing areas in Nevada. Pahrump is home to the **Pahrump Valley Winery** (☎ 702-727-6900), the state's only winery, which produces white and rosé wines and offers free tours, as well as lunch and dinner.

Two casinos, Saddle West and Mountain View, draw business from the California side, but a high proportion of short-term visitors aren't here for gambling action. Pahrump is in Nye County and has the closest legal brothels to Las Vegas, 70 miles away. (Las Vegas is in Clark County, where prostitution has been outlawed since the 1940s.)

Well-publicized in Sin City, the brothels in and around Pahrump offer limo service to entice potential customers. The most famous of the brothels is the **Chicken Ranch**, which

gobbled, pecked and plucked for more than 130 years in La Grange, TX, before moving here in 1976, much to the vocal chagrin of many locals and the silent enthusiasm of many others.

JEAN & PRIMM

For those who just can't wait to start gambling, casinos have sprung up along I-15, on the 45 miles between the California state line and Las Vegas. Right on the border, in Primm, three casinos – Primadonna, Whiskey Pete's and Buffalo Bill's – face each other across the freeway, each with bizarre theme-park gimmicks. Primm gets its name from its founders, the Primm family.

About 15 miles from the border, I-15's exit 12 will leave you in Jean, where the big and garish Gold Strike Hotel & Casino looms on one side of the road and the big and garish Nevada Landing sits on the other. Both have late-19th-century themed decor. The Jean Visitor Center (☎ 702-874-1360) will give you lots of information about Las Vegas. The small Jean Airport is also the base of the Las Vegas Skydiving Center (☎ 702-877-1010), which offers tandem jumps for $179, accelerated freefall jumps for $300 and static-line jumps for $195.

Lake Mead & Around

BOULDER CITY

About 30 miles southeast of Las Vegas, this pretty town of 13,000 was founded in 1931 as a residential community for Hoover Dam workers. Still the main gateway to Hoover Dam, Boulder City is unique in Nevada because it has never allowed gambling. Back in 1931 it was felt that only a strict moral code would ensure the workers' productivity.

With its grassy parks, trees and quiet streets, it's a lovely piece of old-fashioned, small town America. A few of the original buildings, including the Boulder Dam Hotel, frame Hotel Plaza. The **Hoover Dam Museum** (☎ 702-294-1988), 444 Hotel Plaza, preserves artifacts and records from the early days of the dam's construction and the town. Hours are 10 am to 4 pm daily; a donation is encouraged. The visitors' center (☎ 702-294-1252) is at 100 Nevada Hwy.

There are a few places to stay. The historic **Boulder Dam Hotel** *(☎ 702-293-3510, 1305 Arizona St)* reopened in 1999 after restoration and is the most interesting. The **Sands Motel** *(☎ 702-293-2589, 809 Nevada Hwy)* has some of the cheapest rooms in town (from $37 to $52). A bit nicer is **El Rancho Boulder Motel** *(☎ 702-293-1085)*, which charges from $60 to $150. The **Happy Days Diner** at 512 Nevada Hwy has tasty, low-priced American fare.

LAKE MEAD NATIONAL RECREATION AREA

It's less than an hour's drive down Hwy 95/93 from Las Vegas to Lake Mead and Hoover Dam. They are the most visited sites within the 2337 sq mile Lake Mead National Recreation Area, which encompasses both 110-mile-long Lake Mead and 67-mile-long Lake Mohave, and many miles of desert around the lakes. The Colorado River and the two lakes form a natural border with Arizona to the east. Motels, camp-grounds, restaurants, marinas, stores and gas stations are sparse.

Boulder Dam (at the time the world's largest, and later renamed Hoover Dam) was built between 1931 and '35, backing up the Colorado River to form Lake Mead. In 1953, the smaller Davis Dam was completed, forming Lake Mohave.

Highway 93, which connects Kingman, Arizona, with Las Vegas, crosses the dam, passing the main visitors' center. Another important road is Hwy 68, which runs between Kingman and Laughlin, at the southern tip of the recreation area. There is a $3 fee to enter the recreation area.

Lake Mead

Lake Mead has 500 miles of shoreline and a capacity of 9.2 trillion gallons, equal to two years of the normal flow of the Colorado River. Popular activities include swimming, fishing, boating, waterskiing and even scuba diving. The lake is surrounded by beautiful scenery, most of which is undeveloped and protected as part of the recreation area.

The Alan Bible Visitor Center (☎ 702-293-8990), on Hwy 93 about 26 miles east of Las Vegas, is a wellspring of information on

Playing and relaxing at Lake Mead

NORMAN GODWIN

recreational options, camping and natural history. It's open from 8:30 am to 5 pm (4:30 pm in winter) daily. Don't miss the free documentary on the history and construction of Hoover Dam.

The usual scenic drive is along N Shore Road, which starts near the visitors' center and leads up to Valley of Fire State Park and Overton. Lake Mead Cruises (☎ 702-293-6180) operates sightseeing trips ($14.50) and a variety of cruises from the Lake Mead Resort Marina.

Shoreside campgrounds are at Boulder Beach, Las Vegas Wash, Callville Bay, Echo Bay and Temple Bar (in Arizona). Accommodations, from around $70, are available at *Echo Bay Resort* (☎ *702-394-4000, near Overton)* and at *Lake Mead Resort & Marina* (☎ *702-293-2074, near Boulder Beach)*. The toll-free number for both is ☎ 800-752-9669.

Hoover Dam

At 726 feet high, the concrete Hoover Dam is one of the tallest in the world. It has a striking beauty, with its imposing, graceful curve filling a dramatic red rock canyon, backed by the brilliant blue waters of Lake Mead. Its simple form and art deco embellishments and design sit beautifully within the stark landscape. Its construction in the 1930s provided much-needed employment as the country struggled through the Great Depression. When the dam opened in 1936, it was possibly the only public works project completed ahead of schedule: by two years and under budget by $14 million (total cost: $165 million).

Flood control, irrigation, electricity and a regulated water supply were the main purposes for Hoover Dam's construction, and they remain the dam's primary functions today. The waters of the lower Colorado irrigate some one million acres of land in the US and half a million in Mexico; provide water to 25 million people primarily in Las Vegas, Los Angeles, San Diego, Phoenix and Tucson; and generate 4 billion kilowatt hours a year for Southern California, Arizona and Nevada.

Two types of tours leave from the snazzy new visitor center (☎ 702-294-3524) atop the dam. The 35-minute basic tour takes you down into the power plant at the bottom of the dam wall, opening up a truly magnificent view of the dam and the canyon from below.

Hoover Dam intake towers

Hoover Dam and the Colorado River

Tours cost $8 for adults and $2 for children under 16; they leave continuously between 9 am and 6 pm. Long waits are common during summer months. The 75-minute 'Hard Hat Tour' provides a more in-depth look; it operates daily between 9:30 am and 4 pm, and costs $25.

The visitors' center provides very little free background information and functions primarily as a ticket office. The Hoover Dam film that's shown here, which is also shown at the Alan Bible Visitors Center (see Lake Mead, above), is open to tour ticket holders only. Perhaps all this would be less vexing if it hadn't taken $125 million in tax dollars to build this facility, which was a four-fold cost overrun and, incidentally, only $40 million less than Hoover Dam cost.

If you come by car, leave it in the multi-level parking lot *before* you reach the dam. Bus tours from Vegas are a good deal (about $20) and guarantee tickets to the basic tour. The *Snacketeria* at the Nevada spillway on the north side of the dam wall sells food, film and books.

Lake Mohave

South of Hoover Dam, the Colorado River is impounded by the Davis Dam, near Laughlin, creating the narrow, 67-mile-long Lake Mohave. Access to the lake is from

side roads off Hwy 95, one of which (SR164) goes to Cottonwood Cove, site of a campground and boat rentals.

Farther south, a rough road travels east over the Christmas Tree Pass, then south past Grapevine Canyon. A pleasant half-mile walk from the parking lot here leads to a small canyon brimming with petroglyphs. The Katherine Landing Visitors Center (☎ 520-754-3272) is in Arizona – reached via SR 163 – 3 miles north of Davis Dam; it's open from 8 am to 4 pm daily (Mountain Time=+1 hour). Information is also available from ranger stations throughout the area. For advance information, call ☎ 702-293-8906.

LAUGHLIN

About 80 miles south of Las Vegas is the gambling resort town of Laughlin, population 3000. In 1966, Don Laughlin bought the land along the Colorado river and started a gambling operation in a dilapidated hotel catering primarily to Arizonans hungry for their turn at blackjack and poker.

A dozen hotel-casinos now line the west bank of the Colorado River, which is thick with boats and jet skis. The entertainment tends toward country music. Comfortable casino accommodations are cheap here, and swimming in the lake is an option in summer. There is, however, no other reason to come here unless you want to gamble and you can't stand Las Vegas.

The visitors' bureau (☎ 702-298-3022, 800-452-8445, fax 702-298-0013, 1555 S Casino Drive) is open from 8 am to 5 pm daily. A unique way of getting around Laughlin is via water taxis that shuttle between hotels and also cruise the river at sunset.

Places to Stay

All hotels listed here are on S Casino Drive. The *Riverside Resort Hotel & Casino* (☎ 702-298-2535, 800-227-3849, fax 702-298-2614, at No 1650) is one of the original Laughlin casinos, with lots of slots, restaurants and the Losers' Bar. Rooms run from $17 to $109. The *Ramada Express Hotel & Casino* (☎ 702-298-4200, 800-243-6846, fax 702-298-6403, at No 2121), has a railroad theme; their locomotive-shaped pool and a train ride around the parking lot amuse kids (rooms: $16 to $49). The *Colorado Belle Hotel & Casino* (☎ *702-298-4000, 800-477-4837, fax 702-298-5822, at No 2100*) is a big place pretending to be a Mississippi riverboat (rooms $18 to $75).

Valley of Fire State Park

VALLEY OF FIRE STATE PARK

Near the north end of Lake Mead National Recreation Area, this park is a masterpiece of desert scenery, a fantasyland of wonderful shapes carved in psychedelic sandstone. It's similar in appearance and geology to the desert landscapes of Utah, Arizona and New Mexico, but it's easily accessible from Las Vegas and not crowded with tourists.

Early residents included a tribe called the Basketmakers and Anasazi Indians. Several petroglyphs survive throughout the park as a reminder of these early native peoples.

The visitors' center (☎ 702-397-2088) is just off SR169, which runs through the park. Open daily from 8:30 am to 4:30 pm, it has excellent exhibits, general information and hiking suggestions. Some of the most interesting formations are **Elephant Rock**, the **Seven Sisters** and **Rainbow Vista**. Especially scenic is the winding side road to **White Domes**, and **Atlatl Rock** has some very distinct and artistic petroglyphs. There's a $5 day-use fee per vehicle.

The valley is most vibrant at dawn and dusk, so staying in one of the campgrounds ($7 for tent sites) is a good move. Nearby Overton has accommodations, but Las Vegas is only 55 miles away. The quickest route is via I-15 and SR169, though the drive on Lake Mead's Northshore Rd and SR169 is more scenic and hooks up with Hwy 95 near Henderson, south of Vegas.

OVERTON

More than a thousand years ago, a community of Anasazi Indians farmed here and built structures resembling the pueblos of the Southwest found nowhere else in Nevada. For an unknown reason, the Anasazi left the area, which was later occupied by Paiute people. Mormons settled the Muddy (or Moapa) River in 1864, but after seven years they also moved on, and it wasn't until 1880 that new settlers came and stayed. Today, Overton is a small agricultural town of 1800 people with a couple of motels, bars and other businesses along the dusty main street.

The foundations of Pueblo Grande de Nevada were noted by Jedediah Smith in the 1820s. Outside the **Lost City Museum** (☎ 702-397-2193, 721 S Moapa Valley Blvd), some adobe dwellings reconstructed on original foundations provide an idea of what the original settlement looked like. Inside is a collection of artifacts dating back 10,000 years, information on the original inhabitants and early European settlers, and photos of archaeological excavations. The museum is open daily from 8:30 am to 4:30 pm; $2.

MESQUITE

East of the Lake Mead recreation area, Mesquite is typical of a Nevada-style boom town, having been put on the map only in the 1980s with the construction of the Peppermill Hotel-Casino. Now metamorphosed into *Si Redd's Oasis Hotel* (☎ 702-346-5232, 800-216-2747, fax 702-346-5722, 1137 Mesquite Blvd), it has rooms for $39 to $69 and two 18-hole golf courses. It's since been joined by four other hotel-casinos, and there's no end to the boom in sight.

The **Desert Valley Museum** (☎ 702-346-5705; closed Sunday), 35 Mesquite Blvd, documents area history with pioneer and Native American artifacts. Mesquite, on the state line and 70 miles from Vegas, is a good base for exploring Zion and Bryce Canyon national parks in Utah, though the resort really seems to be banking on entertainment-starved visitors from Utah and Arizona. The visitors' center (☎ 702-346-2702) is at 460 N Sandhill.

Grand Canyon National Park

The Grand Canyon is Arizona's most famous sight indeed, it is arguably the best-known natural attraction in the entire US. At 277 miles long, roughly 10 miles wide and a mile deep, the canyon is an incredible spectacle of differently colored rock strata. The many buttes and peaks within the canyon itself and its meandering rims give access to fantastic views. Descending into the canyon on a short hike or a multiday backpacking trip offers an even better sense of the breathtaking variety in the landscape, wildlife and climate.

Although the rims are only 10 miles apart, as the crow flies, it is a 215-mile, five-hour drive on narrow roads from the visitors' center on the South Rim to the visitors' center on the North Rim. Thus, the Grand Canyon National Park is essentially two separate areas and is treated as such here.

In addition, though the South Rim has more facilities and is the most visited side of the canyon, the North Rim is actually a little closer to Las Vegas, and it's a lot closer to Utah's Zion and Bryce Canyon National Parks. Vegas travelers hoping to see more than just the Grand Canyon should consider skipping the South Rim.

Geology

The oldest rocks, near the bottom of the inner canyon, are 1.7 billion years old, but most of the canyon wall layers were laid during the Paleozoic Era, about 250 million to 570 million years ago. These strata were in place well before the Americas began drifting apart from the Old World, roughly 200 million years ago.

Some 60 to 70 million years ago, the massive Colorado Plateau emerged. For millions of years after this uplift, rivers flowed north from the north side of the plateau and south from the south side. The Grand Canyon began to form about 5.5 million years ago when a shifting of the San Andreas Fault created the Gulf of California. South-flowing rivers combined to form the lower Colorado River and emptied into this new sea.

Over time, the headwaters of the lower Colorado eroded through the Grand Wash Cliffs (northeast of Lake Mead) and connected with the upper Colorado system. This altered the river's course from its northward flow into Utah to southward into the Gulf of California, and the erosion of the combined rivers created the Grand Canyon.

GRAND CANYON – SOUTH RIM

The elevation of the South Rim ranges from 7000 to more than 7400 feet and is lower and much more accessible than the North Rim. About 90% of park visitors go to the South Rim.

The foremost attraction is the rim itself, paralleled by a 33-mile scenic drive with numerous parking areas, scenic views and trailheads. However, this drive has become overcrowded and, by the year 2000 or 2001, a light railroad is planned to take visitors from nearby Tusayan to the South Rim. (See The Grand Canyon in the 21st Century boxed text.)

Another attraction is Grand Canyon Village, with both early-20th-century hotels and modern amenities. The canyon is accessed via hiking trails (see below). If you'd rather get away from the topside traffic, hike down to the canyon bottom and stay at Phantom Ranch or at one of several campgrounds, although advance reservations are definitely necessary. Other activities, including mule rides, river running and backcountry backpacking, also require advance planning.

Orientation

It's about a five-hour drive, not counting stops, to get from Las Vegas to the Grand Canyon's South Rim. From Hoover Dam, which is less than an hour from Vegas, it's 71 miles along Hwy 93 to Kingman, AZ. Kingman has plenty of places to stay and eat, especially on Route 66, which runs through the center of the town as Andy Devine Ave. From Kingman, pick up I-40 and go east 110 miles to Williams; then it's another 60 miles north on Hwys 64 and 180 to Grand Canyon National Park. At Grand Canyon Village, Hwy 64 turns east and becomes Rim Drive. As it exits the park, Hwy 64 continues east through the Kaibab National Forest and the Navajo Indian Reservation to Cameron. It's 53 miles from Grand Canyon Village to Cameron, and an additional 51 miles south on Hwy 89 to Flagstaff.

Information

Visitor Centers The main visitor center is in Grand Canyon Village, about 6 miles north of the South Entrance Station. A bulletin board provides information on lodging, weather, tours, talks and a host of other things. If you can't find the information you need, rangers are available to assist you between 8 am and 5 pm daily, with longer hours added from April to November. Park maps and *The Guide* newspaper, with up-to-date park information, are available for free.

A smaller visitor center at Desert View, near the east entrance of the park, is open daily in summer and is usually closed in winter. You'll also get assistance at ranger stations near the Grand Canyon Railway depot, Indian Garden below the South Rim,

the River ranger station and Phantom Ranch at the canyon's bottom, and Cottonwood Campground below the North Rim.

The main park number (☎ 520-638-7888) has recorded information on everything from weather conditions to applying for a river-running permit. You can leave your address to receive written information, or you can speak to a real live ranger during business hours. The park's home page is at www.thecanyon.com/nps.

Fees & Permits Entrance to the park is $20 per private vehicle and $10 for bicyclists and pedestrians. Tickets are valid for seven days and can be used at any entrance point, including the North Rim. Golden Access, Age and Eagle passes are honored. Bus and train passengers either pay a lesser fee or may have the fee included in the tour. Note that fees may change when the train shuttle to the rim is implemented.

For backcountry camping, permits are required from the Backcountry Office (see the Grand Canyon-North Rim section for details).

Climate & When to Go The peak season ranges from about April to November, and the park is busiest from Memorial Day to Labor Day – avoid that period if possible. On average, temperatures are 20°F cooler on the South Rim than at the bottom of the canyon. In summer, expect rim highs in the 80°s F and lows around 50°F.

June is the driest month and summer thunderstorms make July and August the wettest. Weather is cooler in fall, and snow and freezing overnight temperatures are likely by November. Winter weather can be beautifully clear, but be prepared for fierce storms and extreme cold.

Visitor Services Grand Canyon Village has most visitor services, but prices are substantially higher and lines longer than in Flagstaff: plan ahead. Services available include hotels, restaurants, campgrounds, coin laundry, showers and transportation services. Car towing and mechanics (☎ 520-638-2631) are available. A gas station is open

Steve Wynn's Grand Canyon...uh, you mean this is *real*???

daily. A medical clinic (☎ 520-638-2551, 520-638-2469) is open from 8 am to 5:30 pm weekdays, and from 9 am to noon Saturday.

Organized Activities

Call the park's information service (☎ 520-638-7888) or ask at a visitor center about free ranger-led activities. Programs include various talks and slide shows as well as guided walks from a few hundred flat yards (40 minutes) to 3 miles below the rim (three to four hours). In summer there are Junior Ranger activities for four to 12 year olds.

Rim Trail

The paved Rim Trail skirts the rim for about 3 miles from **Yavapai Point** to **Maricopa Point**. It extends unpaved almost 7 miles farther west past several viewpoints to Hermits Rest (see below). The Rim Trail is the park's most popular walk and visitors can hike as far as they feel comfortable. The rewards are beautiful views with many interpretive signs. Only foot and wheelchair traffic are allowed – no bicycles. During winter, snow or ice may temporarily cover the trail.

East & West Rim Drives

The West Rim is accessible by road for 8 miles west of Grand Canyon Village (and by the Rim Trail described above). At the end of the drive and trail is **Hermits Rest** with a snack bar and the Hermit Trailhead leading into the canyon; if you don't descend, you must return the way you came.

Cycling along the road is permitted year round, though cars are banned from about mid-March to mid-October; free shuttle buses operate every 15 minutes. In winter you can make this drive in your own car, although planned shuttle-bus services may change this. Narrated bus tours are also available (see Organized Tours, below).

The East Rim is longer and a little less crowded than the West Rim but offers equally spectacular views. At this time, there are no free shuttle buses or walking trails, but you can drive, bike or take a narrated bus tour. The planned shuttle-bus service

The Grand Canyon in the 21st Century

Grand Canyon National Park is by far the most heavily visited of all the national parks in the Southwest. For years, annual visitation has been close to 5 million, which has influenced and strained many aspects of the park.

During the busy summer season, hotels and campgrounds are booked up months in advance and parking lots are often filled to capacity. Drivers may have to wait just to park. People come for terrific views and instead get traffic jams. Clearly, overcrowding is a major concern.

Various solutions have been proposed and considered. The Park Service wants everyone to be able to enjoy the canyon (after all, this is why the national park was created), so limiting the number of visitors is not an option. Instead, a plan is being implemented to limit the number of cars in the park.

In November 1997 the government approved a $67-million program that will change the way most people visit the Grand Canyon. By the year 2000 or 2001, visitors will leave their cars in a huge parking lot (with more than 3000 spaces) in Tusayan, AZ, just outside the south entrance of the park, and use a light-rail system capable of carrying 47,000 passengers a day to the rim of the canyon. Mather Point is proposed as the rail terminal point.

Once at the rim, visitors will be able to continue by foot, bicycle or shuttle bus. The current free shuttle-bus route, which runs along the West Rim from about March through October, will be expanded to run year-round and perhaps along some of the East Rim as well. If you are visiting in 2000 or later, check locally for what's going on.

Cars will not be banned, however. Visitors with overnight reservations will be able to drive up to their motel room or campground. Drivers will still be able to enter via the longer route from the east, though there may be restrictions on this eventually. But the busiest route, the short drive from Tusayan through the south entrance to Grand Canyon Village, will become a short railway trip all the way to the edge of the canyon – and the 21st century.

Rob Rachowiecki

may provide access to the East Rim as well as the West Rim.

Tusayan, the most accessible of the park's approximately two thousand Ancestral Puebloan ruins, is along this road. The East Rim Drive ends at **Desert View**, which is about 25 miles east of Grand Canyon Village and is the highest point on the South Rim. The road then leaves the national park through the Navajo Indian Reservation to Cameron.

Hiking & Backpacking

For backpacking, the Backcountry Office (☎ 520-638-7875) in Grand Canyon Village has all relevant information. It's open from 1 to 5 pm Monday to Friday (see also Backcountry Permits, below).

The easiest walks are on the Rim Trail, described above. Hikes below the rim are arduous. Some people prefer to use mules (see Organized Tours, below). Mule riders have the right of way. Hikers meeting a mule train should stand on the upper side of the trail until the mules have passed.

Keep this in mind when hiking into the canyon: First, it's easy to stride down the trail for a few hours, but the steep uphill return during the heat of the day when you are tired is much more demanding. Allow at least two hours to return uphill for every hour of hiking downhill. Second, it's a lot hotter inside the gorge than at the rim and water is scarce. Carry plenty of water and sun protection. In summer, temperatures can exceed 110°F in the inner gorge.

The most popular below-the-rim trails are Bright Angel Trail and South Kaibab Trail. Both are well maintained and suitable for either day hikes or, with a permit and advance reservation, overnight backpacking trips. No permit is needed for a day trip. Mule riders also use these trails. Though steep, they are the easiest rim-to-river trails in the canyon. Day hikers should not expect to reach the river and return in one day.

Bright Angel Trail The trail leaves from the Rim Trail a few yards west of Bright Angel Lodge in Grand Canyon Village. From the trailhead at about 6900 feet, the trail drops to Indian Garden 4.6 miles away at about 3800 feet, where there's a ranger station, campground, restrooms and water. From Indian Garden, an almost flat trail goes 1½ miles to Plateau Point with its exceptional views into the inner gorge. The 12.2-mile roundtrip from the rim to Plateau Point is a strenuous all-day hike. There are resthouses after 1½ miles (1130-foot elevation drop) and 3 miles (2110-foot elevation drop). The 1½-mile resthouse has restrooms; both have water in summer only.

From Indian Garden, Bright Angel Trail continues down to the Colorado River (2450 feet elevation), which is crossed by a suspension bridge – the only bridge within the park. The Bright Angel Campground is a short jaunt north of the bridge and 9½ miles from the South Rim. Just beyond is Phantom Ranch with its welcoming water, food, accommodations and a ranger station.

South Kaibab Trail This trail leaves the South Rim from near Yaki Point, about 4½ miles east of Grand Canyon Village. From the trailhead at 7262 feet it's a 4800-foot descent to the river and Bright Angel Campground, but the distance is only 6.7 miles. Clearly, this makes South Kaibab a much steeper trail than Bright Angel but it follows a ridge with glorious views. The first 1½ miles drop 1300 feet to Cedar Ridge, and this makes a good short half-day hike.

North Kaibab Trail From the Bright Angel Campground on the north side of the river,

the North Kaibab Trail climbs to the North Rim at 8200 feet in 14 miles – allowing a rim-to-rim crossing of the canyon. Descending from the South Rim to the river and returning or making a rim-to-rim crossing in one long day is discouraged, especially for inexperienced hikers.

Backcountry Permits Permits are necessary for any overnight camping trip. Written applications are the only way to obtain a permit. Applications can either be turned into the Backcountry Office in Grand Canyon Village in person; mailed to the Backcountry Office, PO Box 129, Grand Canyon, AZ 86023; or faxed (☎ 520-638-2125). Space is limited, so apply as far in advance as possible (reservations are accepted up to five months ahead). If you arrive without a permit, get on a waiting list

Let the mules do the work.

for cancellations – sometimes you'll get lucky, especially if you can wait several days.

The three most popular backcountry campgrounds are Indian Garden (space for 46 campers), Bright Angel (104 campers) and Cottonwood (33 campers). Numerous other smaller, less-developed campsites are available on unmaintained trails below the rim. Call or write for a complete listing.

River Running

Well over 20,000 visitors a year run the river, almost all of them with commercial operators. These aren't cheap; expect to pay up to $200 per person per day. Companies authorized to run the Colorado River through the national park include: Arizona Raft Adventures (☎ 520-526-8200, 800-786-7238), Grand Canyon Expeditions Co (☎ 801-644-2691, 800-544-2691) and OARS/Grand Canyon Dories (☎ 209-736-0805, 800-346-6277). Trips can fill up as much as a year in advance.

Organized Tours

Within the park, most tours are run by a company called Amfac (☎ 303-297-2757, fax 303-297-3175), which has a transportation desk (☎ 520-638-2631) at the Bright Angel Lodge and information desks at the visitors' centers. Narrated bus tours leave from lodges in Grand Canyon Village. These include a two-hour West Rim tour, a 3¾-hour East Rim tour or a combination of both. Both leave twice daily year-round and cost $12 and $19. Sunset tours ($8) are offered in summer. Reservations are advised in summer.

For air tours over the Grand Canyon – as well as other sites – most companies operate out of Las Vegas and promote their tours heavily. The main options are a flight over Hoover Dam, Lake Mead and the western portion of the Grand Canyon for about $75, or an air and ground tour, which involves a similar flight, but also lands at Grand Canyon Airport and includes sightseeing at the South Rim, from about $130. Overnight trips, some with hiking or rafting options, cost $200 to $300. Some operators to try include Air Nevada (☎ 702-736-8900, 800-

634-6377), Vision Air (☎ 702-261-3850) and Scenic Airlines (☎ 702-638-3200).

One-day bus tours from Las Vegas are available to the Grand Canyon, Bryce Canyon, Zion or Death Valley; they usually take about 10 hours and cost from about $90. One large bus operator is Gray Line (☎ 702-384-1234).

Places to Stay

Reservations are essential in summer and are a good idea in winter. Cancellations provide a lucky few with last-minute rooms. Call to check. If you can't find accommodations in the national park, try Tusayan (4 miles south of the South Entrance Station), Valle (31 miles south), Cameron (53 miles east), Williams (60 miles south) and Flagstaff (about 80 miles south).

Camping Campers should be ready for freezing winter nights. Backcountry camping is available by reservation and permit (see Hiking & Backpacking, above). In Grand Canyon Village, *Mather Campground* has 320 sites (no hookups) for $12 to $15. Make reservations (☎ 301-722-1257, 800-365-2267) up to five months in advance. Otherwise it's first-come, first-served.

The *Desert View Campground* near the east entrance has 75 campsites on a first-come, first-served basis from April to October, though they're often full by early morning. There is water but no showers or RV hookups, and fees are $10.

Lodges About a thousand rooms are available on the South Rim in several lodges run by Amfac Grand Canyon National Park Lodges (☎ 520-638-2631 for same-day information, 303-297-2757, fax 303-297-3175 for advance reservations). Grand Canyon Village has six lodges. Prices range from $120 to $180 for stays at the historic *El Tovar Hotel* to $40 to $60 for simple lodge rooms at the 1935 *Bright Angel Lodge*. *Phantom Ranch*, at the bottom of the canyon, has basic cabins sleeping four to 10 people and segregated dorms sleeping 10 people in bunk beds. Dorm rates are $21 per person, including bedding, soap and towels.

Meals are available by advance reservation only. If you lack a reservation, try showing up at the Bright Angel Lodge transportation desk at 5:45 am to snag a canceled bunk. Snacks, limited supplies, beer and wine are also sold.

Places to Eat

By far the best place for quality food in an elegant and historic setting is the *El Tovar Dining Room*, which has main courses in the $15 to $25 range; dinner reservations are recommended. More moderate prices and an American menu are available all day at the *Bright Angel Restaurant*. Next door to the Bright Angel Lodge, the *Arizona Steakhouse* serves steaks and seafood from 5 to 10 pm from March through December. Canyonside snacks and sandwiches are sold from 8 am to 4 pm at the *Bright Angel Fountain* near the Bright Angel trailhead from March to October. Self-service dining is available at the *Maswik Cafeteria* and at the *Yavapai Cafeteria & Grill* from March through December.

Hermits Rest Snack Bar, at the end of the West Rim Drive, and *Desert View Fountain* near the east entrance, are open daily for snacks and fast food; hours vary by season.

Getting Around

Free shuttles operate along three routes from mid-March to mid-October (dates may be extended in the future). One goes around Grand Canyon Village, stopping at lodges, campgrounds, the visitor center, Yavapai Observation Station and other points. Buses leave every 15 minutes from 6:30 am to 9:45 pm and take 50 minutes for the entire loop.

The village loop bus connects with the West Rim shuttle at the Bright Angel trailhead (called the West Rim Interchange Stop). The West Rim shuttle operates every 15 minutes from 7:30 am to sunset, stops at eight scenic points and takes 90 minutes roundtrip.

Shuttles also run every 30 minutes from the Backcountry Office, stopping at Yavapai Lodge and finishing at the South Kaibab trailhead and Yaki Point. Operating from one hour before sunrise to one hour after sunset, these are especially useful to hikers on the South Kaibab trail.

GRAND CANYON – NORTH RIM

The differences between the North and South Rims of the Grand Canyon are elevation and accessibility. The North Rim is more than 8000 feet above sea level. There is only one road in, so visitors must backtrack more than 60 miles after their visit. Winters are colder, the climate is wetter and the spruce and fir forest above the rim is thicker than the forests of the South Rim. Winter snows close the roads to car traffic from December 1 (sometimes earlier) until mid-May.

For visitors from Las Vegas, the North Rim is slightly more accessible than the South Rim, though it's a much longer drive from all of the other major cities and airports, and so only 10% of Grand Canyon visitors come to the North Rim. However, the views here are spectacular. Because of the lack of huge crowds, visiting the North Rim is a more peaceful, if more spartan, experience of the canyon's majesty.

Orientation

From Las Vegas, it's 263 miles one-way to the North Rim. Take I-15 north out of the city to Hwy 9, just past St George, UT; this takes about two hours and passes through some breathtaking artificial canyons chiseled deep into red-rock slopes. From Hwy 9, pick up Hwy 59 south, and then Alt Hwy 89 south at Fredonia, where you can visit Kanab Canyon. Alt Hwy 89 brings you to Hwy 67, which winds another 44 miles south to the Grand Canyon Lodge; another 30 miles of paved roads lead to overlooks to the east. Alternatively, from St George, you can continue on Hwy 9 and pass through Zion National Park before continuing south on Alt Hwy 89 to the Grand Canyon.

From the junction of Alt Hwy 89 and Hwy 67, you can continue on Alt Hwy 89 to the Navajo Indian Reservation. A few miles after crossing the Colorado River, Alt Hwy 89 becomes Hwy 89 and leads south to Cameron.

Information

The Visitors Center (☎ 520-638-7864) is in the Grand Canyon Lodge (the North Rim's only hotel) and is open 8 am to 8 pm from mid-May through mid-October. The usual Park Service activities and information are available in those months.

The North Rim's Backcountry Office (for backpackers) is in the ranger station near the campground, 1½ miles north of the visitor center/lodge. Other services available at the North Rim (in season) are a restaurant, gas station, post office, bookstore, general store, coin laundry and showers, medical clinic and tours. After October 15, all services are closed except the campground, which remains open, weather permitting. After December 1, everything is closed.

During winter, you can ski in and, with a backcountry camping permit, camp. It takes about three days to ski in from where the road closes, so this journey is for adventurous and highly experienced winter campers/skiers.

Park headquarters are at the South Rim. See that section earlier in this chapter for details, fees and permits. The park's automated telephone system (☎ 520-638-7888) has both South and North Rim information.

Climate & When to Go

North Rim overnight temperatures drop below freezing as late as May and as early as October. The hottest month, July, sees average highs in the upper 70°s F and lows in the mid 40°s F. The North Rim is wetter than the South Rim, although the rain pattern is similar. Snowfall is heaviest from late December to early March, when overnight temperatures usually fall into the teens.

North Rim Drives

The drive on Hwy 67 through the Kaibab Plateau to Bright Angel Point takes you through thick forest. There are excellent canyon views from the point, but to reach other overlooks you need to drive north for almost 3 miles and take the signed turn east to **Point Imperial** and **Cape Royal**. It is 9 miles to Point Imperial (8803 feet), the park's highest overlook.

One of the most spectacular of these remote overlooks is the **Toroweap Overlook** at **Tuweep**, far to the west of the main park facilities. A dirt road, usually navigable for cars, leaves Hwy 389 about 9 miles west of Fredonia and heads 55 miles to the Tuweep Ranger Station, which is staffed year-round. It's 5 miles more to the overlook, which has spartan camping (no water).

Hiking & Backpacking

The most popular quick hike is the paved half-mile trail from the Grand Canyon Lodge south to the extreme tip of **Bright Angel Point**, which offers great views at sunset. The 1½-mile **Transept Trail** goes north from the lodge through forest to the North Rim Campground.

Two trailheads are at a parking lot 2 miles north of the lodge. The **Ken Patrick Trail** travels through rolling forested country northeast to Point Imperial, about 10 miles away. This trail may be overgrown and can require route-finding skills. About a mile along this trail, a fork to the right (east) becomes the **Uncle Jim Trail**, a fairly rugged 5-mile loop offering fine views.

The **North Kaibab Trail** descends sharply from the parking lot down to Phantom Ranch at the Colorado River, 5750 feet below and 14 miles away. This is the only maintained rim-to-river trail accessed from the North Rim and it connects with trails to the South Rim. The first 4.7 miles are the steepest, dropping well over 3000 feet to **Roaring Springs** – a popular all-day hike and mule-ride destination. Water is available at Roaring Springs from May to September only. If you prefer a shorter day hike below the rim, you can walk just three-quarters of a mile down to **Coconino Overlook** or 1 mile to the **Supai Tunnel**, 1400 feet below the rim, to get a flavor of steep, inner-canyon hiking.

Cottonwood Campground is 7 miles and 4200 feet below the rim and is the only campground between the North Rim and the river. Phantom Lodge and the Bright Angel Campground are 7 and 7½ miles, respectively, below Cottonwood (see the South Rim section).

Backcountry Permits In winter, the trails of the North Rim are backcountry use areas, as snow can be five feet deep. The North Rim Campground (see Places to Stay, below) is still open for backcountry use, though there are only two ways to get to the campground in winter – either by hiking from the South Rim up to the North Rim via the North Kaibab Trail (only for the truly Nordic) or cross-country skiing 52 miles from Jacob Lake, a route that takes three days.

Permits for Cottonwood Campground and any other backcountry campgrounds must be applied for in writing as early as possible with the Backcountry Office on the South Rim (see the South Rim section for full details). If you don't have an advance permit, get on the waiting list at the Backcountry Office (open from 8 am to noon and from 1 to 5 pm daily during the season) in the North Rim ranger station near the campground as soon as you arrive. Your chances of getting a Cottonwood or Bright Angel Campground permit for the next day are slim; however, if you can wait two to four days, you'll likely get one. The ranger station can advise you of more remote backcountry campgrounds along the North Rim, most of which require a long drive on dirt roads followed by a hike.

Organized Tours
In season, daily three-hour narrated tours to Point Imperial and Cape Royal leave from the lodge and cost $20 for adults, half that for children. A schedule is posted in the lobby.

Trail Rides (☎ 520-638-9875 in season, 801-679-8665 otherwise) offers mule rides for $15 for an hour, $35 for a half day and $85 for an all-day tour into the Grand Canyon, including lunch. All tours have minimum-age requirements. Advance reservations are recommended, or stop by their desk (open from 7 am to 7 pm) in the Grand Canyon Lodge to see what is available.

Places to Stay & Eat
The *North Rim Campground*, 1½ miles north of the Grand Canyon Lodge, has 82 sites costing $12. There is water, a store, snack bar and coin-operated showers and laundry, but no hookups. Make reservations (☎ 301-722-1257, 800-365-2267) up to five months in advance. Without a reservation, show up before 10 am and hope for the best. All other campgrounds require a backcountry permit.

The historic *Grand Canyon Lodge* (☎ 520-638-2611 in season, 303-297-2757, fax 303-297-3175 year-round for reservations) is usually full and reservations should be made as far in advance as possible. It has about 200 units, both motel rooms and cabins sleeping up to five people, all with private baths. Rates vary from $55 to $95 for a double and $70 to $110 for five people. There's a snack bar, restaurant and bar at the lodge.

AROUND GRAND CANYON NATIONAL PARK
Williams
About 110 miles east of Kingman is Williams, from where it's either a 60-mile drive north to Grand Canyon National Park on Hwys 64 and 180, or a 2¼-hour train ride aboard the **Grand Canyon Railway**, which uses turn-of-the-19th-century steam locomotives from late May through September and 1950s diesels the rest of the year. Roundtrips depart Williams daily at 9:30 am and allow about 3½ hours at the canyon before putting you back into Williams by 5:30 pm.

Grand Canyon Railway

Most passengers travel coach class ($49.50 roundtrip, $19.50 for two to 16 year olds) in a 1923 car. Three other, fancier classes offer roomier and more comfortable seating, breakfast and other amenities and range in price from $64 to $114. Tax is an additional 8.8%, and national park admission is $6 extra for adults. It's a short walk from the Grand Canyon train depot to the rim. Narrated bus tours of various lengths are available, as are overnight packages with accommodations at either Williams or the Grand Canyon. Contact the railway (☎ 520-773-1976, 800-843-8724, fax 520-773-1610) for more information or reservations.

Williams has numerous places to eat and stay, including most of the popular hotel chains. Reservations are advised in summer unless you arrive by early afternoon.

Navajo Indian Reservation

Driving from Grand Canyon Village along East Rim Drive/Hwy 64 offers many spectacular views. East Rim Drive ends at Desert View, then proceeds as Hwy 64 through the Navajo Indian Reservation to Cameron. Along the way is the Little Colorado River Gorge Navajo Tribal Park with a scenic overlook; it's worth a stop.

From Cameron, heading north on Hwy 89 leads through the vast countryside of the Navajo reservation, which covers about 27,000 sq miles – the entire northeast corner of Arizona. As befits the nation's largest tribe (about one in seven American Indians is Navajo), this is the largest reservation in the US. About 75% is high desert and the remainder is high forest. Today, over half of the approximately 170,000 members of the Navajo nation live here.

Information Information about the entire reservation is available from Navajoland Tourism Department (☎ 520-871-6436, 520-871-7371, fax 520-871-7381), PO Box 663, Window Rock, AZ 86515. Window Rock is on the Arizona/New Mexico border on Hwy 264.

Photography is permitted almost anywhere there's tourism. Taking photographs of people, however, is not appropriate unless you ask for – and receive permission from – the individual involved. A tip is expected.

Alcohol and drugs are strictly prohibited throughout the reservation. It is a violation of federal, state and tribal laws to disturb, destroy, injure, deface or remove any natural feature or prehistoric object.

Shopping There are numerous stands along Hwy 89 with Navajos offering their wares, including hand-woven rugs, traditional silverwork (often with turquoise and coral), jewelry, blankets and so on. There are also 'official' stores, although there is no guarantee that the quality of items in the stores will be any better than those at the roadside stalls. When you buy direct, you may find that you pay less and the sellers may still make more than if they had sold their wares through the official merchants.

Kanab Canyon

Marked on most maps as Kanab Creek, this is actually the largest canyon leading to the Colorado River's north side. In places, Kanab Canyon is 3500 feet deep, splitting the relatively developed eastern Arizona Strip from the remote western part. From Fredonia, Arizona, Kanab Canyon goes south for 60 miles to the Grand Canyon; many canyoneers enjoy hiking this route, while drivers of 4WD vehicles can drive through Kaibab National Forest to Hack and Jumpup Canyons, two popular entry points into the lower part of Kanab Canyon. Permits are required in some stretches. For more information, contact the Kaibab National Forest District Headquarters (☎ 520-643-7395) in Fredonia.

Utah's Canyon Country

ZION NATIONAL PARK

From St George, UT, it's about 43 miles northeast along I-15 and Hwy 9 to Zion National Park, where the white, pink and red rocks are so huge, overpowering and magnificent that they are at once a photographer's dream and despair. Few photos can do justice to the magnificent scenery found in this, the first national park established in Utah.

The highlight is Zion Canyon, a half-mile-deep slash formed by the Virgin River cutting through the sandstone. Everyone wants to follow the narrow paved road at the bottom, straining their neck at vistas of looming cliffs, domes and mountains. So popular is this route that it became over-crowded with cars and the Park Service began implementing a shuttle bus service in 1999 to mitigate the problem. Other scenic drives are less crowded and just as magnificent. For those with the time and energy, day and overnight hikes can take you into spectacularly wild country.

The nearby Mormon city of St George has plenty of accommodations and makes a good base for exploring Zion and the other national parks. The tiny town of Springdale, just outside of the entrance to Zion, also has a number of decent hotels catering to park visitors.

The Three Patriarchs, Zion National Park

Orientation

Three roads enter the park. Hiking trails depart from all three roads, leading you farther into the splendor. At the southern end, the paved Zion-Mt Carmel Hwy (Hwy 9 between Mt Carmel Junction and Springdale) is the most popular route and leads past the entrance of Zion Canyon. This road has fine views, but it is also exceptionally steep, twisting and narrow. A tunnel on the east side of Zion Canyon is so narrow that escorts must accompany vehicles over 7 feet, 10 inches wide or 11 feet, 4 inches tall (call ☎ 435-772-3256 in advance to arrange an escort; a fee is charged). Bicycles are prohibited in the tunnel unless transported on a vehicle.

The main visitor center and campgrounds lie at the mouth of Zion Canyon; lodging is nearby, either in the canyon or in Springdale. The elevation in Zion Canyon is about 4000 feet, and at the east entrance, 5700 feet.

For the middle of the park, paved **Kolob Terrace Rd** leaves Hwy 9 at the village of Virgin, climbs north into the Kolob Plateau

for about 9 miles and then becomes gravel for a few more miles to Lava Point, with a ranger station and primitive campground. This road (closed by snow from about November to May) continues out of the park past Kolob Reservoir, to Hwy 14 and Cedar City as a dirt road that becomes impassable after rain.

At the north end, paved **Kolob Canyons Rd** leaves I-15 at exit 40 and extends 5 miles into the park. There is a visitors' center at the start of the road, but no camping. The road climbs to more than 5000 feet, is open all year, and has several lookouts over the Finger Canyon formations.

Information

The main visitors' center (☎ 435-772-3256) is on Hwy 9 near the park's southern entrance. Hours are 8 am to 4:30 pm daily, later in summer. The smaller Kolob Canyons Visitors Center (☎ 435-586-9548), at the beginning of Kolob Canyons Rd, is open from 8 am to 4:30 pm.

JOHN ELK III

Zion Canyon was sculpted by the humble Virgin River.

Entrance to the park is $5 per person or $10 per car. Tickets are valid for seven days, and Golden Age, Eagle and Access passes are accepted. The south and east entry stations (at either end of the Zion-Mt Carmel Hwy) and the visitors' centers provide park maps and brochures.

Climate & When to Go

From as early as March to as late as November, campgrounds may fill to capacity, often by late morning in high season. Almost half of the park's annual visitors arrive in the Memorial Day to Labor Day period, while only about 7% come between December and February.

Summer weather is hot (well over 100°F is common), so bring plenty of water and sun protection. Temperatures drop into the 60°s F at night, even in midsummer. Summers are generally dry, except from late July to early September, when the so-called monsoons – short but heavy rainstorms – occur.

There is snow in winter, but the main roads are plowed, and though it may freeze at night, daytime temperatures usually rise to about 50°F. Hikers climbing up from the roads will find colder and more wintry (snow and ice) conditions.

Spring weather is variable and hard to predict; rainstorms and hot sunny spells are both likely. May is the peak of the wildflower blooming. Spring and early summer are also the peak of the bug season – bring insect repellent.

Fall is magnificent, with beautiful foliage colors peaking in September on the Kolob Plateau and October in the Zion Canyon. By then, daytime weather is pleasantly hot and nights are in the 40°s and 50°s F.

Zion Canyon

From the visitors' center, it's a 7-mile drive to the north end of the canyon. The narrow road follows the Virgin River and the only places to stop are at nine parking areas; most are signed trailheads. In order of increasing difficulty, the best trails accessible from the Zion Canyon road are outlined below. All have superb views. Distances listed below are one-way.

You can stroll along the paved **Pairus Trail**, which parallels the road for almost 2 miles from the Watchman Campground to the main park junction. Take an easy walk near the canyon's end along the paved and very popular **Riverside Walk**, about a mile long, fairly flat and partly wheelchair-accessible. (You can continue farther along into The Narrows – see Backpacking, below.) The quarter-mile-long **Weeping Rock Trail** climbs 100 feet to a lovely area of moist hanging gardens. **Emerald Pools** can be reached by a mile-long paved trail or a shorter unpaved one climbing 200 feet to the lower pool; a shorter trail scrambles another 200 feet up to the upper pool. Swimming is not allowed here.

Hidden Canyon Trail has a few long drop-offs and climbs 750 feet in just over a mile to a very narrow and shady canyon. **Angels Landing Trail** is 2½ miles with a 1500-foot elevation gain. Allow three to four hours roundtrip. There are steep and exposed drop-offs with chains to hold on to for security. Views are superb, but don't go if you're afraid of heights. **Observation Point Trail** is almost 4 miles long with a 2150-foot elevation gain; it's less exposed than Angels Landing and offers great views too.

Zion-Mt Carmel Hwy

The road east of Zion Canyon is somewhat of an engineering feat, with switchbacks and a long tunnel (check the Orientation section for vehicle restrictions). East of the tunnel, the geology changes into slickrock, with many carved and etched formations of which the mountainous Checkerboard Mesa is a memorable example. The road travels for about 10 miles from the Zion Canyon turnoff to the east exit of the park with several parking areas along the road. Only one, just east of the mile-long tunnel, has a marked trail – the half-mile-long **Canyon Overlook Trail**, which climbs more than 100 feet and gives fine views into Zion Canyon, 1000 feet lower.

Backpacking

You can backpack and wilderness camp along the more than a hundred miles of trails in Zion. Starting from Lee Pass on the Kolob Canyons Rd in the north, you could backpack along a number of connected trails emerging at the east entrance of the park. This entire traverse of the park is about 50 miles. Park rangers can suggest a variety of shorter backpacking options.

The most famous backpacking trip is through **The Narrows**, a 16-mile journey through canyons along the North Fork of the Virgin River. In places, the canyon walls are only 20 feet apart and tower hundreds of feet above you. The hike requires wading (sometimes swimming) the river many times. It is usually done from Chamberlain's Ranch (outside the park) to the Riverside Walk Trail at the north end of Zion Canyon, to allow hikers to move with the river current. The trip takes about 12 hours and camping for a night is recommended. This hike is limited to June to October and may be closed from late July to early September because of flash-flood danger. The few miles at the north end of Zion Canyon can get very crowded with hundreds of day hikers.

Backpackers need a permit ($5 per person per night) from either visitors' center. These are usually issued the day before or the morning of the trip; problems with selecting a route are rare (although there may be a day or two wait for The Narrows). Camping is allowed in most areas; ask a ranger. Zion's springs and rivers flow year-round but their water must be boiled or treated. Day hikes do not require a permit with the exception of people attempting The Narrows in one day.

Campfires are not allowed, so carry a camping stove or food that doesn't need to be cooked. Sun protection is essential – sun-block, hat, dark glasses and long sleeves. Insect repellent is priceless in spring and early summer.

Many backpacking trips require either retracing your footsteps or leaving a vehicle at either end of the trip. If you don't have two vehicles, a 'Ride Board' at the main visitor center in Zion Canyon can connect you with other backpackers. Also, Zion Lodge (see below) has a shuttle desk and will arrange a ride for a fee.

Places to Stay & Eat

Between the south entrance and the main visitors' center are two campgrounds,

JOHN ELK III

Zion Lodge

Watchman (170 sites; open year-round) and **South** (141 sites; March to October) with water and toilets, but no showers. Both are run by the Park Service. Sites are $10, available first-come, first-served and usually all claimed by the afternoon.

Zion Lodge (☎ 435-772-3213, reservations at 303-297-2757, fax 435-772-2001) has motel rooms ($80 to $95) and cabins ($75 to $95), most with views and porches. Book early – summer dates may fill up months ahead. The lodge's restaurants serve breakfast, lunch and dinner.

Outside the east entrance and 5 miles north from Hwy 9 on North Fork County Rd is the new **Zion Ponderosa Ranch Resort** (☎ 435-648-2700, 800-293-5444), with pool, hot tub, restaurant and a cornucopia of activities, including horseback riding, mountain biking and a climbing wall. Tent sites are $45 to $49 per person, cowboy cabins with shared bath cost from $49 to $89 per person, and log cabins with private bath are $79 to $139. Spring and fall rates are lower. Rates include most activities. The resort is closed in January and February.

In nearby Springdale, **Pioneer Lodge** (☎ 435-772-3233, 800-772-3233, fax 435-772-3165, 838 Zion Park Blvd), is popular, with about 40 standard double rooms in the upper $50s during the summer high season. The pleasant **Bumbleberry Inn** (☎ 435-772-3224, 800-828-1534, fax 435-772-3947, 897 Zion Park Blvd), has a popular restaurant and 48 clean rooms for $59 to $75. The

Canyon Ranch Motel (☎ 435-772-3357, fax 435-772-3057, 668 Zion Park Blvd), has rooms in homey cottages, some with kitchenettes. Doubles are $59 to $69.

BRYCE CANYON NATIONAL PARK

The Grand Staircase – a series of steplike uplifted rock layers stretching north from the Grand Canyon – culminates in the Pink Cliffs formation at Bryce Canyon. These cliffs were deposited as a 2000-foot-deep sediment in a huge prehistoric lake some 50 to 60 million years ago, slowly lifted up to over 7000 and 9000 feet above sea level, and then eroded into wondrous ranks of pinnacles and points, steeples and spires, cliffs and crevices. And then there are the wondrous 'hoodoos.' These are phalanxes of oddly luminous stone towers that line up as if awaiting some kind of blessing. It's a Stonehenge perspective rendered in roseate stone. The oddly shaped 'hoodoos' are made up of reddish-pink rock that is incredibly variable; a shaft of sunlight can suddenly transform the view from merely magnificent to almost otherworldly.

Orientation

From Zion National Park, it takes about two hours to drive to Bryce; follow Hwy 9 to Hwy 89 north to Hwy 12 east. Scenic Hwy 12 is the main paved road to the park and cuts across its northern portion. (There's no entrance fee for driving across the northern corner.) From Hwy 12 (14 miles east of Hwy 89), Hwy 63 heads south to the official park entrance, 3 miles away. From here, an 18-mile dead-end drive continues along the rim of the canyon. Rim Rd climbs past turnoffs to the visitors' center (at about 8000 feet), the lodge, campgrounds, viewpoints and trailheads, ending at Rainbow Point, 9115 feet above sea level. Trailers are allowed only as far as Sunset Campground, 3 miles south of the entrance. Vehicles over 25 feet in length have access restrictions to Paria View in summer.

The 122-mile-long Hwy 12 is one of the most scenic roads in Utah. It continues northeast past Bryce Canyon and terminates at Torrey on Hwy 24, about 4 miles from Capitol Reef National Park, where more red-rock cliffs await. This road is not conducive to fast driving.

Information

The visitors' center (☎ 435-834-5322, fax 435-834-4102) is the first main building along Hwy 63 after you officially enter the park. It's open from 8 am to 4:30 pm (except Thanksgiving, Christmas and New Year's Day), with extended hours from late spring to early fall. Entry to the park is $5 per person or $10 per car. Tickets are valid for seven days, and Golden Age, Eagle and Access passes are honored. The entrance station and visitor center provide free maps and brochures.

Climate & When to Go

The park is open year-round, with the period of May to September seeing about 75% of the approximately 1.6 million annual visitors. Summer high temperatures at the 8000 to 9000 foot elevation of the rim may reach the 80°s F – and even hotter below the rim – so carry water and sun protection. Summer nights have temperatures in the 40°s F. June is relatively dry, but July and August see sudden, but usually brief, torrential storms.

Snow blankets the ground from about November to April, but most of the park's roads remain open. A few are unplowed and designated for cross-country skiing or snowshoeing. The main Rim Rd is occasionally closed after heavy snow, but only until the plows have done their job. January is the slowest month.

Scenic Drives

Almost all visitors take all or part of the Rim Rd drive, normally in their own cars, although a shuttle bus system may be implemented soon.

Near the visitor center, short side roads go to several popular viewpoints overlooking the Bryce Amphitheater. Beyond, the Rim Rd passes half a dozen small parking areas and viewpoints on its way to Rainbow Point – all are worth a look.

Breathtaking Bryce Amphitheater

Hiking & Backpacking

Views from the rim are superb, but you gain a completely different perspective during a hike, either along the rim or, better still, below it. Hikes below the rim descend for quite a ways and the uphill return at more than 8000 feet can be strenuous, so allow enough time and carry extra water. Also remember that most trails skirt steep drop-offs; if you suffer from fear of heights, these trails are not for you. During the July-August thunderstorm season, early morning departures are a good way to avoid the storms, which usually occur in the afternoon.

The easiest hike is along the **Rim Trail**, which is 5½ miles long (one-way) and skirts the Bryce Amphitheater. It passes several viewpoints near the visitors' center, so shorter sections can be done. The 1-mile section between the North Campground and Sunset Point is the most level.

One of the most popular trails below the rim is the three-quarters of a mile from Sunrise Point at 8000 feet down to the **Queen's Garden**, 320 feet below. From here, you can return the way you came or continue descending, connecting with the **Navajo Trail** for a more arduous hike. These trails tend to be fairly heavily used in summer and may remain open even in winter.

One trail suitable even for those with a fear of heights is the mile-long **Whiteman Connecting Trail**, which leaves Rim Rd about 9 miles south of the visitor center. This trail follows an old dirt road that connects with the Under-the-Rim Trail; the descent is about 500 feet and you return the way you came.

If you really want to get away from the crowds, shoulder a pack and get down below the rim for a night or two. There are 10 designated campsites and most can accommodate up to six backpackers. Permits are $5. Backpackers must register at the visitor center. Park rangers will issue your permit, discuss your route, tell you where to find water and where camping is permitted. Note that campgrounds are primitive – no facilities at all. All water below the rim must be purified, no fires are allowed, and you must carry out *all* your trash.

From November to April, backcountry camping can be hard because many trails are snow-covered. One or two campsites should be accessible even then; the rangers will know.

Organized Tours

Canyon Trail Rides (☎ 435-679-8665), PO Box 128, Tropic, UT 84776, operates mule tours into the backcountry. Two-hour rides to the canyon floor cost $25, half-day loop tours cost $35. Bus tours on the park roads start at $10. The Bryce Canyon Lodge (see Places to Stay & Eat, below) also has information – the tours start there. Trail rides are also offered by lodges outside the park.

Places to Stay & Eat

Inside the Park The Park Service operates *North Campground* near the visitor center and *Sunset Campground* about 1 mile south, both with toilets and drinking water and over 200 sites between them. Sites are $10 and often fill up by noon in summer. Between the two campgrounds is a *General Store* for basic food, camping supplies – and coin-operated showers and laundry in summer. (See Outside the Park, below, for places to shower in winter.)

The 1924 *Bryce Canyon Lodge* (☎ 435-834-5361, fax 435-834-5464), near the visitor center, is open April through October with 120 units, a restaurant, coin laundry and rates from $80 to $115. Reservations (☎ 303-297-2757) are more or less essential.

Outside the Park Bryce Central Reservations (☎ 800-462-7923) can find places to stay in the whole area.

The *Best Western Ruby's Inn & Campground* (☎ 435-834-5341, fax 435-834-5265) is a huge, popular and unrelentingly 'Western' complex on Hwy 63 about 1 mile north of the park entrance. Facilities include a pool, spa, post office and coin laundry. Horse, bike and ski rentals are available. Open from April to October, the campground has 200 sites costing $14 (tents) and $22 (hookups) – its coin showers and laundry stay open all year. Pleasant rooms at the motel are $90 to $110 in summer (make reservations early), dropping to half that from January to March.

Pink Cliffs Village (☎ 435-834-5351, 800-834-0043, fax 435-834-5256) is near the junction of Hwys 12 and 63, about 3 miles north of the park. It has an RV park, about 70 rooms, coin laundry, a pool and a restaurant/bar at prices a little lower than Ruby's Inn, but the facilities are much more modest. Dorm beds start at $15.

Other places to try are *Foster's Motel & Restaurant (☎ 435-834-5227, fax 435-834-5304)*, on Hwy 12 a couple of miles west of the junction with Hwy 63, with simple but clean rooms and *Bryce Canyon Pines Motel & Campground (☎ 435-834-5441, fax 435-834-5330)*, on Hwy 12 about 3 miles west of Hwy 63. Both have restaurants and charge about $60 per room in summer, less in winter.

LONELY PLANET

Guides by Region

Lonely Planet is known worldwide for publishing practical, reliable and no-nonsense travel information in our guides and on our Web site. The Lonely Planet list covers just about every accessible part of the world. Currently there are nine series: travel guides, shoestring guides, walking guides, city guides, phrasebooks, audio packs, travel atlases, diving and snorkeling guides and travel literature.

AFRICA Africa – the South • Africa on a shoestring • Arabic (Egyptian) phrasebook • Arabic (Moroccan) phrasebook • Cairo • Cape Town • Central Africa • East Africa • Egypt • Egypt travel atlas • Ethiopian (Amharic) phrasebook • The Gambia & Senegal • Kenya • Kenya travel atlas • Malawi, Mozambique & Zambia • Morocco • North Africa • South Africa, Lesotho & Swaziland • South Africa, Lesotho & Swaziland travel atlas • Swahili phrasebook • Trekking in East Africa • Tunisia • West Africa • Zimbabwe, Botswana & Namibia • Zimbabwe, Botswana & Namibia travel atlas
Travel Literature: The Rainbird: A Central African Journey • Songs to an African Sunset: A Zimbabwean Story • Mali Blues: Traveling to an African Beat

AUSTRALIA & THE PACIFIC Australia • Australian phrasebook • Bushwalking in Australia • Bushwalking in Papua New Guinea • Fiji • Fijian phrasebook • Islands of Australia's Great Barrier Reef • Melbourne • Micronesia • New Caledonia • New South Wales & the ACT • New Zealand • Northern Territory • Outback Australia • Papua New Guinea • Papua New Guinea (Pidgin) phrasebook • Queensland • Rarotonga & the Cook Islands • Samoa • Solomon Islands • South Australia • Sydney • Tahiti & French Polynesia • Tasmania • Tonga • Tramping in New Zealand • Vanuatu • Victoria • Western Australia
Travel Literature: Islands in the Clouds • Sean & David's Long Drive

CENTRAL AMERICA & THE CARIBBEAN Bahamas and Turks & Caicos • Bermuda • Central America on a shoestring • Costa Rica • Cuba • Dominican Republic & Haiti • Eastern Caribbean • Guatemala, Belize & Yucatán: La Ruta Maya • Jamaica • Mexico • Mexico City • Panama • Puerto Rico
Travel Literature: Green Dreams: Travels in Central America

EUROPE Amsterdam • Andalucía • Austria • Baltic States phrasebook • Berlin • Britain • Central Europe • Central Europe phrasebook • Czech & Slovak Republics • Denmark • Dublin • Eastern Europe • Eastern Europe phrasebook • Edinburgh • Estonia, Latvia & Lithuania • Europe • Finland • France • French phrasebook • Germany • German phrasebook • Greece • Greek phrasebook • Hungary • Iceland, Greenland & the Faroe Islands • Ireland • Italian phrasebook • Italy • Lisbon • London • Mediterranean Europe • Mediterranean Europe phrasebook • Paris • Poland • Portugal • Portugal travel atlas • Prague • Romania & Moldova • Russia, Ukraine & Belarus • Russian phrasebook • Scandinavian & Baltic Europe • Scandinavian Europe phrasebook • Scotland • Slovenia • Spain • Spanish phrasebook • St Petersburg • Switzerland • Trekking in Spain • Ukrainian phrasebook • Vienna • Walking in Britain • Walking in Italy • Walking in Switzerland • Western Europe • Western Europe phrasebook
Travel Literature: The Olive Grove: Travels in Greece

INDIAN SUBCONTINENT Bangladesh • Bengali phrasebook • Bhutan • Delhi • Goa • Hindi/Urdu phrasebook • India • India & Bangladesh travel atlas • Indian Himalaya • Karakoram Highway • Nepal • Nepali phrasebook • Pakistan • Rajasthan • South India • Sri Lanka • Sri Lanka phrasebook • Trekking in the Indian Himalaya • Trekking in the Karakoram & Hindukush • Trekking in the Nepal Himalaya
Travel Literature: In Rajasthan • Shopping for Buddhas

LONELY PLANET

Mail Order

Lonely Planet products are distributed worldwide. They are also available by mail order from Lonely Planet, so if you have difficulty finding a title please write to us. North and South American residents should write to 150 Linden St, Oakland, CA 94607, USA; European and African residents should write to 10a Spring Place, London NW5 3BH, UK; and residents of other countries to PO Box 617, Hawthorn, Victoria 3122, Australia.

ISLANDS OF THE INDIAN OCEAN Madagascar & Comoros • Maldives • Mauritius, Réunion & Seychelles

MIDDLE EAST & CENTRAL ASIA Arab Gulf States • Central Asia • Central Asia phrasebook • Iran • Israel & the Palestinian Territories • Israel & the Palestinian Territories travel atlas • Istanbul • Jerusalem • Jordan & Syria • Jordan, Syria & Lebanon travel atlas • Lebanon • Middle East on a shoe string • Turkey • Turkish phrasebook • Turkey travel atlas • Yemen
Travel Literature: The Gates of Damascus • Kingdom of the Film Stars: Journey into Jordan

NORTH AMERICA Alaska • Backpacking in Alaska • Baja California • California & Nevada • Canada • Chicago • Deep South • Florida • Hawaii • Honolulu • Los Angeles • Miami • New England USA • New Orleans • New York City • New York, New Jersey & Pennsylvania • Pacific Northwest USA • Rocky Mountain States • San Francisco • Seattle • Southwest USA • Texas • USA • USA phrasebook • Vancouver • Washington, DC & the Capital Region
Travel Literature: Drive Thru America

NORTH-EAST ASIA Beijing • Cantonese phrasebook • China • Hong Kong • Hong Kong, Macau & Guangzhou • Japan • Japanese phrasebook • Japanese audio pack • Korea • Korean phrasebook • Kyoto • Mandarin phrasebook • Mongolia • Mongolian phrasebook • North-East Asia on a shoestring • Seoul • South-West China • Taiwan • Tibet • Tibetan phrasebook • Tokyo
Travel Literature: Lost Japan

SOUTH AMERICA Argentina, Uruguay & Paraguay • Bolivia • Brazil • Brazilian phrasebook • Buenos Aires • Chile & Easter Island • Chile & Easter Island travel atlas • Colombia • Ecuador & the Galapagos Islands • Latin American Spanish phrasebook • Peru • Quechua phrasebook • Rio de Janeiro • South America on a shoestring • Trekking in the Patagonian Andes • Venezuela
Travel Literature: Full Circle: A South American Journey

SOUTH-EAST ASIA Bali & Lombok • Bangkok • Burmese phrasebook • Cambodia • Hill Tribes phrasebook • Ho Chi Minh City • Indonesia • Indonesian phrasebook • Indonesian audio pack • Jakarta • Java • Laos • Lao phrasebook • Laos travel atlas • Malay phrasebook • Malaysia, Singapore & Brunei • Myanmar (Burma) • Philippines • Pilipino (Tagalog) phrasebook • Singapore • South-East Asia on a shoestring • South-East Asia phrasebook • Thailand • Thailand's Islands & Beaches • Thailand travel atlas • Thai phrasebook • Thai audio pack • Vietnam • Vietnamese phrasebook • Vietnam travel atlas

ALSO AVAILABLE: Antarctica • Brief Encounters: Stories of Love, Sex & Travel • Chasing Rickshaws • Not the Only Planet: Travel Stories from Science Fiction • Travel with Children • Traveller's Tales

LONELY PLANET

Phrasebooks

Lonely Planet phrasebooks are packed with essential words and phrases to help travellers communicate with the locals. With color tabs for quick reference, an extensive vocabulary and use of script, these handy pocket-sized language guides cover day-to-day travel situations.

- handy pocket-sized books
- easy to understand Pronunciation chapter
- clear & comprehensive Grammar chapter
- romanization alongside script to allow ease of pronunciation
- script throughout so users can point to phrases for every situation
- full of cultural information and tips for the traveller

'...vital for a real DIY spirit and attitude in language learning'
– *Backpacker*

'the phrasebooks have good cultural backgrounders and offer solid advice for challenging situations in remote locations'
– *San Francisco Examiner*

Arabic (Egyptian) • Arabic (Moroccan) • Australian *(Australian English, Aboriginal and Torres Strait languages)* • Baltic States *(Estonian, Latvian, Lithuanian)* • Bengali • Brazilian • Burmese • Cantonese • Central Asia • Central Europe *(Czech, French, German, Hungarian, Italian, Slovak)* • Eastern Europe *(Bulgarian, Czech, Hungarian, Polish, Romanian, Slovak)* • Ethiopian (Amharic) • Fijian • French • German • Greek • Hill Tribes • Hindi/Urdu • Indonesian • Italian • Japanese • Korean • Lao • Latin American Spanish • Malay • Mandarin • Mediterranean Europe *(Albanian, Croatian, Greek, Italian, Macedonian, Maltese, Serbian, Slovene)* • Mongolian • Nepali • Papua New Guinea • Pilipino (Tagalog) • Quechua • Russian • Scandinavian Europe *(Danish, Finnish, Icelandic, Norwegian, Swedish)* • South Pacific Languages • South-East Asia *(Burmese, Indonesian, Khmer, Lao, Malay, Tagalog Pilipino, Thai, Vietnamese)* • Spanish (Castilian) *(also includes Catalan, Galician and Basque)* • Sri Lanka • Swahili • Thai • Tibetan • Turkish • Ukrainian • USA *(US English, Vernacular, Native American languages, Hawaiian)* • Vietnamese • Western Europe *(Basque, Catalan, Dutch, French, German, Greek, Irish)*

LONELY PLANET

Lonely Planet Journeys

JOURNEYS is a unique collection of travel writing – published by the company that understands travel better than anyone else. It is a series for anyone who has ever experienced – or dreamed of – the magical moment when they encountered a strange culture or saw a place for the first time. They are tales to read while you're planning a trip, while you're on the road or while you're in an armchair in front of a fire.

These outstanding titles explore our planet through the eyes of a diverse group of international writers. JOURNEYS books catch the spirit of a place, illuminate a culture, recount a crazy adventure or introduce a fascinating way of life. They always entertain, and always enrich the experience of travel.

FULL CIRCLE
A South American Journey
Luis Sepúlveda (translated by Chris Andrews)

'A journey without a fixed itinerary' with Chilean writer Luis Sepúlveda. Extravagant characters and extraordinary situations are memorably evoked: gauchos organising a tournament of lies, a scheming heiress on the lookout for a husband, a pilot with a corpse on board his plane ... *Full Circle* brings us the distinctive voice of one of South America's most compelling writers.

WINNER 1996 Astrolabe – Etonnants Voyageurs award for the best work of travel literature published in France.

GREEN DREAMS
Travels in Central America
Stephen Benz

On the Amazon, in Costa Rica, Honduras and on the Mayan trail from Guatemala to Mexico, Stephen Benz describes his encounters with water, mud, insects and other wildlife – and not least with the ecotourists themselves. With witty insights into modern travel, *Green Dreams* discusses the paradox of cultural and 'green' tourism.

DRIVE THRU AMERICA
Sean Condon

If you've ever wanted to drive across the USA but couldn't find the time (or afford the gas), *Drive Thru America* is perfect for you. In his search for American myths and realities – along with comfort, cable TV and good, reasonably priced coffee – Sean Condon paints a hilarious road-portrait of the USA.

'entertaining and laugh-out-loud funny'– *Alex Wilber, Travel editor, Amazon.com*

SEAN & DAVID'S LONG DRIVE
Sean Condon

Sean and David are young townies who have rarely strayed beyond city limits. One day, for no good reason, they set out to discover their homeland, and what follows is a wildly entertaining adventure that covers half of Australia.

'a hilariously detailed log of two burned out friends' – *Rolling Stone*

LONELY PLANET

Lonely Planet On-line
www.lonelyplanet.com *or* AOL keyword: lp

Whether you've just begun planning your next trip, or you're chasing down specific info on currency regulations or visa requirements, check out Lonely Planet On-line for up-to-the-minute travel information.

As well as mini guides to more than 250 destinations, you'll find maps, photos, travel news, health and visa updates, travel advisories, and discussion of the ecological and political issues you need to be aware of as you travel. You'll also find timely upgrades to popular guidebooks which you can print out and stick in the back of your book.

There's also an on-line travellers' forum where you can share your experience of life on the road, meet travel companions and ask other travellers for their recommendations and advice.

And of course we have a complete and up-to-date list of all Lonely Planet travel products including travel guides, diving and snorkeling guides, phrasebooks, city maps, travel atlases, travel literature and videos, and a simple on-line ordering facility if you can't find the book you want elsewhere.

Lonely Planet Diving & Snorkeling Guides

Beautifully illustrated with full-color photos throughout, Lonely Planet's **Pisces Books** explore the world's best diving and snorkeling areas and prepare divers for what to expect when they get there, both topside and underwater.

Dive sites are described in detail with specifics on depths, visibility, level of difficulty, special conditions, underwater photography tips, and common and unusual marine life present. You'll also find practical logistical information and coverage on topside activities and attractions, sections on diving health and safety, plus listings for diving services, live-aboards, dive resorts and tourist offices.

LONELY PLANET

Lonely Planet Travel Atlases

Lonely Planet has long been famous for the number and quality of its guidebook maps. Now we've gone one step further and produced a handy companion series: Lonely Planet travel atlases – maps of a country produced in book form.

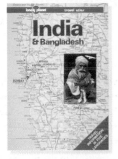

Unlike other maps, which look good but lead travellers astray, our travel atlases have been researched on the road by Lonely Planet's experienced team of writers. All details are carefully checked to ensure the atlas corresponds with the equivalent Lonely Planet guidebook.

- full-color throughout
- maps researched and checked by Lonely Planet authors
- place names correspond with Lonely Planet guidebooks
- no confusing spelling differences
- legend and traveling information in English, French, German, Japanese and Spanish
- size: 230 x 160 mm

Available now: Chile & Easter Island • Egypt • India & Bangladesh • Israel & the Palestinian Territories • Jordan, Syria & Lebanon • Kenya • Laos • Portugal • South Africa, Lesotho & Swaziland • Thailand • Turkey • Vietnam • Zimbabwe, Botswana & Namibia

Lonely Planet TV Series & Videos

Lonely Planet travel guides have been brought to life on television screens around the world. Like our guides, the programs are based on the joy of independent travel, and look honestly at some of the most exciting, picturesque and frustrating places in the world. Each show is presented by one of three travellers from Australia, England or the USA and combines an innovative mixture of video, Super-8 film, atmospheric soundscapes and original music.

Videos of each episode – containing additional footage not shown on television – are available from good book and video shops, but the availability of individual videos varies with regional screening schedules.

Video destinations include: Alaska • American Rockies • Australia – The South-East • Baja California & the Copper Canyon • Brazil • Central Asia • Chile & Easter Island • Corsica, Sicily & Sardinia – The Mediterranean Islands • East Africa (Tanzania & Zanzibar) • Ecuador & the Galapagos Islands • Greenland & Iceland • Indonesia • Israel & the Sinai Desert • Jamaica • Japan • La Ruta Maya • Morocco • New York • North India • Pacific Islands (Fiji, Solomon Islands & Vanuatu) • South India • South West China • Turkey • Vietnam • West Africa • Zimbabwe, Botswana • Namibia

The Lonely Planet TV series is produced by: Pilot Productions
The Old Studio
18 Middle Row
London W10 5AT, UK

LONELY PLANET

FREE Lonely Planet Newsletters

We love hearing from you and think you'd like to hear from us.

Planet Talk

Our FREE quarterly printed newsletter is full of tips from travelers and anecdotes from Lonely Planet guidebook authors. Every issue is packed with up-to-date travel news and advice, and includes:

- a postcard from Lonely Planet co-founder Tony Wheeler
- a swag of mail from travellers
- a look at life on the road through the eyes of a Lonely Planet author
- topical health advice
- prizes for the best travel yarn
- news about forthcoming Lonely Planet events
- a complete list of Lonely Planet books and other titles

To join our mailing list, residents of the UK, Europe and Africa can email us at go@lonelyplanet.co.uk; residents of North and South America can email us at info@lonelyplanet.com; the rest of the world can email us at talk2us@lonelyplanet.com.au, or contact any Lonely Planet office.

Comet

Our FREE monthly email newsletter brings you all the latest travel news, features, interviews, competitions, destination ideas, travelers' tips & tales, Q&As, raging debates and related links. Find out what's new on the Lonely Planet Web site and which books are about to hit the shelves.

Subscribe from your desktop: www.lonelyplanet.com/comet

Index

Text

Bold indicates maps.

Imagine: A Theatrical Odyssey 164
Jubilee! 164
King Arthur's Tournament 164
Lance Burton: Master Magician 101, 164–5
Legends in Concert 165
Mystère 165–6
O 166
Siegfried & Roy 166–7
Spellbound 167
Splash 167–8
Viva Las Vegas 168
Siegel, Benjamin ('Bugsy') 15, 20, 32, 93
Siegfried & Roy 24, 99, 100, 166–7
simulators
  Sahara Speedworld 104–5
  Star Trek: The Experience 112
Sinatra, Frank 22, 25, 32, 167
skating, ice 179
skiing 191–2
slot clubs 121–2
slot machines 40–1, 84
Smith, Jedediah 16
sneakers 157, 171
souvenirs 186
Spanish Trail 16–17, 18
special events 65–8
Spellbound 167
Splash 167–8
sports, spectator 177–80. *See also individual sports*
  betting on 41
  radio stations 56
Spring Mountain Ranch State Park 191, **192**
Stardust 105
  entertainment 163
  restaurant 146
  rooms 129
Star Trek: The Experience 112
Stratosphere 105–6
  entertainment 161, 168
  restaurants 145, 149

rooms 129–30
The Strip, **Map 2**
  accommodations 125–34
  attractions 85–110
  entertainment 158–69
  restaurants 143–9
stripper apparel 183
student cards 47
Studio 54 159

T

taxes 51–2
taxis 80
telephones 52–4
Thompson, Hunter S 31
time zones 58
tipping 51
toilets 58
Toiyabe National Forest 191–2, **192**
Tommy Rocker's Cantina & Grill 175
Top of the World Lounge 157, 161
tourist offices 45
tours, organized 74–5, 82, 202, 205
trains 74, 205–6
transportation
  air travel 69–71, 72–3
  bicycles 80–1
  buses 71, 74, 76–7
  cars 74, 78–9
  hitchhiking 74
  motorcycles 74, 79–80
  taxis 80
  trains 74, 205–6
  trolleys 78
  walking 81
traveler's checks 50, 64
travel insurance 47
Treasure Island 106–8
  entertainment 165–6
  rooms 130
Triple 7 BrewPub 176
trolleys 78
Tropicana 108–9
  entertainment 163
  restaurant 148
  rooms 130
TV 56–7

U

University of Nevada, Las Vegas (UNLV) 29–30
  basketball 177–8
  football 178
Utopia 159

V

Valley of Fire State Park 196, **190**
The Venetian 109, 134
Vertical Reality 93
video 57
video poker 41
visas 46–7
Viva Las Vegas 168
volleyball 180
VooDoo Lounge 157, 176

W

walking 81
water 45
websites 54–5
weddings 111, 118–9
weights 58
West of The Strip, **Map 4**
  accommodations 137–8
  attractions 113–5
  entertainment 173–6
  restaurants 152–5
Wet 'n' Wild 109–10
What's On 56–7
wildlife 28
Williams 205–6, **190**
wines 184–5, 192
women travelers 60
work 68
World of Coca-Cola 110, 182
Wynn, Steve 13–4, 24, 86, 87, 94, 99, 140, 166

Y

Young, Brigham 17, 18
Yucca Mountain 26

Z

Zion National Park 206–10, **190**

Bold indicates maps.

Boxed Text

Las Vegas Map Section

JOHN ELK III

MAP 1 GREATER LAS VEGAS

157

To Reno, Death Valley National Park, CA

95

Las Vegas Valley

Red Rock
Canyon
National
Conservation
Area

W Ann Rd

Camino al Norte

W Craig Rd

NORTH
LAS VEGAS

▲ Lone Mtn
3342ft

95

N Rancho Drive (Tonopah Hwy)

W Cheyenne Ave

N Martin Luther King Blvd

Civic Center Drive

North Las
Vegas Airport

147

Anasazi Drive

Tournament
Players Club

W Lake Mead Blvd

Vegas Drive

BUS
95

H St

N Eastern Ave

N Bruce St

Summerlin Parkway

Oran K Gragson Hwy

W Bonanza Rd

95

Main St

Fremont St

93 95 515

159

W Charleston Blvd

S Rancho Drive

S Las Vegas Blvd (The Strip)

S Main St

MAP 5
Downtown
Las Vegas

Red Rock
Canyon
National
Conservation
Area

Town Center Drive

Rampart Blvd

S Durango Drive

W Sahara Ave

S Rainbow Blvd

S Jones Blvd

S Decatur Blvd

589

W Desert Inn Rd

595

W Flamingo Rd

592

E Flamingo Rd

605

S Maryland Parkway

S Eastern Ave

Paradice Rd

UNLV

▲ Blue Diamond Hill
4957ft

W Tropicana Ave

593

E Tropicana Ave

McCarran
International
Airport

MAP 2
The Strip

MAP 4
West of the Strip

W Russell Rd

MAP 3
East of the Strip

E Russell Rd

E Patrick Lane

562

Sunset
Park

W Warm Springs Rd

Las Vegas Beltway

215

159

S Decatur Blvd

Blue Diamond Rd

15

604

160

To Pahrump

160

● Arden

Red Rock
Canyon
National
Conservation
Area

W Lake Mead Drive

✈ Henderson
Executive
Airport

To Jean, Primm,
Los Angeles, CA

Nellis Air Force Base
Small Arms Range

To Mesquite,
St George, UT

Las Vegas Dunes
Recreation Area

Speedway Blvd

93   15

Las Vegas
Motor Speedway

604

Nellis Air Force Base

0   2   4 km
0   1   2 miles

E Craig Rd

N Las Vegas Blvd

N Nellis Blvd

N Llamo Blvd

N Pecos Rd

Sunrise Mtn ▲
1868ft

E Lake Mead Blvd

N Hollywood Blvd

147

Sunrise Mountain
Natural Area

E Owens Ave

E Bonanza Rd

▲ Frenchman Mtn
4054ft

E Charleston Blvd   159

167

E Sahara Ave

582

Lava Butte ▲
2870ft

Northshore Rd

Sand Hill Rd

S Nellis Blvd

Las Vegas Valley

Lake
Las
Vegas

Lakeshore Rd

Lake Mead

166

River Mountains

93

95

Boulder Hwy Rd

Sam Boyd
Stadium

Boulder Highway

147

E Sunset Rd

515

S Pecos Rd

E Warm Springs Rd

Gibson Rd

E Lake Mead Drive

Racetrack Rd

Lake Mead
National
Recreation
Area

Green Valley Parkway

146

582

(Under
Contruction)

Horizon Ridge Parkway

HENDERSON

Horizon Drive

College
Drive

Black Mtn ▲
3634ft

To Hoover
Dam

Mission Drive

Railroad Pass
2367ft

BOULDER
CITY

93

Adams Blvd

Buchanan Blvd

95

MAP 2 THE STRIP

PLACES TO EAT

1 Liberty Café
2 Montana's Café & Grill,
   Top of the World
4 Holy Cow!
7 Ristorante Italiano
8 Tony Roma's: A Place for Ribs
12 Monte Carlo Room
13 Chin's, Morton's of Chicago, Dive!
17 Noodle Kitchen
18 The Range
19 La Piazza Food Court,
   Stage Deli of Las Vegas, Hyakumi,
   Palace Court, The Palm, Spago,
   Planet Hollywood
21 Hamada of Japan
23 Aqua, Picasso, Prime, Le Cirque
26 Country Star American Music Grill
29 Harley-Davidson Café
32 Dragon Noodle Company
36 GameWorks Grill
37 All-Star Café
38 Chin Chin
39 Coyote Café & Grill Room, Emeril
   Lagasse's New Orleans Fish House,
   Gatsby's, Rain Forest Café
41 Mizuno's
43 Aureole

PLACES TO STAY

2 Stratosphere
5 Sahara
6 Circus Circus
7 Riviera
8 Stardust
12 Desert Inn
14 Treasure Island
16 The Venetian
17 The Mirage
18 Harrah's
19 Caesars Palace
20 Imperial Palace
21 Flamingo Hilton
22 Barbary Coast
23 Bellagio
24 Bally's Las Vegas
25 Paris-Las Vegas
27 Aladdin
28 Holiday Inn Casino Boardwalk
32 Monte Carlo
33 New York-New York
39 MGM Grand
40 Excalibur
41 Tropicana
42 Luxor
43 Mandalay Bay,
   Four Seasons Hotel
44 Warren Motel Apartments

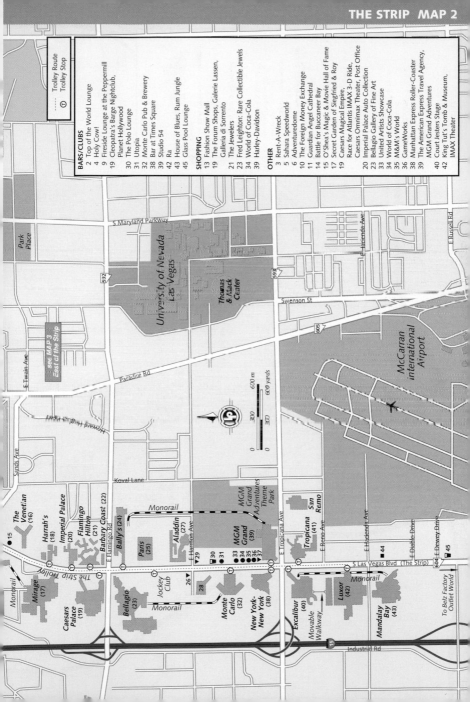

····· Trolley Route
ⓣ Trolley Stop

BARS/CLUBS
2 Top of the World Lounge
4 Holy Cow!
9 Fireside Lounge at the Peppermill
19 Cleopatra's Barge Nightclub,
    Planet Hollywood
30 The Polo Lounge
31 Utopia
32 Monte Carlo Pub & Brewery
38 Bar at Times Square
39 Studio 54
42 Ra
43 House of Blues, Rum Jungle
45 Glass Pool Lounge

SHOPPING
13 Fashion Show Mall
19 The Forum Shops, Galerie Lassen,
    Galleria di Sorrento
21 The Jewelers
23 Fred Leighton: Rare Collectible Jewels
34 World of Coca-Cola
39 Harley-Davidson

OTHER
3 Rent-A-Wreck
5 Sahara Speedworld
6 Adventuredome
10 The Foreign Money Exchange
11 Guardian Angel Cathedral
14 Battle for Buccaneer Bay
15 O'Shea's Magic & Movie Hall of Fame
17 Secret Garden of Siegfried & Roy
19 Caesars Magical Empire,
    Race for Atlantis IMAX 3-D Ride,
    Caesars Omnimax Theater, Post Office
20 Imperial Palace Auto Collection
23 Bellagio Gallery of Fine Art
33 United Artists Showcase
34 World of Coca-Cola
35 M&M's World
36 GameWorks
38 Manhattan Express Roller-Coaster
39 The American Express Travel Agency,
    MGM Grand Adventures
40 Court Jesters Stage
42 King Tut's Tomb & Museum,
    IMAX Theater

Park
Place

S Maryland Parkway

University of Nevada
Las Vegas

Thomas
& Mack
Center

Swenson St

E Twain Ave

Sands Ave

E Hacienda Ave

E Russell Rd

see MAP 3
East of the Strip

Paradise Rd

Howard Hughes Pkwy

605

McCarran
International
Airport

Koval Lane

600 m
600 yards
0   300   600

Monorail

MGM
Grand
Adventures
Theme
Park

San
Remo

Fashion Show Mall

The Venetian
(16)

Harrah's
(18)

Imperial Palace
(20)

Flamingo
Hilton
(21)

Barbary Coast (22)

Bally's (24)

Aladdin
(27)

E Harmon Ave

MGM Grand
(39)

E Tropicana Ave

Tropicana
(41)

E Reno Ave

E Hacienda Ave

44

E Diablo Drive

E Dewey Drive

45

The Strip Trolley

S Las Vegas Blvd (The Strip)

Monorail

Monorail

Mirage
(17)

Caesars
Palace
(19)

Bellagio
(23)

Jockey
Club

Monte
Carlo
(32)

New York-
New York
(38)

Excalibur
(40)

Luxor
(42)

Mandalay
Bay
(43)

Movable
Walkway

To Belz Factory
Outlet World

Industrial Rd

15

E Flamingo Rd

Paris
(25)

29

30

31

33
34
35
36
37

26

28

MAP 3 EAST OF THE STRIP

PLACES TO STAY
4 Brooks Residential Motel
9 Village Green
10 Las Vegas Hilton
17 Budget Suites
28 Woodbridge Inn Apartments
33 Super 8 Motel
42 Harbor Island
43 Hard Rock Café & Hotel
48 San Remo
49 Motel 6 Tropicana

PLACES TO EAT
1 Pamplemousse
5 La Barca Mexican Seafood Restaurant
6 Komol
10 Bistro Le Montrachet
11 Nippon
13 Allie's American Grille
19 Kabuki
20 Gordon-Biersch Brewing Company
21 Z'Tejas Grill
22 Yolie's Brazilian Steak House
23 Shalimar
24 Lawry's The Prime Rib
25 McCormick & Schmick's
26 Cozymel's
27 Gandhi India's Cuisine
29 Celebrity Deli & Restaurant
34 P.F. Chang's
35 Mediterranean Café & Market
38 The Tillerman
40 Wild Oats Community Market
41 Drink!
43 Hard Rock Café
47 Einstein Bros Bagels
51 Toto's
55 Ricardo's
57 Freed's Bakery
60 Fireside at Carollo's

------ Trolley Route

SHOPPING
7 Psychic Eye Bookshop
10 The Jewelers
18 The Boulevard Mall, The Jewelers
43 Hard Rock Hotel Store

OTHER
3 Gay & Lesbian Community Center
8 Sahara Camera Center
10 Star Trek: The Experience
15 Las Vegas Convention Center,
   Las Vegas Convention & Visitors
   Authority
16 Sunrise Hospital & Medical Center
32 McGhie's Bikes
37 The Clark County Library
39 Desert Springs Hospital
50 Rent-A-Vette
53 Liberace Museum
54 Lambda Business Association
58 Dollar Cinema
61 INS Office

BARS/CLUBS
2 PT's Pub
1C The Nightclub
12 Gold Mine Bar & Grill
14 The Beach
3C Lone Star Steakhouse & Saloon
31 T.G.I. Friday's
3E Favorites
41 Drink!
43 Hard Rock Cafe, The Joint
44 The Gipsy
45 Angles, Lace
4E Double Down Saloon
52 Goodtimes Bar & Grill
56 Sneakers
59 Las Vegas Eagle

MAP 4 WEST OF THE STRIP

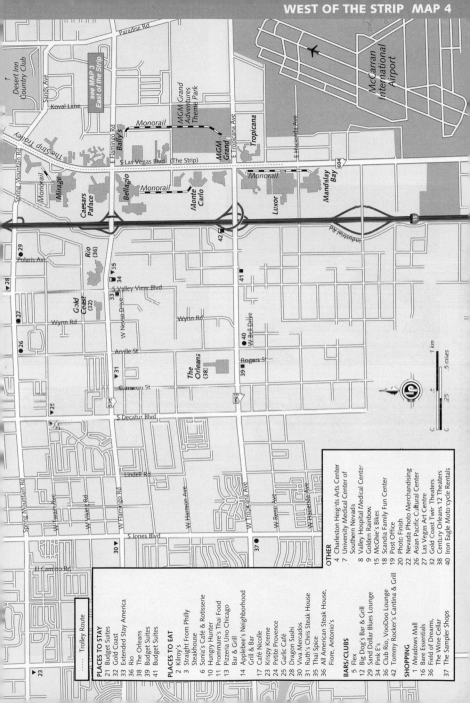

McCarran International Airport

Desert Inn Country Club

Paradise Rd

Sands Ave

Koval Lane

see MAP 3 East of the Strip

Monorail

MGM Grand Adventures Theme Park

Bally's

Flamingo Rd

The Strip Trolley

Monorail

Spring Mountain Rd

S Las Vegas Blvd (The Strip)

E Tropicana Ave

Tropicana

MGM Grand

Monorail

Mirage

Caesars Palace

Bellagio

Monte Carlo

Monorail

Luxor

Mandalay Bay

E Hacienda Ave

604

Industrial Rd

15

42 ■

29 ■

Polaris Ave

28 ▶

Rio (36)

27 ■
26 ■

Gold Coast (32)

Wynn Rd

Arville St

Cimmeron St

25 ▼

S Decatur Blvd

35 ▶▼
34

33

S Valley View Blvd

W Nelson Drive

Wynn Rd

41 ■

W Bell Drive

40 ●

Rogers St

39 ■

The Orleans (38)

31 ▼

Spring Mountain Rd

W Twain Ave

W Viking Rd

W Flamingo Rd

S Jones Blvd

30 ▶

Lindell Rd

W Harmon Ave

W Tropicana Ave

W Rene Ave

37 ●

W Hacienda Ave

El Camino Rd

23 ▶

1 km
.5 miles

PLACES TO STAY
21 Budget Suites
32 Gold Coast
33 Extended Stay America
36 Rio
38 The Orleans
39 Budget Suites
41 Budget Suites

PLACES TO EAT
2 Kilroy's
3 Straight From Philly Steakhouse
6 Sonia's Café & Rotisserie
10 Hungry Hunter
11 Prommare's Thai Food
13 Pizzeria Uno Chicago Bar & Grill
14 Applebee's Neighborhood Grill & Bar
17 Café Nicolle
23 Krispy Kreme
24 Petite Provence
25 Garlic Café
28 Dragon Sushi
30 Viva Mercados
31 Ruth's Chris Steak House
35 Thai Spice
36 All American Steak House, Fiore, Antonio's

BARS/CLUBS
5 Flex
12 Big Dog's Bar & Grill
29 Sand Dollar Blues Lounge
34 Pink E's
36 Club Rio, VooDoo Lounge
42 Tommy Rocker's Cantina & Grill

SHOPPING
1 Meadows Mall
16 Bare Essentials
36 Field of Dreams
   The Wine Cellar
37 The Sampler Shops

OTHER
4 Charleston Heights Arts Center
7 University Medical Center of Southern Nevada
8 Valley Hospital Medical Center
9 Golden Rainbow
15 McGhie's Bikes
18 Scandia Family Fun Center
19 Post Office
20 Photo Finish
22 Nevada Photo Merchandising
26 Asian Pacific Cultural Center
27 Las Vegas Art Centre
32 Gold Coast Twin Theaters
38 Century Orleans 12 Theaters
40 Iron Eagle Moto-cycle Rentals

Trolley Route

Bathing beauty at Playa Harrah's

A quick little drive-thru wedding

Everyone seems to wear the King's clothing.

The Conservatory at the Bellagio

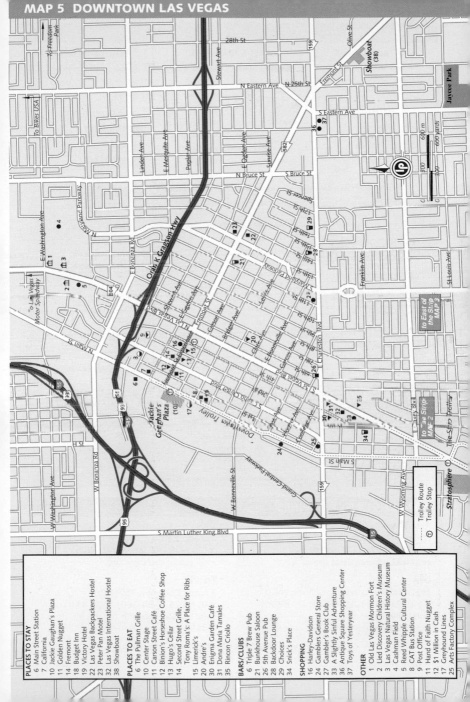

MAP 5 DOWNTOWN LAS VEGAS

PLACES TO STAY
6 Main Street Station
7 California
10 Jackie Gaughan's Plaza
11 Golden Nugget
14 Fremont
18 Budget Inn
19 Victory Hotel
22 Las Vegas Backpackers Hostel
23 Peter Pan Motel
32 Las Vegas International Hostel
38 Showboat

PLACES TO EAT
6 The Pullman Grille
10 Center Stage
11 Carson Street Café
12 Binion's Horseshoe Coffee Shop
13 Hugo's Cellar
14 Second Street Grille,
   Tony Roma's: A Place for Ribs
15 Limerick's
20 Andre's
30 Enigma Garden Café
31 Dona Maria Tamales
35 Rincon Criollo

BARS/CLUBS
6 Triple 7 Brew Pub
21 Bunkhouse Saloon
26 5th Avenue Pub
28 Backdoor Lounge
29 Choices
34 Snick's Place

SHOPPING
16 Harley-Davidson
24 Gamblers General Store
27 Gambler's Book Club
33 A Slightly Sinful Adventure
36 Antique Square Shopping Center
37 Toys of Yesteryear

OTHER
1 Old Las Vegas Mormon Fort
2 Lied Discovery Children's Museum
3 Las Vegas Natural History Museum
4 Cashman Field
5 Reed Whipple Cultural Center
8 CAT Bus Station
9 Post Office
11 Hand of Faith Nugget
12 $1 Million in Cash
17 Greyhound Lines
25 Arts Factory Complex

MAP LEGEND

BOUNDARIES

▬▬▬▬▬	International
▬▬▬	State
▬ ▬ ▬	County

HYDROGRAPHY

	Water
	Coastline
	Beach
	River, Waterfall
	Swamp, Spring

ROUTES & TRANSPORT

▬▬▬	Freeway
	Toll Freeway
	Primary Road
	Secondary Road
	Tertiary Road
===== -----	Unpaved Road
	Pedestrian Mall
----------	Trail
------(T)------	Trolley Route & Stop
+++▬▬+++	Railway, Train Station
▬▬(M)▬▬	Mass Transit Line & Station

ROUTE SHIELDS

15	Interstate		State Highways
101	US Highway	66	Nevada
N1	County Road	99	Utah, Arizona

AREA FEATURES

	Park, Garden
	Ecological Reserve
	Cemetery
	Military
	Plaza
	Golf Course

MAP SYMBOLS

✪	NATIONAL CAPITAL	✛	Airfield	⚓	Mission
◉	State, Provincial Capital	✈	Airport		Monument
●	LARGE CITY	∴	Archaeological Site, Ruins		Mosque
●	Medium City	$	Bank	▲	Mountain
•	Small City		Baseball Diamond	🏛	Museum
•	Town, Village	↗	Beach		Observatory
○	Point of Interest		Border Crossing	←	One-Way Street
			Bus Depot, Bus Stop		Park
			Cathedral	P	Parking
			Cave	)(	Pass
■	Place to Stay	†	Church		Picnic Area
⚠	Campground		Dive Site	★	Police Station
	RV Park		Embassy		Pool
			Fish Hatchery		Post Office
▼	Place to Eat	⋈	Foot Bridge		Shopping Mall
	Bar (Place to Drink)		Garden		Skiing (Alpine)
	Café		Gas Station		Skiing (Nordic)
		⊕	Hospital, Clinic		Stately Home
		❶	Information		Trailhead
			Lighthouse		Winery
		☀	Lookout		Zoo

Note: Not all symbols displayed above appear in this book.

LONELY PLANET OFFICES

Australia
PO Box 617, Hawthorn 3122, Victoria
☎ 03 9819 1877 fax 03 9819 6459
email talk2us@lonelyplanet.com.au

USA
150 Linden Street, Oakland, California 94607
☎ 510 893 8555, TOLL FREE 800 275 8555
fax 510 893 8572
email info@lonelyplanet.com

UK
10A Spring Place, London NW5 3BH
☎ 020 7428 4800 fax 020 7428 4828
email go@lonelyplanet.co.uk

France
1 rue du Dahomey, 75011 Paris
☎ 01 55 25 33 00 fax 01 55 25 33 01
email bip@lonelyplanet.fr
3615 lonelyplanet (1,29 F TTC/min)

World Wide Web: www.lonelyplanet.com or AOL keyword: lp
Lonely Planet Images: lpi@lonelyplanet.com.au